FINANCIAL POST

FPequities
Preferreds
& Derivatives

Additional Publications
For more detailed information or to place an order, see the back of the book.

CANADIAN ALMANAC & DIRECTORY 2024
Répetoire et almanach canadien
2,367 pages, 8 ½ x 11, Hardcover
177th edition, December 2023
ISBN 978-1-63700-702-0
ISSN 0068-8193
A combination of textual material, charts, colour photographs and directory listings, the *Canadian Almanac & Directory* provides the most comprehensive picture of Canada, from physical attributes to economic and business summaries to leisure and recreation.

CANADIAN WHO'S WHO 2024
1,200 pages, 8 3/8 x 10 7/8, Hardcover
December 2023
ISBN 978-1-63700-704-4
ISSN 0068-9963
Published for over 100 years, this authoritative annual publication offers access to the top 10,000 notable Canadians in all walks of life, including details such as date and place of birth, education, family details, career information, memberships, creative works, honours, languages, and awards, together with full addresses. Included are outstanding Canadians from business, academia, politics, sports, the arts and sciences, and more, selected because of the positions they hold in Canadian society, or because of the contributions they have made to Canada.

FINANCIAL POST DIRECTORY OF DIRECTORS 2024
Répertoire des administrateurs
1,759 pages, 5 7/8 x 9, Hardcover
77th edition, September 2023
ISBN 978-1-63700-700-6
ISSN 0071-5042
Published biennially and annually since 1931, this comprehensive resource offers readers access to approximately 16,900 executive contacts from Canada's top 1,400 corporations. The directory provides a definitive list of directorships and offices held by noteworthy Canadian business people, as well as details on prominent Canadian companies (both public and private), including company name, contact information and the names of executive officers and directors. Includes all-new front matter and three indexes.

MAJOR CANADIAN CITIES: COMPARED & RANKED
Comparaison et classement des principales villes canadiennes
1,372 pages, 8 ½ x 11, Softcover
2nd edition, January 2024
ISBN 978-8-89179-049-0
This second edition of *Major Canadian Cities: Compared and Ranked* has been completely revised with 2021 census data, including new tables and a refreshed layout. It provides an in-depth comparison and analysis of the 50 most populated cities in Canada. Each chapter incorporates information from dozens of resources to create the following major sections: Background, Study Rankings, and Statistical Tables.

CANADIAN PARLIAMENTARY GUIDE 2024
Guide parlementaire canadien
1,334 pages, 6 x 9, Hardcover
158th edition, March 2024
ISBN 978-1-63700-918-5
ISSN 0315-6168
Published annually since before Confederation, this indispensable guide to government in Canada provides information on federal and provincial governments, with biographical sketches of government members, descriptions of government institutions, and historical text and charts. With significant bilingual sections, the Guide covers elections from Confederation to the present, including the most recent provincial elections.

ASSOCIATIONS CANADA 2024
Associations du Canada
2,144 pages, 8 ½ x 11, Softcover
45th edition, February 2024
ISBN 978-1-63700-916-1
ISSN 1484-2408
Over 20,000 entries profile Canadian and international organizations active in Canada. Over 2,000 subject classifications index activities, professions and interests served by associations. Includes listings of NGOs, institutes, coalitions, social agencies, federations, foundations, trade unions, fraternal orders, and political parties. Fully indexed by subject, acronym, budget, conference, executive name, geographic location, mailing list availability, and registered charitable organization.

FINANCIAL SERVICES CANADA 2023-2024
Services financiers au Canada
1,516 pages, 8 ½ x 11, Softcover
25th edition, May 2023
ISBN 978-1-63700-692-4
ISSN 1484-2408
This directory of Canadian financial institutions and organizations includes banks and depository institutions, non-depository institutions, investment management firms, financial planners, insurance companies, accountants, major law firms, associations, and financial technology companies. Fully indexed.

LIBRARIES CANADA 2023-2024
Bibliothèques Canada
900 pages, 8 ½ x 11, Softcover
37th edition, July 2023
ISBN 978-1-67300-690-0
ISSN 1920-2849
Libraries Canada offers comprehensive information on Canadian libraries, resource centres, business information centres, professional associations, regional library systems, archives, library schools, government libraries, and library technical programs.

CAREERS & EMPLOYMENT CANADA 2021
Carrières et emploi Canada
970 pages, 8 ½ x 11, Softcover
1st edition, October 2020
ISBN 978-1-61925-713-5
Careers & Employment Canada is a go-to resource for job-seekers across Canada, with detailed, current information on everything from industry associations to summer job opportunities. Divided into five helpful sections, plus three indexes, this guide contains 10,000 organizations and 20,000 industry contacts to aid in research and jump-start careers in a variety of fields.

FINANCIAL POST

FPequities
Preferreds & Derivatives

2024

GREY HOUSE PUBLISHING CANADA

Grey House Publishing Canada
PUBLISHER: Leslie Mackenzie
GENERAL MANAGER: Bryon Moore

Grey House Publishing
EDITORIAL DIRECTOR: Stuart Paterson
MARKETING DIRECTOR: Jessica Moody

Grey House Publishing Canada
3 – 1500 Upper Middle Road
PO Box 76017
Oakville, ON L6M 3H5
866-433-4739
FAX 416-644-1904
www.greyhouse.ca
e-mail: info@greyhouse.ca

Grey House Publishing Canada Inc. is a wholly owned subsidiary of Grey House Publishing Inc. USA.

While every effort has been made to ensure the reliability of the information presented in this publication, Grey House Publishing Canada Inc. and Postmedia Network Inc. neither guarantees the accuracy of the data contained herein nor assumes any responsibility for errors, omissions or discrepancies.

Errors brought to the attention of the publisher and verified to the satisfaction of the publisher will be corrected in future editions.

Except by express prior written permission of the Copyright Proprietor no part of this work may be copied by any means of publication or communication now known or developed hereafter including, but not limited to, use in any compilation or other print or electronic publication, in any information storage and retrieval system, in any other electronic device, or in any visual or audio-visual device or product or internet product.

This publication is an original and creative work, copyrighted by Postmedia Network Inc. and Grey House Publishing Canada Inc. and is fully protected by all applicable copyright laws, as well as by laws covering misappropriation, trade secrets and unfair competition.

Grey House Publishing Canada Inc. has added value to the underlying factual material through one or more of the following efforts: unique and original selection; expression; arrangement; coordination; and classification.

Postmedia Network Inc. and Grey House Publishing Inc. will defend their rights in this publication.

© 2024, Postmedia Network Inc.
365 Bloor St. East
Toronto, ON M4W 3L4
Email: fpadvisor@postmedia.com
legacy-fpadvisor.financialpost.com

Text © 2024 by Postmedia Network Inc.
Texte © 2024 par Postmedia Network Inc.
Cover, Front Matter and Back Matter © 2024 by Grey House Publishing Canada Inc.
Couverture, matière première et publicités de produits © 2024 par Grey House Publishing Canada Inc.

Published in print form by Grey House Publishing Canada Inc. under exclusive license from Postmedia Network Inc. All rights reserved.
Publié sous forme imprimé par Grey House Publishing Canada Inc. sous licence exclusive de Postmedia Network Inc. Tous droits réservés.

Printed in Canada by Marquis Book Printing Inc.

ISSN: 1492-5338
ISBN: 978-1-63700-936-9

Cataloguing in Publication Data is available from Libraries and Archives Canada.

Contents

MARKET PARTICIPANTS SURVEY—FIRST QUARTER OF 2024 vii
Latest results from the Bank of Canada's quarterly survey of financial market participants, reflecting views on macroeconomic and financial variables and monetary policy.

INTRODUCTION 1
Description of the contents of the book.

Preferred Shares

PREFERRED SHARES DESCRIPTION. 3
A brief description of preferred shares and their features.

COMPANIES REFERENCED. 5
A list of the companies and their former names, with page references.

PREFERRED SHARES DETAILS 7
A detailed description of their features.

PENDING REDEMPTIONS 112
A list of preferred shares and preferred securities which have been called for redemption.

CONVERTIBLE ISSUES TABLE, BY ISSUER. 113
Table of outstanding issues of convertible preferred shares. Listed alphabetically, by issuer.

RETRACTABLE ISSUES TABLE, BY ISSUER 114
Table of outstanding issues of retractable preferred shares. Listed alphabetically, by issuer.

EXCHANGEABLE ISSUES TABLE, BY ISSUER. 115
Table of outstanding issues of exchangeable preferred shares. Listed alphabetically, by issuer.

Ratings

DBRS RATINGS SCALE: PREFERRED SHARES DESCRIPTION . . . 121

DBRS PREFERRED SHARE/SECURITIES RATINGS TABLE, BY ISSUER 122
As supplied by Dominion Bond Rating Service Limited, in table format. Listed alphabetically by issuer.

DBRS PREFERRED SHARE/SECURITIES RATINGS TABLE, BY RATING 125
As supplied by Dominion Bond Rating Service Limited, in table format. Listed by rating.

Derivatives

PREFERRED SECURITIES DESCRIPTION 128
A brief description of preferred securities and their features.

PREFERRED SECURITIES TABLE, BY ISSUER 129
Table of preferred securities. Listed alphabetically by issuer.

PREFERRED SECURITIES DETAILS 130
A detailed description of their features.

STRUCTURED PRODUCTS DESCRIPTION. 131
A brief description of structured products and their features.

STRUCTURED PRODUCTS DETAILS 132
A detailed description of their features.

INCOME TRUSTS DESCRIPTION............................ 149
A brief description of income trust products and their features.

INCOME TRUSTS TABLE, BY ISSUER....................... 150
Table of trusts. Listed alphabetically by issuer.

WARRANTS DESCRIPTION 160
A brief description of warrants and their features.

WARRANTS TABLE, BY EXPIRY DATE 161
Table of warrants. Listed by expiry date.

WARRANTS TABLE, BY ISSUER 165
Table of warrants. Listed alphabetically by issuer.

Market Participants Survey—First Quarter of 2024

April 22, 2024

Results of the first-quarter 2024 survey conducted from March 7 to 15, 2024.

The Market Participants Survey results are based on questionnaire responses from about 30 financial market participants. You can view the latest quarterly data here.

Economic scenario

1.1 What is your forecast for real GDP growth (year-over-year percentage change) in Canada?

GDP growth in Canada
(year-over-year % change)

	End of 2024 (n = 26)	End of 2025 (n = 25)
25th percentile of responses	0.5	1.9
Median of responses	1.0	2.1
75th percentile of responses	1.3	2.3

Note: Respondents were asked to calculate the four-quarter (year-over-year) growth rate based on the end of Q4. GDP is gross domestic product.

1.2 What is the probability of real GDP growth in Canada being in each of the following ranges at the end of 2024 and 2025?

GDP growth in Canada, average probability in each range (%)

Range of GDP growth	End of 2024 (n = 25)	End of 2025 (n = 24)
Below 0.00%	17.9	6.1
0.01% to 1.00%	38.2	17.3
1.01% to 2.00%	32.2	34.3
2.01% to 3.00%	9.2	32.9
3.01% to 4.00%	1.8	7.8
4.01% to 5.00%	0.5	1.0
Above 5.01%	0.2	0.6

Note: GDP is gross domestic product.

1.3 Please identify up to three upside risks to your growth outlook for Canada.

Top upside risks	Share of respondents (%)* (n = 27)
Strong housing market	70.4
Easing of financial conditions	48.1
Higher commodity prices	44.4

* Share of respondents who selected each risk

1.4 Please identify up to three downside risks to your growth outlook for Canada.

Top downside risks	Share of respondents (%)* (n = 27)
Weaker housing market	59.3
Tightening of financial conditions	51.9
Increased geopolitical risks	40.7

* Share of respondents who selected each risk

1.5 How would you characterize the current level of Canadian GDP relative to potential output?

Characterization of output gap	Percentage of respondents (%) (n = 26)
Positive output gap (current GDP is greater than potential GDP)	7.7
Negative output gap (current GDP is less than potential GDP)	73.1
No output gap (current GDP is equal to potential GDP)	19.2

Note: GDP is gross domestic product. The output gap is the difference between the current level of Canadian GDP and the level of potential output.

1.6 What is the probability of the Canadian economy being in a recession in each of the following individual time frames?*

Probability of a recession in Canada (%)

	In 0 to 6 months (n = 25)	In 6 to 12 months (n = 25)	In 12 to 18 months (n = 25)	In 18 to 24 months (n = 24)
25th percentile of responses	25	25	20	10
Median of responses	35	40	25	20
75th percentile of responses	45	50	35	25

* A recession is defined as two consecutive quarters of negative economic growth, as measured by real gross domestic product.

1.7 What is your forecast for annual total CPI inflation in Canada?

Headline CPI inflation in Canada (%)	End of 2024 (n = 26)	End of 2025 (n = 26)	5 years ahead (n = 24)
25th percentile of responses	2.2	2.0	2.0
Median of responses	2.3	2.1	2.1
75th percentile of responses	2.5	2.3	2.2

Note: Respondents were asked to estimate, based on the end of Q4, the four-quarter (year-over-year) consumer price index (CPI) inflation in Canada.

1.8 What is the probability of annual total CPI inflation in Canada being in each of the following ranges at the end of 2024 and 2025?

Annual CPI inflation in Canada, average probability in each range (%)

Range of CPI inflation	End of 2024 (n = 25)	End of 2025 (n = 25)
Below 0.00%	1.2	1.8
0.01% to 1.00%	3.9	6.5
1.01% to 2.00%	24.3	30.7
2.01% to 3.00%	49.7	44.8
3.01% to 4.00%	18.2	13.8
Above 4.01%	2.7	2.5

Note: CPI is the consumer price index.

Monetary policy

2.1 What is your forecast for the Bank of Canada's policy interest rate?

Policy interest rate (%)

2024	25th percentile of responses	Median of responses	75th percentile of responses	Number of responses
April	5.00	5.00	5.00	27
June	4.75	4.75	5.00	27
July	4.50	4.50	4.75	27
September	4.25	4.50	4.50	27
October	4.00	4.25	4.38	27
December	4.00	4.00	4.25	27
2025				
January	3.75	4.00	4.00	26
March	3.50	3.75	3.94	26
Q2	3.25	3.50	3.75	26
Q3	3.00	3.25	3.50	25
Q4	2.75	3.00	3.38	25
2026				
Q1	2.75	2.88	3.16	24
Q2	2.50	2.75	3.00	24

2.2 How would you describe the balance of risks around your forecast for the Bank of Canada's policy interest rate?

Balance of risks	Percentage of respondents (%) (n = 27)
Skewed to a higher path	44.5
Skewed to a lower path	14.8
Risks are broadly balanced	40.7

2.3 At what level do you expect the policy rate to peak in the current cycle in Canada?

	Peak level of the policy rate (%) (n = 27)
25th percentile of responses	5.00
Median of responses	5.00
75th percentile of responses	5.00

2.4 What is your estimate of the long-term nominal neutral rate in Canada?

	Nominal neutral rate (%) (n = 25)
25th percentile of responses	2.50
Median of responses	2.75
75th percentile of responses	3.00

Financial assets

Financial assets

3. According to your economic scenario, what is your point estimate for the following?

Point estimates

End of 2024	25th percentile of responses	Median of responses	75th percentile of responses	Number of responses
2-year Canadian bond yield	3.29%	3.50%	3.79%	24
5-year Canadian bond yield	3.09%	3.30%	3.55%	24
10-year Canadian bond yield	3.10%	3.30%	3.50%	25
30-year Canadian bond yield	3.15%	3.30%	3.50%	23
Oil price per barrel (West Texas Intermediate)	US$75	US$80	US$84	26
Canadian dollar	US$0.74	US$0.75	US$0.77	26
End of 2025				
2-year Canadian bond yield	2.80%	3.00%	3.36%	21
5-year Canadian bond yield	2.89%	3.18%	3.47%	22
10-year Canadian bond yield	3.03%	3.35%	3.55%	22
30-year Canadian bond yield	3.10%	3.45%	3.60%	21
Oil price per barrel (West Texas	US$74	US$80	US$83	24

End of 2024	Point estimates			Number of responses
	25th percentile of responses	Median of responses	75th percentile of responses	
Intermediate)				
Canadian dollar	US$0.75	US$0.77	US$0.80	24

Content Type(s): Publications, Market Participants Survey

Reproduced with the permission of the Bank of Canada, 2024.

FP Equities — Preferreds & Derivatives 2024   1

Introduction

The 2024 edition of FP Equities – Preferreds & Derivatives, the ninth edition to be published by Grey House Publishing Canada, is organized into four main sections:

Introductory material includes Bank of Canada content on the current state of financial markets in Canada.

The **Preferred Shares** section lists outstanding publicly and privately held preferred shares with detailed descriptions of their features. Separate tables list convertible, exchangeable and retractable preferred share issues.

The **Ratings** section consists of ratings supplied by **Dominion Bond Rating Service Limited**, dated **May 9, 2024**, (listed by company and by rating).

The **Derivatives** section covers four distinct areas:

> **Preferred securities** – also called hybrid securities as they contain features of both debt and preferred shares – are presented in a tabular format and also with detailed descriptions of their features.
>
> **Structured products** – trusts created to hold a portfolio of a single or group of similar companies – are presented with detailed descriptions of their features.
>
> **Income trusts** are presented in a tabular format with each entity listed alphabetically within their area of operations, such as oil and gas, real estate, etc. Details include the trading symbol, description of the assets held, number of units outstanding and a recent closing price.
>
> **Warrants** which are publicly traded and are outstanding are listed by expiry date. A second table presents warrants alphabetically, by company. Subscription basis, exercise price, expiry date, stock exchange listings and trading symbol are provided for each warrant.

All shares, preferred securities, structured products, Income Trusts and warrants outstanding as at **May 9, 2024** have been included. Trading prices reflect closing price on or recent to **May 9, 2024**.

Abbreviations

A.	annually	O.	Canadian Securities Exchange
cl.	class	o/s.	outstanding
convert.	convertible	pfd.	preferred
cum.	cumulative	pref.	preferred
divd(s).	dividend(s)	pfce.	preference
exchange.	exchangeable	Q.	quarterly
F.R.	floating rate	redeem.	redeemable
M.	monthly	reset.	resettable
max.	maximum	retract.	retractable
min.	minimum	S.	semi-annually
N.	New York Stock Exchange	ser.	series
NEO	NEO Exchange	sh(s).	share(s)
NYSE	New York Stock Exchange	T.	Toronto Stock Exchange
NAV	Net Asset Value	TSX	Toronto Stock Exchange

FP Equities — Preferreds & Derivatives 2024

TSX-VEN............TSX Venture Exchange
V........................TSX Venture Exchange
V.R. ....variable rate
vtg. ....voting
W.......................................NEO Exchange
wt(s). ....warrant(s)

Preferred Shares

Preferred shares are fixed income securities. Whereas common share dividends are tied to the earnings of the issuing company, preferred shares entitle the holder to a fixed dividend income. Preferred dividends are not a legal obligation of the company and can therefore be omitted. Most preferred dividends are cumulative, however, meaning that unpaid dividends accumulate and the company is prohibited from paying dividends on its common shares until the arrears have been paid in full.

Preferred shares have a prior claim to assets over common shares in the event of a company's liquidation, dissolution or winding-up. The extent of this claim is limited to a specific dollar amount which is generally at or above par (depending on whether liquidation is voluntary or involuntary). The claim of preferred shares to assets is however subordinate to the claims of creditors and debtholders.

While almost all preferred shares are non-voting, most issues provide for limited voting rights when dividend payments are in arrears and some give shareholders the right to vote, as a class, to elect one or more directors to the board.

Redemption features give the company the right to call, on notice, preferred shares for redemption at a premium over paid-up value. The premium required on redemption usually reduces to nothing over time. On redemption, the company must also pay all dividend arrears and all dividends which have accrued to the date of redemption.

Purchase obligations are another standard feature of preferred share issues. They require the company to purchase for cancellation, in the open market a specified number of shares each year, at or below a stated price, if available. Purchase obligations can be either cumulative or non-cumulative.

In addition to these basic features, a number of sweeteners such as conversion and retraction privileges and floating rate dividends can be incorporated into an issue to make preferred shares even more appealing from the investor's point of view.

Instead of paying fixed-rate dividends, the issuer can elect to pay dividends at variable or floating rates which are tied to prime lending rates. **Floating rate dividends** provide an obvious benefit to shareholders in times of rising interest rates. Most floating rate issues offer the protection of a minimum dividend rate, should interest rates fall.

Conversion privileges give shareholders the option of exchanging preferred shares for another class of shares (usually common) at a specified price or conversion rate during a specified time period. The value of the conversion feature depends upon the length of the conversion period and the value of the underlying shares.

Retraction privileges allow the shareholder to force redemption of the preferred shares on a specified date at a specified price. Retractable preferred share issues can carry multiple retraction privileges and frequently contain provisions which allow for the introduction of new conversion features or increased dividend rates, on or about the retraction date.

4   FP Equities — Preferreds & Derivatives 2024

Coverage of preferred shares is presented in the following format:

Note: Features and details appear only when applicable. Unless otherwise indicated, accrued and unpaid dividends are payable in additon to the redemption/retraction prices.

1. **5.4% Cum. Class A Pfce., Series 12**
2. **DBRS Rating:**   Pfd-2 low   Apr 24, 2012
3. Issued: 7,000,000 shs.   Feb 19, 2003 $25.000
4. O/S: 7,000,000 shs.   Dec 31, 2011
5. Dividend: $1.35   (Q)   Mar 31/Jun 30/Sep 30/Dec 31
6. Dividend Details:
7. Private Placement
8. **Redemption:** Redeem. on and after the following dates on min. 30 and max. 60 days' notice as follows:
   Mar 31, 2014.....................$26.00   Mar 31, 2015.............................$25.75
9. **Retraction:** Retract. on the following dates as follows:
   Sep 30, 2014.....................$25.00   On or before Aug 31, 2014
   Sep 30, 2015.....................$25.00   On or before Aug 31, 2015
10. Purchase Fund:
11. **Convertible:** Convert. into com sh as follows:
    Jan 2, 2002 - Jul 30, 2003.....$10.00.......0.3   From Jul 31, 2003.........$15.00..........0.2
12. **Exchange:** (same as conversion)
13. Participation:
14. Note:
15. Lead Underwriter(s):
16. Transfer Agent:
17. Registrar:
18. Exchange(s):
19. Symbol:
20. CUSIP:

Description:
1. Security Name
2. DBRS Rating and date rating was last updated
3. **a** Shares issued **b** Date issued **c** Par or stated value
4. **a** Shares outstanding **b** Date outstanding
5. **a** Annual dividend rate or feature (adjusted for splits) **b** Dividend payment frequency **c** Dividend payment cycle (Dividend payment dates are approximate; the 30th/31st indicates payment at the end of the month or on the last business day of the month)
6. Notes on non-fixed dividend rates or other dividend details
7. Private placement indicator
8. **a** Redemption date **b** Redemption price
9. **a** Retraction date **b** Retraction price **c** Retraction exercise period
10. Purchase fund details
11. **a** Conversion period **b** Conversion price per share **c** Conversion basis per pref. share
12. **a** Exchange period **b** Exchange price per share **c** Exchange basis per pref. share
13. Participation in further dividend payments
14. Additional notes
15. Lead Underwriter(s)
16. Transfer Agent
17. Registrar
18. Exchanges on which security is listed
19. Trading Symbol
20. CUSIP Number

FP Equities — Preferreds & Derivatives 2024

Companies Referenced

Companies with one of more security appearing in this publication are listed, alphabetically by current name in this Table of Contents. A supplementary listing of their former name is also found.

Aimia Inc.	7
Algonquin Power & Utilities Corp.	8
AltaGas Ltd.	8
Artis Real Estate Investment Trust	10
BCE Inc.	11
BIP Investment Corporation	18
Bank of Montreal	18
Bombardier Inc.	21
Brookfield Corporation	22
(formerly Brookfield Asset Management Inc.)	
Brookfield Infrastructure Partners L.P.	29
Brookfield Investments Corporation	30
Brookfield Office Properties Inc.	30
Brookfield Property Split Corp.	34
Brookfield Renewable Power Preferred Equity Inc.	36
CU Inc.	37
Canaccord Genuity Group Inc.	38
Canadian Imperial Bank of Commerce	39
Canadian Utilities Limited	41
Canadian Western Bank	43
Capital Power Corporation	44
Capstone Infrastructure Corporation	45
Cenovus Energy Inc.	46
Co-operators General Insurance Company	48
Dundee Corporation	48
E-L Financial Corporation Limited	49
ECN Capital Corp.	50
EQB Inc.	50
(formerly Equitable Group Inc.)	
Element Fleet Management Corp.	51
Emera Incorporated	51
The Empire Life Insurance Company	54
Enbridge Inc.	54
Fairfax Financial Holdings Limited	61
First National Financial Corporation	65
Fortis Inc.	66
Great-West Lifeco Inc.	68
Industrial Alliance Insurance and Financial Services Inc.	72
Innergex Renewable Energy Inc.	72
Intact Financial Corporation	73
Laurentian Bank of Canada	75
Loblaw Companies Limited	75
Manulife Financial Corporation	76
Montfort Capital Corp.	80
(formerly Timia Capital Corp.)	
National Bank of Canada	80
Northland Power Inc.	83
Pembina Pipeline Corporation	83
Power Corporation of Canada	87
Power Financial Corporation	89
RF Capital Group Inc.	93
(formerly GMP Capital Inc.)	
Royal Bank of Canada	93
Sagen MI Canada Inc.	96
(formerly Genworth MI Canada Inc.)	
Sonor Investments Limited	97
Sun Life Financial Inc.	97
TC Energy Corporation	100
Thomson Reuters Corporation	103
The Toronto-Dominion Bank	103
TransAlta Corporation	107
United Corporations Limited	109
VersaBank	109
George Weston Limited	110
Algonquin Power & Utilities Corp.	130
Top 10 Split Trust	130
Big Banc Split Corp.	132
Big Pharma Split Corp.	132
Brompton Energy Split Corp.	132
(formerly Brompton Oil Split Corp.)	
Brompton Lifeco Split Corp.	133
Brompton Split Banc Corp.	133
Canadian Banc Corp.	134
Canadian Large Cap Leaders Split Corp.	134
Canadian Life Companies Split Corp.	135
Canoe EIT Income Fund	135
Dividend 15 Split Corp.	136
Dividend 15 Split Corp. II	136
Dividend Growth Split Corp.	137
E Split Corp.	137
Financial 15 Split Corp.	137
Global Dividend Growth Split Corp.	138
Life & Banc Split Corp.	138
M Split Corp.	139
New Commerce Split Fund	140
North American Financial 15 Split Corp.	141
Partners Value Split Corp.	141
Premium Income Corporation	144
Prime Dividend Corp.	145

Real Estate Split Corp 145
   (formerly Real Estate & E-Commerce Split Corp.)
S Split Corp 146
Sustainable Power & Infrastructure Split Corp 146
TDb Split Corp 146
US Financial 15 Split Corp 147
World Financial Split Corp 147

Aimia Inc.

4.802% Cum. 5-Year Rate Reset Pref., Series 1

Issued:	6,900,000 shs.	Jan 20, 2010	$25.000
O/S:	5,083,140 shs.	Dec 31, 2023	
Dividend:	$1.2005 (Q)	Mar 31/Jun 30/Sep 30/Dec 31	

Dividend Details: Reset on Mar 31, 2025. Dividend rate will be reset in every fifth year thereafter. The annual dividend rate will be equal to the sum of the five-year Government of Canada Bond Yield plus 3.75%. Dividends are payable on the last business day of March, June, September and December. Previously, annual divd. rate was 1.125000 per sh until Mar 30, 2020.
Redemption: Redeem. on the following dates on min. 30 and max. 60 days' notice as follows:
Mar 31, 2015...$25.00   Mar 31, 2020...$25.00
Redeem. on March 31 in every fifth year thereafter on min. 30 and max. 60 days' notice at $25.00 per share.
Exchange: Was exchange. on min. 30 days' notice into pfd ser 2 sh as follows:
On Mar 31, 2015....................$25.00....................1   On Mar 31, 2020....................$25.00....................1
Exchange. on March 31 in every fifth year thereafter.
Lead Underwriter(s): CIBC World Markets Inc., RBC Capital Markets, TD Securities Inc.
Transfer Agent: TSX Trust Company
Registrar: TSX Trust Company
Exchanges: TSX
Symbol: AIM.PR.A
CUSIP: 00900Q202

7.773% Cum. 5-Year Rate Reset Pref., Series 3

Issued:	6,000,000 shs.	Jan 15, 2014	$25.000
O/S:	1,649,151 shs.	Apr 1, 2024	
Dividend:	$1.94325 (Q)	Mar 31/Jun 30/Sep 30/Dec 31	

Dividend Details: Reset on Mar 31, 2029. Dividend rate will be reset in every fifth year thereafter. The annual dividend rate will be equal to the sum of the five-year Government of Canada Bond Yield plus 4.20%. Dividends are payable on the last business day of March, June, September and December. Previously, annual divd. rate was 1.502500 per sh until Mar 30, 2024.
Redemption: Redeem. on the following dates on min. 30 and max. 60 days' notice as follows:
Mar 31, 2019...$25.00   Mar 31, 2024...$25.00
Redeem. on March 31 in every fifth year thereafter on min. 30 and max. 60 days' notice at $25.00 per share.
Exchange: Was exchange. on min. 30 days' notice into pfd ser 4 as follows:
On Mar 31, 2019....................$25.00....................1   On Mar 31, 2024....................$25.00....................1
Exchange. on March 31 in every fifth year thereafter.
Lead Underwriter(s): CIBC World Markets Inc., TD Securities Inc., RBC Capital Markets, BMO Capital Markets
Transfer Agent: TSX Trust Company
Registrar: TSX Trust Company
Exchanges: TSX
Symbol: AIM.PR.C
CUSIP: 00900Q400

Floating Rate Cum. Pref., Series 4

Issued:	2,706,112 shs.	Apr 1, 2024	$25.000
O/S:	2,706,112 shs.	Apr 1, 2024	
Dividend:	F.R. (Q)	Mar 31/Jun 30/Sep 30/Dec 31	

Dividend Details: Quarterly divd. rate is T-bill plus 4.2%.
Redemption: Redeem. on the following dates on min. 30 and max. 60 days' notice as follows:
Mar 31, 2029...$25.00   Mar 31, 2034...$25.00
Redeem. on March 31 in every fifth year thereafter on min. 30 and max. 60 days' notice at $25.00 per share.
On any date after March 31, 2024 that is not an Exchange Date, the company may redeem all or any part of the outstanding Series 4 Preferred Shares, at $25.50 per sh. together with all declared and unpaid dividends to, but excluding, the redemption date (less tax, if any, required to be deducted and withheld).

Exchange: Exchange. on min. 30 days' notice into pfd ser 3 sh as follows:
On Mar 31, 2029.....................$25.00.....................1   On Mar 31, 2034.....................$25.00.....................1
Exchange. on March 31 in every fifth year thereafter.
Note: Issued upon exchange of an equal number of Preferred Shares, Series 3.
Transfer Agent: TSX Trust Company
Registrar: TSX Trust Company
Exchanges: TSX
Symbol: AIM.PR.D
CUSIP: 00900Q509

Algonquin Power & Utilities Corp.

6.469% Cum. 5-Year Rate Reset Pref., Series A

DBRS Rating:	Pfd-3	Feb 6, 2024	
Issued:	4,800,000 shs.	Nov 9, 2012	$25.000
O/S:	4,800,000 shs.	Dec 31, 2023	
Dividend:	$1.61725 (Q)	Mar 31/Jun 30/Sep 30/Dec 31	

Dividend Details: Reset on Dec 31, 2028. Dividend rate will be reset in every fifth year thereafter. The annual dividend rate will be equal to the sum of the five-year Government of Canada Bond Yield plus 2.94%. Dividends are payable on the last business day of March, June, September and December. Previously, annual divd. rate was 1.290500 per sh until Dec 30, 2023.

Redemption: Redeem. on the following dates on min. 30 and max. 60 days' notice as follows:
Dec 31, 2018.....................$25.00   Dec 31, 2023.....................$25.00
Redeem. on Dec. 31 in every fifth year thereafter on min. 30 and max. 60 days' notice at $25.00 per share.

Exchange: Was exchange. on min. 30 days' notice into pfd ser B as follows:
On Dec 31, 2018.....................$25.00.....................1   On Dec 31, 2023.....................$25.00.....................1
Exchange. on Dec. 31 in every fifth year thereafter.
Lead Underwriter(s): Scotia Capital Inc., TD Securities Inc.
Transfer Agent: TSX Trust Company
Registrar: TSX Trust Company
Exchanges: TSX
Symbol: AQN.PR.A
CUSIP: 015857303

6.853% Cum. 5-Year Rate Reset Pref., Series D

DBRS Rating:	Pfd-3	Feb 6, 2024	
Issued:	4,000,000 shs.	Mar 5, 2014	$25.000
O/S:	4,000,000 shs.	Dec 31, 2023	
Dividend:	$1.71325 (Q)	Mar 31/Jun 30/Sep 30/Dec 31	

Dividend Details: Reset on Mar 31, 2029. Dividend rate will be reset in every fifth year thereafter. The annual dividend rate will be equal to the sum of the five-year Government of Canada Bond Yield plus 3.28%. Dividends are payable on the last business day of March, June, September and December. Previously, annual divd. rate was 1.477500 per sh until Mar 30, 2024.

Redemption: Redeem. on the following dates on min. 30 and max. 60 days' notice as follows:
Mar 31, 2019.....................$25.00   Mar 31, 2024.....................$25.00
Redeem. on March 31 in every fifth year thereafter on min. 30 and max. 60 days' notice at $25.00 per share.

Exchange: Was exchange. on min. 30 days' notice into pfd ser E as follows:
On Mar 31, 2019.....................$25.00.....................1   On Mar 31, 2024.....................$25.00.....................1
Exchange. on March 31 in every fifth year thereafter.
Lead Underwriter(s): CIBC World Markets Inc., TD Securities Inc.
Transfer Agent: TSX Trust Company
Registrar: TSX Trust Company
Exchanges: TSX
Symbol: AQN.PR.D
CUSIP: 015857501

AltaGas Ltd.

3.06% Cum. 5-Year Rate Reset Pref., Series A

Issued:	8,000,000 shs.	Aug 19, 2010	$25.000
O/S:	6,746,679 shs.	Dec 31, 2023	
Dividend:	$0.765 (Q)	Mar 31/Jun 30/Sep 30/Dec 31	

Dividend Details: Reset on Sep 30, 2025. Dividend rate will be reset in every fifth year thereafter. The annual dividend rate will be equal to the sum of the five-year Government of Canada Bond Yield plus 2.66%. Previously, annual divd. rate was 0.845000 per sh until Sep 29, 2020.
Redemption: Redeem. on the following dates on min. 30 and max. 60 days' notice as follows:
Sep 30, 2015....................................$25.00   Sep 30, 2020................................$25.00
Redeem. on Sept. 30 in every fifth year thereafter on min. 30 and max. 60 days' notice at $25.00 per share.
Exchange: Was exchange. on min. 30 days' notice into pfd ser B sh as follows:
On Sep 30, 2015....................$25.00....................1   On Sep 30, 2020....................$25.00....................1
Exchange. on Sept. 30 in every fifth year thereafter.
Lead Underwriter(s): TD Securities Inc., RBC Capital Markets, CIBC World Markets Inc.
Transfer Agent: Computershare Trust Company of Canada Inc.
Registrar: Computershare Trust Company of Canada Inc.
Exchanges: TSX
Symbol: ALA.PR.A
CUSIP: 021361209

4.242% Cum. 5-Year Rate Reset Pref., Series G

Issued:	8,000,000 shs.	Jul 3, 2014	$25.000
O/S:	6,885,823 shs.	Dec 31, 2023	
Dividend:	$1.0605 (Q)	Mar 31/Jun 30/Sep 30/Dec 31	

Dividend Details: Reset on Sep 30, 2024. Dividend rate will be reset in every fifth year thereafter. The annual dividend rate will be equal to the sum of the five-year Government of Canada Bond Yield plus 3.06%. Previously, annual divd. rate was 1.187500 per sh until Sep 29, 2019.
Redemption: Redeem. on the following dates on min. 30 and max. 60 days' notice as follows:
Sep 30, 2019..$25.00   Sep 30, 2024..$25.00
Redeem. on Sept. 30 in every fifth year thereafter on min. 30 and max. 60 days' notice at $25.00 per share.
Exchange: Exchange. on min. 30 days' notice into pfd ser H as follows:
On Sep 30, 2019....................$25.00....................1   On Sep 30, 2024....................$25.00....................1
Exchange. on Sept. 30 in every fifth year thereafter.
Lead Underwriter(s): RBC Capital Markets, Scotia Capital Inc., TD Securities Inc.
Transfer Agent: Computershare Trust Company of Canada Inc.
Registrar: Computershare Trust Company of Canada Inc.
Exchanges: TSX
Symbol: ALA.PR.G
CUSIP: 021361886

Floating Rate Cum. Pref., Series B

Issued:	2,488,780 shs.	Sep 30, 2015	$25.000
O/S:	1,253,321 shs.	Dec 31, 2023	
Dividend:	F.R. (Q)	Mar 31/Jun 30/Sep 30/Dec 31	

Dividend Details: Quarterly divd. rate is T-bill plus 2.66%.
Redemption: Redeem. on the following dates on min. 30 and max. 60 days' notice as follows:
Sep 30, 2020..$25.00   Sep 30, 2025................................$25.00
Redeem. on Sept. 30 in every fifth year thereafter on min. 30 and max. 60 days' notice at $25.00 per share.
Exchange: Exchange. on min. 30 days' notice into pfd ser A sh as follows:
On Sep 30, 2020....................$25.00....................1   On Sep 30, 2025....................$25.00....................1
Exchange. on Sept. 30 in every fifth year thereafter.
Note: Issued upon exchange of an equal number of Preferred Shares, Series A.
Transfer Agent: Computershare Trust Company of Canada Inc.
Registrar: Computershare Trust Company of Canada Inc.
Exchanges: TSX
Symbol: ALA.PR.B
CUSIP: 021361308

Floating Rate Cum. Pref., Series H

Issued:	1,114,177 shs.	Sep 30, 2019	$25.000
O/S:	1,114,177 shs.	Dec 31, 2023	
Dividend:	F.R. (Q)	Mar 31/Jun 30/Sep 30/Dec 31	

Dividend Details: Quarterly divd. rate is T-bill plus 3.06%.

Redemption: Redeem. on the following dates on min. 30 and max. 60 days' notice as follows:
Sep 30, 2024..$25.00   Sep 30, 2029..$25.00
Redeem. on Sept. 30 in every fifth year thereafter on min. 30 and max. 60 days' notice at $25.00 per share.
Exchange: Exchange. on min. 30 days' notice into pfd ser G sh as follows:
On Sep 30, 2024.....................$25.00.....................1   On Sep 30, 2029.....................$25.00.....................1
Exchange. on Sept. 30 in every fifth year thereafter.
Note: Issued upon exchange of an equal number of Pref Shs, Series G.
Transfer Agent: Computershare Trust Company of Canada Inc.
Registrar: Computershare Trust Company of Canada Inc.
Exchanges: TSX
Symbol: ALA.PR.H
CUSIP: 021361878

Artis Real Estate Investment Trust

7.198% Cum. 5-Year Rate Reset Pref. Units, Series E

DBRS Rating:	Pfd-3 low	Feb 2, 2024
Issued:	4,000,000 shs.	Mar 21, 2013 $25.000
O/S:	3,248,009 shs.	Dec 31, 2023
Dividend:	$1.7995 (Q)	Mar 31/Jun 30/Sep 30/Dec 31

Dividend Details: Reset on Oct 1, 2028. Dividend rate will be reset in every fifth year thereafter. The annual dividend rate will be equal to the sum of the five-year Government of Canada Bond Yield plus 3.30%. Previously, annual divd. rate was 1.368000 per sh until Sep 30, 2023.
Redemption: Redeem. on the following dates on min. 30 and max. 60 days' notice as follows:
Sep 30, 2018..$25.00   Sep 30, 2023..$25.00
Redeem. on Sept. 30 in every fifth year thereafter on min. 30 and max. 60 days' notice at $25.00 per share.
Exchange: Was exchange. on min. 30 days' notice into pfd ser F as follows:
On Sep 30, 2018.....................$25.00.....................1   On Sep 30, 2023.....................$25.00.....................1
Exchange. on Sept. 30 in every fifth year thereafter.
Lead Underwriter(s): RBC Capital Markets, CIBC World Markets Inc.
Transfer Agent: TSX Trust Company
Registrar: TSX Trust Company
Exchanges: TSX
Symbol: AX.PR.E
CUSIP: 04315L709

6.993% Cum. 5-Year Rate Reset Pref. Units, Series I

DBRS Rating:	Pfd-3 low	Feb 2, 2024
Issued:	5,000,000 shs.	Jan 31, 2018 $25.000
O/S:	4,670,040 shs.	Dec 31, 2023
Dividend:	$1.74825 (Q)	Jan 31/Apr 30/Jul 31/Oct 31

Dividend Details: Reset on May 1, 2028. Dividend rate will be reset in every fifth year thereafter. The annual dividend rate will be equal to the greater of (i) the sum of the five-year Government of Canada Bond Yield plus 3.93% and (ii) 6.0%. Previously, annual divd. rate was 1.500000 per sh until Apr 30, 2023.
Redemption: Redeem. on the following dates on min. 30 and max. 60 days' notice as follows:
Apr 30, 2023..$25.00   Apr 30, 2028..$25.00
Redeem. on April 30 in every fifth year thereafter on min. 30 and max. 60 days' notice at $25.00 per share.
Exchange: Exchange. on min. 30 days' notice into pfd ser J as follows:
On Apr 30, 2023.....................$25.00.....................1   On Apr 30, 2028.....................$25.00.....................1
Exchange. on April 30 in every fifth year thereafter.
Lead Underwriter(s): TD Securities Inc., RBC Capital Markets, Scotia Capital Inc.
Transfer Agent: TSX Trust Company
Registrar: TSX Trust Company
Exchanges: TSX
Symbol: AX.PR.I
CUSIP: 04315L865

BCE Inc.

Floating Rate Cum. Redeem. First Pref., Series S

DBRS Rating: Pfd-3   Mar 28, 2024
Issued: 8,000,000 shs.   Oct 21, 1996 $25.000
O/S: 2,054,167 shs.   Dec 31, 2023
Dividend: F.R. (M)   Payable on the 12th day of each month

Dividend Details: The annual floating dividend rate for the first month was equal to 80% of prime. Subsequently, the dividend rate floats in relation to changes in prime and is adjusted upwards or downwards on a monthly basis by an adjustment factor whenever the Calculated Trading Price of shares is $24.875 or less or $25.125 or more, respectively. The maximum monthly adjustment for changes in the Calculated Trading Price is +/- 4.00% of prime. The annual floating dividend rate applicable for a month will in no event be less than 50% of prime or greater than prime. Previously, annual divd. rate was 1.320000 per sh until Oct 31, 2001. Dividend was payable quarterly.

Redemption: Redeem. at any time on min. 45 and max. 60 days' notice at $25.50 per sh.

Exchange: Was exchange. on min. 45 days' notice into pfd 1st ser T sh as follows:
On Nov 1, 2011.....................$25.00.....................1   On Nov 1, 2016.....................$25.00.....................1
On Nov 1, 2021.....................$25.00.....................1
Exchange. on Nov. 1 in every fifth year thereafter.

Lead Underwriter(s): BMO Capital Markets
Transfer Agent: Computershare Trust Company of Canada Inc.
Registrar: Computershare Trust Company of Canada Inc.
Exchanges: TSX
Symbol: BCE.PR.S
CUSIP: 05534B869

Floating Rate Cum. Redeem. First Pref., Series Y

DBRS Rating: Pfd-3   Mar 28, 2024
Issued: 10,000,000 shs.   Dec 18, 1997 $25.000
O/S: 6,451,752 shs.   Dec 31, 2023
Dividend: F.R. (M)   Payable on the 12th day of each month

Dividend Details: The annual floating dividend rate for the first month was equal to 80% of prime. Subsequently, the dividend rate floats in relation to changes in prime and is adjusted upwards or downwards on a monthly basis by an adjustment factor whenever the Calculated Trading Price of shares is $24.875 or less or $25.125 or more, respectively. The maximum monthly adjustment for changes in the Calculated Trading Price is +/- 4.00% of prime. The annual floating dividend rate applicable for a month will in no event be less than 50% of prime or greater than prime. Previously, annual divd. rate was 1.150000 per sh until Nov 30, 2002. Dividend was payable quarterly.

Redemption: Redeem. at any time on min. 45 and max. 60 days' notice at $25.50 per sh.

Exchange: Was exchange. on min. 45 days' notice into pfd 1st ser Z sh as follows:
On Dec 1, 2012.....................$25.00.....................1   On Dec 1, 2017.....................$25.00.....................1
Exchange. on Dec. 1 in every fifth year thereafter.

Lead Underwriter(s): Scotia Capital Inc., BMO Capital Markets, RBC Capital Markets
Transfer Agent: Computershare Trust Company of Canada Inc.
Registrar: Computershare Trust Company of Canada Inc.
Exchanges: TSX
Symbol: BCE.PR.Y
CUSIP: 05534B851

3.018% Cum. Redeem. 5-Year Rate Reset First Pref., Series R

DBRS Rating: Pfd-3   Mar 28, 2024
Issued: 8,000,000 shs.   Nov 23, 2000 $25.000
O/S: 7,764,800 shs.   Dec 31, 2023
Dividend: $0.7545 (Q)   Mar 1/Jun 1/Sep 1/Dec 1

Dividend Details: Reset on Dec 1, 2025. Dividend rate will be reset in every fifth year thereafter. Minimum dividend rate will be not less than 80% of the five-year Government of Canada Bond Yield. Previously, annual divd. rate was 1.032500 per sh until Nov 30, 2020.

Redemption: Redeem. on the following dates as follows:
Dec 1, 2010..$25.00   Dec 1, 2015..$25.00
Dec 1, 2020..................................$25.00
Redeem. on Dec. 1 in every fifth year thereafter.

Exchange: Was exchange. on min. 45 days' notice into pfd 1st ser Q sh as follows:
On Dec 1, 2010......................$25.00......................1   On Dec 1, 2015......................$25.00......................1
On Dec 1, 2020......................$25.00......................1
Exchange. on Dec. 1 in every fifth year thereafter.
Note: Issued upon exchange of the 6.9% First Preferred Shares, Series Q.
Transfer Agent: Computershare Trust Company of Canada Inc.
Registrar: Computershare Trust Company of Canada Inc.
Exchanges: TSX
Symbol: BCE.PR.R
CUSIP: 05534B703

4.94% Cum. 5-Year Rate Reset Pref., Series AA

DBRS Rating:	Pfd-3	Mar 28, 2024	
Issued:	20,000,000 shs.	Mar 1, 2002	$25.500
O/S:	11,482,631 shs.	Dec 31, 2023	
Dividend:	$1.235 (Q)	Mar 1/Jun 1/Sep 1/Dec 1	

Dividend Details: Reset on Sep 1, 2027. Dividend rate will be reset in every fifth year thereafter. Minimum dividend rate will be not less than 80% of the five-year Government of Canada Bond Yield. Previously, annual divd. rate was 0.902500 per sh until Aug 31, 2022.
Redemption: Redeem. on the following dates on min. 45 and max. 60 days' notice as follows:
Sep 1, 2012..$25.00   Sep 1, 2017..$25.00
Redeem. on Sept. 1 in every fifth year thereafter.
Exchange: Was exchange. on min. 45 days' notice into pfd 1st ser AB sh as follows:
On Sep 1, 2012......................$25.00......................1   On Sep 1, 2017......................$25.00......................1
Exchange. on Sept. 1 in every fifth year thereafter.
Note: Issued 12,000,000 shs. upon exchange of the 5.45% First Preferred Shares, Series W.
Lead Underwriter(s): TD Securities Inc.
Transfer Agent: Computershare Trust Company of Canada Inc.
Registrar: Computershare Trust Company of Canada Inc.
Exchanges: TSX
Symbol: BCE.PR.A
CUSIP: 05534B794

5.346% Cum. Redeem. 5-Year Rate Reset First Pref., Series Z

DBRS Rating:	Pfd-3	Mar 28, 2024	
Issued:	8,852,620 shs.	Nov 22, 2002	$25.000
O/S:	2,708,031 shs.	Dec 31, 2023	
Dividend:	$1.3365 (Q)	Mar 1/Jun 1/Sep 1/Dec 1	

Dividend Details: Reset on Dec 1, 2027. Dividend rate will be reset in every fifth year thereafter. Minimum dividend rate will be not less than 80% of the five-year Government of Canada Bond Yield. Previously, annual divd. rate was 0.976000 per sh until Nov 30, 2022.
Redemption: Redeem. on the following dates as follows:
Dec 1, 2012..$25.00   Dec 1, 2017..$25.00
Redeem. on Dec. 1 in every fifth year thereafter.
Exchange: Was exchange. on min. 45 days' notice into pfd 1st ser Y sh as follows:
On Dec 1, 2012......................$25.00......................1   On Dec 1, 2017......................$25.00......................1
Exchange. on Dec. 1 in every fifth year thereafter.
Note: Issued upon exchange of the 4.6% First Preferred Shares, Series Y.
Transfer Agent: Computershare Trust Company of Canada Inc.
Registrar: Computershare Trust Company of Canada Inc.
Exchanges: TSX
Symbol: BCE.PR.Z
CUSIP: 05534B828

5.08% Cum. Redeem. 5-Year Rate Reset First Pref., Series AC

DBRS Rating:	Pfd-3	Mar 28, 2024	
Issued:	20,000,000 shs.	Feb 28, 2003	$25.500
O/S:	6,482,274 shs.	Dec 31, 2023	
Dividend:	$1.27 (Q)	Mar 1/Jun 1/Sep 1/Dec 1	

Dividend Details: Reset on Mar 1, 2028. Dividend rate will be reset in every fifth year thereafter. Minimum dividend rate will be not less than 80% of the five-year Government of Canada Bond Yield. Previously, annual divd. rate was 1.095000 per sh until Feb 28, 2023.
Redemption: Redeem. on the following dates on min. 45 and max. 60 days' notice as follows:
Mar 1, 2013..$25.00   Mar 1, 2018...$25.00
Redeem. on March 1 in every fifth year thereafter.
Exchange: Was exchange. on min. 45 days' notice into pfd 1st ser AD sh as follows:
On Mar 1, 2013......................$25.50.....................1   On Mar 1, 2018......................$25.50.......................1
Exchange. on March 1 in every fifth year thereafter.
Lead Underwriter(s): RBC Capital Markets
Transfer Agent: Computershare Trust Company of Canada Inc.
Registrar: Computershare Trust Company of Canada Inc.
Exchanges: TSX
Symbol: BCE.PR.C
CUSIP: 05534B786

4.99% Cum. Redeem. 5-Year Rate Reset First Pref., Series T
DBRS Rating:	Pfd-3	Mar 28, 2024	
Issued:	6,188,651 shs.	Nov 1, 2006	$25.000
O/S:	5,301,633 shs.	Dec 31, 2023	
Dividend:	$1.2475 (Q)	Feb 1/May 1/Aug 1/Nov 1	

Dividend Details: Reset on Nov 1, 2026. Dividend rate will be reset in every fifth year thereafter. Minimum dividend rate will be not less than 80% of the five-year Government of Canada Bond Yield. Previously, annual divd. rate was 0.754750 per sh until Oct 31, 2021.
Redemption: Redeem. on the following dates as follows:
Nov 1, 2011..$25.00   Nov 1, 2016..$25.00
Redeem. at $25.00 per sh. on Nov. 1 in every fifth year thereafter.
Exchange: Exchange. on min. 45 days' notice into pfd 1st ser S sh as follows:
On Nov 1, 2011......................$25.00.....................1   On Nov 1, 2016......................$25.00.......................1
On Nov 1, 2021......................$25.00.....................1   On Nov 1, 2025......................$25.00.......................1
Exchange. on Nov. 1 in every fifth year thereafter.
Note: Issued upon exchange of the Floating Rate First Preferred Shares, Series S.
Transfer Agent: Computershare Trust Company of Canada Inc.
Registrar: Computershare Trust Company of Canada Inc.
Exchanges: TSX
Symbol: BCE.PR.T
CUSIP: 05534B810

Floating Rate Cum. First Pref., Series AE
DBRS Rating:	Pfd-3	Mar 28, 2024	
Issued:	1,914,218 shs.	Feb 1, 2007	$25.000
O/S:	6,022,513 shs.	Dec 31, 2023	
Dividend:	F.R. (M)	Payable on the 12th day of each month	

Dividend Details: The dividend rate will float in relation to changes in prime and will be adjusted upwards or downwards on a monthly basis by an adjustment factor (the "Adjustment Factor") whenever the Calculated Trading Price of shares is $24.875 or less or $25.125 or more, respectively. The maximum monthly adjustment for changes in the Calculated Trading Price will be +/- 4.00% of prime. The annual floating dividend rate applicable for a month will in no event be less than 50% of prime or greater than prime. The Adjustment Factor for a month will be based on the Calculated Trading Price of shares for the preceding month. Dividends for the first and second months following issue were equal to that certain percentage of prime that would have been applicable to the Bell Canada class A preferred shares, series 15 had the share exchange not occurred.
Redemption: Redeem. at any time on min. 45 and max. 60 days' notice at $25.50 per sh.
Exchange: Was exchange. on min. 45 days' notice into pfd 1st ser AF sh as follows:
On Feb 1, 2010......................$25.00.....................1   On Feb 1, 2015......................$25.00.......................1
Exchange. on Feb. 1 in every fifth year thereafter.
Note: Issued upon exchange of Bell Canada Class A Preferred Shares, Series 15.
Transfer Agent: Computershare Trust Company of Canada Inc.
Registrar: Computershare Trust Company of Canada Inc.
Exchanges: TSX
Symbol: BCE.PR.E
CUSIP: 05534B752

3.865% Cum. 5-Year Rate Reset First Pref., Series AF

DBRS Rating: Pfd-3 Mar 28, 2024
  Issued: 18,085,782 shs. Feb 1, 2007 $25.000
  O/S: 9,076,087 shs. Dec 31, 2023
  Dividend: $0.96625 (Q) Feb 1/May 1/Aug 1/Nov 1

Dividend Details: Reset on Feb 1, 2025. Dividend rate will be reset in every fifth year thereafter. Minimum dividend rate will be not less than 80% of the five-year Government of Canada Bond Yield. Previously, annual divd. rate was 0.777500 per sh until Jan 31, 2020.

Redemption: Redeem. on the following dates as follows:
Feb 1, 2010...$25.00   Feb 1, 2015...$25.00
Redeem. on Feb. 1 in every fifth year thereafter.

Exchange: Was exchange. on min. 45 days' notice into pfd 1st ser AE sh as follows:
On Feb 1, 2010.....................$25.00.....................1   On Feb 1, 2015.....................$25.00.......................1
Exchange. on Feb. 1 in every fifth year thereafter.

Note: Issued upon exchange of Bell Canada Class A Preferred Shares, Series 16.

Transfer Agent: Computershare Trust Company of Canada Inc.
Registrar: Computershare Trust Company of Canada Inc.
Exchanges: TSX
Symbol: BCE.PR.F
CUSIP: 05534B745

3.37% Cum. 5-Year Rate Reset First Pref., Series AG

DBRS Rating: Pfd-3 Mar 28, 2024
  Issued: 10,051,751 shs. Feb 1, 2007 $25.000
  O/S: 8,442,830 shs. Dec 31, 2023
  Dividend: $0.8425 (Q) Feb 1/May 1/Aug 1/Nov 1

Dividend Details: Reset on May 1, 2026. Dividend rate will be reset in every fifth year thereafter. Minimum dividend rate will be not less than 80% of the five-year Government of Canada Bond Yield. Previously, annual divd. rate was 0.700000 per sh until Apr 30, 2021.

Redemption: Redeem. on the following dates as follows:
May 1, 2011...$25.00   May 1, 2016...$25.00
Redeem. on May 1 in every fifth year thereafter.

Exchange: Was exchange. on min. 45 days' notice into pfd 1st ser AH sh as follows:
On May 1, 2011.....................$25.00.....................1   On May 1, 2016.....................$25.00.......................1
Exchange. on May 1 in every fifth year thereafter.

Note: Issued upon exchange of Bell Canada Class A Preferred Shares, Series 17.

Transfer Agent: Computershare Trust Company of Canada Inc.
Registrar: Computershare Trust Company of Canada Inc.
Exchanges: TSX
Symbol: BCE.PR.G
CUSIP: 05534B737

Floating Rate Cum. First Pref., Series AH

DBRS Rating: Pfd-3 Mar 28, 2024
  Issued: 3,948,249 shs. Feb 1, 2007 $25.000
  O/S: 4,784,070 shs. Dec 31, 2023
  Dividend: F.R. (M) Payable on the 12th day of each month

Dividend Details: The dividend rate will float in relation to changes in prime and will be adjusted upwards or downwards on a monthly basis by an adjustment factor (the "Adjustment Factor") whenever the Calculated Trading Price of shares is $24.875 or less or $25.125 or more, respectively. The maximum monthly adjustment for changes in the Calculated Trading Price will be +/- 4.00% of prime. The annual floating dividend rate applicable for a month will in no event be less than 50% of prime or greater than prime. The Adjustment Factor for a month will be based on the Calculated Trading Price of shares for the preceding month. Dividends for the first and second months following issue were equal to that certain percentage of prime that would have been applicable to the Bell Canada class A preferred shares, series 18 had the share exchange not occurred.

Redemption: Redeem. at any time on min. 45 and max. 60 days' notice at $25.50 per sh.

Exchange: Was exchange. on min. 45 days' notice into pfd 1st ser AG sh as follows:
On May 1, 2011......................$25.00.....................1   On May 1, 2016......................$25.00......................1
Exchange. on May 1 in every fifth year thereafter.
Note: Issued upon exchange of Bell Canada Class A Preferred Shares, Series 18.
Transfer Agent: Computershare Trust Company of Canada Inc.
Registrar: Computershare Trust Company of Canada Inc.
Exchanges: TSX
Symbol: BCE.PR.H
CUSIP: 05534B729

3.39% Cum. 5-Year Rate Reset First Pref., Series AI

DBRS Rating:	Pfd-3	Mar 28, 2024
Issued:	14,000,000 shs.	Feb 1, 2007 $25.000
O/S:	9,246,640 shs.	Dec 31, 2023
Dividend:	$0.8475 (Q)	Feb 1/May 1/Aug 1/Nov 1

Dividend Details: Reset on Aug 1, 2026. Dividend rate will be reset in every fifth year thereafter. Minimum dividend rate will be not less than 80% of the five-year Government of Canada Bond Yield. Previously, annual divd. rate was 0.687500 per sh until Jul 31, 2021.
Redemption: Redeem. on the following dates as follows:
Aug 1, 2011..$25.00   Aug 1, 2016..$25.00
Redeem. on Aug. 1 in every fifth year thereafter.
Exchange: Was exchange. on min. 45 days' notice into pfd 1st ser AJ as follows:
On Aug 1, 2011....................$25.00.....................1   On Aug 1, 2016......................$25.00......................1
Exchange. on Aug. 1 in every fifth year thereafter.
Note: Issued upon exchange of Bell Canada Class A Preferred Shares, Series 19.
Transfer Agent: Computershare Trust Company of Canada Inc.
Registrar: Computershare Trust Company of Canada Inc.
Exchanges: TSX
Symbol: BCE.PR.I
CUSIP: 05534B711

Floating Rate Cum. Redeem. First Pref., Series AB

DBRS Rating:	Pfd-3	Mar 28, 2024
Issued:	9,918,414 shs.	Aug 28, 2007 $25.000
O/S:	6,918,839 shs.	Dec 31, 2023
Dividend:	F.R. (M)	Payable on the 12th day of each month

Dividend Details: The annual floating dividend rate for the first month was equal to 80% of prime. Subsequently, the dividend rate floats in relation to changes in prime and is adjusted upwards or downwards on a monthly basis by an adjustment factor (the "Adjustment Factor") whenever the Calculated Trading Price of shares is $24.875 or less or $25.125 or more, respectively. The maximum monthly adjustment for changes in the Calculated Trading Price is +/- 4.00% of prime. The annual floating dividend rate applicable for a month will in no event be less than 50% of prime or greater than prime.
Redemption: Redeem. at any time on min. 45 and max. 60 days' notice at $25.50 per sh.
Exchange: Was exchange. into pfd 1st ser AA sh as follows:
On Sep 1, 2012....................$25.00.....................1   On Sep 1, 2017......................$25.00......................1
Exchange. on Sept. 1 in every fifth year thereafter.
Note: Issued upon exchange of the 5.45% First Preferred Shares, Series AA.
Transfer Agent: Computershare Trust Company of Canada Inc.
Registrar: Computershare Trust Company of Canada Inc.
Exchanges: TSX
Symbol: BCE.PR.B
CUSIP: 05534B695

Floating Rate Cum. Redeem. First Pref., Series AD

DBRS Rating:	Pfd-3	Mar 28, 2024
Issued:	14,755,445 shs.	Mar 1, 2008 $25.000
O/S:	12,513,726 shs.	Dec 31, 2023
Dividend:	F.R. (M)	Payable on the 12th day of each month

Dividend Details: The annual floating dividend rate for the first month was equal to 80% of prime. Subsequently, the dividend rate floats in relation to changes in prime and will be adjusted upwards or downwards on a monthly basis by an adjustment factor (the "Adjustment Factor") whenever the Calculated Trading Price of shares is $24.875 or less or $25.125 or more, respectively. The maximum monthly adjustment for changes in the Calculated Trading Price will be +/- 4.00% of prime. The annual floating dividend rate applicable for a month will in no event be less than 50% of prime or greater than prime. The Adjustment Factor for a month will be based on the Calculated Trading Price of shares for the preceding month determined in accordance with the following table:

Redemption: Redeem. at any time on min. 45 and max. 60 days' notice at $25.50 per sh.
Exchange: Was exchange. on min. 45 days' notice into pfd 1st ser AC sh as follows:
On Mar 1, 2013......................$25.00.....................1   On Mar 1, 2018......................$25.00......................1
Exchange. on March 1 in every fifth year thereafter.
Note: Issued upon exchange of the 5.54% First Preferred Shares, Series AC.
Transfer Agent: Computershare Trust Company of Canada Inc.
Registrar: Computershare Trust Company of Canada Inc.
Exchanges: TSX
Symbol: BCE.PR.D
CUSIP: 05534B687

3.306% Cum. 5-Year Rate Reset First Pref., Series AK

DBRS Rating:	Pfd-3	Mar 28, 2024	
Issued:	25,000,000 shs.	Jul 5, 2011	$25.000
O/S:	22,303,812 shs.	Dec 31, 2023	
Dividend:	$0.8265 (Q)	Mar 31/Jun 30/Sep 30/Dec 31	

Dividend Details: Reset on Dec 31, 2026. Dividend rate will be reset in every fifth year thereafter. The annual dividend rate will be equal to the sum of the five-year Government of Canada Bond Yield plus 1.88%. Previously, annual divd. rate was 0.738500 per sh until Dec 30, 2021.
Redemption: Redeem. on the following dates on min. 30 and max. 60 days' notice as follows:
Dec 31, 2016.................................$25.00   Dec 31, 2021..$25.00
Redeem. on Dec. 31 in every fifth year thereafter on min. 30 and max. 60 days' notice at $25.00 per share.
Exchange: Was exchange. on min. 30 days' notice into pfd 1st ser AL as follows:
On Dec 31, 2016....................$25.00.....................1   On Dec 31, 2021......................$25.00......................1
Exchange. on Dec. 31 in every fifth year thereafter.
Lead Underwriter(s): CIBC World Markets Inc., RBC Capital Markets, Scotia Capital Inc.
Transfer Agent: Computershare Trust Company of Canada Inc.
Registrar: Computershare Trust Company of Canada Inc.
Exchanges: TSX
Symbol: BCE.PR.K
CUSIP: 05534B679

Floating Rate Cum. Pref., Series AJ

DBRS Rating:	Pfd-3	Mar 28, 2024	
Issued:	3,245,010 shs.	Aug 2, 2011	$25.000
O/S:	4,118,260 shs.	Dec 31, 2023	
Dividend:	F.R. (M)	Payable on the 12th day of each month	

Dividend Details: The annual floating dividend rate for the first month was equal to 80% of prime. Subsequently, the dividend rate floats in relation to changes in prime and is adjusted upwards or downwards on a monthly basis by an adjustment factor (the "Adjustment Factor") whenever the Calculated Trading Price of shares is $24.875 or less or $25.125 or more respectively. The maximum monthly adjustment for changes in the Calculated Trading Price is +/- 4.00% of prime. The annual floating dividend rate applicable for a month will in no event be less than 50% of prime or greater than prime.
Redemption: Redeem. at any time on min. 45 and max. 60 days' notice at $25.50 per sh.
Exchange: Was exchange. on min. 45 days' notice into pfd 1st ser Al sh as follows:
On Aug 1, 2016......................$25.00.....................1   On Aug 1, 2021......................$25.00......................1
Exchange. on Aug. 1 in every fifth year thereafter.
Note: Issued upon exchange of an equal number of First Preferred Shares, Series AI.
Transfer Agent: CIBC Mellon Trust Company
Registrar: CIBC Mellon Trust Company
Exchanges: TSX
Symbol: BCE.PR.J
CUSIP: 05534B653

FP Equities — Preferreds & Derivatives 2024

2.939% Cum. 5-Year Rate Reset First Pref., Series AM

DBRS Rating:	Pfd-3	Mar 28, 2024
Issued:	shs.	Sep 25, 2014
O/S:	10,183,378 shs.	Dec 31, 2023
Dividend:	$0.73475 (Q)	Mar 31/Jun 30/Sep 30/Dec 31

Dividend Details: Reset on Mar 31, 2026. Dividend rate will be reset in every fifth year thereafter. The annual dividend rate will be equal to the sum of the five-year Government of Canada Bond Yield plus 2.09%. Previously, annual divd. rate was 0.691000 per sh until Mar 30, 2021.

Redemption: Redeem. on the following dates on min. 30 and max. 60 days' notice as follows:
Mar 31, 2016...$25.00   Mar 31, 2021...$25.00
Redeem. on March 31 in every fifth year thereafter on min. 30 and max. 60 days' notice at $25.00 per share.

Exchange: Was exchange. on min. 30 days' notice into pfd 1st ser AN as follows:
On Mar 31, 2016....................$25.00....................1   On Mar 31, 2021.....................$25.00.....................1
Exchange. on March 31 in every fifth year thereafter.

Note: Issued upon exchange of an equal number of Bell Aliant Preferred Equity Inc. 5-Year Rate Reset Pref shares, Series A.

Transfer Agent: TSX Trust Company
Registrar: TSX Trust Company
Exchanges: TSX
Symbol: BCE.PR.M
CUSIP: 05534B646

6.538% Cum. 5-Year Rate Reset First Pref., Series AQ

DBRS Rating:	Pfd-3	Mar 28, 2024
Issued:	shs.	Sep 25, 2014
O/S:	8,303,614 shs.	Dec 31, 2023
Dividend:	$1.6345 (Q)	Mar 31/Jun 30/Sep 30/Dec 31

Dividend Details: Reset on Sep 30, 2028. Dividend rate will be reset in every fifth year thereafter. The annual dividend rate will be equal to the sum of the five-year Government of Canada Bond Yield plus 2.64%. Previously, annual divd. rate was 1.203000 per sh until Sep 29, 2023.

Redemption: Redeem. on the following dates on min. 30 and max. 60 days' notice as follows:
Sep 30, 2018...$25.00   Sep 30, 2023...$25.00
Redeem. on Sept. 30 in every fifth year thereafter on min. 30 and max. 60 days' notice at $25.00 per share.

Exchange: Was exchange. on min. 30 days' notice into pfd 1st ser AR as follows:
On Sep 30, 2018....................$25.00....................1   On Sep 30, 2023.....................$25.00.....................1
Exchange. on Sept. 30 in every fifth year thereafter.

Note: Issued upon exchange of an equal number of Bell Aliant Preferred Equity Inc. 5-Year Rate Reset Pref shares, Series E.

Transfer Agent: TSX Trust Company
Registrar: TSX Trust Company
Exchanges: TSX
Symbol: BCE.PR.Q
CUSIP: 05534B596

Floating Rate Cum. Pref., Series AN

Issued:	1,953,385 shs.	Mar 31, 2016	$25.000
O/S:	1,035,822 shs.	Dec 31, 2023	
Dividend:	F.R. (Q)	Mar 31/Jun 30/Sep 30/Dec 31	

Dividend Details: Quarterly divd. rate is T-bill plus 2.09%.

Redemption: Redeem. on the following dates on min. 30 and max. 60 days' notice as follows:
Mar 31, 2021...$25.00   Mar 31, 2026...$25.00
Redeem. on March 31 in every fifth year thereafter on min. 30 and max. 60 days' notice at $25.00 per share. After March 31, 2021, other than on an Exchange Date, redeem. at $25.50 per sh., plus declared and unpaid dividends thereon to the date of redemption.

Exchange: Exchange. on min. 30 days' notice into pfd 1st ser AM sh as follows:
On Mar 31, 2021......................$25.00......................1   On Mar 31, 2026......................$25.00......................1
Exchange. on March 31 in every fifth year thereafter.
Note: Issued upon exchange of an equal number of First Preferred Shares, Series AM.
Transfer Agent: TSX Trust Company
Registrar: TSX Trust Company
Exchanges: TSX
Symbol: BCE.PR.N
CUSIP: 05534B638

Floating Rate Cum. Pref., Series AL

Issued:	2,254,079 shs.	Jan 3, 2017	$25.000
O/S:	1,755,688 shs.	Dec 31, 2023	
Dividend:	F.R. (Q)	Mar 31/Jun 30/Sep 30/Dec 31	

Dividend Details: Quarterly divd. rate is T-bill plus 1.88%.
Redemption: Redeem. on the following dates on min. 30 and max. 60 days' notice as follows:
Dec 31, 2021......................$25.00   Dec 31, 2026......................$25.00
Redeem. on Dec. 31 in every fifth year thereafter on min. 30 and max. 60 days' notice at $25.00 per share. After Dec. 31, 2016, other than on an Exchange Date, redeem. at $25.50 per sh., plus declared and unpaid dividends thereon to the date of redemption.
Exchange: Exchange. on min. 30 days' notice into pfd 1st ser AK sh as follows:
On Dec 31, 2021......................$25.00......................1   On Dec 31, 2026......................$25.00......................1
Exchange. on Dec. 31 in every fifth year thereafter.
Note: Issued upon exchange of an equal number of First Preferred Shares, Series AK.
Transfer Agent: TSX Trust Company
Registrar: TSX Trust Company
Exchanges: TSX
Symbol: BCE.PR.L
CUSIP: 05534B661

BIP Investment Corporation

7.475% 5-Year Rate Reset Pref., Series 1

Issued:	4,000,000 shs.	Feb 5, 2019	$25.000
O/S:	4,000,000 shs.	Dec 31, 2023	
Dividend:	$1.86875 (Q)	Mar 31/Jun 30/Sep 30/Dec 31	

Dividend Details: Reset on Apr 1, 2029. Dividend rate will be reset in every fifth year thereafter. The annual dividend rate will be equal to the greater of (i) the sum of the five-year Government of Canada Bond Yield plus 3.96% and (ii) 5.85%. Previously, annual divd. rate was 1.462500 per sh until Mar 31, 2024.
Redemption: Redeem. on the following dates on min. 30 and max. 60 days' notice as follows:
Mar 31, 2024......................$25.00   Mar 31, 2029......................$2.00
Redeem. on March 31 in every fifth year thereafter on min. 30 and max. 60 days' notice at $25.00 per share.
Exchange: Exchange. on min. 30 days' notice into pfd ser 2 as follows:
On Mar 31, 2024......................$25.00......................1   On Mar 31, 2029......................$25.00......................1
Exchange. on March 31 in every fifth year thereafter.
Lead Underwriter(s): TD Securities Inc., BMO Capital Markets, CIBC World Markets Inc., RBC Capital Markets, Scotia Capital Inc.
Transfer Agent: Computershare Investor Services Inc.
Registrar: Computershare Investor Services Inc.
Exchanges: TSX
Symbol: BIK.PR.A
CUSIP: 09075W209

Bank of Montreal

3.852% Non-Cum. 5-Year Rate Reset Class B Pref., Series 27

DBRS Rating:		Pfd-2	Jun 2, 2023
Issued:	20,000,000 shs.	Apr 23, 2014	$25.000
O/S:	20,000,000 shs.	Jan 31, 2024	
Dividend:	$0.963 (Q)	Feb 25/May 25/Aug 25/Nov 25	

FP Equities — Preferreds & Derivatives 2024

Dividend Details: Reset on May 25, 2024. Dividend rate will be reset in every fifth year thereafter. The annual dividend rate will be equal to the sum of the five-year Government of Canada Bond Yield plus 2.33%. Previously, annual divd. rate was 1.000000 per sh until May 24, 2019.
Redemption: Redeem. on the following dates on min. 30 and max. 60 days' notice, conditional on the approval of the Superintendent of Financial Institutions, as follows:
May 25, 2019..$25.00   May 25, 2024..$25.00
Redeem. on May 25 in every fifth year thereafter on min. 30 and max. 60 days' notice at $25.00 per share, conditional on approval of the Superintendent of Financial Institutions.
Convertible: Automatically convertible into common shares upon occurrence of a Non-Viability Contingent Capital (NVCC) trigger event as defined by OFSI.
Exchange: Exchange. on min. 30 days' notice into pfd B ser 28 as follows:
On May 25, 2019....................$25.00....................1   On May 25, 2024....................$25.00....................1
Exchange. on May 25 in every fifth year thereafter. Exchange. after notice from the Bank given with approval from the Superintendent of Financial Institutions.
Lead Underwriter(s): BMO Capital Markets, CIBC World Markets Inc.
Transfer Agent: Computershare Trust Company of Canada Inc.
Registrar: Computershare Trust Company of Canada Inc.
Exchanges: TSX
Symbol: BMO.PR.S
CUSIP: 063679401

3.624% Non-Cum. 5-Year Rate Reset Class B Pref., Series 29

DBRS Rating:	Pfd-2	Jun 2, 2023	
Issued:	16,000,000 shs.	Jun 6, 2014	$25.000
O/S:	16,000,000 shs.	Jan 31, 2024	
Dividend:	$0.906 (Q)	Feb 25/May 25/Aug 25/Nov 25	

Dividend Details: Reset on Aug 25, 2024. Dividend rate will be reset in every fifth year thereafter. The annual dividend rate will be equal to the sum of the five-year Government of Canada Bond Yield plus 2.24%. Previously, annual divd. rate was 0.975000 per sh until Aug 24, 2019.
Redemption: Redeem. on the following dates on min. 30 and max. 60 days' notice, conditional on the approval of the Superintendent of Financial Institutions, as follows:
Aug 25, 2019..$25.00   Aug 25, 2024..$25.00
Redeem. on Aug. 25 in every fifth year thereafter on min. 30 and max. 60 days' notice at $25.00 per share, conditional on approval of the Superintendent of Financial Institutions.
Convertible: Automatically convertible into common shares upon occurrence of a Non-Viability Contingent Capital (NVCC) trigger event as defined by OFSI.
Exchange: Exchange. on min. 30 days' notice into pfd B ser 30 as follows:
On Aug 25, 2019....................$25.00....................1   On Aug 25, 2024....................$25.00....................1
Exchange. on Aug. 25 in every fifth year thereafter. Exchange. after notice from the Bank given with approval from the Superintendent of Financial Institutions.
Lead Underwriter(s): BMO Capital Markets
Transfer Agent: Computershare Trust Company of Canada Inc.
Registrar: Computershare Trust Company of Canada Inc.
Exchanges: TSX
Symbol: BMO.PR.T
CUSIP: 063679609

3.851% Non-Cum. 5-Year Rate Reset Class B Pref., Series 31

DBRS Rating:	Pfd-2	Jun 2, 2023	
Issued:	12,000,000 shs.	Jul 30, 2014	$25.000
O/S:	12,000,000 shs.	Jan 31, 2024	
Dividend:	$0.96275 (Q)	Feb 25/May 25/Aug 25/Nov 25	

Dividend Details: Reset on Nov 25, 2024. Dividend rate will be reset in every fifth year thereafter. The annual dividend rate will be equal to the sum of the five-year Government of Canada Bond Yield plus 2.22%. Previously, annual divd. rate was 0.950000 per sh until Nov 24, 2019.
Redemption: Redeem. on the following dates on min. 30 and max. 60 days' notice, conditional on the approval of the Superintendent of Financial Institutions, as follows:
Nov 25, 2019..$25.00   Nov 25, 2024..$25.00
Redeem. on Nov. 25 in every fifth year thereafter on min. 30 and max. 60 days' notice at $25.00 per share, conditional on approval of the Superintendent of Financial Institutions.

Convertible: Automatically convertible into common shares upon occurrence of a Non-Viability Contingent Capital (NVCC) trigger event as defined by OFSI.
Exchange: Exchange. on min. 30 days' notice into pfd B ser 32 as follows:
On Nov 25, 2019.....................$25.00.....................1   On Nov 25, 2024......................$25.00......................1
Exchange. on Nov. 25 in every fifth year thereafter. Exchange. after notice from the Bank given with approval from the Superintendent of Financial Institutions.
Lead Underwriter(s): BMO Capital Markets
Transfer Agent: Computershare Trust Company of Canada Inc.
Registrar: Computershare Trust Company of Canada Inc.
Exchanges: TSX
Symbol: BMO.PR.W
CUSIP: 063679880

3.054% Non-Cum. 5-Year Rate Reset Class B Pref., Series 33

DBRS Rating:	Pfd-2	Jun 2, 2023	
Issued:	8,000,000 shs.	Jun 5, 2015	$25.000
O/S:	8,000,000 shs.	Jan 31, 2024	
Dividend:	$0.7635 (Q)	Feb 25/May 25/Aug 25/Nov 25	

Dividend Details: Reset on Aug 25, 2025. Dividend rate will be reset in every fifth year thereafter. The annual dividend rate will be equal to the sum of the five-year Government of Canada Bond Yield plus 2.71%. Previously, annual divd. rate was 0.950000 per sh until Aug 24, 2020.
Redemption: Redeem. on the following dates on min. 30 and max. 60 days' notice, conditional on the approval of the Superintendent of Financial Institutions, as follows:
Aug 25, 2020..$25.00   Aug 25, 2025..$25.00
Redeem. on Aug. 25 in every fifth year thereafter on min. 30 and max. 60 days' notice at $25.00 per share, conditional on approval of the Superintendent of Financial Institutions.
Convertible: Automatically convertible into common shares upon occurrence of a Non-Viability Contingent Capital (NVCC) trigger event as defined by OFSI.
Exchange: Exchange. on min. 30 days' notice into pfd B ser 34 as follows:
On Aug 25, 2020.....................$25.00.....................1   On Aug 25, 2025......................$25.00......................1
Exchange. on Aug. 25 in every fifth year thereafter. Exchange. after notice from the Bank given with approval from the Superintendent of Financial Institutions.
Lead Underwriter(s): BMO Capital Markets
Transfer Agent: Computershare Trust Company of Canada Inc.
Registrar: Computershare Trust Company of Canada Inc.
Exchanges: TSX
Symbol: BMO.PR.Y
CUSIP: 06367X200

6.816% Non-Cum. 5-Year Rate Reset Class B Pref., Series 44

DBRS Rating:	Pfd-2	Jun 2, 2023	
Issued:	16,000,000 shs.	Sep 17, 2018	$25.000
O/S:	16,000,000 shs.	Jan 31, 2024	
Dividend:	$1.704 (Q)	Feb 25/May 25/Aug 25/Nov 25	

Dividend Details: Reset on Nov 25, 2028. Dividend rate will be reset in every fifth year thereafter. The annual dividend rate will be equal to the sum of the five-year Government of Canada Bond Yield plus 2.68%. Previously, annual divd. rate was 1.212500 per sh until Nov 24, 2023.
Redemption: Redeem. on the following dates on min. 30 and max. 60 days' notice, conditional on the approval of the Superintendent of Financial Institutions, as follows:
Nov 25, 2023..$25.00   Nov 25, 2028..$25.00
Redeem. on Nov. 25 in every fifth year thereafter on min. 30 and max. 60 days' notice at $25.00 per share, conditional on approval of the Superintendent of Financial Institutions.
Convertible: Automatically convertible into common shares upon occurrence of a Non-Viability Contingent Capital (NVCC) trigger event as defined by OFSI.
Exchange: Exchange. on min. 30 days' notice into pfd B ser 45 as follows:
On Nov 25, 2023.....................$25.00.....................1   On Nov 25, 2028......................$25.00......................1
Exchange. on Nov. 25 in every fifth year thereafter. Exchange. after notice from the Bank given with approval from the Superintendent of Financial Institutions.

Lead Underwriter(s): BMO Capital Markets
Transfer Agent: Computershare Trust Company of Canada Inc.
Registrar: Computershare Trust Company of Canada Inc.
Exchanges: TSX
Symbol: BMO.PR.E
CUSIP: 06368B207

5.10% 5-Year Rate Reset Class B Pref., Series 46

DBRS Rating:	Pfd-2	Jun 2, 2023	
Issued:	14,000,000 shs.	Apr 17, 2019	$25.000
O/S:	14,000,000 shs.	Jan 31, 2024	
Dividend:	$1.275 (Q)	Feb 25/May 25/Aug 25/Nov 25	

Dividend Details: Reset on May 25, 2024. Dividend rate will be reset in every fifth year thereafter. The annual dividend rate will be equal to the sum of the five-year Government of Canada Bond Yield plus 3.51%.
Redemption: Redeem. on the following dates on min. 30 and max. 60 days' notice, conditional on the approval of the Superintendent of Financial Institutions, as follows:
May 25, 2024...$25.00   May 25, 2029..$25.00
Redeem. on May 25 in every fifth year thereafter on min. 30 and max. 60 days' notice at $25.00 per share, conditional on approval of the Superintendent of Financial Institutions.
Convertible: Automatically convertible into common shares upon occurrence of a Non-Viability Contingent Capital (NVCC) trigger event as defined by OFSI.
Exchange: Exchange. on min. 30 days' notice into pfd ser 47 as follows:
On May 25, 2024...................$25.00....................1   On May 25, 2029....................$25.00....................1
Exchange. on May 25 in every fifth year thereafter. Exchange. after notice from the Bank given with approval from the Superintendent of Financial Institutions.
Lead Underwriter(s): BMO Capital Markets
Transfer Agent: Computershare Trust Company of Canada Inc.
Registrar: Computershare Trust Company of Canada Inc.
Exchanges: TSX
Symbol: BMO.PR.F
CUSIP: 06368B108

Bombardier Inc.

Floating Rate Cum. Redeem. Pref., Series 2

Issued:	12,000,000 shs.	May 22, 1997	$25.000
O/S:	2,684,527 shs.	Dec 31, 2023	
Dividend:	F.R. (M)	Payable on the 15th day of each month	

Dividend Details: The annual floating dividend rate for the first month was equal to 80% of prime. Subsequently, the dividend rate floats in relation to changes in prime and is adjusted upwards or downwards on a monthly basis by an adjustment factor whenever the Calculated Trading Price of shares is $24.90 or less or $25.10 or more, respectively. The maximum monthly adjustment for changes in the Calculated Trading Price is +/- 4.00% of prime. The annual floating dividend rate applicable for a month will in no event be less than 50% of prime or greater than prime. Previously, annual divd. rate was 1.375000 per sh until Jul 31, 2002. Dividend was payable quarterly.
Redemption: Redeem. on and after the following dates on min. 45 days' notice as follows:
Aug 1, 2002..$25.00   Aug 2, 2002..$25.50
Exchange: Exchange. on min. 45 days' notice into pfd ser 3 sh as follows:
On Aug 1, 2012....................$25.00....................1   On Aug 1, 2017.....................$25.00....................1
On Aug 1, 2022....................$25.00....................1   On Aug 1, 2027.....................$25.00....................1
Exchange. on Aug. 1 in every fifth year thereafter.
Lead Underwriter(s): Midland Walwyn Capital Inc., Scotia Capital Inc.
Transfer Agent: Computershare Investor Services Inc.
Registrar: Computershare Investor Services Inc.
Exchanges: TSX
Symbol: BBD.PR.B
CUSIP: 097751507

6.25% Cum. Redeem. Pref., Series 4

Issued:	9,400,000 shs.	Mar 8, 2002	$25.000
O/S:	9,400,000 shs.	Dec 31, 2023	
Dividend:	$1.5625 (Q)	Jan 31/Apr 30/Jul 31/Oct 31	

Redemption: Redeem. on and after the following dates on min. 30 and max. 60 days' notice as follows:
Mar 31, 2007..$26.00   Mar 31, 2008..$25.75
Mar 31, 2009..$25.50   Mar 31, 2010..$25.25
Mar 31, 2011..$25.00

Convertible: Convert. by company on min. 30 days' notice into cl B sh. Conversion rate is determined by dividing the then applicable redemption price, plus declared and unpaid divds. to but excluding the date of conversion, by the greater of $2 and 95% of the weighted average trading price of the com. shs. on the Toronto Stock Exchange for the 20 consecutive trading days ending on the last trading day ending on or before the fourth day prior to the date of conversion. In lieu of fractional shs., cash payment will be made.

Exchange: Exchange. on min. 45 days' notice into 1 new pfd per pref. sh, being an exchange price per new pfd of $25.00.

Lead Underwriter(s): CIBC World Markets Inc., Scotia Capital Inc.
Transfer Agent: Computershare Investor Services Inc.
Registrar: Computershare Investor Services Inc.
Exchanges: TSX
Symbol: BBD.PR.C
CUSIP: 097751705

4.588% Cum. Redeem. Pref., Series 3

Issued:	9,402,093 shs.	Jul 26, 2002	$25.000
O/S:	9,315,473 shs.	Dec 31, 2023	
Dividend:	$1.147 (Q)	Jan 31/Apr 30/Jul 31/Oct 31	

Dividend Details: Reset on Aug 1, 2027. For the five-year period from August 1, 2017 and including July 31, 2022, the Series 3 Cumulative Redeemable Preferred Shares carry fixed cumulative preferential cash dividends at a rate of 3.983% or $0.99575 Cdn per share per annum, payable quarterly on the last day of January, April, July and October of each year at a rate of $0.2489375 Cdn, if declared. For each succeeding five year period, the applicable fixed annual rate of the cumulative preferential cash dividends calculated by the Corporation shall not be less than 80% of the Government of Canada bond yield, as defined in the Articles of Incorporation. Previously, annual divd. rate was 0.995750 per sh until Jul 31, 2022.

Redemption: Redeem. on the following dates on min. 45 and max. 60 days' notice as follows:
Aug 1, 2012..$25.00   Aug 1, 2017..$25.00
Redeem. on Aug. 1 in every fifth year thereafter.

Exchange: Exchange. on min. 14 days' notice into pfd ser 2 sh as follows:
On Aug 1, 2012.....................$25.00.....................1   On Aug 1, 2017.....................$25.00.....................1
On Aug 1, 2022.....................$25.00.....................1   On Aug 1, 2027.....................$25.00.....................1
Exchange. on Aug. 1 in every fifth year thereafter.

Note: Issued upon exchange of the pref. shs., series 2.
Transfer Agent: Computershare Investor Services Inc.
Registrar: Computershare Investor Services Inc.
Exchanges: TSX
Symbol: BBD.PR.D
CUSIP: 097751606

Brookfield Corporation
(formerly Brookfield Asset Management Inc.)

Floating Rate Cum. Class A Pfce., Series 4

DBRS Rating:	Pfd-2	Nov 22, 2023	
Issued:	4,000,000 shs.	Jun 30, 1984	$25.000
O/S:	3,983,910 shs.	Dec 31, 2023	
Dividend:	F.R. (Q)	Mar 31/Jun 30/Sep 30/Dec 31	

Dividend Details: Quarterly divd. rate is one quarter of 70% of prime times $25.00.

FP Equities — Preferreds & Derivatives 2024

Redemption: Redeem. at any time on min. 30 and max. 60 days' notice at $25.00 per sh.
Note: Formerly 1981 pfce. shs., series D of Brascan Limited. Outstanding shs. include class A pref. shs., series 7.
Transfer Agent: TSX Trust Company
Registrar: TSX Trust Company
Exchanges: TSX
Symbol: BN.PR.C
CUSIP: 11271J305

Floating Rate Cum. Class A Pfce., Series 2

DBRS Rating:	Pfd-2	Nov 22, 2023	
Issued:	10,465,100 shs.	Nov 9, 1984	$25.000
O/S:	10,220,175 shs.	Dec 31, 2023	
Dividend:	F.R. (Q)	Mar 31/Jun 30/Sep 30/Dec 31	

Dividend Details: Quarterly divd. rate is one quarter of 70% of prime times $25.00.
Redemption: Redeem. at any time on min. 30 and max. 60 days' notice at $25.00 per sh.
Note: Formerly cl. A pfce. shs., series E of Edper Group Limited. In 1986, cl. A series B and cl. A series C pfce. shs. were converted into cl. A, series E pfce. shs. on a 1-for-0.4 basis. Cl. A, series F pfce. shs. were converted to cl. A, series E pfce. shs. on a 1-for-1 basis. An additional 6,020,000 cl. A, series E pfce. shs. were issued due to these conversions. An additional 45,100 shs. were issued in 1996 upon conversion of class A series D shs.
Transfer Agent: TSX Trust Company
Registrar: TSX Trust Company
Exchanges: TSX
Symbol: BN.PR.B
CUSIP: 11271J206

Floating Rate Cum. Class A Pfce, Series 13

DBRS Rating:	Pfd-2	Nov 22, 2023	
Issued:	9,999,000 shs.	Jan 24, 2005	$25.000
O/S:	8,792,596 shs.	Dec 31, 2023	
Dividend:	F.R. (Q)	Mar 31/Jun 30/Sep 30/Dec 31	

Dividend Details: Quarterly divd. rate is one quarter of 70% of prime times $25.00.
Redemption: Redeem. at any time on min. 30 and max. 60 days' notice at $25.00 per sh.
Note: Issued upon exchange of Brascan Financial Corporation floating rate class I preferred shares, series A and class II preferred shares, series 3.
Transfer Agent: TSX Trust Company
Registrar: TSX Trust Company
Exchanges: TSX
Symbol: BN.PR.K
CUSIP: 11271J602

4.75% Cum. Class A Pref., Series 17

DBRS Rating:	Pfd-2	Nov 22, 2023	
Issued:	8,000,000 shs.	Nov 20, 2006	$25.000
O/S:	7,840,204 shs.	Dec 31, 2023	
Dividend:	$1.1875 (Q)	Mar 31/Jun 30/Sep 30/Dec 31	

Redemption: Redeem. on and after the following dates on min. 30 and max. 60 days' notice as follows:
Dec 31, 2011 ....$26.00   Dec 31, 2012 ....$25.75
Dec 31, 2013 ....$25.50   Dec 31, 2014 ....$25.25
Dec 31, 2015 ....$25.00

Convertible: Convert. into pfd sh designated by the company. The company may at any time give the holders of the series 17 preferred shares the right, at their option, to convert such shares into a further series of preferred shares designated by the company.

Convertible: Convert. by company on min. 30 days' notice into cl A sh. Conversion rate is determined by dividing the then applicable redemption price, plus declared and unpaid divds. to but excluding the date of conversion, by the greater of $2 and 95% of the weighted average trading price of the class A shares on the Toronto Stock Exchange for the 20 trading days ending on or before the fourth day prior to the date of conversion. In lieu of fractional shs., cash payment will be made.

Exchange: Exchange. into 1 new pfd per pref. sh, being an exchange price per new pfd of $25.00.

Lead Underwriter(s): RBC Capital Markets, CIBC World Markets Inc.
Transfer Agent: TSX Trust Company
Registrar: TSX Trust Company
Exchanges: TSX
Symbol: BN.PR.M
CUSIP: 11271J701

4.75% Cum. Class A Pref., Series 18

DBRS Rating:	Pfd-2	Nov 22, 2023	
Issued:	8,000,000 shs.	May 9, 2007	$25.000
O/S:	7,681,088 shs.	Dec 31, 2023	
Dividend:	$1.1875 (Q)	Mar 31/Jun 30/Sep 30/Dec 31	

Redemption: Redeem. on and after the following dates on min. 30 and max. 60 days' notice as follows:
Jun 30, 2012..$26.00   Jun 30, 2013..$25.75
Jun 30, 2014..$25.50   Jun 30, 2015..$25.25
Jun 30, 2016..$25.00

Convertible: Convert. by company on min. 30 days' notice into cl A sh. Conversion rate is determined by dividing the then applicable redemption price, plus declared and unpaid dividends to but excluding the date of conversion, by the greater of $2 and 95% of the weighted average trading price of the common shares on the Toronto Stock Exchange for the 20 trading days ending on or immediately prior to the fifth day prior to the date of conversion. In lieu of fractional shs., cash payment will be made.

Exchange: Exchange. into 1 new pfd per pref. sh, being an exchange price per new pfd of $25.00.
Lead Underwriter(s): CIBC World Markets Inc., RBC Capital Markets
Transfer Agent: TSX Trust Company
Registrar: TSX Trust Company
Exchanges: TSX
Symbol: BN.PR.N
CUSIP: 11271J800

3.237% Cum. 6.5-Year Rate Reset Class A Pref., Series 24

DBRS Rating:	Pfd-2	Nov 22, 2023	
Issued:	11,000,000 shs.	Jan 14, 2010	$25.000
O/S:	10,808,027 shs.	Dec 31, 2023	
Dividend:	$0.80925 (Q)	Mar 31/Jun 30/Sep 30/Dec 31	

Dividend Details: Reset on Jul 1, 2026. Dividend rate will be reset in every fifth year thereafter. The annual dividend rate will be equal to the sum of the five-year Government of Canada Bond Yield plus 2.30%. Previously, annual divd. rate was 0.753500 per sh until Jun 30, 2021.

Redemption: Redeem. on the following dates on min. 30 and max. 60 days' notice as follows:
Jun 30, 2016..$25.00   Jun 30, 2021..$25.00
Redeem. on June 30 in every fifth year thereafter on min. 30 and max. 60 days' notice at $25.00 per share.

Exchange: Was exchange. on min. 30 days' notice into pfd A ser 25 as follows:
On Jun 30, 2016.....................$25.00....................1   On Jun 30, 2021......................$25.00......................1
Exchange. on June 30 in every fifth year thereafter.
Lead Underwriter(s): Scotia Capital Inc., CIBC World Markets Inc., RBC Capital Markets, TD Securities Inc.
Transfer Agent: TSX Trust Company
Registrar: TSX Trust Company
Exchanges: TSX
Symbol: BN.PR.R
CUSIP: 11271J883

3.846% Cum. 5-Year Rate Reset Class A Pref., Series 26

DBRS Rating:	Pfd-2	Nov 22, 2023	
Issued:	10,000,000 shs.	Oct 29, 2010	$25.000
O/S:	9,770,928 shs.	Dec 31, 2023	
Dividend:	$0.9615 (Q)	Mar 31/Jun 30/Sep 30/Dec 31	

Dividend Details: Reset on Apr 1, 2027. Dividend rate will be reset in every fifth year thereafter. The annual dividend rate will be equal to the sum of the five-year Government of Canada Bond Yield plus 2.31%. Previously, annual divd. rate was 0.867750 per sh until Mar 31, 2022.

Redemption: Redeem. on the following dates on min. 30 and max. 60 days' notice as follows:
Mar 31, 2017..$25.00   Mar 31, 2022..$25.00
Redeem. on March 31 in every fifth year thereafter on min. 30 and max. 60 days' notice at $25.00 per share.

FP Equities — Preferreds & Derivatives 2024

Exchange: Was exchange. on min. 30 days' notice into pfd A ser 27 as follows:
On Mar 31, 2017....................$25.00....................1   On Mar 31, 2022....................$25.00....................1
Exchange. on March 31 in every fifth year thereafter.
Lead Underwriter(s): CIBC World Markets Inc., RBC Capital Markets, Scotia Capital Inc., TD Securities Inc.
Transfer Agent: TSX Trust Company
Registrar: TSX Trust Company
Exchanges: TSX
Symbol: BN.PR.T
CUSIP: 11271J867

4.606% Cum. 5-Year Rate Reset Class A Pref., Series 28

DBRS Rating:	Pfd-2	Nov 22, 2023
Issued:	9,400,000 shs.	Feb 8, 2011 $25.000
O/S:	9,233,927 shs.	Dec 31, 2023
Dividend:	$1.1515 (Q)	Mar 31/Jun 30/Sep 30/Dec 31

Dividend Details: Reset on Jul 1, 2027. Dividend rate will be reset in every fifth year thereafter. The annual dividend rate will be equal to the sum of the five-year Government of Canada Bond Yield plus 1.80%. Previously, annual divd. rate was 0.681750 per sh until Jun 30, 2022.
Redemption: Redeem. on the following dates on min. 30 and max. 60 days' notice as follows:
Jun 30, 2017...$25.00   Jun 30, 2022...$25.00
Redeem. on June 30 in every fifth year thereafter on min. 30 and max. 60 days' notice at $25.00 per share.
Exchange: Was exchange. on min. 30 days' notice into pfd A ser 29 as follows:
On Jun 30, 2017....................$25.00....................1   On Jun 30, 2022....................$25.00....................1
Exchange. on June 30 in every fifth year thereafter.
Lead Underwriter(s): TD Securities Inc., CIBC World Markets Inc., RBC Capital Markets, Scotia Capital Inc.
Transfer Agent: TSX Trust Company
Registrar: TSX Trust Company
Exchanges: TSX
Symbol: BN.PR.X
CUSIP: 11271J842

6.089% Cum. 5-Year Rate Reset Class A Pref., Series 30

DBRS Rating:	Pfd-2	Nov 22, 2023
Issued:	10,000,000 shs.	Nov 2, 2011 $25.000
O/S:	9,787,090 shs.	Dec 31, 2023
Dividend:	$1.52225 (Q)	Mar 31/Jun 30/Sep 30/Dec 31

Dividend Details: Reset on Jan 1, 2028. Dividend rate will be reset in every fifth year thereafter. The annual dividend rate will be equal to the sum of the five-year Government of Canada Bond Yield plus 2.96%. Previously, annual divd. rate was 1.171250 per sh until Dec 31, 2022.
Redemption: Redeem. on the following dates on min. 30 and max. 60 days' notice as follows:
Dec 31, 2017...$25.00   Dec 31, 2022...$25.00
Redeem. on Dec. 31 in every fifth year thereafter on min. 30 and max. 60 days' notice at $25.00 per share.
Exchange: Was exchange. on min. 30 days' notice into pfd A ser 31 as follows:
On Dec 31, 2017....................$25.00....................1   On Dec 31, 2022....................$25.00....................1
Exchange. on Dec. 31 in every fifth year thereafter.
Lead Underwriter(s): CIBC World Markets Inc., RBC Capital Markets, Scotia Capital Inc., TD Securities Inc.
Transfer Agent: TSX Trust Company
Registrar: TSX Trust Company
Exchanges: TSX
Symbol: BN.PR.Z
CUSIP: 11271J826

6.744% Cum. 5-Year Rate Reset Class A Pref., Series 32

DBRS Rating:	Pfd-2	Nov 22, 2023
Issued:	12,000,000 shs.	Mar 13, 2012 $25.000
O/S:	11,750,299 shs.	Dec 31, 2023
Dividend:	$1.686 (Q)	Mar 31/Jun 30/Sep 30/Dec 31

Dividend Details: Reset on Oct 1, 2028. Dividend rate will be reset in every fifth year thereafter. The annual dividend rate will be equal to the sum of the five-year Government of Canada Bond Yield plus 2.90%. Previously, annual divd. rate was 1.265250 per sh until Sep 30, 2023.

Redemption: Redeem. on the following dates on min. 30 and max. 60 days' notice as follows:
Sep 30, 2018...$25.00   Sep 30, 2023...$25.00
Redeem. on Sept. 30 in every fifth year thereafter on min. 30 and max. 60 days' notice at $25.00 per share.
Exchange: Was exchange. on min. 30 days' notice into pfd A ser 33 as follows:
On Sep 30, 2018.....................$25.00...................1   On Sep 30, 2023.....................$25.00...................1
Exchange. on Sept. 30 in every fifth year thereafter.
Lead Underwriter(s): RBC Capital Markets, CIBC World Markets Inc., Scotia Capital Inc., TD Securities Inc.
Transfer Agent: TSX Trust Company
Registrar: TSX Trust Company
Exchanges: TSX
Symbol: BN.PF.A
CUSIP: 11271J792

6.145% Cum. 5-Year Rate Reset Class A Pref., Series 34

DBRS Rating:	Pfd-2	Nov 22, 2023	
Issued:	10,000,000 shs.	Sep 12, 2012	$25.000
O/S:	9,876,735 shs.	Dec 31, 2023	
Dividend:	$1.53625 (Q)	Mar 31/Jun 30/Sep 30/Dec 31	

Dividend Details: Reset on Apr 1, 2029. Dividend rate will be reset in every fifth year thereafter. The annual dividend rate will be equal to the sum of the five-year Government of Canada Bond Yield plus 2.63%. Previously, annual divd. rate was 1.109250 per sh until Mar 31, 2024.
Redemption: Redeem. on the following dates on min. 30 and max. 60 days' notice as follows:
Mar 31, 2019...$25.00   Mar 31, 2024...$25.00
Redeem. on March 31 in every fifth year thereafter on min. 30 and max. 60 days' notice at $25.00 per share.
Exchange: Was exchange. on min. 30 days' notice into pfd A ser 35 as follows:
On Mar 31, 2019.....................$25.00...................1   On Mar 31, 2024.....................$25.00...................1
Exchange. on March 31 in every fifth year thereafter.
Lead Underwriter(s): TD Securities Inc., CIBC World Markets Inc., RBC Capital Markets, Scotia Capital Inc.
Transfer Agent: TSX Trust Company
Registrar: TSX Trust Company
Exchanges: TSX
Symbol: BN.PF.B
CUSIP: 11271J776

4.85% Cum. Class A Pfce., Series 36

DBRS Rating:	Pfd-2	Nov 22, 2023	
Issued:	8,000,000 shs.	Nov 27, 2012	$25.000
O/S:	7,842,909 shs.	Dec 31, 2023	
Dividend:	$1.2125 (Q)	Mar 31/Jun 30/Sep 30/Dec 31	

Redemption: Redeem. on and after the following dates on min. 30 and max. 60 days' notice as follows:
Mar 31, 2018...$26.00   Mar 31, 2019...$25.75
Mar 31, 2020...$25.50   Mar 31, 2021...$25.25
Mar 31, 2022...$25.00
Lead Underwriter(s): Scotia Capital Inc., CIBC World Markets Inc., RBC Capital Markets, TD Securities Inc.
Transfer Agent: TSX Trust Company
Registrar: TSX Trust Company
Exchanges: TSX
Symbol: BN.PF.C
CUSIP: 11271J750

4.9% Cum. Class A Pfce., Series 37

DBRS Rating:	Pfd-2	Nov 22, 2023	
Issued:	8,000,000 shs.	Jun 13, 2013	$25.000
O/S:	7,830,091 shs.	Dec 31, 2023	
Dividend:	$1.225 (Q)	Mar 31/Jun 30/Sep 30/Dec 31	

Redemption: Redeem. on and after the following dates on min. 30 and max. 60 days' notice as follows:
Sep 30, 2018...$26.00   Sep 30, 2019...$25.75
Sep 30, 2020...$25.50   Sep 30, 2021...$25.25
Sep 30, 2022...$25.00

FP Equities — Preferreds & Derivatives 2024

Lead Underwriter(s): CIBC World Markets Inc., RBC Capital Markets, Scotia Capital Inc., TD Securities Inc.
Transfer Agent: TSX Trust Company
Registrar: TSX Trust Company
Exchanges: TSX
Symbol: BN.PF.D
CUSIP: 11271J743

3.568% Cum. 5-Year Rate Reset Class A Pref., Series 38

DBRS Rating:	Pfd-2	Nov 22, 2023	
Issued:	8,000,000 shs.	Mar 13, 2014	$25.000
O/S:	7,906,132 shs.	Dec 31, 2023	
Dividend:	$0.892 (Q)	Mar 31/Jun 30/Sep 30/Dec 31	

Dividend Details: Reset on Apr 1, 2025. Dividend rate will be reset in every fifth year thereafter. The annual dividend rate will be equal to the sum of the five-year Government of Canada Bond Yield plus 2.55%. Previously, annual divd. rate was 1.100000 per sh until Mar 31, 2020.

Redemption: Redeem. on the following dates on min. 30 and max. 60 days' notice as follows:
Mar 31, 2020..$25.00   Mar 31, 2025..$25.00
Redeem. on March 31 in every fifth year thereafter on min. 30 and max. 60 days' notice at $25.00 per share.

Exchange: Exchange. on min. 30 days' notice into pfd A ser 39 as follows:
On Mar 31, 2020.....................$25.00.....................1   On Mar 31, 2025.....................$25.00.....................1
Exchange. on March 31 in every fifth year thereafter.

Lead Underwriter(s): TD Securities Inc., CIBC World Markets Inc., RBC Capital Markets, Scotia Capital Inc.
Transfer Agent: TSX Trust Company
Registrar: TSX Trust Company
Exchanges: TSX
Symbol: BN.PF.E
CUSIP: 11271J735

4.029% Cum. 5-Year Rate Reset Class A Pref., Series 40

DBRS Rating:	Pfd-2	Nov 22, 2023	
Issued:	12,000,000 shs.	Jun 5, 2014	$25.000
O/S:	11,841,025 shs.	Dec 31, 2023	
Dividend:	$1.00725 (Q)	Mar 31/Jun 30/Sep 30/Dec 31	

Dividend Details: Reset on Oct 1, 2024. Dividend rate will be reset in every fifth year thereafter. The annual dividend rate will be equal to the sum of the five-year Government of Canada Bond Yield plus 2.86%. Previously, annual divd. rate was 1.125000 per sh until Sep 30, 2019.

Redemption: Redeem. on the following dates on min. 30 and max. 60 days' notice as follows:
Sep 30, 2019..$25.00   Sep 30, 2024..$25.00
Redeem. on Sept. 30 in every fifth year thereafter on min. 30 and max. 60 days' notice at $25.00 per share.

Exchange: Exchange. on min. 30 days' notice into pfd A ser 41 as follows:
On Sep 30, 2019.....................$25.00.....................1   On Sep 30, 2024.....................$25.00.....................1
Exchange. on Sept. 30 in every fifth year thereafter.

Lead Underwriter(s): RBC Capital Markets, CIBC World Markets Inc., Scotia Capital Inc., TD Securities Inc.
Transfer Agent: TSX Trust Company
Registrar: TSX Trust Company
Exchanges: TSX
Symbol: BN.PF.F
CUSIP: 11271J719

3.254% Cum. 5-Year Rate Reset Class A Pref., Series 42

DBRS Rating:	Pfd-2	Nov 22, 2023	
Issued:	12,000,000 shs.	Oct 8, 2014	$25.000
O/S:	11,887,500 shs.	Dec 31, 2023	
Dividend:	$0.8135 (Q)	Mar 31/Jun 30/Sep 30/Dec 31	

Dividend Details: Reset on Jul 1, 2025. Dividend rate will be reset in every fifth year thereafter. The annual dividend rate will be equal to the sum of the five-year Government of Canada Bond Yield plus 2.84%. Previously, annual divd. rate was 1.125000 per sh until Jun 30, 2020.

Redemption: Redeem. on the following dates on min. 30 and max. 60 days' notice as follows:
Jun 30, 2020..$25.00   Jun 30, 2025..$25.00
Redeem. on June 30 in every fifth year thereafter on min. 30 and max. 60 days' notice at $25.00 per share.

Exchange: Exchange. on min. 30 days' notice into pfd A ser 43 as follows:
On Jun 30, 2020......................$25.00......................1   On Jun 30, 2025......................$25.00......................1
Exchange. on June 30 in every fifth year thereafter.
Lead Underwriter(s): TD Securities Inc., RBC Capital Markets, CIBC World Markets Inc., Scotia Capital Inc.
Transfer Agent: TSX Trust Company
Registrar: TSX Trust Company
Exchanges: TSX
Symbol: BN.PF.G
CUSIP: 11271J685

5.0% Cum. 5-Year Rate Reset Class A Pref., Series 44

DBRS Rating:	Pfd-2	Nov 22, 2023	
Issued:	10,000,000 shs.	Oct 2, 2015	$25.000
O/S:	9,831,929 shs.	Dec 31, 2023	
Dividend:	$1.25 (Q)	Mar 31/Jun 30/Sep 30/Dec 31	

Dividend Details: Reset on Jan 1, 2026. Dividend rate will be reset in every fifth year thereafter. The annual dividend rate will be equal to the greater of (i) the sum of the five-year Government of Canada Bond Yield plus 4.17% and (ii) 5.00%. Previously, annual divd. rate was 1.250000 per sh until Dec 31, 2020.
Redemption: Redeem. on the following dates on min. 30 and max. 60 days' notice as follows:
Dec 31, 2020......................................$25.00   Dec 31, 2025......................................$25.00
Redeem. on Dec. 31 in every fifth year thereafter on min. 30 and max. 60 days' notice at $25.00 per share.
Exchange: Exchange. on min. 30 days' notice into pfd A ser 45 as follows:
On Dec 31, 2020......................$25.00......................1   On Dec 31, 2025......................$25.00......................1
Exchange. on Dec. 31 in every fifth year thereafter.
Lead Underwriter(s): Scotia Capital Inc., CIBC World Markets Inc., RBC Capital Markets, TD Securities Inc.
Transfer Agent: TSX Trust Company
Registrar: TSX Trust Company
Exchanges: TSX
Symbol: BN.PF.H
CUSIP: 11271J669

5.386% Cum. 5-Year Rate Reset Class A Pref., Series 46

DBRS Rating:	Pfd-2	Nov 22, 2023	
Issued:	12,000,000 shs.	Nov 18, 2016	$25.000
O/S:	11,740,797 shs.	Dec 31, 2023	
Dividend:	$1.3465 (Q)	Mar 31/Jun 30/Sep 30/Dec 30	

Dividend Details: Reset on Apr 1, 2027. Dividend rate will be reset in every fifth year thereafter. The annual dividend rate will be equal to the greater of (i) the sum of the five-year Government of Canada Bond Yield plus 3.85% and (ii) 4.80%. Previously, annual divd. rate was 1.200000 per sh until Mar 31, 2022.
Redemption: Redeem. on the following dates on min. 30 and max. 60 days' notice as follows:
Mar 31, 2022......................................$25.00   Mar 31, 2027......................................$25.00
Redeem. on March 31 in every fifth year thereafter on min. 30 and max. 60 days' notice at $25.00 per share.
Exchange: Exchange. on min. 30 days' notice into pfd A ser 47 as follows:
On Mar 31, 2022......................$25.00......................1   On Mar 31, 2027......................$25.00......................1
Exchange. on March 31 in every fifth year thereafter.
Lead Underwriter(s): TD Securities Inc., Scotia Capital Inc.
Transfer Agent: TSX Trust Company
Registrar: TSX Trust Company
Exchanges: TSX
Symbol: BN.PF.I
CUSIP: 11271J644

6.229% Cum. 5-Year Rate Reset Class A Pref., Series 48

DBRS Rating:	Pfd-2	Nov 22, 2023	
Issued:	12,000,000 shs.	Sep 13, 2017	$25.000
O/S:	11,885,972 shs.	Dec 31, 2023	
Dividend:	$1.55725 (Q)	Mar 31/Jun 30/Sep 30/Dec 31	

Dividend Details: Reset on Jan 1, 2028. Dividend rate will be reset in every fifth year thereafter. The annual dividend rate will be equal to the greater of (i) the sum of the five-year Government of Canada Bond Yield plus 3.10% and (ii) 4.75%. Previously, annual divd. rate was 1.187500 per sh until Dec 31, 2022.

Redemption: Redeem. on the following dates on min. 30 and max. 60 days' notice as follows:
Dec 31, 2022..$25.00   Dec 31, 2027..$25.00
Redeem. on Dec. 31 in every fifth year thereafter on min. 30 and max. 60 days' notice at $25.00 per share.
Exchange: Exchange. on min. 30 days' notice into pfd A ser 49 as follows:
On Dec 31, 2022...................$25.00...................1   On Dec 31, 2027...................$25.00...................1
Exchange. on Dec. 31 in every fifth year thereafter.
Lead Underwriter(s): CIBC World Markets Inc., RBC Capital Markets, Scotia Capital Inc., TD Securities Inc.
Transfer Agent: TSX Trust Company
Registrar: TSX Trust Company
Exchanges: TSX
Symbol: BN.PF.J
CUSIP: 11271J628

Brookfield Infrastructure Partners L.P.

3.974% Cum. 5-Year Rate Reset Class A Preferred Limited Partnership Units, Series 1

Issued:	5,000,000 shs.	Mar 12, 2015	$25.000
O/S:	4,989,265 shs.	Dec 31, 2023	
Dividend:	$0.9935 (Q)	Mar 31/Jun 30/Sep 30/Dec 31	

Dividend Details: Reset on Jul 1, 2025. Dividend rate will be reset in every fifth year thereafter. The annual dividend rate will be equal to the sum of the five-year Government of Canada Bond Yield plus 3.56%. Previously, annual divd. rate was 1.125000 per sh until Jun 30, 2020.
Redemption: Redeem. on the following dates on min. 25 and max. 60 days' notice as follows:
Jun 30, 2020..$25.00   Jun 30, 2025..$25.00
Redeem. on June 30 in every fifth year thereafter on min. 25 and max. 60 days' notice at $25.00 per share.
Exchange: Exchange. on min. 25 days' notice into pfd A ser 2 as follows:
On Jun 30, 2020...................$25.00...................1   On Jun 30, 2025...................$25.00...................1
Exchange. on June 30 in every fifth year thereafter.
Lead Underwriter(s): CIBC World Markets Inc., RBC Capital Markets, Scotia Capital Inc., TD Securities Inc.
Transfer Agent: Computershare Investor Services Inc.
Registrar: Computershare Investor Services Inc.
Exchanges: TSX
Symbol: BIP.PR.A
CUSIP: G16252127

5.5% Cum. 5-year Rate Reset Class A Preferred Limited Partnership Units, Series 3

Issued:	5,000,000 shs.	Dec 8, 2015	$25.000
O/S:	4,989,262 shs.	Dec 31, 2023	
Dividend:	$1.375 (Q)	Mar 31/Jun 30/Sep 30/Dec 31	

Dividend Details: Reset on Jan 1, 2026. Dividend rate will be reset in every fifth year thereafter. The annual dividend rate will be equal to the greater of (i) the sum of the five-year Government of Canada Bond Yield plus 4.53% and (ii) 5.50%. Previously, annual divd. rate was 1.375000 per sh until Dec 31, 2020.
Redemption: Redeem. on the following dates on min. 25 and max. 60 days' notice as follows:
Dec 31, 2020..$25.00   Dec 31, 2025..$25.00
Redeem. on Dec. 31 in every fifth year thereafter on min. 25 and max. 60 days' notice at $25.00 per share.
Exchange: Exchange. on min. 25 days' notice into pfd A ser 4 as follows:
On Dec 31, 2020...................$25.00...................1   On Dec 31, 2025...................$25.00...................1
Exchange. on Dec. 31 in every fifth year thereafter.
Lead Underwriter(s): RBC Capital Markets, CIBC World Markets Inc., Scotia Capital Inc., TD Securities Inc.
Transfer Agent: Computershare Investor Services Inc.
Registrar: Computershare Investor Services Inc.
Exchanges: TSX
Symbol: BIP.PR.B
CUSIP: G16252143

6.642% Cum. 5-year Rate Reset Class A Preferred Limited Partnership Units, Series 9

Issued:	8,000,000 shs.	Jan 23, 2018	$25.000
O/S:	7,986,595 shs.	Dec 31, 2023	
Dividend:	$1.6605 (Q)	Mar 31/Jun 30/Sep 30/Dec 31	

Dividend Details: Reset on Apr 1, 2028. Dividend rate will be reset in every fifth year thereafter. The annual dividend rate will be equal to the greater of (i) the sum of the five-year Government of Canada Bond Yield plus 3.00% and (ii) 5.00%. Previously, annual divd. rate was 1.250000 per sh until Mar 31, 2023.

Redemption: Redeem. on the following dates on min. 25 and max. 60 days' notice as follows:
Mar 31, 2023..$25.00   Mar 31, 2028..$25.00
Redeem. on March 31 in every fifth year thereafter on min. 25 and max. 60 days' notice at $25.00 per share.

Exchange: Exchange. on min. 25 days' notice into pfd A ser 10 as follows:
On Mar 31, 2023.....................$25.00.....................1   On Mar 31, 2028.....................$25.00.....................1
Exchange. on March 31 in every fifth year thereafter.

Lead Underwriter(s): CIBC World Markets Inc., BMO Capital Markets, RBC Capital Markets, Scotia Capital Inc., TD Securities Inc.

Transfer Agent: Computershare Investor Services Inc.
Registrar: Computershare Investor Services Inc.
Exchanges: TSX
Symbol: BIP.PR.E
CUSIP: G16252200

6.446% Cum. 5-year Rate Reset Class A Preferred Limited Partnership Units, Series 11

Issued:	10,000,000 shs.	Sep 12, 2018	$25.000
O/S:	9,936,190 shs.	Dec 31, 2023	
Dividend:	$1.6115 (Q)	Mar 31/Jun 30/Sep 30/Dec 31	

Dividend Details: Reset on Dec 31, 2028. Dividend rate will be reset in every fifth year thereafter. The annual dividend rate will be equal to the greater of (i) the sum of the five-year Government of Canada Bond Yield plus 2.92% and (ii) 5.10%. Previously, annual divd. rate was 1.275000 per sh until Dec 30, 2023.

Redemption: Redeem. on the following dates on min. 25 and max. 60 days' notice as follows:
Dec 31, 2023..$25.00   Dec 31, 2028..$25.00
Redeem. on Dec. 31 in every fifth year thereafter on min. 25 and max. 60 days' notice at $25.00 per share.

Exchange: Exchange. on min. 25 days' notice into pfd A ser 12 as follows:
On Dec 31, 2023.....................$25.00.....................1   On Dec 31, 2028.....................$25.00.....................1
Exchange. on Dec. 31 in every fifth year thereafter.

Lead Underwriter(s): Scotia Capital Inc., BMO Capital Markets, CIBC World Markets Inc., RBC Capital Markets, TD Securities Inc.

Transfer Agent: Computershare Investor Services Inc.
Registrar: Computershare Investor Services Inc.
Exchanges: TSX
Symbol: BIP.PR.F
CUSIP: G16252226

Brookfield Investments Corporation

4.70% Cum. Class 1 Senior Pref., Series A

DBRS Rating:	Pfd-2	Nov 22, 2023	
Issued:	5,990,785 shs.	Jan 4, 2007	$25.000
O/S:	5,711,940 shs.	Dec 31, 2023	
Dividend:	$1.175 (Q)	Mar 31/Jun 30/Sep 30/Dec 31	

Redemption: Redeem. at any time on min. 30 and max. 60 days' notice at $25.00 per sh.

Note: Issued upon exchange of Brookfield Investments (formerly Brascade Corporation) class 1 senior series B preferred shares and Diversified Canadian Financial II Corp. class A senior preferred shares. On Jan 4, 2007, the company amalgamated with Diversified Canadian Financial II Corp.

Transfer Agent: CIBC Mellon Trust Company
Registrar: CIBC Mellon Trust Company
Exchanges: TSX-VEN
Symbol: BRN.PR.A
CUSIP: 112741202

Brookfield Office Properties Inc.

4.01% Cum. 6.5-Year Rate Reset Class AAA Pref., Series N

DBRS Rating:	Pfd-3 low	May 15, 2023	
Issued:	11,000,000 shs.	Jan 20, 2010	$25.000
O/S:	11,000,000 shs.	Dec 31, 2023	
Dividend:	$1.0025 (Q)	Mar 31/Jun 30/Sep 30/Dec 31	

Dividend Details: Reset on Jul 1, 2026. Dividend rate will be reset in every fifth year thereafter. The annual dividend rate will be equal to the sum of the five-year Government of Canada Bond Yield plus 3.07%. Previously, annual divd. rate was 0.945500 per sh until Jun 30, 2021.

Redemption: Redeem. on the following dates on min. 30 and max. 60 days' notice as follows:
Jun 30, 2016...$25.00   Jun 30, 2021..$25.00
Redeem. on June 30 in every fifth year thereafter on min. 30 and max. 60 days' notice at $25.00 per share.

Exchange: Was exchange. on min. 30 days' notice into pfd AAA ser O as follows:
On Jun 30, 2016....................$25.00....................1   On Jun 30, 2021.....................$25.00......................1
Exchange. on June 30 in every fifth year thereafter.

Lead Underwriter(s): TD Securities Inc., CIBC World Markets Inc., RBC Capital Markets, Scotia Capital Inc.
Transfer Agent: TSX Trust Company
Registrar: TSX Trust Company
Exchanges: TSX
Symbol: BPO.PR.N
CUSIP: 112900832

4.536% Cum. 6.5-Year Rate Reset Class AAA Pref., Series P

DBRS Rating:	Pfd-3 low	May 15, 2023	
Issued:	12,000,000 shs.	Oct 21, 2010	$25.000
O/S:	12,000,000 shs.	Dec 31, 2023	
Dividend:	$1.134 (Q)	Mar 31/Jun 30/Sep 30/Dec 31	

Dividend Details: Reset on Apr 1, 2027. Dividend rate will be reset in every fifth year thereafter. The annual dividend rate will be equal to the sum of the five-year Government of Canada Bond Yield plus 3.0%. Previously, annual divd. rate was 1.040250 per sh until Mar 31, 2022.

Redemption: Redeem. on the following dates on min. 30 and max. 60 days' notice as follows:
Mar 31, 2017...$25.00   Mar 31, 2022..$25.00
Redeem. on March 31 in every fifth year thereafter on min. 30 and max. 60 days' notice at $25.00 per share.

Exchange: Was exchange. on min. 30 days' notice into pfd AAA ser Q as follows:
On Mar 31, 2017....................$25.00....................1   On Mar 31, 2022.....................$25.00......................1
Exchange. on March 31 in every fifth year thereafter.

Lead Underwriter(s): RBC Capital Markets, CIBC World Markets Inc., Scotia Capital Inc., TD Securities Inc.
Transfer Agent: TSX Trust Company
Registrar: TSX Trust Company
Exchanges: TSX
Symbol: BPO.PR.P
CUSIP: 112900816

4.3% Cum. 5-Year Rate Reset Class AAA Pref., Series R

DBRS Rating:	Pfd-3 low	May 15, 2023	
Issued:	10,000,000 shs.	Sep 2, 2011	$25.000
O/S:	10,000,000 shs.	Dec 31, 2023	
Dividend:	$1.075 (Q)	Mar 31/Jun 30/Sep 30/Dec 31	

Dividend Details: Reset on Oct 1, 2026. Dividend rate will be reset in every fifth year thereafter. The annual dividend rate will be equal to the sum of the five-year Government of Canada Bond Yield plus 3.48%. Previously, annual divd. rate was 1.038750 per sh until Sep 30, 2021.

Redemption: Redeem. on the following dates on min. 30 and max. 60 days' notice as follows:
Sep 30, 2016...$25.00   Sep 30, 2021..$25.00
Redeem. on Sept. 30 in every fifth year thereafter on min. 30 and max. 60 days' notice at $25.00 per share.

Exchange: Was exchange. on min. 30 days' notice into pfd AAA ser S as follows:
On Sep 30, 2016....................$25.00....................1   On Sep 30, 2021.....................$25.00......................1
Exchange. on Sept. 30 in every fifth year thereafter.

Lead Underwriter(s): RBC Capital Markets, CIBC World Markets Inc., Scotia Capital Inc., TD Securities Inc.
Transfer Agent: TSX Trust Company
Registrar: TSX Trust Company
Exchanges: TSX
Symbol: BPO.PR.R
CUSIP: 112900782

FP Equities — Preferreds & Derivatives 2024

6.79% Cum. 5-Year Rate Reset Class AAA Pref., Series T

DBRS Rating:	Pfd-3 low	May 15, 2023	
Issued:	10,000,000 shs.	Sep 13, 2012	$25.000
O/S:	10,000,000 shs.	Dec 31, 2023	
Dividend:	$1.6975 (Q)	Mar 31/Jun 30/Sep 30/Dec 31	

Dividend Details: Reset on Jan 1, 2029. Dividend rate will be reset in every fifth year thereafter. The annual dividend rate will be equal to the sum of the five-year Government of Canada Bond Yield plus 3.16%. Previously, annual divd. rate was 1.345750 per sh until Dec 31, 2023.
Redemption: Redeem. on the following dates on min. 30 and max. 60 days' notice as follows:
Dec 31, 2018...$25.00   Dec 31, 2023...$25.00
Redeem. on Dec. 31 in every fifth year thereafter on min. 30 and max. 60 days' notice at $25.00 per share.
Exchange: Was exchange. on min. 30 days' notice into pfd AAA ser U as follows:
On Dec 31, 2018......................$25.00....................1   On Dec 31, 2023.....................$25.00......................1
Exchange. on Dec 31 in every fifth year thereafter.
Lead Underwriter(s): CIBC World Markets Inc., RBC Capital Markets, Scotia Capital Inc., TD Securities Inc.
Transfer Agent: TSX Trust Company
Registrar: TSX Trust Company
Exchanges: TSX
Symbol: BPO.PR.T
CUSIP: 112900766

Floating Rate Cum. Class AAA Pref., Series V

Issued:	1,805,489 shs.	May 1, 2013	$25.000
O/S:	1,805,489 shs.	Dec 31, 2023	
Dividend:	F.R. (Q)	Feb 14/May 14/Aug 14/Nov 14	

Dividend Details: Quarterly divd. rate is one quarter of 70% of prime times $25.00.
Redemption: Redeem. on and after May 2, 2013 on min. 30 days' notice at $25.00 per sh.
Note: Issued upon exchange of BPO Properties Ltd. Preferred Shares, Series G.
Transfer Agent: TSX Trust Company
Registrar: TSX Trust Company
Exchanges: TSX
Symbol: BPO.PR.X
CUSIP: 112900741

Floating Rate Cum. Class AAA Pref., Series W

Issued:	3,816,527 shs.	May 1, 2013	$25.000
O/S:	3,816,527 shs.	Dec 31, 2023	
Dividend:	F.R. (Q)	Feb 14/May 14/Aug 14/Nov 14	

Dividend Details: Quarterly divd. rate is one quarter of 70% of prime times $25.00.
Redemption: Redeem. on and after May 2, 2013 on min. 30 days' notice at $25.00 per sh.
Note: Issued upon exchange of BPO Properties Ltd. Preferred Shares, Series J.
Transfer Agent: TSX Trust Company
Registrar: TSX Trust Company
Exchanges: TSX
Symbol: BPO.PR.W
CUSIP: 112900733

Floating Rate Cum. Class AAA Pref., Series Y

Issued:	2,847,711 shs.	May 1, 2013
O/S:	2,847,711 shs.	Dec 31, 2023
Dividend:	F.R. (Q)	Feb 14/May 14/Aug 14/Nov 14

Dividend Details:
Redemption: Redeem. on and after May 2, 2013 on min. 30 days' notice at $25.00 per sh.
Note: Issued upon exchange of BPO Properties Ltd. Preferred Shares, Series M.
Transfer Agent: TSX Trust Company
Registrar: TSX Trust Company
Exchanges: TSX
Symbol: BPO.PR.Y
CUSIP: 112900717

4.709% Cum. 5-Year Rate Reset Class AAA Pref., Series AA

DBRS Rating:	Pfd-3 low	May 15, 2023	
Issued:	12,000,000 shs.	Oct 23, 2014	$25.000
O/S:	12,000,000 shs.	Dec 31, 2023	
Dividend:	$1.17725 (Q)	Mar 31/Jun 30/Sep 30/Dec 31	

Dividend Details: Reset on Jan 1, 2025. Dividend rate will be reset in every fifth year thereafter. The annual dividend rate will be equal to the sum of the five-year Government of Canada Bond Yield plus 3.15%. Previously, annual divd. rate was 1.187500 per sh until Dec 31, 2019.

Redemption: Redeem. on the following dates on min. 30 and max. 60 days' notice as follows:
Dec 31, 2019...$25.00   Dec 31, 2024..$25.00
Redeem. on Dec 31 in every fifth year thereafter on min. 30 and max. 60 days' notice at $25.00 per share.

Exchange: Exchange. on min. 30 days' notice into pfd AAA ser BB as follows:
On Dec 31, 2019....................$25.00....................1   On Dec 31, 2024....................$25.00......................1
Exchange. on Dec. 31 in every fifth year thereafter.

Lead Underwriter(s): RBC Capital Markets, CIBC World Markets Inc., Scotia Capital Inc., TD Securities Inc.
Transfer Agent: TSX Trust Company
Registrar: TSX Trust Company
Exchanges: TSX
Symbol: BPO.PR.A
CUSIP: 112900683

6.12% Cum. Class AAA 5-Year Rate Reset Pref., Series CC

DBRS Rating:	Pfd-3 low	May 15, 2023	
Issued:	8,000,000 shs.	Apr 27, 2016	$25.000
O/S:	8,000,000 shs.	Dec 31, 2023	
Dividend:	$1.53 (Q)	Mar 31/Jun 30/Sep 30/Dec 31	

Dividend Details: Reset on Jul 1, 2026. Dividend rate will be reset in every fifth year thereafter. The annual dividend rate will be equal to the greater of (i) the sum of the five-year Government of Canada Bond Yield plus 5.18% and (ii) 6.00%. Previously, annual divd. rate was 1.500000 per sh until Jun 30, 2021.

Redemption: Redeem. on the following dates on min. 30 and max. 60 days' notice as follows:
Jun 30, 2021..$25.00   Jun 30, 2026..$25.00
Redeem. on June 30 in every fifth year thereafter on min. 30 and max. 60 days' notice at $25.00 per share.

Exchange: Exchange. on min. 30 days' notice into pfd AAA ser DD as follows:
On Jun 30, 2021....................$25.00....................1   On Jun 30, 2026....................$25.00......................1
Exchange. on June 30 in every fifth year thereafter.

Lead Underwriter(s): TD Securities Inc., CIBC World Markets Inc., RBC Capital Markets, Scotia Capital Inc.
Transfer Agent: TSX Trust Company
Registrar: TSX Trust Company
Exchanges: TSX
Symbol: BPO.PR.C
CUSIP: 112900667

5.496% Cum. Class AAA 5-Year Rate Reset Pref., Series EE

DBRS Rating:	Pfd-3 low	May 15, 2023	
Issued:	11,000,000 shs.	Feb 17, 2017	$25.000
O/S:	11,000,000 shs.	Dec 31, 2023	
Dividend:	$1.374 (Q)	Mar 31/Jun 30/Sep 30/Dec 31	

Dividend Details: Reset on Apr 1, 2027. Dividend rate will be reset in every fifth year thereafter. The annual dividend rate will be equal to the greater of (i) the sum of the five-year Government of Canada Bond Yield plus 3.96% and (ii) 5.10%. Previously, annual divd. rate was 1.275000 per sh until Mar 31, 2022.

Redemption: Redeem. on the following dates on min. 30 and max. 60 days' notice as follows:
Mar 31, 2022..$25.00   Mar 31, 2027..$25.00
Redeem. on March 31 in every fifth year thereafter on min. 30 and max. 60 days' notice at $25.00 per share.

Exchange: Exchange. on min. 30 days' notice into pfd AAA ser FF as follows:
On Mar 31, 2022....................$25.00....................1   On Mar 31, 2027....................$25.00......................1
Exchange. on March 31 in every fifth year thereafter.

Lead Underwriter(s): Scotia Capital Inc., CIBC World Markets Inc., RBC Capital Markets, TD Securities Inc.
Transfer Agent: TSX Trust Company
Registrar: TSX Trust Company
Exchanges: TSX
Symbol: BPO.PR.E
CUSIP: 112900642

6.546% Cum. 5-Year Rate Reset Class AAA Pref., Series GG

DBRS Rating:	Pfd-3 low	May 15, 2023
Issued:	11,000,000 shs.	May 4, 2017 $25.000
O/S:	11,000,000 shs.	Dec 31, 2023
Dividend:	$1.6365 (Q)	Mar 31/Jun 30/Sep 30/Dec 31

Dividend Details: Reset on Jul 1, 2027. Dividend rate will be reset in every fifth year thereafter. The annual dividend rate will be equal to the greater of (i) the sum of the five-year Government of Canada Bond Yield plus 3.74% and (ii) 4.85%. Previously, annual divd. rate was 1.212500 per sh until Jun 30, 2022.
Redemption: Redeem. on the following dates on min. 30 and max. 60 days' notice as follows:
Jun 30, 2022..$25.00   Jun 30, 2027...$25.00
Redeem. on June 30 in every fifth year thereafter on min. 30 and max. 60 days' notice at $25.00 per share.
Exchange: Exchange. on min. 30 days' notice into pfd AAA ser HH as follows:
On Jun 30, 2022.....................$25.00.....................1   On Jun 30, 2027.....................$25.00.....................1
Exchange. on June 30 in every fifth year thereafter.
Lead Underwriter(s): TD Securities Inc., CIBC World Markets Inc., RBC Capital Markets, Scotia Capital Inc.
Transfer Agent: TSX Trust Company
Registrar: TSX Trust Company
Exchanges: TSX
Symbol: BPO.PR.G
CUSIP: 112900626

6.359% Cum. 5-Year Rate Reset Class AAA Pref., Series II

DBRS Rating:	Pfd-3 low	May 15, 2023
Issued:	10,000,000 shs.	Dec 7, 2017 $25.000
O/S:	10,000,000 shs.	Dec 31, 2023
Dividend:	$1.58975 (Q)	Mar 31/Jun 30/Sep 30/Dec 31

Dividend Details: Dividend rate will be reset in every fifth year thereafter. The annual dividend rate will be equal to the greater of (i) the sum of the five-year Government of Canada Bond Yield plus 3.23% and (ii) 4.85%. Reset on Jan 1, 2028. Previously, annual divd. rate was 1.212500 per sh until Dec 31, 2022.
Redemption: Redeem. on the following dates on min. 30 and max. 60 days' notice as follows:
Dec 31, 2022..$25.00   Dec 31, 2027...$25.00
Redeem. on Dec. 31 in every fifth year thereafter on min. 30 and max. 60 days' notice at $25.00 per share.
Exchange: Exchange. on min. 30 days' notice into pfd AAA ser JJ as follows:
On Dec 31, 2022.....................$25.00.....................1   On Dec 31, 2027.....................$25.00.....................1
Exchange. on Dec. 31 in every fifth year thereafter.
Lead Underwriter(s): Scotia Capital Inc., CIBC World Markets Inc., RBC Capital Markets, TD Securities Inc.
Transfer Agent: TSX Trust Company
Registrar: TSX Trust Company
Exchanges: TSX
Symbol: BPO.PR.I
CUSIP: 112900592

Brookfield Property Split Corp.

Cum. Class A Pref., Series 1

Issued:	1,000,000 shs.	Jun 11, 2014 US$25.000
O/S:	636,328 shs.	Dec 31, 2023
Dividend:	US$1.3125 (Q)	Mar 31/Jun 30/Sep 30/Dec 31

Redemption: Redeem. on and after the following dates on min. 30 days' notice as follows:
Jun 11, 2014..US$25.33   Jun 30, 2014...US$25.00

FP Equities — Preferreds & Derivatives 2024

Retraction: Retract. on and after the following dates as follows:
Jun 11, 2014...US$23.75   Sep 30, 2015...US$25.00
Note: Issued upon exchange of Brookfield Office Properties Inc. class AAA pref. shares series G, series H, Series J or series K shares.
Transfer Agent: TSX Trust Company
Registrar: TSX Trust Company
Exchanges: TSX
Symbol: BPS.PR.U
CUSIP: 112827209

Cum. Class A Pref., Series 2

Issued:	1,000,000 shs.	Jun 11, 2014	$25.000
O/S:	362,546 shs.	Dec 31, 2023	
Dividend:	$1.4375 (Q)	Mar 31/Jun 30/Sep 30/Dec 31	

Redemption: Redeem. on and after the following dates on min. 30 days' notice as follows:
Jun 11, 2014..$25.33   Dec 31, 2014..$25.00
Retraction: Retract. on and after the following dates as follows:
Jun 11, 2014..$23.75   Dec 31, 2015..$25.00
Note: Issued upon exchange of Brookfield Office Properties Inc. class AAA pref. shares series G, series H, Series J or series K shares.
Transfer Agent: TSX Trust Company
Registrar: TSX Trust Company
Exchanges: TSX
Symbol: BPS.PR.A
CUSIP: 112827308

Cum. Class A Pref., Series 3

Issued:	1,000,000 shs.	Jun 11, 2014	$25.000
O/S:	408,962 shs.	Dec 31, 2023	
Dividend:	$1.25 (Q)	Mar 31/Jun 30/Sep 30/Dec 31	

Redemption: Redeem. on and after the following dates as follows:
Jun 11, 2014..$25.25   Jun 30, 2014..$25.00
Retraction: Retract. on and after the following dates as follows:
Jun 11, 2014..$23.75   Dec 31, 2014..$25.00
Note: Issued upon exchange of Brookfield Office Properties Inc. class AAA pref. shares series G, series H, Series J or series K shares.
Transfer Agent: TSX Trust Company
Registrar: TSX Trust Company
Exchanges: TSX
Symbol: BPS.PR.B
CUSIP: 112827407

Cum. Class A Pref., Series 4

Issued:	1,000,000 shs.	Jun 11, 2014	$25.000
O/S:	365,661 shs.	Dec 31, 2023	
Dividend:	$1.30 (Q)	Mar 31/Jun 30/Sep 30/Dec 31	

Redemption: Redeem. on and after the following dates on min. 30 days' notice as follows:
Jun 11, 2014..$25.67   Dec 31, 2014..$25.33
Dec 31, 2015..$25.00
Retraction: Retract. on and after the following dates as follows:
Jun 11, 2014..$23.75   Dec 31, 2016..$25.00
Note: Issued upon exchange of Brookfield Office Properties Inc. class AAA pref. shares series G, series H, Series J or series K shares.
Transfer Agent: TSX Trust Company
Registrar: TSX Trust Company
Exchanges: TSX
Symbol: BPS.PR.C
CUSIP: 112827506

Brookfield Renewable Power Preferred Equity Inc.

3.137% Cum. 5-Year Rate Reset Class A Pref., Series 1

DBRS Rating:	Pfd-3 high	May 26, 2023
Issued:	10,000,000 shs.	Mar 10, 2010 $25.000
O/S:	6,849,533 shs.	Dec 31, 2023
Dividend:	$0.78425 (Q)	Jan 31/Apr 30/Jul 31/Oct 31

Dividend Details: Reset on May 1, 2025. Dividend rate will be reset in every fifth year thereafter. The annual dividend rate will be equal to the sum of the five-year Government of Canada Bond Yield plus 2.62%. Previously, annual divd. rate was 0.838750 per sh until Apr 30, 2020.

Redemption: Redeem. on the following dates on min. 30 and max. 60 days' notice as follows:
Apr 30, 2015...$25.00   Apr 30, 2020...$25.00
Redeem. on April 30 in every fifth year thereafter on min. 30 and max. 60 days' notice at $25.00 per share.

Exchange: Was exchange. on min. 30 days' notice into pfd A ser 2 sh as follows:
On Apr 30, 2015....................$25.00....................1   On Apr 30, 2020....................$25.00....................1
Exchange. on April 30 in every fifth year thereafter.

Note: The payment of dividends and principal (upon redemption or liquidation, dissolution and winding-up of the company) is guaranteed by Brookfield Renewable Power Fund.

Lead Underwriter(s): Scotia Capital Inc., CIBC World Markets Inc., RBC Capital Markets, TD Securities Inc.
Transfer Agent: Computershare Investor Services Inc.
Registrar: Computershare Investor Services Inc.
Exchanges: TSX
Symbol: BRF.PR.A
CUSIP: 11283Q206

4.351% Cum. 5-Year Rate Reset Class A Pref., Series 3

DBRS Rating:	Pfd-3 high	May 26, 2023
Issued:	10,000,000 shs.	Oct 11, 2012 $25.000
O/S:	9,961,399 shs.	Dec 31, 2023
Dividend:	$1.08775 (Q)	Jan 31/Apr 30/Jul 31/Oct 31

Dividend Details: Reset on Aug 1, 2024. Dividend rate will be reset in every fifth year thereafter. The annual dividend rate will be equal to the sum of the five-year Government of Canada Bond Yield plus 2.94%. Previously, annual divd. rate was 1.100000 per sh until Jul 31, 2019.

Redemption: Redeem. on the following dates on min. 30 and max. 60 days' notice as follows:
Jul 31, 2019...$25.00   Jul 31, 2024...$25.00
Redeem. on July 31 in every fifth year thereafter on min. 30 and max. 60 days' notice at $25.00 per share.

Exchange: Exchange. on min. 30 days' notice into pfd A ser 4 as follows:
On Jul 31, 2019....................$25.00....................1   On Jul 31, 2024....................$25.00....................1
Exchange. on July 31 in every fifth year thereafter.

Lead Underwriter(s): TD Securities Inc., CIBC World Markets Inc., RBC Capital Markets, Scotia Capital Inc.
Transfer Agent: Computershare Trust Company of Canada Inc.
Registrar: Computershare Trust Company of Canada Inc.
Exchanges: TSX
Symbol: BRF.PR.C
CUSIP: 11283Q404

5% Cum. Class A Pref., Series 5

DBRS Rating:	Pfd-3 high	May 26, 2023
Issued:	7,000,000 shs.	Jan 29, 2013 $25.000
O/S:	4,114,504 shs.	Dec 31, 2023
Dividend:	$1.25 (Q)	Jan 31/Apr 30/Jul 31/Oct 31

Redemption: Redeem. on and after the following dates on min. 30 and max. 60 days' notice as follows:
Apr 30, 2018...$26.00   Apr 30, 2019...$25.75
Apr 30, 2020...$25.50   Apr 30, 2021...$25.25
Apr 30, 2022...$25.00

Lead Underwriter(s): RBC Capital Markets, CIBC World Markets Inc., Scotia Capital Inc., TD Securities Inc.
Transfer Agent: Computershare Investor Services Inc.
Registrar: Computershare Investor Services Inc.
Exchanges: TSX
Symbol: BRF.PR.E
CUSIP: 11283Q602

FP Equities — Preferreds & Derivatives 2024

5% Cum. Class A Pref., Series 6

DBRS Rating:	Pfd-3 high	May 26, 2023
Issued:	7,000,000 shs.	May 1, 2013	$25.000
O/S:	7,000,000 shs.	Dec 31, 2023
Dividend:	$1.25 (Q)	Jan 31/Apr 30/Jul 31/Oct 31

Redemption: Redeem. on and after the following dates on min. 30 and max. 60 days' notice as follows:
Jul 31, 2018................................$26.00 Jul 31, 2019...................................$25.75
Jul 31, 2020................................$25.50 Jul 31, 2021...................................$25.25
Jul 31, 2022................................$25.00
Lead Underwriter(s): Scotia Capital Inc., CIBC World Markets Inc., RBC Capital Markets, TD Securities Inc.
Transfer Agent: Computershare Investor Services Inc.
Registrar: Computershare Investor Services Inc.
Exchanges: TSX
Symbol: BRF.PR.F
CUSIP: 11283Q701

Floating Rate Cum. Class A Pref., Series 2

Issued:	4,518,289 shs.	May 1, 2015	$25.000
O/S:	3,110,531 shs.	Dec 31, 2023
Dividend:	F.R. (Q)	Jan 31/Apr 30/Jul 31/Oct 31

Dividend Details: Quarterly divd. rate is T-bill plus 2.62%.
Redemption: Redeem. on the following dates on min. 30 and max. 60 days' notice as follows:
Apr 30, 2020................................$25.00 Apr 30, 2025...................................$25.00
Redeem. on April 30 in every fifth year thereafter on min. 30 and max. 60 days' notice at $25.00 per share.
Exchange: Exchange. on min. 30 days' notice into pfd A ser 1 sh as follows:
On Apr 30, 2020.................$25.00...................1   On Apr 30, 2025...................$25.00.....................1
Exchange. on April 30 in every fifth year thereafter.
Note: Issued upon exchange of an equal number of Preferred Shares, Series 1.
Transfer Agent: Computershare Investor Services Inc.
Registrar: Computershare Investor Services Inc.
Exchanges: TSX
Symbol: BRF.PR.B
CUSIP: 11283Q305

CU Inc.

4.60% Cum. Pref., Series 1

DBRS Rating:	Pfd-2 high	Jul 25, 2023
Issued:	4,600,000 shs.	Apr 18, 2007	$25.000
O/S:	4,600,000 shs.	Dec 31, 2023
Dividend:	$1.15 (Q)	Mar 1/Jun 1/Sep 1/Dec 1

Redemption: Redeem. on and after the following dates on min. 30 and max. 60 days' notice as follows:
Jun 1, 2012................................$26.00 Jun 1, 2013...................................$25.75
Jun 1, 2014................................$25.50 Jun 1, 2015...................................$25.25
Jun 1, 2016................................$25.00
Lead Underwriter(s): BMO Capital Markets
Transfer Agent: TSX Trust Company
Registrar: TSX Trust Company
Exchanges: TSX
Symbol: CIU.PR.A
CUSIP: 22944C205

2.29% Cum. 5-Year Rate Reset Pref., Series 4

DBRS Rating:	Pfd-2 high	Jul 25, 2023
Issued:	3,000,000 shs.	Dec 2, 2010	$25.000
O/S:	3,000,000 shs.	Dec 31, 2023
Dividend:	$0.5725 (Q)	Mar 1/Jun 1/Sep 1/Dec 1

Dividend Details: Reset on Jun 1, 2025. Dividend rate will be reset in every fifth year thereafter. The annual dividend rate will be equal to the sum of the five-year Government of Canada Bond Yield plus 1.36%. Previously, annual divd. rate was 0.560000 per sh until May 31, 2021.

Redemption: Redeem. on the following dates on min. 30 and max. 60 days' notice as follows:
Jun 1, 2016...$25.00   Jun 1, 2021...$25.00
Redeem. on June 1 in every fifth year thereafter on min. 30 and max. 60 days' notice at $25.00 per share.
Exchange: Was exchange. on min. 30 days' notice into pfd ser 5 as follows:
On Jun 1, 2016.........................$25.00.....................1   On Jun 1, 2021.......................$25.00........................1
Exchange. on June 1 in every fifth year thereafter. The holders of the Cum. Redeemable Pref. Shares, Series 5 will be entitled to receive quarterly floating rate cash dividends as and when declared by the board of directors.
Lead Underwriter(s): BMO Capital Markets, RBC Capital Markets
Transfer Agent: TSX Trust Company
Registrar: TSX Trust Company
Exchanges: TSX
Symbol: CIU.PR.C
CUSIP: 22944C502

Canaccord Genuity Group Inc.

4.028% Cum. 5-Year Rate Reset First Pref., Series A

Issued:	4,540,000 shs.	Jun 23, 2011	$25.000
O/S:	4,540,000 shs.	Dec 31, 2023	
Dividend:	$1.007 (Q)	Mar 31/Jun 30/Sep 30/Dec 31	

Dividend Details: Reset on Oct 1, 2026. Dividend rate will be reset in every fifth year thereafter. The annual dividend rate will be equal to the sum of the five-year Government of Canada Bond Yield plus 3.21%. Previously, annual divd. rate was 0.971250 per sh until Sep 30, 2021.
Redemption: Redeem. on the following dates on min. 30 and max. 60 days' notice as follows:
Sep 30, 2016..$25.00   Sep 30, 2021...$25.00
Redeem. on Sept. 30 in every fifth year thereafter on min. 30 and max. 60 days' notice at $25.00 per share.
Exchange: Was exchange. on min. 30 days' notice into pfd 1st ser B as follows:
On Sep 30, 2016.....................$25.00.....................1   On Sep 30, 2021......................$25.00........................1
Exchange. on Sept. 30 in every fifth year thereafter.
Lead Underwriter(s): CIBC World Markets Inc., Canaccord Genuity Corp.
Transfer Agent: Computershare Investor Services Inc.
Registrar: Computershare Investor Services Inc.
Exchanges: TSX
Symbol: CF.PR.A
CUSIP: 134801307

6.837% Cum. 5-Year Rate Reset First Pref., Series C

Issued:	4,000,000 shs.	Apr 10, 2012	$25.000
O/S:	4,000,000 shs.	Dec 31, 2023	
Dividend:	$1.70925 (Q)	Mar 31/Jun 30/Sep 30/Dec 31	

Dividend Details: Reset on Jul 1, 2027. Dividend rate will be reset in every fifth year thereafter. The annual dividend rate will be equal to the sum of the five-year Government of Canada Bond Yield plus 4.03%. Previously, annual divd. rate was 1.248250 per sh until Jun 30, 2022.
Redemption: Redeem. on the following dates on min. 30 and max. 60 days' notice as follows:
Jun 30, 2017..$25.00   Jun 30, 2022...$25.00
Redeem. on June 30 in every fifth year thereafter on min. 30 and max. 60 days' notice at $25.00 per share.
Exchange: Was exchange. on min. 30 days' notice into pfd 1st ser D as follows:
On Jun 30, 2017.....................$25.00.....................1   On Jun 30, 2022......................$25.00........................1
Exchange. on June 30 in every fifth year thereafter.
Lead Underwriter(s): CIBC World Markets Inc., Canaccord Genuity Corp., RBC Capital Markets
Transfer Agent: Computershare Investor Services Inc.
Registrar: Computershare Investor Services Inc.
Exchanges: TSX
Symbol: CF.PR.C
CUSIP: 134801604

Canadian Imperial Bank of Commerce

3.981% Non-Cum. 5-Year Rate Reset Class A Pref., Series 39

DBRS Rating:	Pfd-2	Jun 1, 2023	
Issued:	16,000,000 shs.	Jun 11, 2014	$25.000
O/S:	16,000,000 shs.	Jan 31, 2024	
Dividend:	$0.99525 (Q)	Jan 28/Apr 28/Jul 28/Oct 28	

Dividend Details: Reset on Jul 31, 2024. Dividend rate will be reset in every fifth year thereafter. The annual dividend rate will be equal to the sum of the five-year Government of Canada Bond Yield plus 2.32%. Previously, annual divd. rate was 0.975000 per sh until Jul 30, 2019.

Redemption: Redeem. on the following dates on min. 30 and max. 60 days' notice, conditional on the approval of the Superintendent of Financial Institutions, as follows:
Jul 31, 2019..$25.00   Jul 31, 2024..$25.00
Redeem. on July 31 in every fifth year thereafter on min. 30 and max. 60 days' notice at $25.00 per share, subject to certain conditions including approval of the Superintendent of Financial Institutions.

Convertible: Automatically convertible into common shares upon occurrence of a Non-Viability Contingent Capital (NVCC) trigger event as defined by OFSI.

Exchange: Exchange. into pfd A ser 40 as follows:
On Jul 31, 2019....................$25.00....................1   On Jul 31, 2024.....................$25.00.....................1
Exchange. on min. 15 max. 30 days' notice. Exchange. on July 31 in every fifth year thereafter. Exchange. unless the Bank has announced its intention to redeem.

Lead Underwriter(s): CIBC World Markets Inc.
Transfer Agent: TSX Trust Company
Registrar: TSX Trust Company
Exchanges: TSX
Symbol: CM.PR.O
CUSIP: 136069440

3.909% Non-Cum. 5-Year Rate Reset Class A Pref., Series 41

DBRS Rating:	Pfd-2	Jun 1, 2023	
Issued:	12,000,000 shs.	Dec 16, 2014	$25.000
O/S:	12,000,000 shs.	Jan 31, 2024	
Dividend:	$0.97725 (Q)	Jan 28/Apr 28/Jul 28/Oct 28	

Dividend Details: Reset on Jan 31, 2025. Dividend rate will be reset in every fifth year thereafter. The annual dividend rate will be equal to the sum of the five-year Government of Canada Bond Yield plus 2.24%. Previously, annual divd. rate was 0.937500 per sh until Jan 30, 2020.

Redemption: Redeem. on the following dates on min. 30 and max. 60 days' notice, conditional on the approval of the Superintendent of Financial Institutions, as follows:
Jan 31, 2020...$25.00   Jan 31, 2025..$25.00
Redeem. on Jan. 31 in every fifth year thereafter on min. 30 and max. 60 days' notice at $25.00 per share, subject to certain conditions including the approval of the Superintendent of Financial Institutions.

Convertible: Automatically convertible into common shares upon occurrence of a Non-Viability Contingent Capital (NVCC) trigger event as defined by OFSI.

Exchange: Exchange. into pfd A ser 42 as follows:
On Jan 31, 2020....................$25.00....................1   On Jan 31, 2025.....................$25.00.....................1
Exchange. on min. 15 max. 30 days' notice. Exchange. on Jan. 31 in every fifth year thereafter. Exchange. unless the Bank has announced its intention to redeem.

Lead Underwriter(s): CIBC World Markets Inc.
Transfer Agent: TSX Trust Company
Registrar: TSX Trust Company
Exchanges: TSX
Symbol: CM.PR.P
CUSIP: 136069424

3.143% Non-Cum. 5-Year Rate Reset Class A Pref., Series 43

DBRS Rating:	Pfd-2	Jun 1, 2023	
Issued:	12,000,000 shs.	Mar 11, 2015	$25.000
O/S:	12,000,000 shs.	Jan 31, 2024	
Dividend:	$0.78575 (Q)	Jan 28/Apr 28/Jul 28/Oct 28	

Dividend Details: Reset on Jul 31, 2025. Dividend rate will be reset in every fifth year thereafter. The annual dividend rate will be equal to the sum of the five-year Government of Canada Bond Yield plus 2.79%. Previously, annual divd. rate was 0.900000 per sh until Jul 30, 2020.

Redemption: Redeem. on the following dates on min. 30 and max. 60 days' notice, conditional on the approval of the Superintendent of Financial Institutions, as follows:
Jul 31, 2020...$25.00   Jul 31, 2025...$25.00
Redeem. on July 31 in every fifth year thereafter on min. 30 and max. 60 days' notice at $25.00 per share, subject to certain conditions including the approval of the Superintendent of Financial Institutions.

Convertible: Automatically convertible into common shares upon occurrence of a Non-Viability Contingent Capital (NVCC) trigger event as defined by OFSI.

Exchange: Exchange. into pfd A ser 44 as follows:
On Jul 31, 2020......................$25.00......................1   On Jul 31, 2025......................$25.00......................1
Exchange. on min. 15 max. 30 days' notice. Exchange. on July 31 in every fifth year thereafter. Exchange. unless the Bank has announced its intention to redeem.

Lead Underwriter(s): CIBC World Markets Inc., Scotia Capital Inc.
Transfer Agent: TSX Trust Company
Registrar: TSX Trust Company
Exchanges: TSX
Symbol: CM.PR.Q
CUSIP: 136069390

5.878% Non-Cum. 5-Year Rate Reset Class A Pref., Series 47

DBRS Rating:	Pfd-2	Jun 1, 2023	
Issued:	18,000,000 shs.	Jan 18, 2018	$25.000
O/S:	18,000,000 shs.	Jan 31, 2024	
Dividend:	$1.4695 (Q)	Jan 28/Apr 28/Jul 28/Oct 28	

Dividend Details: Reset on Jan 31, 2028. Dividend rate will be reset in every fifth year thereafter. The annual dividend rate will be equal to the sum of the five-year Government of Canada Bond Yield plus 2.45%. Previously, annual divd. rate was 1.125000 per sh until Jan 30, 2023.

Redemption: Redeem. on the following dates on min. 30 and max. 60 days' notice, conditional on the approval of the Superintendent of Financial Institutions, as follows:
Jan 31, 2023...$25.00   Jan 31, 2028...$25.00
Redeem. on Jan. 31 in every fifth year thereafter on min. 30 and max. 60 days' notice at $25.00 per share, conditional on approval of the Superintendent of Financial Institutions.

Convertible: Automatically convertible into common shares upon occurrence of a Non-Viability Contingent Capital (NVCC) trigger event as defined by OFSI.

Exchange: Exchange. into pfd A ser 48 as follows:
On Jan 31, 2023......................$25.00......................1   On Jan 31, 2028......................$25.00......................1
Exchange. on min. 15 max. 30 days' notice. Exchange. on Jan. 31 in every fifth year thereafter. Exchange. unless the Bank has announced its intention to redeem.

Lead Underwriter(s): CIBC World Markets Inc., BMO Capital Markets, National Bank Financial Inc.
Transfer Agent: TSX Trust Company
Registrar: TSX Trust Company
Exchanges: TSX
Symbol: CM.PR.S
CUSIP: 136070877

5.15% Non-Cum. 5-Year Rate Reset Class A Pref., Series 51

DBRS Rating:	Pfd-2	Jun 1, 2023	
Issued:	10,000,000 shs.	Jun 4, 2019	$25.000
O/S:	10,000,000 shs.	Jan 31, 2024	
Dividend:	$1.2875 (Q)	Jan 28/Apr 28/Jul 28/Oct 28	

Dividend Details: Reset on Jul 31, 2024. Dividend rate will be reset in every fifth year thereafter. The annual dividend rate will be equal to the sum of the five-year Government of Canada Bond Yield plus 3.62%.

Redemption: Redeem. on the following dates on min. 30 and max. 60 days' notice, conditional on the approval of the Superintendent of Financial Institutions, as follows:
Jul 31, 2024...$25.00   Jul 31, 2029...$25.00
Redeem. on July 31 in every fifth year thereafter on min. 30 and max. 60 days' notice at $25.00 per share, conditional on approval of the Superintendent of Financial Institutions.

Convertible: Automatically convertible into common shares upon occurrence of a Non-Viability Contingent Capital (NVCC) trigger event as defined by OFSI.

Exchange: Exchange. into pfd A ser 52 as follows:
On Jul 31, 2024...............$25.00...............1   On Jul 31, 2029...............$25.00...............1
Exchange. on min. 15 max. 30 days' notice. Exchange. on July 31 in every fifth year thereafter. Exchange. unless the Bank has announced its intention to redeem.
Lead Underwriter(s): CIBC World Markets Inc., BMO Capital Markets, National Bank Financial Inc.
Transfer Agent: TSX Trust Company
Registrar: TSX Trust Company
Exchanges: TSX
Symbol: CM.PR.Y
CUSIP: 13607G799

Canadian Utilities Limited

5.2% Cum. 5-Year Rate Reset Second Pref., Series Y

DBRS Rating:	Pfd-2	Aug 29, 2023	
Issued:	13,000,000 shs.	Sep 21, 2011	$25.000
O/S:	13,000,000 shs.	Dec 31, 2023	
Dividend:	$1.30 (Q)	Mar 1/Jun 1/Sep 1/Dec 1	

Dividend Details: Reset on Jun 1, 2027. Dividend rate will be reset in every fifth year thereafter. The annual dividend rate will be equal to the sum of the five-year Government of Canada Bond Yield plus 2.40%. Previously, annual divd. rate was 0.850750 per sh until May 31, 2022.
Redemption: Redeem. on the following dates on min. 30 and max. 60 days' notice as follows:
Jun 1, 2017...............$25.00   Jun 1, 2022...............$25.00
Redeem. on June 1 in every fifth year thereafter on min. 30 and max. 60 days' notice at $25.00 per share.
Exchange: Was exchange. into pfd 2nd ser Z as follows:
On Jun 1, 2017...............$25.00...............1   On Jun 1, 2022...............$25.00...............1
Exchange. on June 1 in every fifth year thereafter.
Lead Underwriter(s): RBC Capital Markets, BMO Capital Markets
Transfer Agent: TSX Trust Company
Registrar: TSX Trust Company
Exchanges: TSX
Symbol: CU.PR.C
CUSIP: 136717691

4.9% Cum. Redeem. Second Pref., Series AA

DBRS Rating:	Pfd-2	Aug 29, 2023	
Issued:	6,000,000 shs.	Jun 18, 2012	$25.000
O/S:	6,000,000 shs.	Dec 31, 2023	
Dividend:	$1.225 (Q)	Mar 1/Jun 1/Sep 1/Dec 1	

Redemption: Redeem. on and after the following dates on min. 30 and max. 60 days' notice as follows:
Sep 1, 2017...............$26.00   Sep 1, 2018...............$25.75
Sep 1, 2019...............$25.50   Sep 1, 2020...............$25.25
Sep 1, 2021...............$25.00
Lead Underwriter(s): BMO Capital Markets, RBC Capital Markets
Transfer Agent: TSX Trust Company
Registrar: TSX Trust Company
Exchanges: TSX
Symbol: CU.PR.D
CUSIP: 136717675

4.9% Cum. Redeem. Second Pref., Series BB

DBRS Rating:	Pfd-2	Aug 29, 2023	
Issued:	6,000,000 shs.	Jul 5, 2012	$25.000
O/S:	6,000,000 shs.	Dec 31, 2023	
Dividend:	$1.225 (Q)	Mar 1/Jun 1/Sep 1/Dec 1	

Redemption: Redeem. on and after the following dates on min. 30 and max. 60 days' notice as follows:
Sep 1, 2017...............$26.00   Sep 1, 2018...............$25.75
Sep 1, 2019...............$25.50   Sep 1, 2020...............$25.25
Sep 1, 2021...............$25.00

Lead Underwriter(s): RBC Capital Markets, BMO Capital Markets
Transfer Agent: TSX Trust Company
Registrar: TSX Trust Company
Exchanges: TSX
Symbol: CU.PR.E
CUSIP: 136717667

4.5% Cum. Redeem. Second Pref., Series CC

DBRS Rating:		Pfd-2	Aug 29, 2023
Issued:	7,000,000 shs.	Mar 19, 2013	$25.000
O/S:	7,000,000 shs.	Dec 31, 2023	
Dividend:	$1.125 (Q)	Mar 1/Jun 1/Sep 1/Dec 1	

Redemption: Redeem. on and after the following dates on min. 30 and max. 60 days' notice as follows:
Jun 1, 2018..$26.00   Jun 1, 2019..$25.75
Jun 1, 2020..$25.50   Jun 1, 2021..$25.25
Jun 1, 2022..$25.00

Lead Underwriter(s): BMO Capital Markets, RBC Capital Markets
Transfer Agent: TSX Trust Company
Registrar: TSX Trust Company
Exchanges: TSX
Symbol: CU.PR.F
CUSIP: 136717659

4.5% Cum. Redeem. Second Pref., Series DD

DBRS Rating:		Pfd-2	Aug 29, 2023
Issued:	9,000,000 shs.	May 15, 2013	$25.000
O/S:	9,000,000 shs.	Dec 31, 2023	
Dividend:	$1.125 (Q)	Mar 1/Jun 1/Sep 1/Dec 1	

Redemption: Redeem. on and after the following dates on min. 30 and max. 60 days' notice as follows:
Sep 1, 2018..$26.00   Sep 1, 2019..$25.75
Sep 1, 2020..$25.50   Sep 1, 2021..$25.25
Sep 1, 2022..$25.00

Lead Underwriter(s): RBC Capital Markets, BMO Capital Markets
Transfer Agent: TSX Trust Company
Registrar: TSX Trust Company
Exchanges: TSX
Symbol: CU.PR.G
CUSIP: 136717642

5.25% Cum. Redeem. Second Pref., Series EE

DBRS Rating:		Pfd-2	Aug 29, 2023
Issued:	5,000,000 shs.	Aug 7, 2015	$25.000
O/S:	5,000,000 shs.	Dec 31, 2023	
Dividend:	$1.3125 (Q)	Mar 1/Jun 1/Sep 1/Dec 1	

Redemption: Redeem. on and after the following dates on min. 30 and max. 60 days' notice as follows:
Sep 1, 2020..$26.00   Sep 1, 2021..$25.75
Sep 1, 2022..$25.50   Sep 1, 2023..$25.25
Sep 1, 2024..$25.00

Lead Underwriter(s): BMO Capital Markets, RBC Capital Markets
Transfer Agent: TSX Trust Company
Registrar: TSX Trust Company
Exchanges: TSX
Symbol: CU.PR.H
CUSIP: 136717634

4.5% Cum. 5-Year Rate Reset Second Pref., Series FF

DBRS Rating:		Pfd-2	Aug 29, 2023
Issued:	10,000,000 shs.	Sep 24, 2015	$25.000
O/S:	10,000,000 shs.	Dec 31, 2023	
Dividend:	$1.125 (Q)	Mar 1/Jun 1/Sep 1/Dec 1	

Dividend Details: Reset on Dec 1, 2025. Dividend rate will be reset in every fifth year thereafter. The annual dividend rate will be equal to the greater of (i) the sum of the five-year Government of Canada Bond Yield plus 3.69% and (ii) 4.5%. Previously, annual divd. rate was 1.125000 per sh until Nov 30, 2020.
Redemption: Redeem. on the following dates on min. 30 and max. 60 days' notice as follows:
Dec 1, 2020.................................$25.00   Dec 1, 2025.................................$25.00
Redeem. on Dec. 1 in every fifth year thereafter on min. 30 and max. 60 days' notice at $25.00 per share.
Exchange: Exchange. on min. 30 days' notice into pfd 2nd ser GG as follows:
On Dec 1, 2020.................$25.00..................1   On Dec 1, 2025.................$25.00..................1
Exchange. on Dec. 1 in every fifth year thereafter.
Lead Underwriter(s): BMO Capital Markets, RBC Capital Markets
Transfer Agent: TSX Trust Company
Registrar: TSX Trust Company
Exchanges: TSX
Symbol: CU.PR.I
CUSIP: 136717626

4.75% Cum. Redeem. Second Pref., Series HH

DBRS Rating:	Pfd-2	Aug 29, 2023	
Issued:	8,050,000 shs.	Dec 9, 2021	$25.000
O/S:	8,050,000 shs.	Dec 31, 2023	
Dividend:	$1.1875 (Q)	Mar 1/Jun 1/Sep 1/Dec 1	

Redemption: Redeem. on and after the following dates on min. 30 and max. 60 days' notice as follows:
Mar 1, 2027...$26.00   Mar 1, 2028...$25.75
Mar 1, 2029...$25.50   Mar 1, 2030...$25.25
Mar 1, 2031...$25.00
Lead Underwriter(s): BMO Capital Markets, RBC Capital Markets
Transfer Agent: TSX Trust Company
Registrar: TSX Trust Company
Exchanges: TSX
Symbol: CU.PR.J
CUSIP: 136717592

Canadian Western Bank

6.371% Non-Cum. 5-Year Rate Reset Pref., Series 5

DBRS Rating:	Pfd-3	Nov 14, 2023	
Issued:	5,000,000 shs.	Feb 10, 2014	$25.000
O/S:	5,000,000 shs.	Apr 15, 2024	
Dividend:	$1.59275 (Q)	Jan 31/Apr 30/Jul 31/Oct 31	

Dividend Details: Reset on May 1, 2029. Dividend rate will be reset in every fifth year thereafter. The annual dividend rate will be equal to the sum of the five-year Government of Canada Bond Yield plus 2.76%. Previously, annual divd. rate was 1.075250 per sh until Apr 30, 2024.
Redemption: Redeem. on the following dates on min. 30 and max. 60 days' notice, conditional on the approval of the Superintendent of Financial Institutions, as follows:
Apr 30, 2019..$25.00   Apr 30, 2024..$25.00
Apr 30, 2029..$25.00
Redeem. on April 30 in every fifth year thereafter on min. 30 and max. 60 days' notice at $25.00 per share, conditional on approval of the Superintendent of Financial Institutions.
Convertible: Automatically convertible into common shares upon occurrence of a Non-Viability Contingent Capital (NVCC) trigger event as defined by OFSI.
Exchange: Exchange. on min. 30 days' notice into pfd ser 6 as follows:
On Apr 30, 2019..................$25.00....................1   On Apr 30, 2024...................$25.00......................1
On Apr 30, 2029..................$25.00....................1
Exchange. on April 30 in every fifth year thereafter. Exchange. after notice from the Bank given with approval from the Superintendent of Financial Institutions.
Lead Underwriter(s): National Bank Financial Inc.
Transfer Agent: Computershare Trust Company of Canada Inc.
Registrar: Computershare Trust Company of Canada Inc.
Exchanges: TSX
Symbol: CWB.PR.B
CUSIP: 136765500

7.651% Non-Cum. 5-Year Rate Reset Pref., Series 9

DBRS Rating:	Pfd-3	Nov 14, 2023
Issued:	5,000,000 shs.	Jan 29, 2019 $25.000
O/S:	5,000,000 shs.	Apr 15, 2024
Dividend:	$1.91275 (Q)	Jan 31/Apr 30/Jul 31/Oct 31

Dividend Details: Reset on May 1, 2029. Dividend rate will be reset in every fifth year thereafter. The annual dividend rate will be equal to the sum of the five-year Government of Canada Bond Yield plus 4.04%. Previously, annual divd. rate was 1.500000 per sh until Apr 30, 2024.

Redemption: Redeem. on the following dates on min. 30 and max. 60 days' notice, conditional on the approval of the Superintendent of Financial Institutions, as follows:
Apr 30, 2024...$25.00   Apr 30, 2029...$25.00
Redeem. on April 30 in every fifth year thereafter on min. 30 and max. 60 days' notice at $25.00 per share, conditional on approval of the Superintendent of Financial Institutions.

Convertible: Automatically convertible into common shares upon occurrence of a Non-Viability Contingent Capital (NVCC) trigger event as defined by OFSI.

Exchange: Exchange. on min. 30 days' notice into pfd ser 10 as follows:
On Apr 30, 2024.....................$25.00....................1   On Apr 30, 2029....................$25.00....................1
Exchange. on April 30 in every fifth year thereafter. Exchange. after notice from the Bank given with approval from the Superintendent of Financial Institutions.

Lead Underwriter(s): National Bank Financial Inc., BMO Capital Markets
Transfer Agent: Computershare Trust Company of Canada Inc.
Registrar: Computershare Trust Company of Canada Inc.
Exchanges: TSX
Symbol: CWB.PR.D
CUSIP: 136765880

Capital Power Corporation

2.621% Cum. 5-Year Rate Reset Pref., Series 1

DBRS Rating:	Pfd-3 low	Apr 5, 2024
Issued:	5,000,000 shs.	Dec 16, 2010 $25.000
O/S:	5,000,000 shs.	Dec 31, 2023
Dividend:	$0.65525 (Q)	Mar 31/Jun 30/Sep 30/Dec 31

Dividend Details: Reset on Dec 31, 2025. Dividend rate will be reset in every fifth year thereafter. The annual dividend rate will be equal to the sum of the five-year Government of Canada Bond Yield plus 2.17%. Previously, annual divd. rate was 0.765000 per sh until Dec 30, 2020.

Redemption: Redeem. on the following dates on min. 30 and max. 60 days' notice as follows:
Dec 31, 2015...$25.00   Dec 31, 2020...$25.00
Redeem. on Dec. 31 in every fifth year thereafter on min. 30 and max. 60 days' notice at $25.00 per share.

Exchange: Was exchange. on min. 30 days' notice into pfd ser 2 as follows:
On Dec 31, 2015.....................$25.00....................1   On Dec 31, 2020....................$25.00....................1
Exchange. on Dec. 31 in every fifth year thereafter.

Lead Underwriter(s): TD Securities Inc., RBC Capital Markets
Transfer Agent: Computershare Trust Company of Canada Inc.
Registrar: Computershare Trust Company of Canada Inc.
Exchanges: TSX
Symbol: CPX.PR.A
CUSIP: 14042M300

6.86% Cum. 5-Year Rate Reset Pref., Series 3

DBRS Rating:	Pfd-3 low	Apr 5, 2024
Issued:	6,000,000 shs.	Dec 18, 2012 $25.000
O/S:	6,000,000 shs.	Dec 31, 2023
Dividend:	$1.715 (Q)	Mar 31/Jun 30/Sep 30/Dec 31

Dividend Details: Reset on Dec 31, 2028. Dividend rate will be reset in every fifth year thereafter. The annual dividend rate will be equal to the sum of the five-year Government of Canada Bond Yield plus 3.23%. Previously, annual divd. rate was 1.363250 per sh until Dec 30, 2023.

Redemption: Redeem. on the following dates on min. 30 and max. 60 days' notice as follows:
Dec 31, 2018...$25.00   Dec 31, 2023...$25.00
Redeem. on Dec. 31 in every fifth year thereafter on min. 30 and max. 60 days' notice at $25.00 per share.

FP Equities — Preferreds & Derivatives 2024

Exchange: Was exchange. on min. 30 days' notice into pfd ser 4 as follows:
On Dec 31, 2018.....................$25.00....................1   On Dec 31, 2023.....................$25.00.....................1
Exchange. on Dec. 31 in every fifth year thereafter.
Lead Underwriter(s): TD Securities Inc., BMO Capital Markets
Transfer Agent: Computershare Trust Company of Canada Inc.
Registrar: Computershare Trust Company of Canada Inc.
Exchanges: TSX
Symbol: CPX.PR.C
CUSIP: 14042M508

6.631% Cum. 5-Year Rate Reset Pref., Series 5

DBRS Rating:	Pfd-3 low	Apr 5, 2024	
Issued:	8,000,000 shs.	Mar 14, 2013	$25.000
O/S:	8,000,000 shs.	Dec 31, 2023	
Dividend:	$1.5775 (Q)	Mar 31/Jun 30/Sep 30/Dec 31	

Dividend Details: Reset on Jun 30, 2028. Dividend rate will be reset in every fifth year thereafter. The annual dividend rate will be equal to the sum of the five-year Government of Canada Bond Yield plus 3.15%. Previously, annual divd. rate was 1.309500 per sh until Jun 29, 2023.
Redemption: Redeem. on the following dates on min. 30 and max. 60 days' notice as follows:
Jun 30, 2018..................................$25.00   Jun 30, 2023..$25.00
Redeem. on June 30 in every fifth year thereafter on min. 30 and max. 60 days' notice at $25.00 per share.
Exchange: Was exchange. on min. 30 days' notice into pfd ser 6 as follows:
On Jun 30, 2018....................$25.00....................1   On Jun 30, 2023.....................$25.00.....................1
Exchange. on June 30 in every fifth year thereafter.
Lead Underwriter(s): RBC Capital Markets, Scotia Capital Inc.
Transfer Agent: Computershare Trust Company of Canada Inc.
Registrar: Computershare Trust Company of Canada Inc.
Exchanges: TSX
Symbol: CPX.PR.E
CUSIP: 14042M706

5.75% Cum. 5-Year Rate Reset Pref., Series 11

DBRS Rating:	Pfd-3 low	Apr 5, 2024	
Issued:	6,000,000 shs.	May 16, 2019	$25.000
O/S:	6,000,000 shs.	Dec 31, 2023	
Dividend:	$1.4375 (Q)	Mar 31/Jun 30/Sep 30/Dec 31	

Dividend Details: Reset on Jun 30, 2024. Dividend rate will be reset in every fifth year thereafter. The annual dividend rate will be equal to the greater of (i) the sum of the five-year Government of Canada Bond Yield plus 4.15% and (ii) 5.75%.
Redemption: Redeem. on the following dates on min. 30 and max. 60 days' notice as follows:
Jun 30, 2024..................................$25.00   Jun 30, 2029..$25.00
Redeem. on June 30 in every fifth year thereafter on min. 30 and max. 60 days' notice at $25.00 per share.
Exchange: Exchange. on min. 30 days' notice into pfd ser 12 as follows:
On Jun 30, 2024....................$25.00....................1   On Jun 30, 2029.....................$25.00.....................1
Exchange. on June 30 in every fifth year thereafter.
Lead Underwriter(s): TD Securities Inc., RBC Capital Markets
Transfer Agent: Computershare Trust Company of Canada Inc.
Registrar: Computershare Trust Company of Canada Inc.
Exchanges: TSX
Symbol: CPX.PR.K
CUSIP: 14042M847

Capstone Infrastructure Corporation

3.702% Cum. 5-Year Rate Reset Pref., Series A

Issued:	3,000,000 shs.	Jun 30, 2011	$25.000
O/S:	3,000,000 shs.	Dec 31, 2023	
Dividend:	$0.9255 (Q)	Jan 31/Apr 30/Jul 31/Oct 31	

Dividend Details: Reset on Jul 31, 2026. Dividend rate will be reset in every fifth year thereafter. The annual dividend rate will be equal to the sum of the five-year Government of Canada Bond Yield plus 2.71%. Previously, annual divd. rate was 0.817750 per sh until Jul 30, 2021.

Redemption: Redeem. on the following dates on min. 30 and max. 60 days' notice as follows:
Jul 31, 2016...$25.00   Jul 31, 2021...$25.00
Redeem. on July 31 in every fifth year thereafter on min. 30 and max. 60 days' notice at $25.00 per share.
Exchange: Was exchange. on min. 30 days' notice into pfd B as follows:
On Jul 31, 2016.....................$25.00......................1   On Jul 31, 2021.......................$25.00........................1
Exchange. on July 31 in every fifth year thereafter.
Lead Underwriter(s): TD Securities Inc., Macquarie Capital Markets Canada Ltd., RBC Capital Markets
Transfer Agent: Computershare Investor Services Inc.
Registrar: Computershare Investor Services Inc.
Exchanges: TSX
Symbol: CSE.PR.A
CUSIP: 14069Q507

Cenovus Energy Inc.

2.577% Cum. 5-Year Rate Reset Pref., Series 1

DBRS Rating:	Pfd-3 high	Dec 18, 2023
Issued:	10,435,932 shs.	Jan 6, 2021	$25.000
O/S:	10,739,654 shs.	Dec 31, 2023
Dividend:	$0.64425 (Q)	Mar 31/Jun 30/Sep 30/Dec 31

Dividend Details: Reset on Mar 31, 2026. Dividend rate will be reset in every fifth year thereafter. The annual dividend rate will be equal to the sum of the five-year Government of Canada Bond Yield plus 1.73%. Previously, annual divd. rate was 0.601000 per sh until Mar 30, 2021.
Redemption: Redeem. on the following dates on min. 30 and max. 60 days' notice as follows:
Mar 31, 2021...$25.00   Mar 31, 2026...$25.00
Redeem. on March 31 in every fifth year thereafter on min. 30 and max. 60 days' notice at $25.00 per share.
Exchange: Exchange. on min. 30 days' notice into pfd 1st ser 2 sh as follows:
On Mar 31, 2021.....................$25.00......................1   On Mar 31, 2026.......................$25.00........................1
Exchange. on March 31 in every fifth year thereafter.
Note: Issued upon exchange of Husky Energy Inc. pref shares, series 1.
Transfer Agent: Computershare Investor Services Inc.
Registrar: Computershare Investor Services Inc.
Exchanges: TSX
Symbol: CVE.PR.A
CUSIP: 15135U307

Floating Rate Cum. Pref., Series 2

DBRS Rating:	Pfd-3 high	Dec 18, 2023
Issued:	1,564,068 shs.	Jan 6, 2021	$25.000
O/S:	1,260,346 shs.	Dec 31, 2023
Dividend:	F.R. (Q)	Mar 31/Jun 30/Sep 30/Dec 31

Dividend Details: Quarterly divd. rate is T-bill plus 1.73%.
Redemption: Redeem. on the following dates on min. 30 and max. 60 days' notice as follows:
Mar 31, 2021...$25.00   Mar 31, 2026...$25.00
Redeem. on March 31 in every fifth year thereafter on min. 30 and max. 60 days' notice at $25.00 per share. After March 31, 2021, other than on an Exchange Date, redeem. at $25.50 per sh., plus declared and unpaid dividends thereon to the date of redemption.
Exchange: Exchange. on min. 30 days' notice into pfd 1st ser 1 sh as follows:
On Mar 31, 2021.....................$25.00......................1   On Mar 31, 2026.......................$25.00........................1
Exchange. on March 31 in every fifth year thereafter.
Note: Issued upon exchange of Husky Energy Inc. pref shares, series 2.
Transfer Agent: Computershare Investor Services Inc.
Registrar: Computershare Investor Services Inc.
Exchanges: TSX
Symbol: CVE.PR.B
CUSIP: 15135U406

4.689% Cum. 5-Year Rate Reset Pref., Series 3

Issued:	10,000,000 shs.	Jan 6, 2021	$25.000
O/S:	10,000,000 shs.	Dec 31, 2023
Dividend:	$1.17225 (Q)	Mar 31/Jun 30/Sep 30/Dec 31

FP Equities — Preferreds & Derivatives 2024

Dividend Details: Reset on Dec 31, 2024. Dividend rate will be reset in every fifth year thereafter. The annual dividend rate will be equal to the sum of the five-year Government of Canada Bond Yield plus 3.13%.
Redemption: Redeem. on the following dates on min. 30 and max. 60 days' notice as follows:
Jan 6, 2021...$25.00   Dec 31, 2024...$25.00
Redeem. on Dec. 31 in every fifth year thereafter on min. 30 and max. 60 days' notice at $25.00 per share.
Exchange: Exchange. on min. 30 days' notice into pfd 1st ser 4 as follows:
On Dec 31, 2024....................$25.00....................1   On Dec 31, 2029....................$25.00....................1
Exchange. on December 31 in every fifth year thereafter.
Note: Issued upon exchange of Husky Energy Inc. pref shares, series 3.
Transfer Agent: Computershare Investor Services Inc.
Registrar: Computershare Investor Services Inc.
Exchanges: TSX
Symbol: CVE.PR.C
CUSIP: 15135U505

4.591% Cum. 5-Year Rate Reset Pref., Series 5

DBRS Rating:	Pfd-3 high	Dec 18, 2023	
Issued:	8,000,000 shs.	Jan 6, 2021	$25.000
O/S:	8,000,000 shs.	Dec 31, 2023	
Dividend:	$1.14775 (Q)	Mar 31/Jun 30/Sep 30/Dec 31	

Dividend Details: Reset on Mar 31, 2025. Dividend rate will be reset in every fifth year thereafter. The annual dividend rate will be equal to the sum of the five-year Government of Canada Bond Yield plus 3.57%.
Redemption: Redeem. on the following dates on min. 30 and max. 60 days' notice as follows:
Jan 6, 2021...$25.00   Mar 31, 2025...$25.00
Redeem. on March 31 in every fifth year thereafter on min. 30 and max. 60 days' notice at $25.00 per share.
Exchange: Exchange. on min. 30 days' notice into pfd 1st ser 6 as follows:
On Mar 31, 2025....................$25.00....................1   On Mar 31, 2030....................$25.00....................1
Exchange. on March 31 in every fifth year thereafter.
Note: Issued upon exchange of Husky Energy Inc. pref shares, series 5.
Transfer Agent: Computershare Investor Services Inc.
Registrar: Computershare Investor Services Inc.
Exchanges: TSX
Symbol: CVE.PR.E
CUSIP: 15135U703

3.935% Cum. 5-Year Rate Reset Pref., Series 7

DBRS Rating:	Pfd-3 high	Dec 18, 2023	
Issued:	6,000,000 shs.	Jan 6, 2021	$25.000
O/S:	6,000,000 shs.	Dec 31, 2023	
Dividend:	$0.98375 (Q)	Mar 31/Jun 30/Sep 30/Dec 31	

Dividend Details: Reset on Jun 30, 2025. Dividend rate will be reset in every fifth year thereafter. The annual dividend rate will be equal to the sum of the five-year Government of Canada Bond Yield plus 3.52%.
Redemption: Redeem. on the following dates on min. 30 and max. 60 days' notice as follows:
Jun 30, 2025...$25.00   Jun 30, 2030...$25.00
Redeem. on June 30 in every fifth year thereafter on min. 30 and max. 60 days' notice at $25.00 per share.
Exchange: Exchange. on min. 30 days' notice into pfd 1st ser 8 as follows:
On Jun 30, 2025....................$25.00....................1   On Jun 30, 2030....................$25.00....................1
Exchange. on June 30 in every fifth year thereafter.
Note: Issued upon exchange of Husky Energy Inc. pref shares, series 7.
Transfer Agent: Computershare Investor Services Inc.
Registrar: Computershare Investor Services Inc.
Exchanges: TSX
Symbol: CVE.PR.G
CUSIP: 15135U885

Co-operators General Insurance Company

5% Non-Cum. Class E Pref., Series C

DBRS Rating:	Pfd-2	Oct 26, 2023	
Issued:	4,000,000 shs.	Jun 12, 2007	$25.000
O/S:	4,000,000 shs.	Dec 31, 2023	
Dividend:	$1.25 (Q)	Mar 31/Jun 30/Sep 30/Dec 31	

Redemption: Redeem. on and after the following dates on min. 30 and max. 60 days' notice, conditional on the approval of the Superintendent of Financial Institutions, as follows:
Jun 30, 2012...$26.00   Jun 30, 2013..$25.75
Jun 30, 2014...$25.50   Jun 30, 2015..$25.25
Jun 30, 2016...$25.00

Exchange: Exchange. on min. 30 days' notice into 1 new pfd per pref. sh, being an exchange price per new pfd of $25.00.
Lead Underwriter(s): Scotia Capital Inc.
Transfer Agent: Computershare Trust Company of Canada Inc.
Registrar: Computershare Trust Company of Canada Inc.
Exchanges: TSX
Symbol: CCS.PR.C
CUSIP: 189906407

Dundee Corporation

5.284% Cum. 5-Year Rate Reset First Pfce., Series 2

Issued:	5,200,000 shs.	Sep 15, 2009	$25.000
O/S:	1,149,162 shs.	Dec 31, 2023	
Dividend:	$1.321 (Q)	Mar 31/Jun 30/Sep 30/Dec 31	

Dividend Details: Reset on Sep 30, 2024. Dividend rate will be reset in every fifth year thereafter. The annual dividend rate will be equal to the sum of the five-year Government of Canada Bond Yield plus 4.10%. Previously, annual divd. rate was 1.422000 per sh until Sep 29, 2019.
Redemption: Redeem. on the following dates on min. 30 and max. 60 days' notice as follows:
Sep 30, 2014...$25.00   Sep 30, 2019..$25.00
Redeem. on Sept. 30 in every fifth year thereafter on min. 30 and max. 60 days' notice at $25.00 per share. If, at any time, the series 2 preference shares become entitled to vote separately as a class with all other first preference shares or separately as a series, the company may redeem, on min. 30 and max. 60 days' notice, all or any number of the then outstanding series 2 preference shares as follows, in each case together with all accrued and unpaid dividends to the date fixed for redemption: $26.25 per share, if redeemed prior to Sept. 30, 2010; $26.00 per share, if redeemed on or after Sept. 30, 2010 and prior to Sept. 30, 2011; $25.75 per share, if redeemed on or after Sept. 30, 2011 and prior to Sept. 30, 2012; $25.50 per share, if redeemed on or after Sept. 30, 2012 and prior to Sept. 30, 2013; $25.25 per share, if redeemed on or after Sept. 30, 2013 and prior to Sept. 30, 2014; or $25.00 per share if redeemed on or after Sept. 30, 2014.
Exchange: Was exchange. on min. 30 days' notice into pfce 1st ser 3 as follows:
On Sep 30, 2014....................$25.00....................1   On Sep 30, 2019......................$25.00......................1
Exchange. on Sept. 30 in every fifth year thereafter on min. 30 days' notice.
Lead Underwriter(s): RF Securities Clearing LP, Scotia Capital Inc.
Transfer Agent: Computershare Investor Services Inc.
Registrar: Computershare Investor Services Inc.
Exchanges: TSX
Symbol: DC.PR.B
CUSIP: 264901703

Floating Rate Cum. Pfce., Series 3

Issued:	shs.	Sep 30, 2014	$25.000
O/S:	724,982 shs.	Dec 31, 2023	
Dividend:	F.R. (Q)	Mar 31/Jun 30/Sep 30/Dec 31	

Dividend Details: Quarterly divd. rate is T-bill plus 4.1%.

Redemption: Redeem. on the following dates on min. 30 and max. 60 days' notice as follows:
Sep 30, 2019...$25.00   Sep 30, 2024...$25.00
Redeem. on Sept. 30 in every fifth year thereafter on min. 30 and max. 60 days' notice at $25.00 per share. If, at any time, the series 3 preference shares become entitled to vote separately as a class with all other first preference shares or separately as a series, the company may redeem, on min. 30 and max. 60 days' notice, all or any number of the then outstanding series 3 preference shares at $25.00 per share together with all accrued and unpaid dividends to the date fixed for redemption.

Exchange: Exchange. on min. 30 days' notice into pfce 1st ser 2 as follows:
On Sep 30, 2019....................$25.00....................1   On Sep 30, 2024....................$25.00....................1
Exchange. on Sept. 30 in every fifth year thereafter.

Note: Issued upon exchange of an equal number of 5-Year Rate Reset First Pfce. shs, series 2.
Transfer Agent: Computershare Investor Services Inc.
Registrar: Computershare Investor Services Inc.
Exchanges: TSX
Symbol: DC.PR.D
CUSIP: 264901802

E-L Financial Corporation Limited

5.3% Non-Cum. First Pfce., Series 1

Issued:	4,000,000 shs.	Nov 30, 2004	$25.000
O/S:	4,000,000 shs.	Dec 31, 2023	
Dividend:	$1.325 (Q)	Jan 17/Apr 17/Jul 17/Oct 17	

Redemption: Redeem. on and after the following dates on min. 30 and max. 60 days' notice as follows:
Oct 17, 2009..$26.00   Oct 17, 2010...$25.75
Oct 17, 2011..$25.50   Oct 17, 2012...$25.25
Oct 17, 2013..$25.00

Convertible: Convert. by company on min. 40 days' notice into com sh. Conversion rate is determined by dividing the then applicable redemption price, plus declared and unpaid divds. to but excluding the date of conversion, by the greater of $1 and 95% of the weighted average trading price of the com. shs. on the Toronto Stock Exchange for the 20 trading days ending on or before the fourth day prior to the date of conversion.

Note: Issued upon exchange of 5.3% pfce. shs., series B.
Transfer Agent: Computershare Investor Services Inc.
Registrar: Computershare Investor Services Inc.
Exchanges: TSX
Symbol: ELF.PR.F
CUSIP: 26857Q309

4.75% Non-Cum. First Pfce., Series 2

Issued:	4,000,000 shs.	Oct 17, 2006	$25.000
O/S:	4,000,000 shs.	Dec 31, 2023	
Dividend:	$1.1875 (Q)	Jan 17/Apr 17/Jul 17/Oct 17	

Redemption: Redeem. on and after the following dates on min. 30 and max. 60 days' notice as follows:
Oct 17, 2011..$26.00   Oct 17, 2012...$25.75
Oct 17, 2013..$25.50   Oct 17, 2014...$25.25
Oct 17, 2015..$25.00

Convertible: Convert. by company on min. 40 days' notice into com sh. Conversion rate is determined by dividing the then applicable redemption price, plus declared and unpaid divds. to but excluding the date of conversion, by the greater of $1 and 95% of the weighted average trading price of the com. shs. on the Toronto Stock Exchange for the 20 trading days ending on or before the fourth day prior to the date of conversion. In lieu of fractional shs., cash payment will be made.

Lead Underwriter(s): RBC Capital Markets
Transfer Agent: Computershare Investor Services Inc.
Registrar: Computershare Investor Services Inc.
Exchanges: TSX
Symbol: ELF.PR.G
CUSIP: 26857Q408

5.50% Non-Cum. First Pfce., Series 3

Issued:	4,000,000 shs.	Apr 2, 2012	$25.000
O/S:	4,000,000 shs.	Dec 31, 2023	
Dividend:	$1.375 (Q)	Jan 17/Apr 17/Jul 17/Oct 17	

Redemption: Redeem. on and after the following dates on min. 30 and max. 60 days' notice as follows:
Apr 17, 2017...$26.00   Apr 17, 2018...$25.75
Apr 17, 2019...$25.50   Apr 17, 2020...$25.25
Apr 17, 2021...$25.00

Convertible: Convert. by company on min. 40 days' notice into com sh. Conversion rate is determined by dividing the then applicable redemption price, plus declared and unpaid divds. to but excluding the date of conversion, by the greater of $1 and 95% of the weighted average trading price of the com. shs. on the Toronto Stock Exchange for the 20 trading days ending on or before the fourth day prior to the date of conversion. In lieu of fractional shs., cash payment will be made.

Lead Underwriter(s): Scotia Capital Inc., TD Securities Inc.
Transfer Agent: Computershare Investor Services Inc.
Registrar: Computershare Investor Services Inc.
Exchanges: TSX
Symbol: ELF.PR.H
CUSIP: 26857Q507

ECN Capital Corp.

7.937% Cum. 5-Year Rate Reset Pref. Series C

DBRS Rating:	Pfd-4 high	Aug 24, 2023
Issued:	4,000,000 shs.	May 25, 2017 $25.000
O/S:	3,712,400 shs.	Dec 31, 2023
Dividend:	$1.98425 (Q)	Mar 31/Jun 30/Sep 30/Dec 31

Dividend Details: Reset on Jun 30, 2027. Dividend rate will be reset in every fifth year thereafter. The annual dividend rate will be equal to the greater of (i) the sum of the five-year Government of Canada Bond Yield plus 5.19% and (ii) 6.25%. Previously, annual divd. rate was 1.562500 per sh until Jun 29, 2022.

Redemption: Redeem. on the following dates on min. 30 and max. 60 days' notice as follows:
Jun 30, 2022...$25.00   Jun 30, 2027...$25.00
Redeem. on June 30 in every fifth year thereafter on min. 30 and max. 60 days' notice at $25.00 per share.

Exchange: Exchange. on min. 30 days' notice into pfd ser D as follows:
On Jun 30, 2022.................$25.00.....................1   On Jun 30, 2027.....................$25.00.......................1
Exchange. on June 30 in every fifth year thereafter.

Lead Underwriter(s): BMO Capital Markets, CIBC World Markets Inc., National Bank Financial Inc., RBC Capital Markets, TD Securities Inc.
Transfer Agent: Computershare Investor Services Inc.
Registrar: Computershare Investor Services Inc.
Exchanges: TSX
Symbol: ECN.PR.C
CUSIP: 26829L602

EQB Inc.
(formerly Equitable Group Inc.)

5.969% Non-Cum. 5-Year Rate Reset Pref., Series 3

Issued:	3,000,000 shs.	Aug 8, 2014 $25.000
O/S:	2,911,800 shs.	Jan 31, 2024
Dividend:	$1.49225 (Q)	Mar 31/Jun 30/Sep 30/Dec 31

Dividend Details: Reset on Sep 30, 2024. Dividend rate will be reset in every fifth year thereafter. The annual dividend rate will be equal to the sum of the five-year Government of Canada Bond Yield plus 4.78%. Previously, annual divd. rate was 1.587500 per sh until Sep 29, 2019.

Redemption: Redeem. on the following dates on min. 30 and max. 60 days' notice as follows:
Sep 30, 2019..$25.00   Sep 30, 2024..$25.00
Redeem. on Sept. 30 in every fifth year thereafter on min. 30 and max. 60 days' notice at $25.00 per share.

Exchange: Exchange. on min. 30 days' notice into pfd ser 4 as follows:
On Sep 30, 2019.................$25.00....................1   On Sep 30, 2024....................$25.00.......................1
Exchange. on Sept. 30 in every fifth year thereafter.

Lead Underwriter(s): TD Securities Inc., Scotia Capital Inc.
Transfer Agent: Computershare Investor Services Inc.
Registrar: Computershare Investor Services Inc.
Exchanges: TSX
Symbol: EQB.PR.C
CUSIP: 26886R203

Element Fleet Management Corp.

6.21% Cum. 5-Year Rate Reset Pref., Series C

DBRS Rating:	Pfd-3 high	Sep 27, 2023	
Issued:	5,126,400 shs.	Mar 7, 2014	$25.000
O/S:	5,126,400 shs.	Dec 31, 2023	
Dividend:	$1.5525 (Q)	Mar 31/Jun 30/Sep 30/Dec 31	

Dividend Details: Reset on Jun 30, 2024. Dividend rate will be reset in every fifth year thereafter. The annual dividend rate will be equal to the sum of the five-year Government of Canada Bond Yield plus 4.81%. Dividends are payable on the last business day of March, June, September and December. Previously, annual divd. rate was 1.625000 per sh until Jun 29, 2019.

Redemption: Redeem. on the following dates on min. 30 and max. 60 days' notice as follows:
Jun 30, 2019...$25.00   Jun 30, 2024..$25.00
Exchange: Exchange. on min. 30 days' notice into pfd ser D as follows:
On Jun 30, 2019....................$25.00....................1   On Jun 30, 2024....................$25.00....................1
Exchange. on June 30 in every fifth year thereafter.

Lead Underwriter(s): RF Securities Clearing LP, National Bank Financial Inc., BMO Capital Markets, CIBC World Markets Inc., RBC Capital Markets, TD Securities Inc.
Transfer Agent: Computershare Investor Services Inc.
Registrar: Computershare Investor Services Inc.
Exchanges: TSX
Symbol: EFN.PR.C
CUSIP: 286181839

5.903% Cum. 5-Year Rate Reset Pref., Series E

DBRS Rating:	Pfd-3 high	Sep 27, 2023	
Issued:	5,321,900 shs.	Jun 18, 2014	$25.000
O/S:	5,321,900 shs.	Dec 31, 2023	
Dividend:	$1.47575 (Q)	Mar 31/Jun 30/Sep 30/Dec 31	

Dividend Details: Reset on Sep 30, 2024. Dividend rate will be reset in every fifth year thereafter. The annual dividend rate will be equal to the sum of the five-year Government of Canada Bond Yield plus 4.72%. Dividends are payable on the last business day of March, June, September and December. Previously, annual divd. rate was 1.600000 per sh until Sep 29, 2019.

Redemption: Redeem. on the following dates on min. 30 and max. 60 days' notice as follows:
Sep 30, 2019...$25.00   Sep 30, 2024..$25.00
Redeem. on Sept. 30 in every fifth year thereafter on min. 30 and max. 60 days' notice at $25.00 per share.
Exchange: Exchange. on min. 30 days' notice into pfd ser F as follows:
On Sep 30, 2019....................$25.00....................1   On Sep 30, 2024....................$25.00....................1
Exchange. on Sept. 30 in every fifth year thereafter.

Lead Underwriter(s): BMO Capital Markets, CIBC World Markets Inc., RF Securities Clearing LP, National Bank Financial Inc., TD Securities Inc.
Transfer Agent: Computershare Investor Services Inc.
Registrar: Computershare Investor Services Inc.
Exchanges: TSX
Symbol: EFN.PR.E
CUSIP: 286181813

Emera Incorporated

2.182% Cum. 5-Year Rate Reset First Pref., Series A

Issued:	6,000,000 shs.	Jun 2, 2010	$25.000
O/S:	4,866,814 shs.	Dec 31, 2023	
Dividend:	$0.5455 (Q)	Feb 15/May 15/Aug 15/Nov 15	

Dividend Details: Dividend rate will be reset in every fifth year thereafter. The annual dividend rate will be equal to the sum of the five-year Government of Canada Bond Yield plus 1.84%. Reset on Aug 15, 2025. Previously, annual divd. rate was 0.638750 per sh until Aug 14, 2020.

Redemption: Redeem. on the following dates on min. 30 and max. 60 days' notice as follows:
Aug 15, 2015..$25.00   Aug 15, 2020..$25.00
Redeem. on Aug. 15 in every fifth year thereafter on min. 30 and max. 60 days' notice at $25.00 per share.

Exchange: Was exchange. on min. 30 days' notice into pfd 1st ser B as follows:
On Aug 15, 2015......................$25.00.....................1   On Aug 15, 2020......................$25.00........................1
Exchange. on Aug. 15 in every fifth year thereafter.

Lead Underwriter(s): Scotia Capital Inc., RBC Capital Markets, CIBC World Markets Inc.
Transfer Agent: TSX Trust Company
Registrar: TSX Trust Company
Exchanges: TSX
Symbol: EMA.PR.A
CUSIP: 290876309

6.434% Cum. 5-Year Rate Reset First Pref. Pref., Series C

Issued:	10,000,000 shs.	Jun 7, 2012	$25.000
O/S:	10,000,000 shs.	Dec 31, 2023	
Dividend:	$1.6085 (Q)	Feb 15/May 15/Aug 15/Nov 15	

Dividend Details: Reset on Aug 15, 2028. Dividend rate will be reset in every fifth year thereafter. The annual dividend rate will be equal to the sum of the five-year Government of Canada Bond Yield plus 2.65%. Previously, annual divd. rate was 1.180240 per sh until Aug 14, 2023.

Redemption: Redeem. on the following dates on min. 30 and max. 60 days' notice as follows:
Aug 15, 2018..$25.00   Aug 15, 2023..$25.00
Redeem. on Aug. 15 in every fifth year thereafter on min. 30 and max. 60 days' notice at $25.00 per share.

Exchange: Was exchange. on min. 30 days' notice into pfd 1st ser D as follows:
On Aug 15, 2018......................$25.00.....................1   On Aug 15, 2023......................$25.00........................1
Exchange. on Aug. 15 in every fifth year thereafter.

Lead Underwriter(s): Scotia Capital Inc., RBC Capital Markets, TD Securities Inc.
Transfer Agent: TSX Trust Company
Registrar: TSX Trust Company
Exchanges: TSX
Symbol: EMA.PR.C
CUSIP: 290876507

4.5% Cum. First Pref., Series E

Issued:	5,000,000 shs.	Jun 10, 2013	$25.000
O/S:	5,000,000 shs.	Dec 31, 2023	
Dividend:	$1.125 (Q)	Feb 15/May 15/Aug 15/Nov 15	

Redemption: Redeem. on and after the following dates on min. 30 and max. 60 days' notice as follows:
Aug 15, 2018...$26.00   Aug 15, 2019..$25.75
Aug 15, 2020...$25.50   Aug 15, 2021..$25.25
Aug 15, 2022...$25.00

Lead Underwriter(s): RBC Capital Markets, CIBC World Markets Inc., Scotia Capital Inc., TD Securities Inc.
Transfer Agent: TSX Trust Company
Registrar: TSX Trust Company
Exchanges: TSX
Symbol: EMA.PR.E
CUSIP: 290876705

4.202% Cum. 5-Year Rate Reset First Pref., Series F

Issued:	8,000,000 shs.	Jun 9, 2014	$25.000
O/S:	8,000,000 shs.	Dec 31, 2023	
Dividend:	$1.0505 (Q)	Feb 15/May 15/Aug 15/Nov 15	

Dividend Details: Reset on Feb 15, 2025. Dividend rate will be reset in every fifth year thereafter. The annual dividend rate will be equal to the sum of the five-year Government of Canada Bond Yield plus 2.63%. Previously, annual divd. rate was 1.062500 per sh until Feb 14, 2020.

Redemption: Redeem. on the following dates on min. 30 and max. 60 days' notice as follows:
Feb 15, 2020..$25.00   Feb 15, 2025..$25.00
Redeem. on Feb. 15 in every fifth year thereafter on min. 30 and max. 60 days' notice at $25.00 per share.

FP Equities — Preferreds & Derivatives 2024

Exchange: Exchange. on min. 30 days' notice into pfd ist ser G as follows:
On Feb 15, 2020.....................$25.00....................1   On Feb 15, 2025......................$25.00.....................1
Exchange. on Feb. 15 in every fifth year thereafter.
Lead Underwriter(s): Scotia Capital Inc.
Transfer Agent: TSX Trust Company
Registrar: TSX Trust Company
Exchanges: TSX
Symbol: EMA.PR.F
CUSIP: 290876804

Floating Rate Cum. Pref., Series B

Issued:	2,135,364 shs.	Aug 17, 2015	$25.000
O/S:	1,133,186 shs.	Dec 31, 2023	
Dividend:	F.R. (Q)	Feb 15/May 15/Aug 15/Nov 15	

Dividend Details: Quarterly divd. rate is T-bill plus 1.84%.
Redemption: Redeem. on the following dates on min. 30 and max. 60 days' notice as follows:
Aug 15, 2020..$25.00   Aug 15, 2025...$25.00
Redeem. on Aug. 15 in every fifth year thereafter on min. 30 and max. 60 days' notice at $25.00 per share.
Exchange: Exchange. on min. 30 days' notice into pfd 1st ser A sh as follows:
On Aug 15, 2020....................$25.00....................1   On Aug 15, 2025......................$25.00.....................1
Exchange. on Aug. 15 in every fifth year thereafter.
Note: Issued upon exchange of an equal number of First Preferred Shares, Series A.
Transfer Agent: TSX Trust Company
Registrar: TSX Trust Company
Exchanges: TSX
Symbol: EMA.PR.B
CUSIP: 290876408

6.324% Cum. 5-Year Rate Reset First Pref., Series H

Issued:	12,000,000 shs.	May 31, 2018	$25.000
O/S:	12,000,000 shs.	Dec 31, 2023	
Dividend:	$1.581 (Q)	Feb 15/May 15/Aug 15/Nov 15	

Dividend Details: Reset on Aug 15, 2028. Dividend rate will be reset in every fifth year thereafter. The annual dividend rate will be equal to the greater of (i) the sum of the five-year Government of Canada Bond Yield plus 2.54% and (ii) 4.90%. Previously, annual divd. rate was 1.225000 per sh until Aug 14, 2023.
Redemption: Redeem. on the following dates on min. 30 and max. 60 days' notice as follows:
Aug 15, 2023..$25.00   Aug 15, 2028...$25.00
Redeem. on Aug. 15 in every fifth year thereafter on min. 30 and max. 60 days' notice at $25.00 per share.
Exchange: Exchange. on min. 30 days' notice into pfd 1st ser I as follows:
On Aug 15, 2023....................$25.00....................1   On Aug 15, 2028......................$25.00.....................1
Exchange. on Aug. 15 in every fifth year thereafter.
Lead Underwriter(s): Scotia Capital Inc., CIBC World Markets Inc., RBC Capital Markets, TD Securities Inc.
Transfer Agent: TSX Trust Company
Registrar: TSX Trust Company
Exchanges: TSX
Symbol: EMA.PR.H
CUSIP: 290876861

4.25% Cum. 5-Year Rate Reset First Pref., Series J

Issued:	8,000,000 shs.	Apr 6, 2021	$25.000
O/S:	8,000,000 shs.	Dec 31, 2023	
Dividend:	$1.0625 (Q)	Feb 15/May 15/Aug 15/Nov 15	

Dividend Details: Reset on May 16, 2026. Dividend rate will be reset in every fifth year thereafter. The annual dividend rate will be equal to the greater of (i) the sum of the five-year Government of Canada Bond Yield plus 3.28% and (ii) 4.25%.
Redemption: Redeem. on the following dates on min. 30 and max. 60 days' notice as follows:
May 15, 2026..$25.00   May 15, 2031...$25.00
Redeem. on May 15 in every fifth year thereafter on min. 30 and max. 60 days' notice at $25.00 per share.
Exchange: Exchange. into Pfd 1st ser K as follows:
On May 15, 2026....................$25.00....................1   On May 15, 2031......................$25.00.....................1
Exchange. on May 15 in every fifth year thereafter.

Lead Underwriter(s): Scotia Capital Inc., RBC Capital Markets
Transfer Agent: TSX Trust Company
Registrar: TSX Trust Company
Exchanges: TSX
Symbol: EMA.PR.J
CUSIP: 290876846

4.6% Cum. First Pref., Series L

Issued:	9,000,000 shs.	Sep 24, 2021	$25.000
O/S:	9,000,000 shs.	Dec 31, 2023	
Dividend:	$1.15 (Q)	Feb 15/May 15/Aug 15/Nov 15	

Redemption: Redeem. on and after the following dates on min. 30 and max. 60 days' notice as follows:
Nov 15, 2026..$26.00   Nov 15, 2027..$25.75
Nov 15, 2028..$25.50   Nov 15, 2029..$25.25
Nov 15, 2030..$25.00
Lead Underwriter(s): TD Securities Inc., CIBC World Markets Inc.
Transfer Agent: TSX Trust Company
Registrar: TSX Trust Company
Exchanges: TSX
Symbol: EMA.PR.L
CUSIP: 290876820

The Empire Life Insurance Company

6.1870% Non-Cum. 5-Year Rate Reset Pref., Series 3

DBRS Rating:	Pfd-2	May 25, 2023	
Issued:	4,000,000 shs.	Nov 1, 2017	$25.000
O/S:	4,000,000 shs.	Dec 31, 2023	
Dividend:	$1.54675 (Q)	Jan 17/Apr 17/Jul 17/Oct 17	

Dividend Details: Reset on Jan 18, 2028. Dividend rate will be reset in every fifth year thereafter. The annual dividend rate will be equal to the sum of the five-year Government of Canada Bond Yield plus 3.24%. Previously, annual divd. rate was 1.225000 per sh until Jan 17, 2023.
Private Placement
Redemption: Redeem. on the following dates on min. 30 and max. 60 days' notice as follows:
Jan 17, 2023..$25.00   Jan 17, 2028..$25.00
Redeem. on Jan. 17 in every fifth year thereafter on min. 30 and max. 60 days' notice at $25.00 per share. All redemptions are subject to the provisions of the Insurance Companies Act (Canada), including the requirement of obtaining the prior consent of the Superintendent of Financial Institutions.
Exchange: Exchange. on min. 15 days' notice into pfd ser 4 as follows:
On Jan 17, 2023.....................$25.00.....................1   On Jan 17, 2028.....................$25.00.....................1
Exchange. on Jan. 17 in every fifth year thereafter. Shareholders need to provide notice of applicable conversion date not more than 30 days and not less than 15 days before such date.
Note: Issued to E-L Financial Corporation.
Lead Underwriter(s): Scotia Capital Inc., CIBC World Markets Inc., TD Securities Inc., BMO Capital Markets
Transfer Agent: TSX Trust Company
Registrar: TSX Trust Company
CUSIP: 291839405

Enbridge Inc.

5.5% Cum. Pfce., Series A

DBRS Rating:	Pfd-3 high	Sep 6, 2023	
Issued:	5,000,000 shs.	Dec 1, 1998	$25.000
O/S:	5,000,000 shs.	Dec 31, 2023	
Dividend:	$1.375 (Q)	Mar 1/Jun 1/Sep 1/Dec 1	

Redemption: Redeem. on and after the following dates on min. 30 and max. 60 days' notice as follows:
Dec 2, 2003..$26.00   Dec 2, 2004..$25.75
Dec 2, 2005..$25.50   Dec 2, 2006..$25.25
Dec 2, 2007..$25.00

Lead Underwriter(s): TD Securities Inc.
Transfer Agent: Computershare Trust Company of Canada Inc.
Registrar: Computershare Trust Company of Canada Inc.
Exchanges: TSX
Symbol: ENB.PR.A
CUSIP: 29250N204

5.202% Cum. 5-Year Rate Reset Pref., Series B

DBRS Rating:	Pfd-3 high	Sep 6, 2023	
Issued:	20,000,000 shs.	Sep 30, 2011	$25.000
O/S:	20,000,000 shs.	Dec 31, 2023	
Dividend:	$1.255 (Q)	Mar 1/Jun 1/Sep 1/Dec 1	

Dividend Details: Reset on Jun 1, 2027. Dividend rate will be reset in every fifth year thereafter. The annual dividend rate will be equal to the sum of the five-year Government of Canada Bond Yield plus 2.40%. Previously, annual divd. rate was 0.853750 per sh until May 31, 2022.
Redemption: Redeem. on the following dates on min. 30 and max. 60 days' notice as follows:
Jun 1, 2017...$25.00   Jun 1, 2022...$25.00
Redeem. on June 1 in every fifth year thereafter on min. 30 and max. 60 days' notice at $25.00 per share.
Exchange: Was exchange. on min. 30 days' notice into pfd ser C as follows:
On Jun 1, 2017......................$25.00......................1   On Jun 1, 2022......................$25.00......................1
Exchange. on June 1 in every fifth year thereafter.
Lead Underwriter(s): Scotia Capital Inc., RBC Capital Markets, TD Securities Inc.
Transfer Agent: Computershare Trust Company of Canada Inc.
Registrar: Computershare Trust Company of Canada Inc.
Exchanges: TSX
Symbol: ENB.PR.B
CUSIP: 29250N709

5.412% Cum. 5-Year Rate Reset Pref., Series D

DBRS Rating:	Pfd-3 high	Sep 6, 2023	
Issued:	18,000,000 shs.	Nov 23, 2011	$25.000
O/S:	18,000,000 shs.	Dec 31, 2023	
Dividend:	$1.353 (Q)	Mar 1/Jun 1/Sep 1/Dec 1	

Dividend Details: Reset on Mar 1, 2028. Dividend rate will be reset in every fifth year thereafter. The annual dividend rate will be equal to the sum of the five-year Government of Canada Bond Yield plus 2.37%. Previously, annual divd. rate was 1.115000 per sh until Feb 28, 2023.
Redemption: Redeem. on the following dates on min. 30 and max. 60 days' notice as follows:
Mar 1, 2018...$25.00   Mar 1, 2023..$25.00
Redeem. on March 1 in every fifth year thereafter on min. 30 and max. 60 days' notice at $25.00 per share.
Exchange: Was exchange. on min. 30 days' notice into pfd ser E as follows:
On Mar 1, 2018......................$25.00......................1   On Mar 1, 2023......................$25.00......................1
Exchange. on March 1 in every fifth year thereafter.
Lead Underwriter(s): TD Securities Inc., RBC Capital Markets, Scotia Capital Inc.
Transfer Agent: Computershare Trust Company of Canada Inc.
Registrar: Computershare Trust Company of Canada Inc.
Exchanges: TSX
Symbol: ENB.PR.D
CUSIP: 29250N881

5.538% Cum. 5-Year Rate Reset Pref., Series F

DBRS Rating:	Pfd-3 high	Sep 6, 2023	
Issued:	20,000,000 shs.	Jan 18, 2012	$25.000
O/S:	18,172,305 shs.	Dec 31, 2023	
Dividend:	$1.3845 (Q)	Mar 1/Jun 1/Sep 1/Dec 1	

Dividend Details: Reset on Jun 1, 2028. Dividend rate will be reset in every fifth year thereafter. The annual dividend rate will be equal to the sum of the five-year Government of Canada Bond Yield plus 2.51%. Previously, annual divd. rate was 1.172250 per sh until May 31, 2023.
Redemption: Redeem. on the following dates on min. 30 and max. 60 days' notice as follows:
Jun 1, 2018...$25.00   Jun 1, 2023...$25.00
Redeem. on June 1 in every fifth year thereafter on min. 30 and max. 60 days' notice at $25.00 per share.

Exchange: Was exchange. on min. 30 days' notice into pfd ser G sh as follows:
On Jun 1, 2018......................$25.00......................1   On Jun 1, 2023......................$25.00......................1
Exchange. on June 1 in every fifth year thereafter.
Lead Underwriter(s): Scotia Capital Inc., RBC Capital Markets, TD Securities Inc.
Transfer Agent: Computershare Trust Company of Canada Inc.
Registrar: Computershare Trust Company of Canada Inc.
Exchanges: TSX
Symbol: ENB.PR.F
CUSIP: 29250N865

6.112% Cum. 5-Year Rate Reset Pref., Series H

DBRS Rating:	Pfd-3 high	Sep 6, 2023
Issued:	14,000,000 shs.	Mar 29, 2012 $25.000
O/S:	11,649,398 shs.	Dec 31, 2023
Dividend:	$1.528 (Q)	Mar 1/Jun 1/Sep 1/Dec 1

Dividend Details: Reset on Sep 1, 2028. Dividend rate will be reset in every fifth year thereafter. The annual dividend rate will be equal to the sum of the five-year Government of Canada Bond Yield plus 2.12%. Previously, annual divd. rate was 1.094000 per sh until Aug 31, 2023.
Redemption: Redeem. on the following dates on min. 30 and max. 60 days' notice as follows:
Sep 1, 2018....................................$25.00   Sep 1, 2023......................................$25.00
Redeem. on Sept. 1 in every fifth year thereafter on min. 30 and max. 60 days' notice at $25.00 per share.
Exchange: Was exchange. on min. 30 days' notice into pfd ser I as follows:
On Sep 1, 2018......................$25.00......................1   On Sep 1, 2023......................$25.00......................1
Exchange. on Sept. 1 in every fifth year thereafter.
Lead Underwriter(s): RBC Capital Markets, Scotia Capital Inc., TD Securities Inc.
Transfer Agent: Computershare Trust Company of Canada Inc.
Registrar: Computershare Trust Company of Canada Inc.
Exchanges: TSX
Symbol: ENB.PR.H
CUSIP: 29250N840

5.8579% Cum. 5-Year Rate Reset Pref., Series L

DBRS Rating:	Pfd-3 high	Sep 6, 2023
Issued:	16,000,000 shs.	May 23, 2012 US$25.000
O/S:	16,000,000 shs.	Dec 31, 2023
Dividend:	US$1.46975 (Q)	Mar 1/Jun 1/Sep 1/Dec 1

Dividend Details: Reset on Sep 1, 2027. Dividend rate will be reset in every fifth year thereafter. The annual dividend rate will be equal to the sum of the five-year United States Government Bond Yield plus 3.15%. Previously, annual divd. rate was 1.239750 per sh until Aug 31, 2022.
Redemption: Redeem. on the following dates on min. 30 and max. 60 days' notice as follows:
Sep 1, 2017................................US$25.00   Sep 1, 2022................................US$25.00
Redeem. on Sept. 1 in every fifth year thereafter on min. 30 and max. 60 days' notice at US$25.00 per share.
Exchange: Was exchange. on min. 30 days' notice into pfd ser M as follows:
On Sep 1, 2017..................US$25.00......................1   On Sep 1, 2022....................US$25.00....................1
Exchange. on Sept. 1 in every fifth year thereafter.
Lead Underwriter(s): Scotia Capital Inc., RBC Capital Markets, TD Securities Inc.
Transfer Agent: Computershare Trust Company of Canada Inc.
Registrar: Computershare Trust Company of Canada Inc.
Exchanges: TSX
Symbol: ENB.PF.U
CUSIP: 29250N790

6.696% Cum. 5-Year Rate Reset Pref., Series N

DBRS Rating:	Pfd-3 high	Sep 6, 2023
Issued:	18,000,000 shs.	Jul 17, 2012 $25.000
O/S:	18,000,000 shs.	Dec 31, 2023
Dividend:	$1.674 (Q)	Mar 1/Jun 1/Sep 1/Dec 1

Dividend Details: Reset on Dec 1, 2028. Dividend rate will be reset in every fifth year thereafter. The annual dividend rate will be equal to the sum of the five-year Government of Canada Bond Yield plus 2.65%. Previously, annual divd. rate was 1.271500 per sh until Nov 30, 2023.

FP Equities — Preferreds & Derivatives 2024

Redemption: Redeem. on the following dates on min. 30 and max. 60 days' notice as follows:
Dec 1, 2018...$25.00   Dec 1, 2023..$25.00
Redeem. on Dec. 1 in every fifth year thereafter on min. 30 and max. 60 days' notice at $25.00 per share.
Exchange: Was exchange. on min. 30 days' notice into pfd ser O as follows:
On Dec 1, 2018....................$25.00....................1   On Dec 1, 2023....................$25.00....................1
Exchange. on Dec 1 in every fifth year thereafter.
Lead Underwriter(s): RBC Capital Markets, CIBC World Markets Inc., Scotia Capital Inc., TD Securities Inc.
Transfer Agent: Computershare Trust Company of Canada Inc.
Registrar: Computershare Trust Company of Canada Inc.
Exchanges: TSX
Symbol: ENB.PR.N
CUSIP: 29250N774

5.918% Cum. 5-Year Rate Reset Pref., Series P

DBRS Rating:	Pfd-3 high	Sep 6, 2023
Issued:	16,000,000 shs.	Sep 13, 2012 $25.000
O/S:	16,000,000 shs.	Dec 31, 2023
Dividend:	$1.4795 (Q)	Mar 1/Jun 1/Sep 1/Dec 1

Dividend Details: Reset on Mar 1, 2029. Dividend rate will be reset in every fifth year thereafter. The annual dividend rate will be equal to the sum of the five-year Government of Canada Bond Yield plus 2.50%. Previously, annual divd. rate was 1.094750 per sh until Feb 29, 2024.
Redemption: Redeem. on the following dates on min. 30 and max. 60 days' notice as follows:
Mar 1, 2019...$25.00   Mar 1, 2024..$25.00
Redeem. on March 1 in every fifth year thereafter on min. 30 and max. 60 days' notice at $25.00 per share.
Exchange: Was exchange. on min. 30 days' notice into pfd ser Q as follows:
On Mar 1, 2019....................$25.00....................1   On Mar 1, 2024....................$25.00....................1
Exchange. on March 1 in every fifth year thereafter.
Lead Underwriter(s): TD Securities Inc., CIBC World Markets Inc., RBC Capital Markets, Scotia Capital Inc.
Transfer Agent: Computershare Trust Company of Canada Inc.
Registrar: Computershare Trust Company of Canada Inc.
Exchanges: TSX
Symbol: ENB.PR.P
CUSIP: 29250N758

4.073% Cum. 5-Year Rate Reset Pref., Series R

DBRS Rating:	Pfd-3 high	Sep 6, 2023
Issued:	16,000,000 shs.	Dec 5, 2012 $25.000
O/S:	16,000,000 shs.	Dec 31, 2023
Dividend:	$1.01825 (Q)	Mar 1/Jun 1/Sep 1/Dec 1

Dividend Details: Reset on Jun 1, 2024. Dividend rate will be reset in every fifth year thereafter. The annual dividend rate will be equal to the sum of the five-year Government of Canada Bond Yield plus 2.50%. Previously, annual divd. rate was 1.000000 per sh until May 31, 2019.
Redemption: Redeem. on the following dates on min. 30 and max. 60 days' notice as follows:
Jun 1, 2019...$25.00   Jun 1, 2024..$25.00
Redeem. on June 1 in every fifth year thereafter on min. 30 and max. 60 days' notice at $25.00 per share.
Exchange: Exchange. on min. 30 days' notice into pfd ser S as follows:
On Jun 1, 2019....................$25.00....................1   On Jun 1, 2024....................$25.00....................1
Exchange. on June 1 in every fifth year thereafter.
Lead Underwriter(s): Scotia Capital Inc., RBC Capital Markets, TD Securities Inc.
Transfer Agent: Computershare Trust Company of Canada Inc.
Registrar: Computershare Trust Company of Canada Inc.
Exchanges: TSX
Symbol: ENB.PR.T
CUSIP: 29250N733

6.7037% Cum. 5-Year Rate Reset Pref., Series 1

DBRS Rating:	Pfd-3 high	Sep 6, 2023
Issued:	16,000,000 shs.	Mar 27, 2013 US$25.000
O/S:	16,000,000 shs.	Dec 31, 2023
Dividend:	US$1.675925 (Q)	Mar 1/Jun 1/Sep 1/Dec 1

Dividend Details: Reset on Jun 1, 2028. Dividend rate will be reset in every fifth year thereafter. The annual dividend rate will be equal to the sum of the five-year United States Government Bond Yield plus 3.14%. Previously, annual divd. rate was 1.487275 per sh until May 31, 2023.

Redemption: Redeem. on the following dates on min. 30 and max. 60 days' notice as follows:
Jun 1, 2018...US$25.00   Jun 1, 2023...US$25.00
Redeem. on June 1 in every fifth year thereafter on min. 30 and max. 60 days' notice at US$25.00 per share.

Exchange: Was exchange. on min. 30 days' notice into pfd ser 2 as follows:
On Jun 1, 2018....................US$25.00....................1   On Jun 1, 2023....................US$25.00....................1
Exchange. on June 1 in every fifth year thereafter.

Lead Underwriter(s): Scotia Capital Inc., CIBC World Markets Inc., RBC Capital Markets, TD Securities Inc.
Transfer Agent: Computershare Trust Company of Canada Inc.
Registrar: Computershare Trust Company of Canada Inc.
Exchanges: TSX
Symbol: ENB.PR.V
CUSIP: 29250N717

3.737% Cum. 5-Year Rate Reset Pref., Series 3

DBRS Rating:	Pfd-3 high	Sep 6, 2023	
Issued:	24,000,000 shs.	Jun 6, 2013	$25.000
O/S:	24,000,000 shs.	Dec 31, 2023	
Dividend:	$0.93425 (Q)	Mar 1/Jun 1/Sep 1/Dec 1	

Dividend Details: Reset on Sep 1, 2024. Dividend rate will be reset in every fifth year thereafter. The annual dividend rate will be equal to the sum of the five-year Government of Canada Bond Yield plus 2.38%. Previously, annual divd. rate was 1.000000 per sh until Aug 31, 2019.

Redemption: Redeem. on the following dates on min. 30 and max. 60 days' notice as follows:
Sep 1, 2019...$25.00   Sep 1, 2024...$25.00
Redeem. on Sept. 1 in every fifth year thereafter on min. 30 and max. 60 days' notice at $25.00 per share.

Exchange: Exchange. on min. 30 days' notice into pfd ser 4 as follows:
On Sep 1, 2019....................$25.00....................1   On Sep 1, 2024....................$25.00....................1
Exchange. on Sept. 1 in every fifth year thereafter.

Lead Underwriter(s): TD Securities Inc., CIBC World Markets Inc., RBC Capital Markets, Scotia Capital Inc.
Transfer Agent: Computershare Trust Company of Canada Inc.
Registrar: Computershare Trust Company of Canada Inc.
Exchanges: TSX
Symbol: ENB.PR.Y
CUSIP: 29250N683

5.3753% Cum. 5-Year Rate Reset Pref., Series 5

DBRS Rating:	Pfd-3 high	Sep 6, 2023	
Issued:	8,000,000 shs.	Sep 27, 2013	US$25.000
O/S:	8,000,000 shs.	Dec 31, 2023	
Dividend:	US$1.67075 (Q)	Mar 1/Jun 1/Sep 1/Dec 1	

Dividend Details: Reset on Mar 1, 2029. Dividend rate will be reset in every fifth year thereafter. The annual dividend rate will be equal to the sum of the five-year United States Government Bond Yield plus 2.82%. Previously, annual divd. rate was 1.343825 per sh until Feb 29, 2024.

Redemption: Redeem. on the following dates on min. 30 and max. 60 days' notice as follows:
Mar 1, 2019...US$25.00   Mar 1, 2024...US$25.00
Redeem. on March 1 in every fifth year thereafter on min. 30 and max. 60 days' notice at $25.00 per share.

Exchange: Was exchange. on min. 30 days' notice into pfd ser 6 as follows:
On Mar 1, 2019....................US$25.00....................1   On Mar 1, 2024....................US$25.00....................1
Exchange. on March 1 in every fifth year thereafter.

Lead Underwriter(s): CIBC World Markets Inc., RBC Capital Markets, Scotia Capital Inc., TD Securities Inc.
Transfer Agent: Computershare Trust Company of Canada Inc.
Registrar: Computershare Trust Company of Canada Inc.
Exchanges: TSX
Symbol: ENB.PF.V
CUSIP: 29250N667

FP Equities — Preferreds & Derivatives 2024   59

5.988% Cum. 5-Year Rate Reset Pref., Series 7
DBRS Rating: Pfd-3 high   Sep 6, 2023
Issued: 10,000,000 shs.   Dec 12, 2013 $25.000
O/S: 10,000,000 shs.   Dec 31, 2023
Dividend: $1.497 (Q)   Mar 1/Jun 1/Jul 1/Dec 1

Dividend Details: Reset on Mar 1, 2029. Dividend rate will be reset in every fifth year thereafter. The annual dividend rate will be equal to the sum of the five-year Government of Canada Bond Yield plus 2.57%. Previously, annual divd. rate was 1.112250 per sh until Feb 29, 2024.

Redemption: Redeem. on the following dates on min. 30 and max. 60 days' notice as follows:
Mar 1, 2019..$25.00   Mar 1, 2024.....................................$25.00
Redeem. on March 1 in every fifth year thereafter on min. 30 and max. 60 days' notice at $25.00 per share.

Exchange: Was exchange. on min. 30 days' notice into pfd ser 8 as follows:
On Mar 1, 2019....................$25.00......................1   On Mar 1, 2024....................$25.00......................1
Exchange. on March 1 in every fifth year thereafter.

Lead Underwriter(s): Scotia Capital Inc., CIBC World Markets Inc., RBC Capital Markets, TD Securities Inc.
Transfer Agent: Computershare Trust Company of Canada Inc.
Registrar: Computershare Trust Company of Canada Inc.
Exchanges: TSX
Symbol: ENB.PR.J
CUSIP: 29250N642

4.097% Cum. 5-Year Rate Reset Pref., Series 9
DBRS Rating: Pfd-3 high   Sep 6, 2023
Issued: 11,000,000 shs.   Mar 13, 2014 $25.000
O/S: 11,000,000 shs.   Dec 31, 2023
Dividend: $1.02425 (Q)   Mar 1/Jun 1/Sep 1/Dec 1

Dividend Details: Reset on Dec 1, 2024. Dividend rate will be reset in every fifth year thereafter. The annual dividend rate will be equal to the sum of the five-year Government of Canada Bond Yield plus 2.66%. Previously, annual divd. rate was 1.100000 per sh until Nov 30, 2019.

Redemption: Redeem. on the following dates on min. 30 and max. 60 days' notice as follows:
Dec 1, 2019..$25.00   Dec 1, 2024.....................................$25.00
Redeem. on Dec. 1 in every fifth year thereafter on min. 30 and max. 60 days' notice at $25.00 per share.

Exchange: Exchange. on min. 30 days' notice into pfd ser 10 as follows:
On Dec 1, 2019....................$25.00......................1   On Dec 1, 2024....................$25.00......................1
Exchange. on Dec. 1 in every fifth year thereafter.

Lead Underwriter(s): TD Securities Inc., CIBC World Markets Inc., RBC Capital Markets, Scotia Capital Inc.
Transfer Agent: Computershare Trust Company of Canada Inc.
Registrar: Computershare Trust Company of Canada Inc.
Exchanges: TSX
Symbol: ENB.PF.A
CUSIP: 29250N626

3.938% Cum. 5-Year Rate Reset Pref., Series 11
DBRS Rating: Pfd-3 high   Sep 6, 2023
Issued: 20,000,000 shs.   May 22, 2014 $25.000
O/S: 20,000,000 shs.   Dec 31, 2023
Dividend: $0.9845 (Q)   Mar 1/Jun 1/Sep 1/Dec 1

Dividend Details: Reset on Mar 1, 2025. Dividend rate will be reset in every fifth year thereafter. The annual dividend rate will be equal to the sum of the five-year Government of Canada Bond Yield plus 2.64%. Previously, annual divd. rate was 1.100000 per sh until Feb 29, 2020.

Redemption: Redeem. on the following dates on min. 30 and max. 60 days' notice as follows:
Mar 1, 2020..$25.00   Mar 1, 2025.....................................$25.00
Redeem. on March 1 in every fifth year thereafter on min. 30 and max. 60 days' notice at $25.00 per share.

Exchange: Exchange. on min. 30 days' notice into pfd ser 12 as follows:
On Mar 1, 2020....................$25.00......................1   On Mar 1, 2025....................$25.00......................1
Exchange. on March 1 in every fifth year thereafter.

Lead Underwriter(s): Scotia Capital Inc., CIBC World Markets Inc., RBC Capital Markets, TD Securities Inc.
Transfer Agent: Computershare Trust Company of Canada Inc.
Registrar: Computershare Trust Company of Canada Inc.
Exchanges: TSX
Symbol: ENB.PF.C
CUSIP: 29250N592

3.043% Cum. 5-Year Rate Reset Pref., Series 13

DBRS Rating:	Pfd-3 high	Sep 6, 2023
Issued:	14,000,000 shs.	Jul 17, 2014 $25.000
O/S:	14,000,000 shs.	Dec 31, 2023
Dividend:	$0.76075 (Q)	Mar 1/Jun 1/Sep 1/Dec 1

Dividend Details: Reset on Jun 1, 2025. Dividend rate will be reset in every fifth year thereafter. The annual dividend rate will be equal to the sum of the five-year Government of Canada Bond Yield plus 2.66%. Previously, annual divd. rate was 1.100000 per sh until May 31, 2020.
Redemption: Redeem. on the following dates on min. 30 and max. 60 days' notice as follows:
Jun 1, 2020...$25.00   Jun 1, 2025...$25.00
Redeem. on June 1 in every fifth year thereafter on min. 30 and max. 60 days' notice at $25.00 per share.
Exchange: Exchange. on min. 30 days' notice into pfd ser 14 as follows:
On Jun 1, 2020.....................$25.00.....................1   On Jun 1, 2025.....................$25.00.....................1
Exchange. on June 1 in every fifth year thereafter.
Lead Underwriter(s): CIBC World Markets Inc., RBC Capital Markets, Scotia Capital Inc., TD Securities Inc.
Transfer Agent: Computershare Trust Company of Canada Inc.
Registrar: Computershare Trust Company of Canada Inc.
Exchanges: TSX
Symbol: ENB.PF.E
CUSIP: 29250N576

2.983% Cum. 5-Year Rate Reset Pref., Series 15

DBRS Rating:	Pfd-3 high	Sep 6, 2023
Issued:	11,000,000 shs.	Sep 23, 2014 $25.000
O/S:	11,000,000 shs.	Dec 31, 2023
Dividend:	$0.74575 (Q)	Mar 1/Jun 1/Sep 1/Dec 1

Dividend Details: Reset on Sep 1, 2025. Dividend rate will be reset in every fifth year thereafter. The annual dividend rate will be equal to the sum of the five-year Government of Canada Bond Yield plus 2.68%. Previously, annual divd. rate was 1.100000 per sh until Aug 31, 2020.
Redemption: Redeem. on the following dates on min. 30 and max. 60 days' notice as follows:
Sep 1, 2020...$25.00   Sep 1, 2025...$25.00
Redeem. on Sept. 1 in every fifth year thereafter on min. 30 and max. 60 days' notice at $25.00 per share.
Exchange: Exchange. on min. 30 days' notice into pfd ser 16 as follows:
On Sep 1, 2020.....................$25.00.....................1   On Sep 1, 2025.....................$25.00.....................1
Exchange. on Sept. 1 in every fifth year thereafter.
Lead Underwriter(s): TD Securities Inc., CIBC World Markets Inc., RBC Capital Markets, Scotia Capital Inc.
Transfer Agent: Computershare Trust Company of Canada Inc.
Registrar: Computershare Trust Company of Canada Inc.
Exchanges: TSX
Symbol: ENB.PF.G
CUSIP: 29250N550

6.212% Cum. 5-Year Rate Reset Pref., Series 19

DBRS Rating:	Pfd-3 high	Sep 6, 2023
Issued:	20,000,000 shs.	Dec 11, 2017 $25.000
O/S:	20,000,000 shs.	Dec 31, 2023
Dividend:	$1.553 (Q)	Mar 1/Jun 1/Sep 1/Dec 1

Dividend Details: Reset on Mar 1, 2028. Dividend rate will be reset in every fifth year thereafter. The annual dividend rate will be equal to the greater of (i) the sum of the five-year Government of Canada Bond Yield plus 3.17% and (ii) 4.90%. Previously, annual divd. rate was 1.225000 per sh until Feb 28, 2023.
Redemption: Redeem. on the following dates on min. 30 and max. 60 days' notice as follows:
Mar 1, 2023...$25.00   Mar 1, 2028...$25.00
Redeem. on March 1 in every fifth year thereafter on min. 30 and max. 60 days' notice at $25.00 per share.

Exchange: Exchange. on min. 30 days' notice into pfd ser 20 as follows:
On Mar 1, 2023......................$25.00......................1   On Mar 1, 2028......................$25.00......................1
Exchange. on March 1 in every fifth year thereafter.
Lead Underwriter(s): Scotia Capital Inc., BMO Capital Markets, CIBC World Markets Inc., National Bank Financial Inc.
Transfer Agent: Computershare Trust Company of Canada Inc.
Registrar: Computershare Trust Company of Canada Inc.
Exchanges: TSX
Symbol: ENB.PF.K
CUSIP: 29250N519

Floating Rate Cum. Pref., Series G

Issued:	1,827,695 shs.	Jun 1, 2023	$25.000
O/S:	1,827,695 shs.	Dec 31, 2023	
Dividend:	F.R. (Q)	Mar 1/Jun 1/Sep 1/Dec 1	

Dividend Details: Quarterly divd. rate is T-bill plus 2.51%.
Redemption: Redeem. on the following dates on min. 30 and max. 60 days' notice as follows:
Jun 1, 2028......................$25.00   Jun 1, 2033......................$25.00
Redeem. on June 1 in every fifth year thereafter on min. 30 and max. 60 days' notice at $25.00 per share. After June 1, 2023, other than on an Exchange Date, redeem. at $25.50 per sh., plus declared and unpaid dividends thereon to the date of redemption.
Exchange: Exchange. on min. 30 days' notice into pfd ser F sh as follows:
On Jun 1, 2028......................$25.00......................1   On Jun 1, 2033......................$25.00......................1
Exchange. on June 1 in every fifth year thereafter.
Note: Issued upon exchange of an equal number of Pref Shs, Series F.
Transfer Agent: Computershare Trust Company of Canada Inc.
Registrar: Computershare Trust Company of Canada Inc.
Exchanges: TSX
Symbol: ENB.PR.G
CUSIP: 29250N857

Floating Rate Cum. Pref., Series I

Issued:	2,350,602 shs.	Sep 1, 2023	$25.000
O/S:	2,350,602 shs.	Dec 31, 2023	
Dividend:	F.R. (Q)	Mar 1/Jun 1/Sep 1/Dec 1	

Dividend Details: Quarterly divd. rate is T-bill plus 2.12%.
Redemption: Redeem. on the following dates on min. 30 and max. 60 days' notice as follows:
Sep 1, 2028......................$25.00   Sep 1, 2033......................$25.00
Redeem. on Sept. 1 in every fifth year thereafter on min. 30 and max. 60 days' notice at $25.00 per share. After Sept. 1, 2028, other than on an Exchange Date, redeem. at $25.50 per sh., plus declared and unpaid dividends thereon to the date of redemption.
Exchange: Exchange. on min. 30 days' notice into pfd ser H sh as follows:
On Sep 1, 2028......................$25.00......................1   On Sep 1, 2033......................$25.00......................1
Exchange. on Sept. 1 in every fifth year thereafter.
Note: Issued upon exchange of an equal number of Pref Shs, Series H.
Transfer Agent: Computershare Trust Company of Canada Inc.
Exchanges: TSX
Symbol: ENB.PR.I
CUSIP: 29250N832

Fairfax Financial Holdings Limited

4.709% Cum. 5-Year Rate Reset Pref., Series C

DBRS Rating:	Pfd-2 low	Dec 1, 2023	
Issued:	10,000,000 shs.	Oct 5, 2009	$25.000
O/S:	7,515,642 shs.	Dec 31, 2023	
Dividend:	$1.17725 (Q)	Mar 31/Jun 30/Sep 30/Dec 31	

Dividend Details: Reset on Jan 1, 2025. Dividend rate will be reset in every fifth year thereafter. The annual dividend rate will be equal to the sum of the then current five-year Government of Canada Bond Yield plus 3.15%. Previously, annual divd. rate was 1.144500 per sh until Dec 31, 2019.

Redemption: Redeem. on the following dates on min. 30 and max. 60 days' notice as follows:
Dec 31, 2014..$25.00   Dec 31, 2019..$25.00
Redeem. on Dec. 31 in every fifth year thereafter on min. 30 and max. 60 days' notice at $25.00 per share.
Exchange: Was exchange. on min. 30 days' notice into pfd ser D sh as follows:
On Dec 31, 2014......................$25.00......................1   On Dec 31, 2019......................$25.00......................1
Exchange. on Dec. 31 in every fifth year thereafter.
Lead Underwriter(s): Scotia Capital Inc., RBC Capital Markets, BMO Capital Markets
Transfer Agent: Computershare Trust Company of Canada Inc.
Registrar: Computershare Trust Company of Canada Inc.
Exchanges: TSX
Symbol: FFH.PR.C
CUSIP: 303901508

3.183% Cum. 5-Year Rate Reset Pref., Series E

DBRS Rating:	Pfd-2 low	Dec 1, 2023	
Issued:	8,000,000 shs.	Feb 1, 2010	$25.000
O/S:	5,440,132 shs.	Dec 31, 2023	
Dividend:	$0.79575 (Q)	Mar 31/Jun 30/Sep 30/Dec 31	

Dividend Details: Reset on Apr 1, 2025. Dividend rate will be reset in every fifth year thereafter. The annual dividend rate will be equal to the sum of the then current five-year Government of Canada Bond Yield plus 2.16%. Previously, annual divd. rate was 0.727500 per sh until Mar 31, 2020.
Redemption: Redeem. on the following dates on min. 30 and max. 60 days' notice as follows:
Mar 31, 2015..$25.00   Mar 31, 2020..$25.00
Redeem. on March 31 in every fifth year thereafter on min. 30 and max. 60 days' notice at $25.00 per share.
Exchange: Was exchange. on min. 30 days' notice into pfd ser F sh as follows:
On Mar 31, 2015......................$25.00......................1   On Mar 31, 2020......................$25.00......................1
Exchange. on March 31 in every fifth year thereafter.
Lead Underwriter(s): BMO Capital Markets, CIBC World Markets Inc., RBC Capital Markets, Scotia Capital Inc.
Transfer Agent: Computershare Trust Company of Canada Inc.
Registrar: Computershare Trust Company of Canada Inc.
Exchanges: TSX
Symbol: FFH.PR.E
CUSIP: 303901888

2.962% Cum. 5-Year Rate Reset Pref., Series G

DBRS Rating:	Pfd-2 low	Dec 1, 2023	
Issued:	10,000,000 shs.	Jul 28, 2010	$25.000
O/S:	7,719,843 shs.	Dec 31, 2023	
Dividend:	$0.7405 (Q)	Mar 31/Jun 30/Sep 30/Dec 31	

Dividend Details: Reset on Oct 1, 2025. Dividend rate will be reset in every fifth year thereafter. The annual dividend rate will be equal to the sum of the then current five-year Government of Canada Bond Yield plus 2.56%. Previously, annual divd. rate was 0.829500 per sh until Sep 30, 2020.
Redemption: Redeem. on the following dates on min. 30 days' notice as follows:
Sep 30, 2015..$25.00   Sep 30, 2020..$25.00
Redeem. on Sept. 30 in every fifth year thereafter on min. 30 and max. 60 days' notice at $25.00 per share.
Exchange: Was exchange. on min. 30 days' notice into pfd ser H sh as follows:
On Sep 30, 2015......................$25.00......................1   On Sep 30, 2020......................$25.00......................1
Exchange. on Sept. 30 in every fifth year thereafter.
Lead Underwriter(s): BMO Capital Markets, CIBC World Markets Inc., RBC Capital Markets, Scotia Capital Inc.
Transfer Agent: Computershare Trust Company of Canada Inc.
Registrar: Computershare Trust Company of Canada Inc.
Exchanges: TSX
Symbol: FFH.PR.G
CUSIP: 303901862

3.327% Cum. 5-Year Rate Reset Pref., Series I

DBRS Rating:	Pfd-2 low	Dec 1, 2023	
Issued:	12,000,000 shs.	Oct 5, 2010	$25.000
O/S:	10,420,101 shs.	Dec 31, 2023	
Dividend:	$0.83175 (Q)	Mar 31/Jun 30/Sep 30/Dec 31	

Dividend Details: Reset on Jan 1, 2026. Dividend rate will be reset in every fifth year thereafter. The annual dividend rate will be equal to the sum of the then current five-year Government of Canada Bond Yield plus 2.85%. Previously, annual divd. rate was 0.927000 per sh until Dec 31, 2020.
Redemption: Redeem. on the following dates on min. 30 and max. 60 days' notice as follows:
Dec 31, 2015..$25.00   Dec 31, 2020...$25.00
Redeem. on Dec. 31 in every fifth year thereafter on min. 30 and max. 60 days' notice at $25.00 per share.
Exchange: Was exchange. on min. 30 days' notice into pfd ser J as follows:
On Dec 31, 2015...................$25.00....................1   On Dec 31, 2020.....................$25.00.....................1
Exchange. on Dec. 31 in every fifth year thereafter.
Lead Underwriter(s): BMO Capital Markets, CIBC World Markets Inc., RBC Capital Markets, Scotia Capital Inc.
Transfer Agent: Computershare Trust Company of Canada Inc.
Registrar: Computershare Trust Company of Canada Inc.
Exchanges: TSX
Symbol: FFH.PR.I
CUSIP: 303901847

5.045% Cum. 5-Year Rate Reset Pref., Series K

DBRS Rating:	Pfd-2 low	Dec 1, 2023	
Issued:	9,500,000 shs.	Mar 21, 2012	$25.000
O/S:	9,500,000 shs.	Dec 31, 2023	
Dividend:	$1.26125 (Q)	Mar 31/Jun 30/Sep 30/Dec 31	

Dividend Details: Reset on Apr 1, 2027. Dividend rate will be reset in every fifth year thereafter. The annual dividend rate will be equal to the sum of the five-year Government of Canada Bond Yield plus 3.51%. Previously, annual divd. rate was 1.167750 per sh until Mar 31, 2022.
Redemption: Redeem. on the following dates on min. 30 and max. 60 days' notice as follows:
Mar 31, 2017..$25.00   Mar 31, 2022...$25.00
Redeem. on March 31 in every fifth year thereafter on min. 30 and max. 60 days' notice at $25.00 per share.
Exchange: Was exchange. on min. 30 days' notice into pfd ser L as follows:
On Mar 31, 2017....................$25.00....................1   On Mar 31, 2022.....................$25.00.....................1
Exchange. on March 31 in every fifth year thereafter.
Lead Underwriter(s): BMO Capital Markets, CIBC World Markets Inc., RBC Capital Markets, Scotia Capital Inc.
Transfer Agent: Computershare Trust Company of Canada Inc.
Registrar: Computershare Trust Company of Canada Inc.
Exchanges: TSX
Symbol: FFH.PR.K
CUSIP: 303901821

Floating Rate Cum. Pref., Series D

Issued:	3,983,616 shs.	Dec 31, 2014	$25.000
O/S:	2,484,358 shs.	Dec 31, 2023	
Dividend:	F.R. (Q)	Mar 31/Jun 30/Sep 30/Dec 31	

Dividend Details: Quarterly divd. rate is T-bill plus 3.15%.
Redemption: Redeem. on the following dates on min. 30 and max. 60 days' notice as follows:
Dec 31, 2019..$25.00   Dec 31, 2024...$25.00
Redeem. on Dec. 31 in every fifth year thereafter on min. 30 and max. 60 days' notice at $25.00 per share.

64 FP Equities — Preferreds & Derivatives 2024

Exchange: Exchange. on min. 30 days' notice into pfd ser C sh as follows:
On Dec 31, 2019.....................$25.00......................1   On Dec 31, 2024......................$25.00......................1
Exchange. on Dec. 31 in every fifth year thereafter.
Note: Issued upon exchange of an equal number of Preferred Shares, Series C.
Transfer Agent: Computershare Trust Company of Canada Inc.
Registrar: Computershare Trust Company of Canada Inc.
Exchanges: TSX
Symbol: FFH.PR.D
CUSIP: 303901607

5.003% Cum. 5-Year Rate Reset Pref., Series M

DBRS Rating:	Pfd-2 low	Dec 1, 2023	
Issued:	9,200,000 shs.	Mar 3, 2015	$25.000
O/S:	9,200,000 shs.	Dec 31, 2023	
Dividend:	$1.25075 (Q)	Mar 31/Jun 30/Sep 30/Dec 31	

Dividend Details: Reset on Apr 1, 2025. Dividend rate will be reset in every fifth year thereafter. The annual dividend rate will be equal to the sum of the five-year Government of Canada Bond Yield plus 3.98%. Previously, annual divd. rate was 1.187500 per sh until Mar 31, 2020.
Redemption: Redeem. on the following dates on min. 30 and max. 60 days' notice as follows:
Mar 31, 2020...$25.00   Mar 31, 2025...$25.00
Redeem. on March 31 in every fifth year thereafter on min. 30 and max. 60 days' notice at $25.00 per share.
Exchange: Exchange. on min. 30 days' notice into pfd ser N as follows:
On Mar 31, 2020......................$25.00......................1   On Mar 31, 2025......................$25.00......................1
Exchange. on March 31 in every fifth year thereafter.
Lead Underwriter(s): BMO Capital Markets, RBC Capital Markets, Scotia Capital Inc.
Transfer Agent: Computershare Trust Company of Canada Inc.
Registrar: Computershare Trust Company of Canada Inc.
Exchanges: TSX
Symbol: FFH.PR.M
CUSIP: 303901797

Floating Rate Cum. Pref., Series F

Issued:	3,572,044 shs.	Mar 31, 2015	$25.000
O/S:	2,099,046 shs.	Dec 31, 2023	
Dividend:	F.R. (Q)	Mar 31/Jun 30/Sep 30/Dec 31	

Dividend Details: Quarterly divd. rate is T-bill plus 2.16%.
Redemption: Redeem. on the following dates on min. 30 and max. 60 days' notice as follows:
Mar 31, 2020...$25.00   Mar 31, 2025...$25.00
Redeem. on March 31 in every fifth year thereafter on min. 30 and max. 60 days' notice at $25.00 per share.
After March 31, 2015, other than an Exchange Date, redeem. at $25.50 per sh. plus accrued and unpaid dividends thereon to but excluding the date fixed for redemption.
Exchange: Exchange. on min. 30 days' notice into pfd ser E sh as follows:
On Mar 31, 2020......................$25.00......................1   On Mar 31, 2025......................$25.00......................1
Exchange. on March 31 in every fifth year thereafter.
Note: Issued upon exchange of an equal number of Preferred Shares, Series E.
Transfer Agent: Computershare Trust Company of Canada Inc.
Registrar: Computershare Trust Company of Canada Inc.
Exchanges: TSX
Symbol: FFH.PR.F
CUSIP: 303901870

Floating Rate Cum. Pref., Series H

Issued:	2,567,048 shs.	Sep 30, 2015	$25.000
O/S:	2,280,157 shs.	Dec 31, 2023	
Dividend:	F.R. (Q)	Mar 31/Jun 30/Sep 30/Dec 31	

Dividend Details: Quarterly divd. rate is T-bill plus 2.56%.
Redemption: Redeem. on the following dates on min. 30 and max. 60 days' notice as follows:
Sep 30, 2020...$25.00   Sep 30, 2025...$25.00
Redeem. on Sept. 30 in every fifth year thereafter on min. 30 and max. 60 days' notice at $25.00 per share.

FP Equities — Preferreds & Derivatives 2024   65

Exchange: Exchange. on min. 30 days' notice into pfd ser G sh as follows:
On Sep 30, 2020....................$25.00....................1   On Sep 30, 2025.....................$25.00.....................1
Exchange. on Sept. 30 in every fifth year thereafter.
Note: Issued upon exchange of an equal number of Preferred Shares, Series G.
Transfer Agent: Computershare Trust Company of Canada Inc.
Registrar: Computershare Trust Company of Canada Inc.
Exchanges: TSX
Symbol: FFH.PR.H
CUSIP: 303901854

Floating Rate Cum. Pref., Series J

Issued:	1,534,447 shs.	Dec 31, 2015	$25.000
O/S:	1,579,899 shs.	Dec 31, 2023	
Dividend:	F.R. (Q)	Mar 31/Jun 30/Sep 30/Dec 31	

Dividend Details: Quarterly divd. rate is T-bill plus 2.85%.
Redemption: Redeem. on the following dates on min. 30 and max. 60 days' notice as follows:
Dec 31, 2020..$25.00   Dec 31, 2025..$25.00
Redeem. on Dec. 31 in every fifth year thereafter on min. 30 and max. 60 days' notice at $25.00 per share.
Exchange: Exchange. on min. 30 days' notice into pfd ser I sh as follows:
On Dec 31, 2020....................$25.00....................1   On Dec 31, 2025.....................$25.00.....................1
Exchange. on Dec. 31 in every fifth year thereafter.
Note: Issued upon exchange of an equal number of Preferred Shares, Series I.
Transfer Agent: Computershare Trust Company of Canada Inc.
Registrar: Computershare Trust Company of Canada Inc.
Exchanges: TSX
Symbol: FFH.PR.J
CUSIP: 303901839

First National Financial Corporation

2.895% Cum. 5-Year Rate Reset Class A Pref., Series 1

DBRS Rating:	Pfd-3	Mar 12, 2024	
Issued:	4,000,000 shs.	Jan 25, 2011	$25.000
O/S:	2,984,835 shs.	Dec 31, 2023	
Dividend:	$0.72375 (Q)	Mar 31/Jun 30/Sep 30/Dec 31	

Dividend Details: Reset on Apr 1, 2026. Dividend rate will be reset in every fifth year thereafter. The annual dividend rate will be equal to the sum of the five-year Government of Canada Bond Yield plus 2.07%. Previously, annual divd. rate was 0.697500 per sh until Mar 31, 2021.
Redemption: Redeem. on the following dates on min. 30 and max. 60 days' notice as follows:
Mar 31, 2016..$25.00   Mar 31, 2021..$25.00
Redeem. on March 31 in every fifth year thereafter on min. 30 and max. 60 days' notice at $25.00 per share.
Exchange: Was exchange. on min. 30 days' notice into pfd A ser 2 as follows:
On Mar 31, 2016....................$25.00....................1   On Mar 31, 2021.....................$25.00.....................1
Exchange. on March 31 in every fifth year thereafter.
Lead Underwriter(s): RBC Capital Markets, Scotia Capital Inc.
Transfer Agent: Computershare Investor Services Inc.
Registrar: Computershare Investor Services Inc.
Exchanges: TSX
Symbol: FN.PR.A
CUSIP: 33564P202

Floating Rate Cum. Class A Pref., Series 2

DBRS Rating:	Pfd-3	Mar 12, 2024	
Issued:	1,112,853 shs.	Apr 1, 2016	$25.000
O/S:	1,015,165 shs.	Dec 31, 2023	
Dividend:	F.R. (Q)	Mar 31/Jun 30/Sep 30/Dec 31	

Dividend Details: Quarterly divd. rate is T-bill plus 2.07%.

Redemption: Redeem. on the following dates on min. 30 and max. 60 days' notice as follows:
Mar 31, 2021...$25.00   Mar 31, 2026...$25.00
Redeem. on March 31 in every fifth year thereafter on min. 30 and max. 60 days' notice at $25.00 per share. After March 31, 2021, other than on an Exchange Date, redeem. at $25.50 per sh., plus declared and unpaid dividends thereon to the date of redemption.

Exchange: Exchange. on min. 30 days' notice into pfd A ser 1 sh as follows:
On Mar 31, 2021.....................$25.00......................1   On Mar 31, 2026.....................$25.00......................1
Exchange. on March 31 in every fifth year thereafter.

Note: Issued upon exchange of an equal number of Class A Preferred Shares, Series 1.
Transfer Agent: Computershare Investor Services Inc.
Registrar: Computershare Investor Services Inc.
Exchanges: TSX
Symbol: FN.PR.B
CUSIP: 33564P301

Fortis Inc.

4.9% Cum. First Pfce., Series F

DBRS Rating:	Pfd-2 low	May 3, 2024
Issued:	5,000,000 shs.	Sep 28, 2006 $25.000
O/S:	5,000,000 shs.	Dec 31, 2023
Dividend:	$1.225 (Q)	Mar 1/Jun 1/Sep 1/Dec 1

Redemption: Redeem. on and after the following dates on min. 30 and max. 60 days' notice as follows:
Dec 1, 2011..$26.00   Dec 1, 2012..$25.75
Dec 1, 2013..$25.50   Dec 1, 2014..$25.25
Dec 1, 2015..$25.00

Lead Underwriter(s): BMO Capital Markets
Transfer Agent: Computershare Trust Company of Canada Inc.
Registrar: Computershare Trust Company of Canada Inc.
Exchanges: TSX
Symbol: FTS.PR.F
CUSIP: 349553867

6.123% Cum. 5-Year Rate Reset First Pfce., Series G

DBRS Rating:	Pfd-2 low	May 3, 2024
Issued:	9,200,000 shs.	May 23, 2008 $25.000
O/S:	9,200,000 shs.	Dec 31, 2023
Dividend:	$1.53075 (Q)	Mar 1/Jun 1/Sep 1/Dec 1

Dividend Details: Reset on Sep 1, 2028. Dividend rate will be reset in every fifth year thereafter. The annual dividend rate will be equal to the sum of the five-year Government of Canada Bond Yield plus 2.13%. Previously, annual divd. rate was 1.098250 per sh until Aug 31, 2023.

Redemption: Redeem. on the following dates on min. 30 and max. 60 days' notice as follows:
Sep 1, 2013..$25.00   Sep 1, 2018..$25.00
Redeem. on Sept. 1 in every fifth year thereafter on min. 30 and max. 60 days' notice at $25.00 per share.

Lead Underwriter(s): Scotia Capital Inc., CIBC World Markets Inc.
Transfer Agent: Computershare Trust Company of Canada Inc.
Registrar: Computershare Trust Company of Canada Inc.
Exchanges: TSX
Symbol: FTS.PR.G
CUSIP: 349553834

1.835% Cum. 5-Year Rate Reset First Pfce., Series H

DBRS Rating:	Pfd-2 low	May 3, 2024
Issued:	10,000,000 shs.	Jan 26, 2010 $25.000
O/S:	7,665,082 shs.	Dec 31, 2023
Dividend:	$0.45875 (Q)	Mar 1/Jun 1/Sep 1/Dec 1

Dividend Details: Reset on Jun 1, 2025. Dividend rate will be reset in every fifth year thereafter. The annual dividend rate will be equal to the sum of the five-year Government of Canada Bond Yield plus 1.45%. Previously, annual divd. rate was 0.625000 per sh until May 31, 2020.

FP Equities — Preferreds & Derivatives 2024

Redemption: Redeem. on the following dates on min. 30 and max. 60 days' notice as follows:
Jun 1, 2015...$25.00   Jun 1, 2020..$25.00
Redeem. on June 1 in every fifth year thereafter on min. 30 and max. 60 days' notice at $25.00 per share.
Exchange: Was exchange. on min. 30 days' notice into pfd 1st ser I as follows:
On Jun 1, 2015......................$25.00........................1   On Jun 1, 2020......................$25.00......................1
Exchange. on June 1 in every fifth year thereafter.
Lead Underwriter(s): TD Securities Inc., Scotia Capital Inc., RBC Capital Markets, CIBC World Markets Inc.
Transfer Agent: Computershare Trust Company of Canada Inc.
Registrar: Computershare Trust Company of Canada Inc.
Exchanges: TSX
Symbol: FTS.PR.H
CUSIP: 349553826

4.75% Cum. First Pfce., Series J

DBRS Rating:	Pfd-2 low	May 3, 2024	
Issued:	8,000,000 shs.	Nov 13, 2012	$25.000
O/S:	8,000,000 shs.	Dec 31, 2023	
Dividend:	$1.1875 (Q)	Mar 1/Jun 1/Sep 1/Dec 1	

Redemption: Redeem. on and after the following dates on min. 30 and max. 60 days' notice as follows:
Dec 1, 2017...$26.00   Dec 1, 2018..$25.75
Dec 1, 2019...$25.50   Dec 1, 2020..$25.25
Dec 1, 2021...$25.00
Lead Underwriter(s): BMO Capital Markets, RBC Capital Markets
Transfer Agent: Computershare Trust Company of Canada Inc.
Registrar: Computershare Trust Company of Canada Inc.
Exchanges: TSX
Symbol: FTS.PR.J
CUSIP: 349553792

5.469% Cum. 5-Year Rate Reset First Pfce., Series K

DBRS Rating:	Pfd-2 low	May 3, 2024	
Issued:	10,000,000 shs.	Jul 18, 2013	$25.000
O/S:	10,000,000 shs.	Dec 31, 2023	
Dividend:	$1.36725 (Q)	Mar 1/Jun 1/Sep 1/Dec 1	

Dividend Details: Reset on Mar 1, 2029. Dividend rate will be reset in every fifth year thereafter. The annual dividend rate will be equal to the sum of the five-year Government of Canada Bond Yield plus 2.05%. Previously, annual divd. rate was 0.981250 per sh until Feb 29, 2024.
Redemption: Redeem. on the following dates on min. 30 and max. 60 days' notice as follows:
Mar 1, 2019...$25.00   Mar 1, 2024..$25.00
Redeem. on March 1 in every fifth year thereafter on min. 30 and max. 60 days' notice at $25.00 per share.
Exchange: Was exchange. into pfd 1st ser L as follows:
On Mar 1, 2019......................$25.00........................1   On Mar 1, 2024......................$25.00......................1
Exchange. on March 1 in every fifth year thereafter.
Lead Underwriter(s): TD Securities Inc., CIBC World Markets Inc., Scotia Capital Inc.
Transfer Agent: Computershare Trust Company of Canada Inc.
Registrar: Computershare Trust Company of Canada Inc.
Exchanges: TSX
Symbol: FTS.PR.K
CUSIP: 349553784

3.913% Cum. 5-Year Rate Reset First Pfce., Series M

DBRS Rating:	Pfd-2 low	May 3, 2024	
Issued:	24,000,000 shs.	Sep 19, 2014	$25.000
O/S:	24,000,000 shs.	Dec 31, 2023	
Dividend:	$0.97825 (Q)	Mar 1/Jun 1/Sep 1/Dec 1	

Dividend Details: Reset on Dec 1, 2024. Dividend rate will be reset in every fifth year thereafter. The annual dividend rate will be equal to the sum of the five-year Government of Canada Bond Yield plus 2.48%. Previously, annual divd. rate was 1.025000 per sh until Nov 30, 2019.
Redemption: Redeem. on the following dates on min. 30 and max. 60 days' notice as follows:
Dec 1, 2019...$25.00   Dec 1, 2024..$25.00
Redeem. on Dec. 1 in every fifth year thereafter on min. 30 and max. 60 days' notice at $25.00 per share.

Exchange: Exchange. on min. 30 days' notice into pfd 1st ser N as follows:
On Dec 1, 2019......................$25.00......................1   On Dec 1, 2024......................$25.00......................1
Exchange. on Dec. 1 in every fifth year thereafter.
Lead Underwriter(s): Scotia Capital Inc., RBC Capital Markets
Transfer Agent: Computershare Trust Company of Canada Inc.
Registrar: Computershare Trust Company of Canada Inc.
Exchanges: TSX
Symbol: FTS.PR.M
CUSIP: 349553768

Floating Rate Cum. Pref., Series I

DBRS Rating:	Pfd-2 low	May 3, 2024	
Issued:	2,975,154 shs.	Jun 1, 2015	$25.000
O/S:	2,334,918 shs.	Dec 31, 2023	
Dividend:	F.R. (Q)	Mar 1/Jun 1/Sep 1/Dec 1	

Dividend Details: Quarterly divd. rate is T-bill plus 1.45%.
Redemption: Redeem. on the following dates on min. 30 and max. 60 days' notice as follows:
Jun 1, 2020......................$25.00   Jun 1, 2025......................$25.00
Redeem. on June 1 in every fifth year thereafter on min. 30 and max. 60 days' notice at $25.00 per share or at $25.50 on any other date on or after June 1, 2015 plus all declared and unpaid dividends.
Exchange: Exchange. on min. 30 days' notice into pfd 1st ser H sh as follows:
On Jun 1, 2020......................$25.00......................1   On Jun 1, 2025......................$25.00......................1
Exchange. on June 1 in every fifth year thereafter.
Note: Issued upon exchange of an equal number of Preferred Shares, Series H.
Transfer Agent: Computershare Trust Company of Canada Inc.
Registrar: Computershare Trust Company of Canada Inc.
Exchanges: TSX
Symbol: FTS.PR.I
CUSIP: 349553818

Great-West Lifeco Inc.

5.2% Non-Cum. First Pref., Series G

DBRS Rating:	Pfd-2 high	Sep 22, 2023	
Issued:	12,000,000 shs.	Sep 14, 2004	$25.000
O/S:	12,000,000 shs.	Dec 31, 2023	
Dividend:	$1.30 (Q)	Mar 31/Jun 30/Sep 30/Dec 31	

Redemption: Redeem. on and after the following dates on min. 30 and max. 60 days' notice as follows:
Dec 31, 2009......................$26.00   Dec 31, 2010......................$25.75
Dec 31, 2011......................$25.50   Dec 31, 2012......................$25.25
Dec 31, 2013......................$25.00
Lead Underwriter(s): BMO Capital Markets, RBC Capital Markets
Transfer Agent: Computershare Investor Services Inc.
Registrar: Computershare Investor Services Inc.
Exchanges: TSX
Symbol: GWO.PR.G
CUSIP: 39138C882

4.85% Non-Cum. First Pref., Series H

DBRS Rating:	Pfd-2 high	Sep 22, 2023	
Issued:	12,000,000 shs.	Aug 12, 2005	$25.000
O/S:	12,000,000 shs.	Dec 31, 2023	
Dividend:	$1.2125 (Q)	Mar 31/Jun 30/Sep 30/Dec 31	

Redemption: Redeem. on and after the following dates on min. 30 and max. 60 days' notice as follows:
Sep 30, 2010......................$26.00   Sep 30, 2011......................$25.75
Sep 30, 2012......................$25.50   Sep 30, 2013......................$25.25
Sep 30, 2014......................$25.00

FP Equities — Preferreds & Derivatives 2024

Lead Underwriter(s): Scotia Capital Inc., BMO Capital Markets
Transfer Agent: Computershare Investor Services Inc.
Registrar: Computershare Investor Services Inc.
Exchanges: TSX
Symbol: GWO.PR.H
CUSIP: 39138C874

4.5% Non-Cum. First Pref., Series I

DBRS Rating:	Pfd-2 high	Sep 22, 2023	
Issued:	12,000,000 shs.	Apr 12, 2006	$25.000
O/S:	12,000,000 shs.	Dec 31, 2023	
Dividend:	$1.125 (Q)	Mar 31/Jun 30/Sep 30/Dec 31	

Redemption: Redeem. on and after the following dates on min. 30 and max. 60 days' notice as follows:
Jun 30, 2011 .... $26.00   Jun 30, 2012 .... $25.75
Jun 30, 2013 .... $25.50   Jun 30, 2014 .... $25.25
Jun 30, 2015 .... $25.00

Lead Underwriter(s): RBC Capital Markets
Transfer Agent: Computershare Investor Services Inc.
Registrar: Computershare Investor Services Inc.
Exchanges: TSX
Symbol: GWO.PR.I
CUSIP: 39138C866

5.65% Non-Cum. First Pref., Series L

DBRS Rating:	Pfd-2 high	Sep 22, 2023	
Issued:	6,800,000 shs.	Oct 2, 2009	$25.000
O/S:	6,800,000 shs.	Dec 31, 2023	
Dividend:	$1.4125 (Q)	Mar 31/Jun 30/Sep 30/Dec 31	

Redemption: Redeem. on and after the following dates on min. 30 and max. 60 days' notice as follows:
Dec 31, 2014 .... $26.00   Dec 31, 2015 .... $25.75
Dec 31, 2016 .... $25.50   Dec 31, 2017 .... $25.25
Dec 31, 2018 .... $25.00

Lead Underwriter(s): BMO Capital Markets, CIBC World Markets Inc., Scotia Capital Inc.
Transfer Agent: Computershare Investor Services Inc.
Registrar: Computershare Investor Services Inc.
Exchanges: TSX
Symbol: GWO.PR.L
CUSIP: 39138C825

5.8% Non-Cum. First Pref., Series M

DBRS Rating:	Pfd-2 high	Sep 22, 2023	
Issued:	6,000,000 shs.	Mar 4, 2010	$25.000
O/S:	6,000,000 shs.	Dec 31, 2023	
Dividend:	$1.45 (Q)	Mar 31/Jun 30/Sep 30/Dec 31	

Redemption: Redeem. on and after the following dates on min. 30 and max. 60 days' notice as follows:
Mar 31, 2015 .... $26.00   Mar 31, 2016 .... $25.75
Mar 31, 2017 .... $25.50   Mar 31, 2018 .... $25.25
Mar 31, 2019 .... $25.00

Lead Underwriter(s): BMO Capital Markets, RBC Capital Markets, Scotia Capital Inc.
Transfer Agent: Computershare Investor Services Inc.
Registrar: Computershare Investor Services Inc.
Exchanges: TSX
Symbol: GWO.PR.M
CUSIP: 39138C817

1.749% Non-Cum. 5-Year Rate Reset First Pref., Series N

DBRS Rating:	Pfd-2 high	Sep 22, 2023	
Issued:	10,000,000 shs.	Nov 23, 2010	$25.000
O/S:	10,000,000 shs.	Dec 31, 2023	
Dividend:	$0.43725 (Q)	Mar 31/Jun 30/Sep 30/Dec 31	

Dividend Details: Reset on Dec 31, 2025. Dividend rate will be reset in every fifth year thereafter. The annual dividend rate will be equal to the sum of the five-year Government of Canada Bond Yield plus 1.30%. Previously, annual divd. rate was 0.544000 per sh until Dec 30, 2020.
Redemption: Redeem. on the following dates on min. 30 and max. 60 days' notice as follows:
Dec 31, 2015...$25.00   Dec 31, 2020..$25.00
Redeem. on Dec. 31 in every fifth year thereafter on min. 30 and max. 60 days' notice at $25.00 per share.
Exchange: Was exchange. on min. 30 days' notice into pfd 1st O as follows:
On Dec 31, 2015.....................$25.00.....................1   On Dec 31, 2020.....................$25.00.....................1
Exchange. on Dec. 31 in every fifth year thereafter.
Lead Underwriter(s): BMO Capital Markets, RBC Capital Markets, Scotia Capital Inc.
Transfer Agent: Computershare Investor Services Inc.
Registrar: Computershare Investor Services Inc.
Exchanges: TSX
Symbol: GWO.PR.N
CUSIP: 39138C791

5.40% Non-Cum. First Pref., Series P

DBRS Rating:	Pfd-2 high	Sep 22, 2023	
Issued:	10,000,000 shs.	Feb 22, 2012	$25.000
O/S:	10,000,000 shs.	Dec 31, 2023	
Dividend:	$1.35 (Q)	Mar 31/Jun 30/Sep 30/Dec 31	

Redemption: Redeem. on and after the following dates on min. 30 and max. 60 days' notice as follows:
Mar 31, 2017...$26.00   Mar 31, 2018...$25.75
Mar 31, 2019...$25.50   Mar 31, 2020...$25.25
Mar 31, 2021...$25.00
Lead Underwriter(s): BMO Capital Markets, RBC Capital Markets, Scotia Capital Inc.
Transfer Agent: Computershare Investor Services Inc.
Registrar: Computershare Investor Services Inc.
Exchanges: TSX
Symbol: GWO.PR.P
CUSIP: 39138C775

5.15% Non-Cum. Pref., Series Q

DBRS Rating:	Pfd-2 high	Sep 22, 2023	
Issued:	8,000,000 shs.	Jul 6, 2012	$25.000
O/S:	8,000,000 shs.	Dec 31, 2023	
Dividend:	$1.2875 (Q)	Mar 31/Jun 30/Sep 30/Dec 31	

Redemption: Redeem. on and after the following dates on min. 30 and max. 60 days' notice as follows:
Sep 30, 2017...$26.00   Sep 30, 2018...$25.75
Sep 30, 2019...$25.25   Sep 30, 2020...$25.25
Sep 30, 2021...$25.00
Lead Underwriter(s): BMO Capital Markets, RBC Capital Markets, Scotia Capital Inc.
Transfer Agent: Computershare Investor Services Inc.
Registrar: Computershare Investor Services Inc.
Exchanges: TSX
Symbol: GWO.PR.Q
CUSIP: 39138C767

4.80% Non-Cum. First Pref., Series R

DBRS Rating:	Pfd-2 high	Sep 22, 2023	
Issued:	8,000,000 shs.	Oct 11, 2012	$25.000
O/S:	8,000,000 shs.	Dec 31, 2023	
Dividend:	$1.20 (Q)	Mar 31/Jun 30/Sep 30/Dec 31	

Redemption: Redeem. on and after the following dates on min. 30 and max. 60 days' notice as follows:
Dec 31, 2017...$26.00   Dec 31, 2018...$25.75
Dec 31, 2019...$25.50   Dec 31, 2020...$25.25
Dec 31, 2021...$25.00

FP Equities — Preferreds & Derivatives 2024

Lead Underwriter(s): BMO Capital Markets, RBC Capital Markets, Scotia Capital Inc.
Transfer Agent: Computershare Investor Services Inc.
Registrar: Computershare Investor Services Inc.
Exchanges: TSX
Symbol: GWO.PR.R
CUSIP: 39138C759

5.25% Non-Cum. First Pref., Series S

DBRS Rating:	Pfd-2 high	Sep 22, 2023	
Issued:	8,000,000 shs.	May 22, 2014	$25.000
O/S:	8,000,000 shs.	Dec 31, 2023	
Dividend:	$1.3125 (Q)	Mar 31/Jun 30/Sep 30/Dec 31	

Redemption: Redeem. on and after the following dates on min. 30 and max. 60 days' notice as follows:
Jun 30, 2019..$26.00   Jun 30, 2020..$25.75
Jun 30, 2021..$25.50   Jun 30, 2022..$25.25
Jun 30, 2023..$25.00

Lead Underwriter(s): BMO Capital Markets, Scotia Capital Inc.
Transfer Agent: Computershare Investor Services Inc.
Registrar: Computershare Investor Services Inc.
Exchanges: TSX
Symbol: GWO.PR.S
CUSIP: 39138C734

5.15% Non-Cum. First Pref., Series T

DBRS Rating:	Pfd-2 high	Sep 22, 2023	
Issued:	8,000,000 shs.	May 18, 2017	$25.000
O/S:	8,000,000 shs.	Dec 31, 2023	
Dividend:	$1.2875 (Q)	Mar 31/Jun 30/Sep 30/Dec 31	

Redemption: Redeem. on and after the following dates on min. 30 and max. 60 days' notice as follows:
Jun 30, 2022..$26.00   Jun 30, 2023..$25.75
Jun 30, 2024..$25.50   Jun 30, 2025..$25.25
Jun 30, 2026..$25.00

Lead Underwriter(s): BMO Capital Markets, CIBC World Markets Inc., Scotia Capital Inc., TD Securities Inc.
Transfer Agent: Computershare Investor Services Inc.
Registrar: Computershare Investor Services Inc.
Exchanges: TSX
Symbol: GWO.PR.T
CUSIP: 39138C726

4.5% Non-Cum. First Pref., Series Y

DBRS Rating:	Pfd-2 high	Sep 22, 2023	
Issued:	8,000,000 shs.	Oct 8, 2021	$25.000
O/S:	8,000,000 shs.	Dec 31, 2023	
Dividend:	$1.125 (Q)	Mar 31/Jun 30/Sep 30/Dec 31	

Redemption: Redeem. on and after the following dates on min. 30 and max. 60 days' notice as follows:
Dec 31, 2026..$26.00   Dec 31, 2027..$25.75
Dec 31, 2028..$25.50   Dec 31, 2029..$25.25
Dec 31, 2030..$25.00

Lead Underwriter(s): BMO Capital Markets, RBC Capital Markets, Scotia Capital Inc., CIBC World Markets Inc., TD Securities Inc.
Transfer Agent: Computershare Investor Services Inc.
Registrar: Computershare Investor Services Inc.
Exchanges: TSX
Symbol: GWO.PR.Y
CUSIP: 39138C692

Industrial Alliance Insurance and Financial Services Inc.

4.6% Non-Cum. Class A Pref., Series B

DBRS Rating:	Pfd-1 low	Feb 27, 2024	
Issued:	5,000,000 shs.	Feb 24, 2006	$25.000
O/S:	5,000,000 shs.	Dec 31, 2023	
Dividend:	$1.15 (Q)	Mar 31/Jun 30/Sep 30/Dec 31	

Redemption: Redeem. on and after the following dates on min. 30 and max. 60 days' notice, conditional on the approval of the Superintendent of Financial Institutions, as follows:
Mar 31, 2011...$26.00　Mar 31, 2012...$25.75
Mar 31, 2013...$25.50　Mar 31, 2014...$25.25
Mar 31, 2015...$25.00

Exchange: Exchange. into 1 new pfd per pref. sh, being an exchange price per new pfd of $25.00.
Lead Underwriter(s): Scotia Capital Inc.
Transfer Agent: Computershare Investor Services Inc.
Registrar: Computershare Investor Services Inc.
Exchanges: TSX
Symbol: IAF.PR.B
CUSIP: 455871301

Innergex Renewable Energy Inc.

3.244% Cum. 5-Year Rate Reset Pref., Series A

Issued:	3,400,000 shs.	Sep 14, 2010	$25.000
O/S:	3,400,000 shs.	Dec 31, 2023	
Dividend:	$0.811 (Q)	Jan 15/Apr 15/Jul 15/Oct 15	

Dividend Details: Reset on Jan 15, 2026. Dividend rate will be reset in every fifth year thereafter. The annual dividend rate will be equal to the sum of the five-year Government of Canada Bond Yield on the 30th day prior to the first day of the subsequent five year fixed period rate plus 2.79%. Previously, annual divd. rate was 0.902000 per sh until Jan 14, 2021.

Redemption: Redeem. on the following dates as follows:
Jan 15, 2016...$25.00　Jan 15, 2021...$25.00
Redeem. on Jan. 15 in every fifth year thereafter on min. 30 and max. 60 days' notice at $25.00 per share.

Exchange: Was exchange. on min. 30 days' notice into pfd ser B as follows:
On Jan 15, 2016......................$25.00.....................1　On Jan 15, 2021......................$25.00.....................1
Exchange. on Jan. 15 in every fifth year thereafter, subject to other conditions as provided in the Prospectus.

Lead Underwriter(s): BMO Capital Markets, TD Securities Inc.
Transfer Agent: Computershare Investor Services Inc.
Registrar: Computershare Investor Services Inc.
Exchanges: TSX
Symbol: INE.PR.A
CUSIP: 45790B500

5.75% Cum. Pref., Series C

Issued:	2,000,000 shs.	Dec 11, 2012	$25.000
O/S:	2,000,000 shs.	Dec 31, 2023	
Dividend:	$1.4376 (Q)	Jan 15/Apr 15/Jul 15/Oct 15	

Redemption: Redeem. on and after the following dates on min. 30 and max. 60 days' notice as follows:
Jan 15, 2018...$26.00　Jan 15, 2019...$25.75
Jan 15, 2020...$25.50　Jan 15, 2021...$25.25
Jan 15, 2022...$25.00

Lead Underwriter(s): TD Securities Inc., National Bank Financial Inc., BMO Capital Markets
Transfer Agent: Computershare Investor Services Inc.
Registrar: Computershare Investor Services Inc.
Exchanges: TSX
Symbol: INE.PR.C
CUSIP: 45790B708

Intact Financial Corporation

4.841% Non-Cum. 5-Year Rate Reset Class A Pref., Series 1

DBRS Rating: Pfd-2 high Oct 10, 2023
Issued: 10,000,000 shs. Jul 12, 2011 $25.000
O/S: 10,000,000 shs. Dec 31, 2023
Dividend: $1.21025 (Q) Mar 31/Jun 30/Sep 30/Dec 31

Dividend Details: Reset on Dec 31, 2027. Dividend rate will be reset in every fifth year thereafter. The annual dividend rate will be equal to the sum of the five-year Government of Canada Bond Yield plus 1.72%. Previously, annual divd. rate was 0.849000 per sh until Dec 30, 2022.

Redemption: Redeem. on the following dates on min. 30 and max. 60 days' notice as follows:
Dec 31, 2017..$25.00   Dec 31, 2022...$25.00
Redeem. on Dec. 31 in every fifth year thereafter on min. 30 and max. 60 days' notice at $25.00 per share.

Exchange: Was exchange. on min. 30 days' notice into pfd A ser 2 as follows:
On Dec 31, 2017...................$25.00....................1   On Dec 31, 2022.....................$25.00.....................1
Exchange. on Dec. 31 in every fifth year thereafter.

Lead Underwriter(s): CIBC World Markets Inc., RBC Capital Markets, Scotia Capital Inc., TD Securities Inc.
Transfer Agent: Computershare Investor Services Inc.
Registrar: Computershare Investor Services Inc.
Exchanges: TSX
Symbol: IFC.PR.A
CUSIP: 45823T304

3.457% Non-Cum. 5-Year Rate Reset Class A Pref., Series 3

DBRS Rating: Pfd-2 high Oct 10, 2023
Issued: 10,000,000 shs. Aug 18, 2011 $25.000
O/S: 10,000,000 shs. Dec 31, 2023
Dividend: $0.86425 (Q) Mar 31/Jun 30/Sep 30/Dec 31

Dividend Details: Reset on Sep 30, 2026. Dividend rate will be reset in every fifth year thereafter. The annual dividend rate will be equal to the sum of the five-year Government of Canada Bond Yield plus 2.66%. Previously, annual divd. rate was 0.833000 per sh until Sep 29, 2021.

Redemption: Redeem. on the following dates on min. 30 and max. 60 days' notice as follows:
Sep 30, 2016..$25.00   Sep 30, 2021...$25.00
Redeem. on Sept. 30 in every fifth year thereafter on min. 30 and max. 60 days' notice at $25.00 per share.

Exchange: Was exchange. on min. 30 days' notice into pfd A ser 4 as follows:
On Sep 30, 2016...................$25.00....................1   On Sep 30, 2021.....................$25.00.....................1
Exchange. on Sept. 30 in every fifth year thereafter.

Lead Underwriter(s): CIBC World Markets Inc., RBC Capital Markets, Scotia Capital Inc., TD Securities Inc.
Transfer Agent: Computershare Investor Services Inc.
Registrar: Computershare Investor Services Inc.
Exchanges: TSX
Symbol: IFC.PR.C
CUSIP: 45823T601

5.20% Non-Cum. Class A Pref., Series 5

DBRS Rating: Pfd-2 high Oct 10, 2023
Issued: 6,000,000 shs. May 24, 2017 $25.000
O/S: 6,000,000 shs. Dec 31, 2023
Dividend: $1.30 (Q) Mar 31/Jun 30/Sep 30/Dec 31

Redemption: Redeem. on and after the following dates on min. 30 and max. 60 days' notice as follows:
Jun 30, 2022..$26.00   Jun 30, 2023...$25.75
Jun 30, 2024..$25.50   Jun 30, 2025...$25.25
Jun 30, 2026..$25.00

Lead Underwriter(s): CIBC World Markets Inc., BMO Capital Markets, National Bank Financial Inc., TD Securities Inc.
Transfer Agent: Computershare Investor Services Inc.
Registrar: Computershare Investor Services Inc.
Exchanges: TSX
Symbol: IFC.PR.E
CUSIP: 45823T809

5.30% Non-Cum. Class A Pref., Series 6

DBRS Rating: Pfd-2 high   Oct 10, 2023
  Issued: 6,000,000 shs.   Aug 18, 2017 $25.000
  O/S: 6,000,000 shs.   Dec 31, 2023
  Dividend: $1.325 (Q)   Mar 31/Jun 30/Sep 30/Dec 31

Redemption: Redeem. on and after the following dates on min. 30 and max. 60 days' notice as follows:
Sep 30, 2022...$26.00   Sep 30, 2023..$25.75
Sep 30, 2024...$25.50   Sep 30, 2025..$25.25
Sep 30, 2026...$25.00

Lead Underwriter(s): CIBC World Markets Inc., BMO Capital Markets, National Bank Financial Inc., TD Securities Inc.
Transfer Agent: Computershare Investor Services Inc.
Registrar: Computershare Investor Services Inc.
Exchanges: TSX
Symbol: IFC.PR.F
CUSIP: 45823T882

6.012% Non-Cum. 5-Year Rate Reset Class A Pref., Series 7

DBRS Rating: Pfd-2 high   Oct 10, 2023
  Issued: 10,000,000 shs.   May 29, 2018 $25.000
  O/S: 10,000,000 shs.   Dec 31, 2023
  Dividend: $1.503 (Q)   Mar 31/Jun 30/Sep 30/Dec 31

Dividend Details: Reset on Jun 30, 2028. Dividend rate will be reset in every fifth year thereafter. The annual dividend rate will be equal to the sum of the five-year Government of Canada Bond Yield plus 2.55%. Previously, annual divd. rate was 1.225000 per sh until Jun 29, 2023.

Redemption: Redeem. on the following dates on min. 30 and max. 60 days' notice as follows:
Jun 30, 2023..$25.00   Jun 30, 2028..$25.00
Redeem. on June 30 in every fifth year thereafter on min. 30 and max. 60 days' notice at $25.00 per share.

Exchange: Exchange. on min. 30 days' notice into pfd A ser 8 as follows:
On Jun 30, 2023.....................$25.00.....................1   On Jun 30, 2028.......................$25.00.......................1
Exchange. on June 30 in every fifth year thereafter.

Lead Underwriter(s): TD Securities Inc., BMO Capital Markets, CIBC World Markets Inc., National Bank Financial Inc.
Transfer Agent: Computershare Investor Services Inc.
Registrar: Computershare Investor Services Inc.
Exchanges: TSX
Symbol: IFC.PR.G
CUSIP: 45823T874

5.40% Class A Pref., Series 9

DBRS Rating: Pfd-2 high   Oct 10, 2023
  Issued: 6,000,000 shs.   Feb 18, 2020 $25.000
  O/S: 6,000,000 shs.   Dec 31, 2023
  Dividend: $1.35 (Q)   Mar 31/Jun 30/Sep 30/Dec 31

Redemption: Redeem. on and after the following dates on min. 30 and max. 60 days' notice as follows:
Mar 31, 2025...$26.00   Mar 31, 2026..$25.75
Mar 31, 2027...$25.50   Mar 31, 2028..$25.25
Mar 31, 2029...$25.00

Lead Underwriter(s): TD Securities Inc., BMO Capital Markets, CIBC World Markets Inc., National Bank Financial Inc., RBC Capital Markets, Scotia Capital Inc.
Transfer Agent: Computershare Investor Services Inc.
Registrar: Computershare Investor Services Inc.
Exchanges: TSX
Symbol: IFC.PR.I
CUSIP: 45823T858

5.25% Class A Pref., Series 11

DBRS Rating: Pfd-2 high   Oct 10, 2023
  Issued: 6,000,000 shs.   Mar 15, 2022 $25.000
  O/S: 6,000,000 shs.   Dec 31, 2023
  Dividend: $1.3125 (Q)   Mar 31/Jun 30/Sep 30/Dec 31

FP Equities — Preferreds & Derivatives 2024   75

Redemption: Redeem. on and after the following dates on min. 30 and max. 60 days' notice as follows:
Mar 31, 2027...$26.00   Mar 31, 2028...$25.75
Mar 31, 2029...$25.50   Mar 31, 2030...$25.25
Mar 31, 2031...$25.00

Lead Underwriter(s): TD Securities Inc., BMO Capital Markets, CIBC World Markets Inc., National Bank Financial Inc., RBC Capital Markets, Scotia Capital Inc.
Transfer Agent: Computershare Investor Services Inc.
Registrar: Computershare Investor Services Inc.
Exchanges: TSX
Symbol: IFC.PR.K
CUSIP: 45823T817

Laurentian Bank of Canada

4.123% Non-Cum. 5-Year Rate Reset Class A Pref., Series 13

DBRS Rating:	Pfd-3	Dec 15, 2023	
Issued:	5,000,000 shs.	Apr 3, 2014	$25.000
O/S:	5,000,000 shs.	Jan 31, 2024	
Dividend:	$1.03075 (Q)	Mar 15/Jun 15/Sep 15/Dec 15	

Dividend Details: Reset on Jun 15, 2024. Dividend rate will be reset in every fifth year thereafter. The annual dividend rate will be equal to the sum of the five-year Government of Canada Bond Yield plus 2.55%. Previously, annual divd. rate was 1.075000 per sh until Jun 14, 2019.

Redemption: Redeem. on the following dates on min. 30 and max. 60 days' notice, conditional on the approval of the Superintendent of Financial Institutions, as follows:
Jun 15, 2019...$25.00   Jun 15, 2024...$25.00
Redeem. on June 15 in every fifth year thereafter on min. 30 and max. 60 days' notice at $25.00 per share, conditional on approval of the Superintendent of Financial Institutions.

Convertible: Automatically convertible into common shares upon occurrence of a Non-Viability Contingent Capital (NVCC) trigger event as defined by OFSI.

Exchange: Exchange. on min. 30 days' notice into pfd A ser 14 as follows:
On Jun 15, 2019.................$25.00......................1   On Jun 15, 2024.....................$25.00.....................1
Exchange. on June 15 in every fifth year thereafter.

Lead Underwriter(s): RBC Capital Markets, BMO Capital Markets, Laurentian Bank Securities Inc.
Transfer Agent: Computershare Investor Services Inc.
Registrar: Computershare Investor Services Inc.
Exchanges: TSX
Symbol: LB.PR.H
CUSIP: 51925D825

Loblaw Companies Limited

5.3% Cum. Second Pref., Series B

DBRS Rating:	Pfd-3 high	May 18, 2023	
Issued:	9,000,000 shs.	Jun 9, 2015	$25.000
O/S:	9,000,000 shs.	Dec 30, 2023	
Dividend:	$1.325 (Q)	Mar 31/Jun 30/Sep 30/Dec 31	

Redemption: Redeem. on and after the following dates on min. 30 and max. 60 days' notice as follows:
Jun 30, 2020...$26.00   Jun 30, 2021...$25.75
Jun 30, 2022...$25.50   Jun 30, 2023...$25.25
Jun 30, 2024...$25.00

Lead Underwriter(s): RBC Capital Markets, Scotia Capital Inc., TD Securities Inc.
Transfer Agent: Computershare Investor Services Inc.
Registrar: Computershare Investor Services Inc.
Exchanges: TSX
Symbol: L.PR.B
CUSIP: 539481705

Manulife Financial Corporation

4.65% Non-Cum. Class A Pref., Series 2

DBRS Rating:	Pfd-2 high	Jul 19, 2023	
Issued:	14,000,000 shs.	Feb 18, 2005	$25.000
O/S:	14,000,000 shs.	Dec 31, 2023	
Dividend:	$1.1625 (Q)	Mar 19/Jun 19/Sep 19/Dec 19	

Redemption: Redeem. on and after the following dates on min. 30 and max. 60 days' notice, conditional on the approval of the Superintendent of Financial Institutions, as follows:

Mar 19, 2010..$26.00   Mar 19, 2011..$25.75
Mar 19, 2012..$25.50   Mar 19, 2013..$25.25
Mar 19, 2014..$25.00

Exchange: Exchange. into 1 new pfd per pref. sh, being an exchange price per new pfd of $25.00. The company will provide notice of applicable conversion date not more than 60 days and not less than 30 days before such date, provided that the company offers such right to holders.

Lead Underwriter(s): Scotia Capital Inc.
Transfer Agent: TSX Trust Company
Registrar: TSX Trust Company
Exchanges: TSX
Symbol: MFC.PR.B
CUSIP: 56501R403

4.5% Non-Cum. Class A Pref., Series 3

DBRS Rating:	Pfd-2 high	Jul 19, 2023	
Issued:	12,000,000 shs.	Jan 3, 2006	$25.000
O/S:	12,000,000 shs.	Dec 31, 2023	
Dividend:	$1.125 (Q)	Mar 19/Jun 19/Sep 19/Dec 19	

Redemption: Redeem. on and after the following dates on min. 30 and max. 60 days' notice, conditional on the approval of the Superintendent of Financial Institutions, as follows:

Mar 19, 2011..$26.00   Mar 19, 2012..$25.75
Mar 19, 2013..$25.50   Mar 19, 2014..$25.25
Mar 19, 2015..$25.00

Exchange: Exchange. into 1 new pfd per pref. sh, being an exchange price per new pfd of $25.00. The company will provide notice of applicable conversion date not more than 60 days and not less than 30 days before such date, provided that the company offers such right to holders.

Lead Underwriter(s): Scotia Capital Inc.
Transfer Agent: TSX Trust Company
Registrar: TSX Trust Company
Exchanges: TSX
Symbol: MFC.PR.C
CUSIP: 56501R502

2.348% Non-Cum. 5-Year Rate Reset Class 1 Pref., Series 3

DBRS Rating:	Pfd-2 high	Jul 19, 2023	
Issued:	8,000,000 shs.	Mar 11, 2011	$25.000
O/S:	6,537,903 shs.	Dec 31, 2023	
Dividend:	$0.587 (Q)	Mar 19/Jun 19/Sep 19/Dec 19	

Dividend Details: Reset on Jun 20, 2026. Dividend rate will be reset in every fifth year thereafter. The annual dividend rate will be equal to the sum of the five-year Government of Canada Bond Yield plus 1.41%. Previously, annual divd. rate was 0.544500 per sh until Jun 19, 2021.

Redemption: Redeem. on the following dates on min. 30 and max. 60 days' notice, conditional on the approval of the Superintendent of Financial Institutions, as follows:

Jun 19, 2016..$25.00   Jun 19, 2021..$25.00

Redeem. on June 19 in every fifth year thereafter on min. 30 and max. 60 days' notice at $25.00 per share, plus all declared and unpaid dividends. All redemptions are subject to the provisions of the Insurance Companies Act (Canada), including the requirement of obtaining the prior consent of the Superintendent of Financial Institutions.

Exchange: Was exchange. into pfd 1 ser 4 as follows:
On Jun 19, 2016....................$25.00.....................1   On Jun 19, 2021.....................$25.00.....................1
Exchange. at shareholders' option on June 19, 2016 and on June 19 in every fifth year thereafter (conversion date) into class 1 series 4 preferred shares on a one-to-one basis, subject to certain conditions. Shareholders need to provide notice not more than 30 days and not less than 15 days before a conversion date.
Lead Underwriter(s): Scotia Capital Inc., RBC Capital Markets
Transfer Agent: TSX Trust Company
Registrar: TSX Trust Company
Exchanges: TSX
Symbol: MFC.PR.F
CUSIP: 56501R858

5.978% Non-Cum. 5-Year Rate Reset Class 1 Pref., Series 9

DBRS Rating:	Pfd-2 high	Jul 19, 2023	
Issued:	10,000,000 shs.	May 24, 2012	$25.000
O/S:	10,000,000 shs.	Dec 31, 2023	
Dividend:	$1.4945 (Q)	Mar 19/Jun 19/Sep 19/Dec 19	

Dividend Details: Reset on Sep 20, 2027. Dividend rate will be reset in every fifth year thereafter. The annual dividend rate will be equal to the sum of the five-year Government of Canada Bond Yield plus 2.86%. Previously, annual divd. rate was 1.087750 per sh until Sep 19, 2022.
Redemption: Redeem. on the following dates on min. 30 and max. 60 days' notice as follows:
Sep 19, 2017..$25.00   Sep 19, 2022...$25.00
Redeem. on Sept. 19 in every fifth year thereafter on min. 30 and max. 60 days' notice at $25.00 per share. All redemptions are subject to the provisions of the Insurance Companies Act (Canada), including the requirement of obtaining the prior consent of the Superintendent of Financial Institutions.
Exchange: Was exchange. into pfd 1 ser 10 as follows:
On Sep 19, 2017....................$25.00.....................1   On Sep 19, 2022.....................$25.00.....................1
Exchange. at shareholders' option on Sept. 19, 2017 and on Sept. 19 every fifth year thereafter (conversion date) into class 1 series 10 preferred shares on a one-to-one basis, subject to certain conditions. Shareholders need to provide notice not more than 30 days and not less than 15 days before a conversion date.
Lead Underwriter(s): Scotia Capital Inc., CIBC World Markets Inc., RBC Capital Markets
Transfer Agent: TSX Trust Company
Registrar: TSX Trust Company
Exchanges: TSX
Symbol: MFC.PR.I
CUSIP: 56501R783

6.159% Non-Cum. 5-Year Rate Reset Class 1 Pref., Series 11

DBRS Rating:	Pfd-2 high	Jul 19, 2023	
Issued:	8,000,000 shs.	Dec 4, 2012	$25.000
O/S:	8,000,000 shs.	Dec 31, 2023	
Dividend:	$1.53975 (Q)	Mar 19/Jun 19/Sep 19/Dec 19	

Dividend Details: Reset on Mar 20, 2028. Dividend rate will be reset in every fifth year thereafter. The annual dividend rate will be equal to the sum of the five-year Government of Canada Bond Yield plus 2.61%. Previously, annual divd. rate was 1.182750 per sh until Mar 19, 2023.
Redemption: Redeem. on the following dates on min. 30 and max. 60 days' notice as follows:
Mar 19, 2018..$25.00   Mar 19, 2023...$25.00
Redeem. on March 19 in every fifth year thereafter on min. 30 and max. 60 days' notice at $25.00 per share. All redemptions are subject to the provisions of the Insurance Companies Act (Canada), including the requirement of obtaining the prior consent of the Superintendent of Financial Institutions.
Exchange: Was exchange. into pfd 1 ser 12 as follows:
On Mar 19, 2018....................$25.00.....................1   On Mar 19, 2023.....................$25.00.....................1
Exchange. at shareholders' option on March 19, 2018 and on March 19 every fifth year thereafter (conversion date) into class 1 series 12 preferred shares on a one-to-one basis, subject to certain conditions. Shareholders need to provide notice not more than 30 days and not less than 15 days before a conversion date.
Lead Underwriter(s): Scotia Capital Inc., RBC Capital Markets, TD Securities Inc.
Transfer Agent: TSX Trust Company
Registrar: TSX Trust Company
Exchanges: TSX
Symbol: MFC.PR.J
CUSIP: 56501R767

6.35% Non-Cum. 5-Year Rate Reset Class 1 Pref., Series 13

DBRS Rating:	Pfd-2 high	Jul 19, 2023
Issued:	8,000,000 shs.	Jun 21, 2013 $25.000
O/S:	8,000,000 shs.	Dec 31, 2023
Dividend:	$1.5875 (Q)	Mar 19/Jun 19/Sep 19/Dec 19

Dividend Details: Reset on Sep 20, 2028. Dividend rate will be reset in every fifth year thereafter. The annual dividend rate will be equal to the sum of the five-year Government of Canada Bond Yield plus 2.22%. Previously, annual divd. rate was 1.103500 per sh until Sep 19, 2023.

Redemption: Redeem. on the following dates on min. 30 and max. 60 days' notice as follows:
Sep 19, 2018..$25.00   Sep 19, 2023..$25.00
Redeem. on Sept. 19 in every fifth year thereafter on min. 30 and max. 60 days' notice at $25.00 per share. All redemptions are subject to the provisions of the Insurance Companies Act (Canada), including the requirement of obtaining the prior consent of the Superintendent of Financial Institutions.

Exchange: Was exchange. into pfd 1 ser 14 as follows:
On Sep 19, 2018.....................$25.00....................1   On Sep 19, 2023.....................$25.00....................1
Exchange. at shareholders' option on Sept. 19, 2018 and on Sept. 19 every fifth year thereafter (conversion date) into class 1 series 14 preferred shares on a one-to-one basis, subject to certain conditions. Shareholders need to provide notice not more than 30 days and not less than 15 days before a conversion date.

Lead Underwriter(s): Scotia Capital Inc., RBC Capital Markets
Transfer Agent: TSX Trust Company
Registrar: TSX Trust Company
Exchanges: TSX
Symbol: MFC.PR.K
CUSIP: 56501R742

3.786% Non-Cum. 5-Year Rate Reset Class 1 Pref., Series 15

DBRS Rating:	Pfd-2 high	Jul 19, 2023
Issued:	8,000,000 shs.	Feb 25, 2014 $25.000
O/S:	8,000,000 shs.	Dec 31, 2023
Dividend:	$0.9465 (Q)	Mar 19/Jun 19/Sep 19/Dec 19

Dividend Details: Reset on Jun 20, 2024. Dividend rate will be reset in every fifth year thereafter. The annual dividend rate will be equal to the sum of the five-year Government of Canada Bond Yield plus 2.16%. Previously, annual divd. rate was 0.975000 per sh until Jun 19, 2019.

Redemption: Redeem. on the following dates on min. 30 and max. 60 days' notice as follows:
Jun 19, 2019..$25.00   Jun 19, 2024..$25.00
Redeem. on June 19 in every fifth year thereafter on min. 30 and max. 60 days' notice at $25.00 per share. All redemptions are subject to the provisions of the Insurance Companies Act (Canada), including the requirement of obtaining the prior consent of the Superintendent of Financial Institutions.

Exchange: Exchange. into pfd 1 ser 16 as follows:
On Jun 19, 2019.....................$25.00....................1   On Jun 19, 2024.....................$25.00....................1
Exchange. at shareholders' option on June 19, 2019 and on June 19 every fifth year thereafter (conversion date) into class 1 series 16 preferred shares on a one-to-one basis, subject to certain conditions. Shareholders need to provide notice not more than 30 days and not less than 15 days before a conversion date.

Lead Underwriter(s): Scotia Capital Inc., CIBC World Markets Inc., RBC Capital Markets
Transfer Agent: TSX Trust Company
Registrar: TSX Trust Company
Exchanges: TSX
Symbol: MFC.PR.L
CUSIP: 56501R726

3.80% Non-Cum. 5-Year Rate Reset Class 1 Pref., Series 17

DBRS Rating:	Pfd-2 high	Jul 19, 2023
Issued:	14,000,000 shs.	Aug 15, 2014 $25.000
O/S:	14,000,000 shs.	Dec 31, 2023
Dividend:	$0.95 (Q)	Mar 19/Jun 19/Sep 19/Dec 19

Dividend Details: Reset on Dec 20, 2024. Dividend rate will be reset in every fifth year thereafter. The annual dividend rate will be equal to the sum of the five-year Government of Canada Bond Yield plus 2.36%. Previously, annual divd. rate was 0.975000 per sh until Dec 19, 2019.

Redemption: Redeem. on the following dates on min. 30 and max. 60 days' notice as follows:
Dec 19, 2019..$25.00   Dec 19, 2024..$25.00
Redeem. on Dec. 19 in every fifth year thereafter on min. 30 and max. 60 days' notice at $25.00 per share. All redemptions are subject to the provisions of the Insurance Companies Act (Canada), including the requirement of obtaining the prior consent of the Superintendent of Financial Institutions.
Exchange: Exchange. into pfd 1 ser 18 as follows:
On Dec 19, 2019.....................$25.00....................1   On Dec 19, 2024.....................$25.00.....................1
Exchange. at shareholders' option on Dec. 19, 2019 and on Dec. 19 every fifth year thereafter (conversion date) into class 1 series 18 preferred shares on a one-to-one basis, subject to certain conditions. Shareholders need to provide notice not more than 30 days and not less than 15 days before a conversion date.
Lead Underwriter(s): Scotia Capital Inc., RBC Capital Markets, TD Securities Inc.
Transfer Agent: TSX Trust Company
Registrar: TSX Trust Company
Exchanges: TSX
Symbol: MFC.PR.M
CUSIP: 56501R692

3.675% Non-Cum. 5-Year Rate Reset Class 1 Pref., Series 19

DBRS Rating:	Pfd-2 high	Jul 19, 2023	
Issued:	10,000,000 shs.	Dec 3, 2014	$25.000
O/S:	10,000,000 shs.	Dec 31, 2023	
Dividend:	$0.91875 (Q)	Mar 19/Jun 19/Sep 19/Dec 19	

Dividend Details: Reset on Mar 20, 2025. Dividend rate will be reset in every fifth year thereafter. The annual dividend rate will be equal to the sum of the five-year Government of Canada Bond Yield plus 2.30%. Previously, annual divd. rate was 0.950000 per sh until Mar 19, 2020.
Redemption: Redeem. on the following dates on min. 30 and max. 60 days' notice as follows:
Mar 19, 2020..$25.00   Mar 19, 2025..$25.00
Redeem. on March 19 in every fifth year thereafter on min. 30 and max. 60 days' notice at $25.00 per share. All redemptions are subject to the provisions of the Insurance Companies Act (Canada), including the requirement of obtaining the prior consent of the Superintendent of Financial Institutions.
Exchange: Exchange. into pfd 1 ser 20 as follows:
On Mar 19, 2020.....................$25.00....................1   On Mar 19, 2025.....................$25.00.....................1
Exchange. at shareholders' option on March 19, 2020 and on March 19 every fifth year thereafter (conversion date) into class 1 series 20 preferred shares on a one-to-one basis, subject to certain conditions. Shareholders need to provide notice not more than 30 days and not less than 15 days before a conversion date.
Lead Underwriter(s): Scotia Capital Inc., CIBC World Markets Inc., RBC Capital Markets
Transfer Agent: TSX Trust Company
Registrar: TSX Trust Company
Exchanges: TSX
Symbol: MFC.PR.N
CUSIP: 56501R676

Floating Rate Non-Cum. Class 1 Pref., Series 4

DBRS Rating:	Pfd-2 high	Jul 19, 2023	
Issued:	1,664,169 shs.	Jun 20, 2016	$25.000
O/S:	1,462,097 shs.	Dec 31, 2023	
Dividend:	F.R. (Q)	Mar 19/Jun 19/Sep 19/Dec 19	

Dividend Details: Quarterly divd. rate is three-month T-Bll plus 1.41%
Redemption: Redeem. on the following dates on min. 30 and max. 60 days' notice, conditional on the approval of the Superintendent of Financial Institutions, as follows:
Jun 19, 2021..$25.00   Jun 19, 2026..$25.00
Redeem. on June 19 in every fifth year thereafter on min. 30 and max. 60 days' notice at (i) $25.00 per share, or (ii) $25.50 in the case of redemption on any other date after June 19, 2016, in each case plus all declared and unpaid dividends. All redemptions are subject to the provisions of the Insurance Companies Act (Canada), including the requirement of obtaining the prior consent of the Superintendent of Financial Institutions.

Exchange: Exchange. into pfd 1 ser 3 sh as follows:
On Jun 19, 2021.....................$25.00.....................1   On Jun 19, 2026.....................$25.00.....................1
Exchange. at shareholders' option on June 19, 2021 and on June 19 every fifth year thereafter (conversion date) into class 1 series 3 preferred shares on a one-to-one basis, subject to certain conditions. Shareholders need to provide notice not more than 30 days and not less than 15 days before a conversion date.
Note: Issued upon exchange of an equal number of Class 1 Pref Shares, Series 3.
Transfer Agent: TSX Trust Company
Registrar: TSX Trust Company
Exchanges: TSX
Symbol: MFC.PR.P
CUSIP: 56501R841

<ins>5.942% Non-Cum. 5-Year Rate Reset Class 1 Pref., Series 25</ins>

DBRS Rating:	Pfd-2 high	Jul 19, 2023	
Issued:	10,000,000 shs.	Feb 20, 2018	$25.000
O/S:	10,000,000 shs.	Dec 31, 2023	
Dividend:	$1.4855 (Q)	Mar 19/Jun 19/Sep 19/Dec 19	

Dividend Details: Reset on Jun 20, 2028. Dividend rate will be reset in every fifth year thereafter. The annual dividend rate will be equal to the sum of the five-year Government of Canada Bond Yield plus 2.55%. Previously, annual divd. rate was 1.175000 per sh until Jun 19, 2023.
Redemption: Redeem. on the following dates on min. 30 and max. 60 days' notice as follows:
Jun 19, 2023.....................$25.00   Jun 19, 2028.....................$25.00
Redeem. on June 19 in every fifth year thereafter on min. 30 and max. 60 days' notice at $25.00 per share. All redemptions are subject to the provisions of the Insurance Companies Act (Canada), including the requirement of obtaining the prior consent of the Superintendent of Financial Institutions.
Exchange: Exchange. on min. 30 days' notice into pfd 1 ser 26 as follows:
On Jun 19, 2023.....................$25.00.....................1   On Jun 19, 2028.....................$25.00.....................1
Exchange. at shareholders' option on June 19, 2023 and on June 19 every fifth year thereafter (conversion date) into class 1 series 26 preferred shares on a one-to-one basis, subject to certain conditions. Shareholders need to provide notice not more than 30 days and not less than 15 days before a conversion date.
Lead Underwriter(s): RBC Capital Markets, Scotia Capital Inc., TD Securities Inc.
Transfer Agent: TSX Trust Company
Registrar: TSX Trust Company
Exchanges: TSX
Symbol: MFC.PR.Q
CUSIP: 56501R619

Montfort Capital Corp.
(formerly Timia Capital Corp.)

<ins>8% Pref., Series A</ins>

Issued:	5,210,994 shs.	Nov 27, 2020	$1.000
O/S:	28,485,994 shs.	Dec 31, 2023	
Dividend:	$0.08 (Q)	Mar 31/Jun 30/Sep 30/Dec 31	

Lead Underwriter(s): Echelon Wealth Partners Inc.
Transfer Agent: Computershare Investor Services Inc.
Registrar: Computershare Investor Services Inc.
Exchanges: TSX-VEN
Symbol: MONT.PR.A
CUSIP: 61288M205

National Bank of Canada

<ins>4.025% Non-Cum. 5-Year Rate Reset First Pref., Series 30</ins>

DBRS Rating:	Pfd-2	Apr 26, 2024	
Issued:	14,000,000 shs.	Feb 7, 2014	$25.000
O/S:	14,000,000 shs.	Jan 31, 2024	
Dividend:	$1.00625 (Q)	Feb 15/May 15/Aug 15/Nov 15	

Dividend Details: Reset on May 16, 2024. Dividend rate will be reset in every fifth year thereafter. The annual dividend rate will be equal to the sum of the five-year Government of Canada Bond Yield plus 2.40%. Previously, annual divd. rate was 1.025000 per sh until May 15, 2019.

FP Equities — Preferreds & Derivatives 2024

Redemption: Redeem. on the following dates on min. 30 and max. 60 days' notice, conditional on the approval of the Superintendent of Financial Institutions, as follows:
May 15, 2019..$25.00   May 15, 2024..$25.00
Redeem. on May 15 in every fifth year thereafter on min. 30 and max. 60 days' notice at $25.00 per share, conditional on approval of the Superintendent of Financial Institutions.
Convertible: Automatically convertible into common shares upon occurrence of a Non-Viability Contingent Capital (NVCC) trigger event as defined by OFSI.
Exchange: Exchange. on min. 15 days' notice into pfd 1st ser 31 as follows:
On May 15, 2019...................$25.00....................1   On May 15, 2024.....................$25.00.......................1
Exchange. on May 15 in every fifth year thereafter. Exchange. after notice from the Bank given with approval from the Superintendent of Financial Institutions.
Lead Underwriter(s): National Bank Financial Inc., RBC Capital Markets
Transfer Agent: Computershare Trust Company of Canada Inc.
Registrar: Computershare Trust Company of Canada Inc.
Exchanges: TSX
Symbol: NA.PR.S
CUSIP: 633067319

3.839% Non-Cum. 5-Year Rate Reset First Pref., Series 32

DBRS Rating:	Pfd-2	Apr 26, 2024	
Issued:	12,000,000 shs.	Oct 9, 2014	$25.000
O/S:	12,000,000 shs.	Jan 31, 2024	
Dividend:	$0.95975 (Q)	Feb 15/May 15/Aug 15/Nov 15	

Dividend Details: Reset on Feb 16, 2025. Dividend rate will be reset in every fifth year thereafter. The annual dividend rate will be equal to the sum of the five-year Government of Canada Bond Yield plus 2.25%. Previously, annual divd. rate was 0.975000 per sh until Feb 15, 2020.
Redemption: Redeem. on the following dates on min. 30 and max. 60 days' notice, conditional on the approval of the Superintendent of Financial Institutions, as follows:
Feb 15, 2020..$25.00   Feb 15, 2025..$25.00
Redeem. on Feb. 15 in every fifth year thereafter on min. 30 and max. 60 days' notice at $25.00 per share, conditional on approval of the Superintendent of Financial Institutions.
Convertible: Automatically convertible into common shares upon occurrence of a Non-Viability Contingent Capital (NVCC) trigger event as defined by OFSI.
Exchange: Exchange. on min. 15 days' notice into pfd 1st ser 33 as follows:
On Feb 15, 2020...................$25.00....................1   On Feb 15, 2025.....................$25.00.......................1
Exchange. on Feb. 15 in every fifth year thereafter. Exchange. after notice from the Bank given with approval from the Superintendent of Financial Institutions.
Lead Underwriter(s): National Bank Financial Inc.
Transfer Agent: Computershare Trust Company of Canada Inc.
Registrar: Computershare Trust Company of Canada Inc.
Exchanges: TSX
Symbol: NA.PR.W
CUSIP: 633067285

7.027% Non-Cum. 5-Year Rate Reset First Pref., Series 38

DBRS Rating:	Pfd-2	Apr 26, 2024	
Issued:	16,000,000 shs.	Jun 13, 2017	$25.000
O/S:	16,000,000 shs.	Jan 31, 2024	
Dividend:	$1.75675 (Q)	Feb 15/May 15/Aug 15/Nov 15	

Dividend Details: Dividend rate will be reset in every fifth year thereafter. The annual dividend rate will be equal to the sum of the five-year Government of Canada Bond Yield plus 3.43%. Reset on Nov 16, 2027. Previously, annual divd. rate was 1.112500 per sh until Nov 15, 2022.
Redemption: Redeem. on the following dates on min. 30 and max. 60 days' notice, conditional on the approval of the Superintendent of Financial Institutions, as follows:
Nov 15, 2022..$25.00   Nov 15, 2027..$25.00
Redeem. on Nov. 15 in every fifth year thereafter on min. 30 and max. 60 days' notice at $25.00 per share, conditional on approval of the Superintendent of Financial Institutions.
Convertible: Automatically convertible into common shares upon occurrence of a Non-Viability Contingent Capital (NVCC) trigger event as defined by OFSI.

Exchange: Exchange. on min. 15 days' notice into pfd 1st ser 39 as follows:
On Nov 15, 2022.....................$25.00......................1   On Nov 15, 2027.......................$25.00.......................1
Exchange. on Nov. 15 in every fifth year thereafter. Exchange. after notice from the Bank given with approval from the Superintendent of Financial Institutions.
Lead Underwriter(s): National Bank Financial Inc.
Transfer Agent: Computershare Trust Company of Canada Inc.
Registrar: Computershare Trust Company of Canada Inc.
Exchanges: TSX
Symbol: NA.PR.C
CUSIP: 633067228

5.818% Non-Cum. 5-Year Rate Reset First Pref., Series 40

DBRS Rating:	Pfd-2	Apr 26, 2024	
Issued:	12,000,000 shs.	Jan 22, 2018	$25.000
O/S:	12,000,000 shs.	Jan 31, 2024	
Dividend:	$1.4545 (Q)	Feb 15/May 15/Aug 15/Nov 15	

Dividend Details: Reset on May 16, 2028. Dividend rate will be reset in every fifth year thereafter. The annual dividend rate will be equal to the sum of the five-year Government of Canada Bond Yield plus 2.58%. Previously, annual divd. rate was 1.150000 per sh until May 15, 2023.
Redemption: Redeem. on the following dates on min. 30 and max. 60 days' notice, conditional on the approval of the Superintendent of Financial Institutions, as follows:
May 15, 2023...$25.00   May 15, 2028...$25.00
Redeem. on May 15 in every fifth year thereafter on min. 30 and max. 60 days' notice at $25.00 per share, conditional on approval of the Superintendent of Financial Institutions.
Convertible: Automatically convertible into common shares upon occurrence of a Non-Viability Contingent Capital (NVCC) trigger event as defined by OFSI.
Exchange: Exchange. on min. 15 days' notice into pfd 1st ser 41 as follows:
On May 15, 2023......................$25.00......................1   On May 15, 2028.......................$25.00.......................1
Exchange. on May 15 in every fifth year thereafter. Exchange. after notice from the Bank given with approval from the Superintendent of Financial Institutions.
Lead Underwriter(s): National Bank Financial Inc.
Transfer Agent: Computershare Trust Company of Canada Inc.
Registrar: Computershare Trust Company of Canada Inc.
Exchanges: TSX
Symbol: NA.PR.E
CUSIP: 633067194

7.056% Non-Cum. 5-Year Rate Reset First Pref., Series 42

Issued:	12,000,000 shs.	Jun 11, 2018	$25.000
O/S:	12,000,000 shs.	Jan 31, 2024	
Dividend:	$1.764 (Q)	Feb 15/May 15/Aug 15/Nov 15	

Dividend Details: Reset on Nov 15, 2028. Dividend rate will be reset in every fifth year thereafter. The annual dividend rate will be equal to the sum of the five-year Government of Canada Bond Yield plus 2.77%. Previously, annual divd. rate was 1.237500 per sh until Nov 14, 2023.
Redemption: Redeem. on the following dates on min. 30 and max. 60 days' notice, conditional on the approval of the Superintendent of Financial Institutions, as follows:
Nov 15, 2023...$25.00   Nov 15, 2028...$25.00
Redeem. on Nov. 15 in every fifth year thereafter on min. 30 and max. 60 days' notice at $25.00 per share, conditional on approval of the Superintendent of Financial Institutions.
Convertible: Automatically convertible into common shares upon occurrence of a Non-Viability Contingent Capital (NVCC) trigger event as defined by OFSI.
Exchange: Exchange. on min. 30 days' notice into pfd 1st ser 43 as follows:
On Nov 15, 2023.....................$25.00......................1   On Nov 15, 2028.......................$25.00.......................1
Exchange. on Nov. 15 in every fifth year thereafter. Exchange. after notice from the Bank given with approval from the Superintendent of Financial Institutions.
Lead Underwriter(s): National Bank Financial Inc.
Transfer Agent: Computershare Trust Company of Canada Inc.
Registrar: Computershare Trust Company of Canada Inc.
Exchanges: TSX
Symbol: NA.PR.G
CUSIP: 63306A205

Northland Power Inc.

3.2% Cum. 5-Year Rate Reset Pref., Series 1

Issued:	6,000,000 shs.	Jul 28, 2010	$25.000
O/S:	4,762,246 shs.	Dec 31, 2023	
Dividend:	$0.80 (Q)	Mar 31/Jun 30/Sep 30/Dec 31	

Dividend Details: Reset on Sep 30, 2025. Dividend rate will be reset in every fifth year thereafter. The annual dividend rate will be equal to the sum of the five-year Government of Canada Bond Yield plus 2.80%. Previously, annual divd. rate was 0.877500 per sh until Sep 29, 2020.

Redemption: Redeem. on the following dates on min. 30 and max. 60 days' notice as follows:
Sep 30, 2015..$25.00   Sep 30, 2020..$25.00
Redeem. on Sept. 30 in every fifth year thereafter on min. 30 and max. 60 days' notice at $25.00 per share.

Exchange: Was exchange. on min. 30 days' notice into pfd ser 2 sh as follows:
On Sep 30, 2015.....................$25.00.....................1   On Sep 30, 2020.....................$25.00.....................1
Exchange. on Sept. 30 in every fifth year thereafter.

Lead Underwriter(s): CIBC World Markets Inc.
Transfer Agent: Computershare Investor Services Inc.
Registrar: Computershare Investor Services Inc.
Exchanges: TSX
Symbol: NPI.PR.A
CUSIP: 666511308

Floating Rate Cum. Pref., Series 2

Issued:	1,498,435 shs.	Sep 30, 2015	$25.000
O/S:	1,237,754 shs.	Dec 31, 2023	
Dividend:	F.R. (Q)	Mar 31/Jun 30/Sep 30/Dec 31	

Dividend Details: Quarterly divd. rate is T-bill plus 2.8%.

Redemption: Redeem. on the following dates on min. 30 and max. 60 days' notice as follows:
Sep 30, 2020..$25.00   Sep 30, 2025..$25.00
Redeem. on Sept. 30 in every fifth year thereafter on min. 30 and max. 60 days' notice at $25.00 per share.

Exchange: Exchange. on min. 30 days' notice into pfd ser 1 sh as follows:
On Sep 30, 2020.....................$25.00.....................1   On Sep 30, 2025.....................$25.00.....................1
Exchange. on Sept. 30 in every fifth year thereafter.

Note: Issued upon exchange of an equal number of Preferred Shares, Series 1.
Transfer Agent: Computershare Trust Company of Canada Inc.
Registrar: Computershare Trust Company of Canada Inc.
Exchanges: TSX
Symbol: NPI.PR.B
CUSIP: 666511506

Pembina Pipeline Corporation

6.525% Cum. 5-Year Rate Reset Class A Pref., Series 1

DBRS Rating:	Pfd-3 high	Apr 26, 2024	
Issued:	10,000,000 shs.	Jul 26, 2013	$25.000
O/S:	10,000,000 shs.	Dec 31, 2023	
Dividend:	$1.63125 (Q)	Mar 1/Jun 1/Sep 1/Dec 1	

Dividend Details: Reset on Dec 1, 2028. Dividend rate will be reset in every fifth year thereafter. The annual dividend rate will be equal to the sum of the five-year Government of Canada Bond Yield plus 2.47%. Previously, annual divd. rate was 1.226500 per sh until Nov 30, 2023.

Redemption: Redeem. on the following dates on min. 30 and max. 60 days' notice as follows:
Dec 1, 2018..$25.00   Dec 1, 2023..$25.00
Redeem. on Dec. 1 in every fifth year thereafter on min. 30 and max. 60 days' notice at $25.00 per share.

Exchange: Was exchange. on min. 30 days' notice into pfd A ser 2 as follows:
On Dec 1, 2018.....................$25.00.....................1   On Dec 1, 2023.....................$25.00.....................1
Exchange. on Dec. 1 in every fifth year thereafter.

Lead Underwriter(s): RBC Capital Markets, Scotia Capital Inc.
Transfer Agent: Computershare Trust Company of Canada Inc.
Registrar: Computershare Trust Company of Canada Inc.
Exchanges: TSX
Symbol: PPL.PR.A
CUSIP: 706327202

6.019% Cum. 5-Year Rate Reset Class A Pref., Series 3

DBRS Rating:	Pfd-3 high	Apr 26, 2024
Issued:	6,000,000 shs.	Oct 2, 2013	$25.000
O/S:	6,000,000 shs.	Dec 31, 2023
Dividend:	$1.50475 (Q)	Mar 1/Jun 1/Sep 1/Dec 1

Dividend Details: Reset on Mar 1, 2029. Dividend rate will be reset in every fifth year thereafter. The annual dividend rate will be equal to the sum of the five-year Government of Canada Bond Yield plus 2.60%. Previously, annual divd. rate was 1.119500 per sh until Feb 29, 2024.
Redemption: Redeem. on the following dates on min. 30 and max. 60 days' notice as follows:
Mar 1, 2019...$25.00   Mar 1, 2024...$25.00
Redeem. on March 1 in every fifth year thereafter on min. 30 and max. 60 days' notice at $25.00 per share.
Exchange: Was exchange. on min. 30 days' notice into pfd A ser 4 as follows:
On Mar 1, 2019......................$25.00.....................1   On Mar 1, 2024.......................$25.00........................1
Exchange. on March 1 in every fifth year thereafter.
Lead Underwriter(s): RBC Capital Markets, Scotia Capital Inc.
Transfer Agent: Computershare Trust Company of Canada Inc.
Registrar: Computershare Trust Company of Canada Inc.
Exchanges: TSX
Symbol: PPL.PR.C
CUSIP: 706327400

4.573% Cum. 5-Year Rate Reset Class A Pref., Series 5

DBRS Rating:	Pfd-3 high	Apr 26, 2024
Issued:	10,000,000 shs.	Jan 16, 2014	$25.000
O/S:	10,000,000 shs.	Dec 31, 2023
Dividend:	$1.14325 (Q)	Mar 1/Jun 1/Sep 1/Dec 1

Dividend Details: Reset on Jun 1, 2024. Dividend rate will be reset in every fifth year thereafter. The annual dividend rate will be equal to the sum of the five-year Government of Canada Bond Yield plus 3.00%. Previously, annual divd. rate was 1.250000 per sh until May 31, 2019.
Redemption: Redeem. on the following dates on min. 30 and max. 60 days' notice as follows:
Jun 1, 2019..$25.00   Jun 1, 2024..$25.00
Redeem. on June 1 in every fifth year thereafter on min. 30 and max. 60 days' notice at $25.00 per share.
Exchange: Exchange. on min. 30 days' notice into pfd A ser 6 as follows:
On Jun 1, 2019......................$25.00.....................1   On Jun 1, 2024.......................$25.00........................1
Exchange. on June 1 in every fifth year thereafter.
Lead Underwriter(s): Scotia Capital Inc., RBC Capital Markets
Transfer Agent: Computershare Trust Company of Canada Inc.
Registrar: Computershare Trust Company of Canada Inc.
Exchanges: TSX
Symbol: PPL.PR.E
CUSIP: 706327111

4.38% Cum. 5-Year Rate Reset Class A Pref., Series 7

DBRS Rating:	Pfd-3 high	Apr 26, 2024
Issued:	10,000,000 shs.	Sep 11, 2014	$25.000
O/S:	10,000,000 shs.	Dec 31, 2023
Dividend:	$1.095 (Q)	Mar 1/Jun 1/Sep 1/Dec 1

Dividend Details: Reset on Dec 1, 2024. Dividend rate will be reset in every fifth year thereafter. The annual dividend rate will be equal to the sum of the five-year Government of Canada Bond Yield plus 2.94%. Previously, annual divd. rate was 1.125000 per sh until Nov 30, 2019.
Redemption: Redeem. on the following dates on min. 30 and max. 60 days' notice as follows:
Dec 1, 2019..$25.00   Dec 1, 2024...$25.00
Redeem. on Dec. 1 in every fifth year thereafter on min. 30 and max. 60 days' notice at $25.00 per share.

Exchange: Exchange. on min. 30 days' notice into pfd A ser 8 as follows:
On Dec 1, 2019.....................$25.00.....................1   On Dec 1, 2024.....................$25.00.....................1
Exchange. on Dec. 1 in every fifth year thereafter.
Lead Underwriter(s): CIBC World Markets Inc., Scotia Capital Inc.
Transfer Agent: Computershare Trust Company of Canada Inc.
Registrar: Computershare Trust Company of Canada Inc.
Exchanges: TSX
Symbol: PPL.PR.G
CUSIP: 706327608

4.302% Cum. 5-Year Rate Reset Class A Pref., Series 9

DBRS Rating:	Pfd-3 high	Apr 26, 2024	
Issued:	9,000,000 shs.	Apr 10, 2015	$25.000
O/S:	9,000,000 shs.	Dec 31, 2023	
Dividend:	$1.0755 (Q)	Mar 1/Jun 1/Sep 1/Dec 1	

Dividend Details: Reset on Dec 1, 2025. Dividend rate will be reset in every fifth year thereafter. The annual dividend rate will be equal to the sum of the five-year Government of Canada Bond Yield plus 3.91%. Previously, annual divd. rate was 1.187500 per sh until Nov 30, 2020.
Redemption: Redeem. on the following dates on min. 30 and max. 60 days' notice as follows:
Dec 1, 2020..$25.00   Dec 1, 2025...$25.00
Redeem. on Dec. 1 in every fifth year thereafter on min. 30 and max. 60 days' notice at $25.00 per share.
Exchange: Exchange. on min. 30 days' notice into pfd A ser 10 as follows:
On Dec 1, 2020.....................$25.00.....................1   On Dec 1, 2025.....................$25.00.....................1
Exchange. on Dec. 1 in every fifth year thereafter.
Lead Underwriter(s): Scotia Capital Inc., RBC Capital Markets
Transfer Agent: Computershare Trust Company of Canada Inc.
Registrar: Computershare Trust Company of Canada Inc.
Exchanges: TSX
Symbol: PPL.PR.I
CUSIP: 706327806

6.164% Cum. 5-Year Rate Reset Class A Pref., Series 15

Issued:	8,000,000 shs.	Oct 2, 2017	$25.000
O/S:	8,000,000 shs.	Dec 31, 2023	
Dividend:	$1.541 (Q)	Mar 31/Jun 30/Sep 30/Dec 31	

Dividend Details: Reset on Sep 30, 2027. Dividend rate will be reset in every fifth year thereafter. The annual dividend rate will be equal to the sum of the five-year Government of Canada Bond Yield plus 2.92%. Previously, annual divd. rate was 1.116000 per sh until Sep 29, 2022.
Redemption: Redeem. on the following dates on min. 30 and max. 60 days' notice as follows:
Sep 30, 2022..$25.00   Sep 30, 2027...$25.00
Redeem. on Sept. 30 in every fifth year thereafter on min. 30 and max. 60 days' notice at $25.00 per share.
Exchange: Exchange. on min. 30 days' notice into pfd A ser 16 as follows:
On Sep 30, 2022.....................$25.00....................1   On Sep 30, 2027.....................$25.00.....................1
Exchange. on Sept. 30 in every fifth year thereafter.
Note: Issued upon exchange of Veresen Inc. preferred shares, series A.
Transfer Agent: Computershare Trust Company of Canada Inc.
Registrar: Computershare Trust Company of Canada Inc.
Exchanges: TSX
Symbol: PPL.PR.O
CUSIP: 706327830

6.605% Cum. 5-Year Rate Reset Class A Pref., Series 17

Issued:	6,000,000 shs.	Oct 2, 2017	$25.000
O/S:	6,000,000 shs.	Dec 31, 2023	
Dividend:	$1.65125 (Q)	Mar 31/Jun 30/Sep 30/Dec 31	

Dividend Details: Reset on Mar 31, 2029. Dividend rate will be reset in every fifth year thereafter. The annual dividend rate will be equal to the sum of the five-year Government of Canada Bond Yield plus 3.01%. Previously, annual divd. rate was 1.205250 per sh until Mar 30, 2024.
Redemption: Redeem. on the following dates on min. 30 and max. 60 days' notice as follows:
Mar 31, 2019..$25.00   Mar 31, 2024...$25.00
Redeem. on March 31 in every fifth year thereafter on min. 30 and max. 60 days' notice at $25.00 per share.

Exchange: Was exchange. on min. 30 days' notice into pfd A ser 18 as follows:
On Mar 31, 2019......................$25.00.....................1   On Mar 31, 2024......................$25.00.....................1
Exchange. on March 31 in every fifth year thereafter.
Note: Issued upon exchange of Veresen Inc. preferred shares, series C.
Transfer Agent: Computershare Trust Company of Canada Inc.
Registrar: Computershare Trust Company of Canada Inc.
Exchanges: TSX
Symbol: PPL.PR.Q
CUSIP: 706327814

4.684% Cum. 5-Year Rate Reset Class A Pref., Series 19

Issued:	8,000,000 shs.	Oct 2, 2017	$25.000
O/S:	8,000,000 shs.	Dec 31, 2023	
Dividend:	$1.171 (Q)	Mar 31/Jun 30/Sep 30/Dec 31	

Dividend Details: Reset on Jun 30, 2025. Dividend rate will be reset in every fifth year thereafter. The annual dividend rate will be equal to the sum of the five-year Government of Canada Bond Yield plus 4.27%. Previously, annual divd. rate was 1.250000 per sh until Jun 29, 2020.
Redemption: Redeem. on the following dates on min. 30 and max. 60 days' notice as follows:
Jun 30, 2020...$25.00   Jun 30, 2025...$25.00
Redeem. on June 30 in every fifth year thereafter on min. 30 and max. 60 days' notice at $25.00 per share.
Exchange: Exchange. on min. 30 days' notice into pfd A ser 20 as follows:
On Jun 30, 2020......................$25.00.....................1   On Jun 30, 2025......................$25.00.....................1
Exchange. on June 30 in every fifth year thereafter.
Note: Issued upon exchange of Veresen Inc. preferred shares, series E.
Transfer Agent: Computershare Trust Company of Canada Inc.
Registrar: Computershare Trust Company of Canada Inc.
Exchanges: TSX
Symbol: PPL.PR.S
CUSIP: 706327780

6.302% Cum. 5-Year Rate Reset Class A Pref., Series 21

DBRS Rating:	Pfd-3 high	Apr 26, 2024	
Issued:	16,000,000 shs.	Dec 7, 2017	$25.000
O/S:	14,971,870 shs.	Dec 31, 2023	
Dividend:	$1.5755 (Q)	Mar 1/Jun 1/Sep 1/Dec 1	

Dividend Details: Reset on Mar 1, 2028. Dividend rate will be reset in every fifth year thereafter. The annual dividend rate will be equal to the greater of (i) the sum of the five-year Government of Canada Bond Yield plus 3.26% and (ii) 4.90%. Previously, annual divd. rate was 1.225000 per sh until Feb 28, 2023.
Redemption: Redeem. on the following dates on min. 30 and max. 60 days' notice as follows:
Mar 1, 2023...$25.00   Mar 1, 2028...$25.00
Redeem. on March 1 in every fifth year thereafter on min. 30 and max. 60 days' notice at $25.00 per share.
Exchange: Exchange. on min. 30 days' notice into pfd A ser 22 as follows:
On Mar 1, 2023......................$25.00.....................1   On Mar 1, 2028......................$25.00.....................1
Exchange. on March 1 in every fifth year thereafter.
Lead Underwriter(s): RBC Capital Markets, CIBC World Markets Inc., Scotia Capital Inc.
Transfer Agent: Computershare Trust Company of Canada Inc.
Registrar: Computershare Trust Company of Canada Inc.
Exchanges: TSX
Symbol: PPL.PF.A
CUSIP: 706327764

6.481% Cum. 5-Year Rate Reset Class A Pref., Series 25

DBRS Rating:	Pfd-3 high	Apr 26, 2024	
Issued:	10,000,000 shs.	Dec 16, 2019	$25.000
O/S:	10,000,000 shs.	Dec 31, 2023	
Dividend:	$1.62025 (Q)	Feb 15/May 15/Aug 15/Nov 15	

Dividend Details: Reset on Feb 15, 2028. Dividend rate will be reset in every fifth year thereafter. The annual dividend rate will be equal to the greater of (i) the sum of the five-year Government of Canada Bond Yield plus 3.51% and (ii) 5.20%. Previously, annual divd. rate was 1.300000 per sh until Feb 14, 2023.

FP Equities — Preferreds & Derivatives 2024   87

Redemption: Redeem. on the following dates on min. 30 and max. 60 days' notice as follows:
Feb 15, 2023..$25.00   Feb 15, 2028..$25.00
Redeem. on Feb. 15 in every fifth year thereafter on min. 30 and max. 60 days' notice at $25.00 per share.
Exchange: Exchange. on min. 30 days' notice into pfd A ser 26 as follows:
On Feb 15, 2023....................$25.00....................1   On Feb 15, 2028....................$25.00....................1
Exchange. on Feb. 15 in every fifth year thereafter.
Note: Issued upon exchange of Kinder Morgan Canada Limited pfd shs, series 3.
Transfer Agent: Computershare Trust Company of Canada Inc.
Registrar: Computershare Trust Company of Canada Inc.
Exchanges: TSX
Symbol: PPL.PF.E
CUSIP: 706327723

Floating Rate Cum. Class A Pref., Series 22

Issued:	1,028,130 shs.	Mar 1, 2023	$25.000
O/S:	1,028,130 shs.	Dec 31, 2023	
Dividend:	F.R. (Q)	Mar 1/Jun 1/Sep 1/Dec 1	

Dividend Details: Quarterly divd. rate is T-bill plus 3.26%.
Redemption: Redeem. on the following dates on min. 30 and max. 60 days' notice as follows:
Mar 1, 2028..$25.00   Mar 1, 2033..$25.00
Redeem. on March 1 in every fifth year thereafter on min. 30 and max. 60 days' notice at $25.00 per share.
Exchange: Exchange. on min. 30 days' notice into pfd A ser 21 sh as follows:
On Mar 1, 2028....................$25.00....................1   On Mar 1, 2033....................$25.00....................1
Exchange. on March 1 in every fifth year thereafter.
Note: Issued upon exchange of an equal number of Class A Preferred Shares, Series 21.
Transfer Agent: Computershare Trust Company of Canada Inc.
Registrar: Computershare Trust Company of Canada Inc.
Exchanges: TSX
Symbol: PPL.PF.B
CUSIP: 706327756

Power Corporation of Canada

Non-Cum. Participating Voting Pref.

DBRS Rating:	Pfd-2	Nov 2, 2023	
Issued:	3,533,421 shs.	Apr 18, 1925	
O/S:	54,860,866 shs.	Dec 31, 2023	
Dividend:	V.R. (Q)		

Dividend Details: Entitled to a non-cum. dividend of $0.009375 per sh. per annum before dividends on the subordinate voting shares.
Participation: Participates equally with subordinate voting shs. in any further divds. after $0.009375 per sh. paid on subordinate voting shs. (adjusted for 2-for-1 splits in 1985, 1986, 1998 and 2004).
Note: Entitled to 10 votes per share.
Transfer Agent: Computershare Investor Services Inc.
Registrar: Computershare Investor Services Inc.
Exchanges: TSX
Symbol: POW.PR.E
CUSIP: 739239408

5.6% Non-Cum. First Pref., Series A

DBRS Rating:	Pfd-2	Nov 2, 2023	
Issued:	6,000,000 shs.	Jun 11, 1999	$25.000
O/S:	6,000,000 shs.	Dec 31, 2023	
Dividend:	$1.40 (Q)	Jan 15/Apr 15/Jul 15/Oct 15	

Redemption: Redeem. on and after the following dates on min. 30 and max. 60 days' notice as follows:
Jun 11, 2004..$26.00   Jun 11, 2005..$25.75
Jun 11, 2006..$25.50   Jun 11, 2007..$25.25
Jun 11, 2008..$25.00

Lead Underwriter(s): BMO Capital Markets, TD Securities Inc.
Transfer Agent: Computershare Investor Services Inc.
Registrar: Computershare Investor Services Inc.
Exchanges: TSX
Symbol: POW.PR.A
CUSIP: 739239887

5.35% Non-Cum. First Pref., Series B

DBRS Rating:	Pfd-2	Nov 2, 2023	
Issued:	8,000,000 shs.	Nov 27, 2001	$25.000
O/S:	8,000,000 shs.	Dec 31, 2023	
Dividend:	$1.3375 (Q)	Jan 15/Apr 15/Jul 15/Oct 15	

Redemption: Redeem. on and after the following dates on min. 30 and max. 60 days' notice as follows:
Nov 28, 2006...$26.00   Nov 28, 2007..$25.75
Nov 28, 2008...$25.50   Nov 28, 2009..$25.25
Nov 28, 2010...$25.00

Lead Underwriter(s): BMO Capital Markets, Scotia Capital Inc.
Transfer Agent: Computershare Investor Services Inc.
Registrar: Computershare Investor Services Inc.
Exchanges: TSX
Symbol: POW.PR.B
CUSIP: 739239804

5.8% Non-Cum. First Pref., Series C

DBRS Rating:	Pfd-2	Nov 2, 2023	
Issued:	6,000,000 shs.	Dec 5, 2002	$25.000
O/S:	6,000,000 shs.	Dec 31, 2023	
Dividend:	$1.45 (Q)	Jan 15/Apr 15/Jul 15/Oct 15	

Redemption: Redeem. on and after the following dates on min. 30 and max. 60 days' notice as follows:
Dec 6, 2007...$26.00   Dec 6, 2008..$25.75
Dec 6, 2009...$25.50   Dec 6, 2010..$25.25
Dec 6, 2011...$25.00

Lead Underwriter(s): BMO Capital Markets
Transfer Agent: Computershare Investor Services Inc.
Registrar: Computershare Investor Services Inc.
Exchanges: TSX
Symbol: POW.PR.C
CUSIP: 739239879

5% Non-Cum. First Pref., Series D

DBRS Rating:	Pfd-2	Nov 2, 2023	
Issued:	10,000,000 shs.	Oct 19, 2005	$25.000
O/S:	10,000,000 shs.	Dec 31, 2023	
Dividend:	$1.25 (Q)	Jan 15/Apr 15/Jul 15/Oct 15	

Redemption: Redeem. on and after the following dates on min. 30 and max. 60 days' notice as follows:
Oct 31, 2010..$26.00   Oct 31, 2011...$25.75
Oct 31, 2012..$25.50   Oct 31, 2013...$25.25
Oct 31, 2014..$25.00

Lead Underwriter(s): BMO Capital Markets
Transfer Agent: Computershare Investor Services Inc.
Registrar: Computershare Investor Services Inc.
Exchanges: TSX
Symbol: POW.PR.D
CUSIP: 739239861

5.60% Non-Cum. First Pref., Series G

DBRS Rating:	Pfd-2	Nov 2, 2023	
Issued:	8,000,000 shs.	Feb 28, 2012	$25.000
O/S:	8,000,000 shs.	Dec 31, 2023	
Dividend:	$1.40 (Q)	Jan 15/Apr 15/Jul 15/Oct 15	

Redemption: Redeem. on and after the following dates on min. 30 and max. 60 days' notice as follows:
Apr 15, 2017..$26.00   Apr 15, 2018..$25.75
Apr 15, 2019..$25.50   Apr 15, 2020..$25.25
Apr 15, 2021..$25.00
Lead Underwriter(s): BMO Capital Markets, RBC Capital Markets, Scotia Capital Inc.
Transfer Agent: Computershare Investor Services Inc.
Registrar: Computershare Investor Services Inc.
Exchanges: TSX
Symbol: POW.PR.G
CUSIP: 739239853

Power Financial Corporation

Floating Rate Cum. First Pref., Series A

DBRS Rating:	Pfd-2 high	Nov 2, 2023	
Issued:	4,000,000 shs.	Dec 5, 1986	$25.000
O/S:	4,000,000 shs.	Dec 31, 2023	
Dividend:	F.R. (Q)	Feb 15/May 15/Aug 15/Nov 15	

Dividend Details: Quarterly divd. rate is one quarter of 70% of prime times $25.00.
Redemption: Redeem. on and after Nov 15, 1991 at $25.00 per sh.
Transfer Agent: Computershare Investor Services Inc.
Registrar: Computershare Investor Services Inc.
Exchanges: TSX
Symbol: PWF.PR.A
CUSIP: 73927C209

5.50% Non-Cum. First Pref., Series D

DBRS Rating:	Pfd-2 high	Nov 2, 2023	
Issued:	6,000,000 shs.	Dec 16, 1997	$25.000
O/S:	6,000,000 shs.	Dec 31, 2023	
Dividend:	$1.375 (Q)	Jan 31/Apr 30/Jul 31/Oct 31	

Redemption: Redeem. on and after Jan 31, 2013 on min. 30 and max. 60 days' notice at $25.00 per sh.
Lead Underwriter(s): BMO Capital Markets
Transfer Agent: Computershare Investor Services Inc.
Registrar: Computershare Investor Services Inc.
Exchanges: TSX
Symbol: PWF.PR.E
CUSIP: 73927C803

5.25% Non-Cum. First Pref., Series E

DBRS Rating:	Pfd-2 high	Nov 2, 2023	
Issued:	8,000,000 shs.	Nov 29, 2001	$25.000
O/S:	8,000,000 shs.	Dec 31, 2023	
Dividend:	$1.3125 (Q)	Jan 31/Apr 30/Jul 31/Oct 31	

Redemption: Redeem. on and after the following dates on min. 30 and max. 60 days' notice as follows:
Nov 30, 2006..$26.00   Nov 30, 2007..$25.75
Nov 30, 2008..$25.50   Nov 30, 2009..$25.25
Nov 30, 2010..$25.00
Lead Underwriter(s): Scotia Capital Inc., BMO Capital Markets
Transfer Agent: Computershare Investor Services Inc.
Registrar: Computershare Investor Services Inc.
Exchanges: TSX
Symbol: PWF.PR.F
CUSIP: 73927C886

5.90% Non-Cum. First Pref., Series F

DBRS Rating:	Pfd-2 high	Nov 2, 2023	
Issued:	6,000,000 shs.	Jul 16, 2002	$25.000
O/S:	6,000,000 shs.	Dec 31, 2023	
Dividend:	$1.475 (Q)	Jan 31/Apr 30/Jul 31/Oct 31	

Redemption: Redeem. on and after the following dates on min. 30 and max. 60 days' notice as follows:
Jul 17, 2007...$26.00 Jul 17, 2008..$25.75
Jul 17, 2009...$25.50 Jul 17, 2010..$25.25
Jul 17, 2011...$25.00
Lead Underwriter(s): BMO Capital Markets
Transfer Agent: Computershare Investor Services Inc.
Registrar: Computershare Investor Services Inc.
Exchanges: TSX
Symbol: PWF.PR.G
CUSIP: 73927C878

5.75% Non-Cum. First Pref., Series H

DBRS Rating:	Pfd-2 high	Nov 2, 2023	
Issued:	6,000,000 shs.	Dec 9, 2002	$25.000
O/S:	6,000,000 shs.	Dec 31, 2023	
Dividend:	$1.4375 (Q)	Jan 31/Apr 30/Jul 31/Oct 31	

Redemption: Redeem. on and after the following dates on min. 30 and max. 60 days' notice as follows:
Dec 10, 2007...$26.00 Dec 10, 2008..$25.75
Dec 10, 2009...$25.50 Dec 10, 2010..$25.25
Dec 10, 2011...$25.00
Lead Underwriter(s): CIBC World Markets Inc., Scotia Capital Inc.
Transfer Agent: Computershare Investor Services Inc.
Registrar: Computershare Investor Services Inc.
Exchanges: TSX
Symbol: PWF.PR.H
CUSIP: 73927C860

4.95% Non-Cum. First Pref., Series K

DBRS Rating:	Pfd-2 high	Nov 2, 2023	
Issued:	10,000,000 shs.	Oct 7, 2005	$25.000
O/S:	10,000,000 shs.	Dec 31, 2023	
Dividend:	$1.2375 (Q)	Jan 31/Apr 30/Jul 31/Oct 31	

Redemption: Redeem. on and after the following dates on min. 30 and max. 60 days' notice as follows:
Oct 31, 2010..$26.00 Oct 31, 2011...$25.75
Oct 31, 2012..$25.50 Oct 31, 2013...$25.25
Oct 31, 2014..$25.00
Lead Underwriter(s): BMO Capital Markets
Transfer Agent: Computershare Investor Services Inc.
Registrar: Computershare Investor Services Inc.
Exchanges: TSX
Symbol: PWF.PR.K
CUSIP: 73927C837

5.10% Non-Cum. First Pref., Series L

DBRS Rating:	Pfd-2 high	Nov 2, 2023	
Issued:	8,000,000 shs.	Aug 4, 2006	$25.000
O/S:	8,000,000 shs.	Dec 31, 2023	
Dividend:	$1.275 (Q)	Jan 31/Apr 30/Jul 31/Oct 31	

Redemption: Redeem. on and after the following dates on min. 30 and max. 60 days' notice as follows:
Oct 31, 2011..$26.00 Oct 31, 2012...$25.75
Oct 31, 2013..$25.50 Oct 31, 2014...$25.25
Oct 31, 2015..$25.00
Lead Underwriter(s): BMO Capital Markets, Scotia Capital Inc.
Transfer Agent: Computershare Investor Services Inc.
Registrar: Computershare Investor Services Inc.
Exchanges: TSX
Symbol: PWF.PR.L
CUSIP: 73927C829

FP Equities — Preferreds & Derivatives 2024   91

5.8% Non-Cum. First Pref., Series O

DBRS Rating:	Pfd-2 high	Nov 2, 2023	
Issued:	6,000,000 shs.	Oct 9, 2009	$25.000
O/S:	6,000,000 shs.	Dec 31, 2023	
Dividend:	$1.45 (Q)	Jan 31/Apr 30/Jul 31/Oct 31	

Redemption: Redeem. on and after the following dates on min. 30 and max. 60 days' notice as follows:
Oct 31, 2014...$26.00   Oct 31, 2015...$25.75
Oct 31, 2016...$25.50   Oct 31, 2017...$25.25
Oct 31, 2018...$25.00
Lead Underwriter(s): BMO Capital Markets, Scotia Capital Inc., RBC Capital Markets
Transfer Agent: Computershare Investor Services Inc.
Registrar: Computershare Investor Services Inc.
Exchanges: TSX
Symbol: PWF.PR.O
CUSIP: 73927C787

1.998% Non-Cum. 5-Year Rate Reset First Pref., Series P

DBRS Rating:	Pfd-2 high	Nov 2, 2023	
Issued:	11,200,000 shs.	Jun 29, 2010	$25.000
O/S:	9,657,516 shs.	Dec 31, 2023	
Dividend:	$0.4995 (Q)	Jan 31/Apr 30/Jul 31/Oct 31	

Dividend Details: Reset on Jan 31, 2026. Dividend rate will be reset in every fifth year thereafter. The annual dividend rate will be equal to the sum of the five-year Government of Canada Bond Yield plus 1.60%. Previously, annual divd. rate was 0.576500 per sh until Jan 30, 2021.
Redemption: Redeem. on the following dates on min. 30 and max. 60 days' notice as follows:
Jan 31, 2016...$25.00   Jan 31, 2021...$25.00
Redeem. on Jan. 31 in every fifth year thereafter on min. 30 and max. 60 days' notice at $25.00 per share.
Exchange: Was exchange. on min. 30 days' notice into pfd 1st ser Q as follows:
On Jan 31, 2016....................$25.00.....................1   On Jan 31, 2021......................$25.00......................1
Exchange. on Jan. 31 in every fifth year thereafter.
Lead Underwriter(s): BMO Capital Markets, RBC Capital Markets, Scotia Capital Inc.
Transfer Agent: Computershare Investor Services Inc.
Registrar: Computershare Investor Services Inc.
Exchanges: TSX
Symbol: PWF.PR.P
CUSIP: 73927C779

5.5% Non-Cum. First Pref., Series R

DBRS Rating:	Pfd-2 high	Nov 2, 2023	
Issued:	10,000,000 shs.	Feb 23, 2012	$25.000
O/S:	10,000,000 shs.	Dec 31, 2023	
Dividend:	$1.375 (Q)	Jan 31/Apr 30/Jul 31/Oct 31	

Redemption: Redeem. on and after the following dates on min. 30 and max. 60 days' notice as follows:
Apr 30, 2017...$26.00   Apr 30, 2018...$25.75
Apr 30, 2019...$25.50   Apr 30, 2020...$25.25
Apr 30, 2021...$25.00
Lead Underwriter(s): BMO Capital Markets, RBC Capital Markets, Scotia Capital Inc.
Transfer Agent: Computershare Investor Services Inc.
Registrar: Computershare Investor Services Inc.
Exchanges: TSX
Symbol: PWF.PR.R
CUSIP: 73927C753

4.80% Non-Cum First Pref., Series S

DBRS Rating:	Pfd-2 high	Nov 2, 2023	
Issued:	12,000,000 shs.	Feb 28, 2013	$25.000
O/S:	12,000,000 shs.	Dec 31, 2023	
Dividend:	$1.20 (Q)	Jan 31/Apr 30/Jul 31/Oct 31	

Redemption: Redeem. on and after the following dates on min. 30 and max. 60 days' notice as follows:
Apr 30, 2018...$26.00   Apr 30, 2019..$25.75
Apr 30, 2020...$25.50   Apr 30, 2021..$25.25
Apr 30, 2022...$25.00
Lead Underwriter(s): BMO Capital Markets, RBC Capital Markets, Scotia Capital Inc.
Transfer Agent: Computershare Investor Services Inc.
Registrar: Computershare Investor Services Inc.
Exchanges: TSX
Symbol: PWF.PR.S
CUSIP: 73927C746

5.595% Non-Cum. 5-Year Rate Reset Pref., Series T

DBRS Rating:	Pfd-2 high	Nov 2, 2023	
Issued:	8,000,000 shs.	Dec 11, 2013	$25.000
O/S:	8,000,000 shs.	Dec 31, 2023	
Dividend:	$1.39875 (Q)	Jan 31/Apr 30/Jul 31/Oct 31	

Dividend Details: Reset on Jan 31, 2029. Dividend rate will be reset in every fifth year thereafter. The annual dividend rate will be equal to the sum of the five-year Government of Canada Bond Yield plus 2.37%. Previously, annual divd. rate was 1.053750 per sh until Jan 30, 2024.
Redemption: Redeem. on the following dates as follows:
Jan 31, 2019..$25.00   Jan 31, 2024..$25.00
Redeem. on Jan. 31 in every fifth year thereafter on min. 30 and max. 60 days' notice at $25.00 per share.
Exchange: Was exchange. on min. 30 days' notice into pfd 1st ser U as follows:
On Jan 31, 2019.....................$25.00....................1   On Jan 31, 2024......................$25.00........................1
Exchange. on Jan. 31 in every fifth year thereafter.
Lead Underwriter(s): BMO Capital Markets, RBC Capital Markets, Scotia Capital Inc.
Transfer Agent: Computershare Investor Services Inc.
Registrar: Computershare Investor Services Inc.
Exchanges: TSX
Symbol: PWF.PR.T
CUSIP: 73927C738

Floating Rate Non-Cum First Pref., Series Q

Issued:	2,234,515 shs.	Feb 1, 2016	$25.000
O/S:	1,542,484 shs.	Dec 31, 2023	
Dividend:	F.R. (Q)	Jan 31/Apr 30/Jul 31/Oct 31	

Dividend Details: Quarterly divd. rate is T-bill plus 1.6%.
Redemption: Redeem. on the following dates on min. 30 and max. 60 days' notice as follows:
Jan 31, 2021..$25.00   Jan 31, 2026..$25.00
Redeem. on Jan. 31 in every fifth year thereafter on min. 30 and max. 60 days' notice at $25.00 per share.
Exchange: Exchange. on min. 30 days' notice into pfd 1st ser P sh as follows:
On Jan 31, 2021.....................$25.00....................1   On Jan 31, 2026......................$25.00........................1
Exchange. on Jan. 31 in every fifth year thereafter.
Note: Issued upon exchange of an equal number of First Preferred Shares, Series P.
Transfer Agent: Computershare Investor Services Inc.
Registrar: Computershare Investor Services Inc.
Exchanges: TSX
Symbol: PWF.PR.Q
CUSIP: 73927C761

5.15% Non Cum. First Pref., Series V

DBRS Rating:	Pfd-2 high	Nov 2, 2023	
Issued:	10,000,000 shs.	May 26, 2017	$25.000
O/S:	10,000,000 shs.	Dec 31, 2023	
Dividend:	$1.2875 (Q)	Jan 31/Apr 30/Jul 31/Oct 31	

Redemption: Redeem. on and after the following dates on min. 30 and max. 60 days' notice as follows:
Jul 31, 2022...$26.00   Jul 31, 2023..$25.75
Jul 31, 2024...$25.50   Jul 31, 2025..$25.25
Jul 31, 2026...$25.00

FP Equities — Preferreds & Derivatives 2024

Lead Underwriter(s): BMO Capital Markets, RBC Capital Markets, Scotia Capital Inc., TD Securities Inc.
Transfer Agent: Computershare Investor Services Inc.
Registrar: Computershare Investor Services Inc.
Exchanges: TSX
Symbol: PWF.PR.Z
CUSIP: 73927C712

4.5% First Pref., Series 23

DBRS Rating:	Pfd-2 high	Nov 2, 2023
Issued:	8,000,000 shs.	Oct 15, 2021 $25.000
O/S:	8,000,000 shs.	Dec 31, 2023
Dividend:	$1.125 (Q)	Jan 31/Apr 30/Jul 31/Oct 31

Redemption: Redeem. on and after the following dates on min. 30 and max. 60 days' notice as follows:
Jan 31, 2027...$26.00   Jan 31, 2028..$25.75
Jan 31, 2029...$25.50   Jan 31, 2030..$25.25
Jan 31, 2031...$25.00
Lead Underwriter(s): BMO Capital Markets, RBC Capital Markets, Scotia Capital Inc.
Transfer Agent: Computershare Investor Services Inc.
Registrar: Computershare Investor Services Inc.
Exchanges: TSX
Symbol: PWF.PF.A
CUSIP: 73927C118

RF Capital Group Inc.
(formerly GMP Capital Inc.)

3.70% Cum. 5-Year Rate Reset Pref., Series B

DBRS Rating:	Pfd-4 high	Jun 28, 2023
Issued:	4,600,000 shs.	Feb 22, 2011 $25.000
O/S:	4,600,000 shs.	Dec 31, 2023
Dividend:	$0.925 (Q)	Mar 31/Jun 30/Sep 30/Dec 31

Dividend Details: Reset on Apr 1, 2026. Dividend rate will be reset in every fifth year thereafter. The annual dividend rate will be equal to the sum of the five-year Government of Canada Bond Yield plus 2.89%. Previously, annual divd. rate was 0.902800 per sh until Mar 31, 2021.
Redemption: Redeem. on the following dates on min. 30 and max. 60 days' notice as follows:
Mar 31, 2016...$25.00   Mar 31, 2021..$25.00
Redeem. on March 31 in every fifth year thereafter on min. 30 and max. 60 days' notice at $25.00 per share.
Exchange: Was exchange. on min. 30 days' notice into pfd ser C as follows:
On Mar 31, 2016....................$25.00....................1   On Mar 31, 2021.....................$25.00.....................1
Exchange. on March 31 in every fifth year thereafter.
Lead Underwriter(s): National Bank Financial Inc., RF Securities Clearing LP, Scotia Capital Inc.
Transfer Agent: TSX Trust Company
Registrar: TSX Trust Company
Exchanges: TSX
Symbol: RCG.PR.B
CUSIP: 74971G203

Royal Bank of Canada

3.70% Non-Cum. 5-Year Rate Reset First Pref., Series AZ

DBRS Rating:	Pfd-2 high	May 12, 2023
Issued:	20,000,000 shs.	Jan 30, 2014 $25.000
O/S:	20,000,000 shs.	Jan 31, 2024
Dividend:	$0.925 (Q)	Feb 24/May 24/Aug 24/Nov 24

Dividend Details: Reset on May 24, 2024. Dividend rate will be reset in every fifth year thereafter. The annual dividend rate will be equal to the sum of the five-year Government of Canada Bond Yield plus 2.21%. Previously, annual divd. rate was 1.000000 per sh until May 23, 2019.

Redemption: Redeem. on the following dates on min. 30 and max. 60 days' notice, conditional on the approval of the Superintendent of Financial Institutions, as follows:
May 24, 2019..$25.00   May 24, 2024..$25.00
Redeem. on May. 24 in every fifth year thereafter on min. 30 and max. 60 days' notice at $25.00 per share, conditional on approval of the Superintendent of Financial Institutions.

Convertible: Automatically convertible into common shares upon occurrence of a Non-Viability Contingent Capital (NVCC) trigger event as defined by OFSI.

Exchange: Exchange. on min. 30 days' notice into pfd 1st ser BA as follows:
On May 24, 2019.....................$25.00.....................1   On May 24, 2024......................$25.00........................1
Exchange. on May 24 in every fifth year thereafter. Exchange. after notice from the Bank given with approval from the Superintendent of Financial Institutions.

Lead Underwriter(s): RBC Capital Markets
Transfer Agent: Computershare Trust Company of Canada Inc.
Registrar: Computershare Trust Company of Canada Inc.
Exchanges: TSX
Symbol: RY.PR.Z
CUSIP: 78012G411

3.65% Non-Cum. 5-Year Rate Reset First Pref., Series BB

DBRS Rating:	Pfd-2 high	May 12, 2023	
Issued:	20,000,000 shs.	Jun 3, 2014	$25.000
O/S:	20,000,000 shs.	Jan 31, 2024	
Dividend:	$0.9125 (Q)	Feb 24/May 24/Aug 24/Nov 24	

Dividend Details: Reset on Aug 24, 2025. Dividend rate will be reset in every fifth year thereafter. The annual dividend rate will be equal to the sum of the five-year Government of Canada Bond Yield plus 2.26%. Previously, annual divd. rate was 0.975000 per sh until Aug 23, 2019.

Redemption: Redeem. on the following dates on min. 30 and max. 60 days' notice, conditional on the approval of the Superintendent of Financial Institutions, as follows:
Aug 24, 2019..$25.00   Aug 24, 2024..$25.00
Redeem. on Aug. 24 in every fifth year thereafter on min. 30 and max. 60 days' notice at $25.00 per share, conditional on approval of the Superintendent of Financial Institutions.

Convertible: Automatically convertible into common shares upon occurrence of a Non-Viability Contingent Capital (NVCC) trigger event as defined by OFSI.

Exchange: Exchange. on min. 30 days' notice into pfd 1st ser BC as follows:
On Aug 24, 2019.....................$25.00.....................1   On Aug 24, 2024......................$25.00........................1
Exchange. on Aug. 24 in every fifth year thereafter. Exchange. after notice from the Bank given with approval from the Superintendent of Financial Institutions.

Lead Underwriter(s): RBC Capital Markets
Transfer Agent: Computershare Trust Company of Canada Inc.
Registrar: Computershare Trust Company of Canada Inc.
Exchanges: TSX
Symbol: RY.PR.H
CUSIP: 78012H567

3.20% Non-Cum. 5-Year Rate Reset First Pref., Series BD

DBRS Rating:	Pfd-2 high	May 12, 2023	
Issued:	24,000,000 shs.	Jan 30, 2015	$25.000
O/S:	24,000,000 shs.	Jan 31, 2024	
Dividend:	$0.80 (Q)	Feb 24/May 24/Aug 24/Nov 24	

Dividend Details: Reset on May 24, 2025. Dividend rate will be reset in every fifth year thereafter. The annual dividend rate will be equal to the sum of the five-year Government of Canada Bond Yield plus 2.74%. Previously, annual divd. rate was 0.900000 per sh until May 23, 2020.

Redemption: Redeem. on the following dates on min. 30 and max. 60 days' notice, conditional on the approval of the Superintendent of Financial Institutions, as follows:
May 24, 2020..$25.00   May 24, 2025..$25.00
Redeem. on May 24 in every fifth year thereafter on min. 30 and max. 60 days' notice at $25.00 per share, conditional on approval of the Superintendent of Financial Institutions.

Convertible: Automatically convertible into common shares upon occurrence of a Non-Viability Contingent Capital (NVCC) trigger event as defined by OFSI.

FP Equities — Preferreds & Derivatives 2024   95

Exchange: Exchange. on min. 30 days' notice into pfd 1st ser BE as follows:
On May 24, 2020...................$25.00....................1   On May 24, 2025.....................$25.00.....................1
Exchange. on May 24 in every fifth year thereafter. Exchange. after notice from the Bank given with approval from the Superintendent of Financial Institutions.
Lead Underwriter(s): RBC Capital Markets, Scotia Capital Inc., TD Securities Inc.
Transfer Agent: Computershare Trust Company of Canada Inc.
Registrar: Computershare Trust Company of Canada Inc.
Exchanges: TSX
Symbol: RY.PR.J
CUSIP: 78012Q112

3.0% Non-Cum. 5-Year Rate Reset First Pref., Series BF

DBRS Rating:	Pfd-2 high	May 12, 2023	
Issued:	12,000,000 shs.	Mar 13, 2015	$25.000
O/S:	12,000,000 shs.	Jan 31, 2024	
Dividend:	$0.75 (Q)	Feb 24/May 24/Aug 24/Nov 24	

Dividend Details: Reset on Nov 24, 2025. Dividend rate will be reset in every fifth year thereafter. The annual dividend rate will be equal to the sum of the five-year Government of Canada Bond Yield plus 2.62%. Previously, annual divd. rate was 0.900000 per sh until Nov 23, 2020.
Redemption: Redeem. on the following dates on min. 30 and max. 60 days' notice, conditional on the approval of the Superintendent of Financial Institutions, as follows:
Nov 24, 2020...$25.00   Nov 24, 2025..$25.00
Redeem. on. Nov. 24 in every fifth year thereafter on min. 30 and max. 60 days' notice at $25.00 per share, conditional on approval of the Superintendent of Financial Institutions.
Convertible: Automatically convertible into common shares upon occurrence of a Non-Viability Contingent Capital (NVCC) trigger event as defined by OFSI.
Exchange: Exchange. on min. 30 days' notice into pfd 1st ser BG as follows:
On Nov 24, 2020...................$25.00....................1   On Nov 24, 2025.....................$25.00.....................1
Exchange. on Nov. 24 in every fifth year thereafter. Exchange. after notice from the Bank given with approval from the Superintendent of Financial Institutions.
Lead Underwriter(s): RBC Capital Markets, Scotia Capital Inc., TD Securities Inc.
Transfer Agent: Computershare Trust Company of Canada Inc.
Registrar: Computershare Trust Company of Canada Inc.
Exchanges: TSX
Symbol: RY.PR.M
CUSIP: 78012T470

4.90% Non-Cum. First Pref., Series BH

DBRS Rating:	Pfd-2 high	May 12, 2023	
Issued:	6,000,000 shs.	Jun 5, 2015	$25.000
O/S:	6,000,000 shs.	Jan 31, 2024	
Dividend:	$1.225 (Q)	Feb 24/May 24/Aug 24/Nov 24	

Redemption: Redeem. on and after the following dates on min. 30 and max. 60 days' notice, conditional on the approval of the Superintendent of Financial Institutions, as follows:
Nov 24, 2020...$26.00   Nov 24, 2021..$25.75
Nov 24, 2022...$25.50   Nov 24, 2023..$25.25
Nov 24, 2024...$25.00
Convertible: Automatically convertible into common shares upon occurrence of a Non-Viability Contingent Capital (NVCC) trigger event as defined by OFSI.
Exchange: Exchange. on min. 30 days' notice into 1 new pfd sh per pref. sh, being an exchange price per new pfd sh of $25.00.
Lead Underwriter(s): RBC Capital Markets
Transfer Agent: Computershare Trust Company of Canada Inc.
Registrar: Computershare Trust Company of Canada Inc.
Exchanges: TSX
Symbol: RY.PR.N
CUSIP: 78013J455

4.90% Non-Cum. First Pref., Series BI

DBRS Rating:	Pfd-2 high	May 12, 2023	
Issued:	6,000,000 shs.	Jul 22, 2015	$25.000
O/S:	6,000,000 shs.	Jan 31, 2024	
Dividend:	$1.225 (Q)	Feb 24/May 24/Aug 24/Nov 24	

Redemption: Redeem. on and after the following dates on min. 30 and max. 60 days' notice, conditional on the approval of the Superintendent of Financial Institutions, as follows:
Nov 24, 2020...$25.75 Nov 24, 2021..$25.75
Nov 24, 2022...$25.50 Nov 24, 2023..$25.25
Nov 24, 2024...$25.00

Convertible: Automatically convertible into common shares upon occurrence of a Non-Viability Contingent Capital (NVCC) trigger event as defined by OFSI.

Exchange: Exchange. on min. 30 days' notice into 1 new pfd sh per pref. sh, being an exchange price per new pfd sh of $25.00.

Lead Underwriter(s): RBC Capital Markets, Scotia Capital Inc.
Transfer Agent: Computershare Trust Company of Canada Inc.
Registrar: Computershare Trust Company of Canada Inc.
Exchanges: TSX
Symbol: RY.PR.O
CUSIP: 78013K601

5.885% Non-Cum. 5-Year Rate Reset Pref., Series BO

DBRS Rating:	Pfd-2 high	May 12, 2023	
Issued:	14,000,000 shs.	Nov 2, 2018	$25.000
O/S:	14,000,000 shs.	Jan 31, 2024	
Dividend:	$1.47125 (Q)	Feb 24/May 24/Aug 24/Nov 24	

Dividend Details: Reset on Feb 24, 2029. Dividend rate will be reset in every fifth year thereafter. The annual dividend rate will be equal to the sum of the five-year Government of Canada Bond Yield plus 2.38%. Previously, annual divd. rate was 1.200000 per sh until Feb 23, 2024.

Redemption: Redeem. on the following dates on min. 30 and max. 60 days' notice, conditional on the approval of the Superintendent of Financial Institutions, as follows:
Feb 24, 2024...$25.00   Feb 24, 2029..$25.00
Redeem. on Feb. 24 in every fifth year thereafter on min. 30 and max. 60 days' notice at $25.00 per share, conditional on approval of the Superintendent of Financial Institutions.

Convertible: Automatically convertible into common shares upon occurrence of a Non-Viability Contingent Capital (NVCC) trigger event as defined by OFSI.

Exchange: Exchange. on min. 30 days' notice into pfd 1st ser BP as follows:
On Feb 24, 2024....................$25.00....................1   On Feb 24, 2029.....................$25.00........................1
Exchange. on Feb. 24 in every fifth year thereafter. Exchange. after notice from the Bank given with approval from the Superintendent of Financial Institutions.

Lead Underwriter(s): RBC Capital Markets
Transfer Agent: Computershare Trust Company of Canada Inc.
Registrar: Computershare Trust Company of Canada Inc.
Exchanges: TSX
Symbol: RY.PR.S
CUSIP: 78013R390

Sagen MI Canada Inc.
(formerly Genworth MI Canada Inc.)

5.4% Pref., Series 1

DBRS Rating:	Pfd-2 high	Apr 26, 2024	
Issued:	4,000,000 shs.	Feb 18, 2021	$25.000
O/S:	4,000,000 shs.	Dec 31, 2023	
Dividend:	$1.35 (Q)	Mar 31/Jun 30/Sep 30/Dec 31	

Redemption: Redeem. on and after the following dates on min. 30 and max. 60 days' notice as follows:
Mar 31, 2026...$26.00   Mar 31, 2027..$25.75
Mar 31, 2028...$25.50   Mar 31, 2029..$25.25
Mar 31, 2030...$25.00

FP Equities — Preferreds & Derivatives 2024

Lead Underwriter(s): BMO Capital Markets, CIBC World Markets Inc., National Bank Financial Inc., RBC Capital Markets, Scotia Capital Inc., TD Securities Inc.
Transfer Agent: TSX Trust Company
Exchanges: TSX
Symbol: MIC.PR.A
CUSIP: 786688309

Sonor Investments Limited

9% Cum. Redeem. Voting First Pfce.

Issued:	240,000 shs.	Jan 1, 1972	$5.000
O/S:	195,600 shs.	Dec 31, 2023	
Dividend:	$0.45 (S)	Mar 15/Sep 15	

Redemption: Redeem. on and after the following dates as follows:
Jan 1, 1972...$5.05   May 1, 1993...$5.00
Purchase Fund: Company to make all reasonable efforts to purchase annually 4,800 shares at a maximum price of $5.00 per share.
Note: Formerly 8% first pfce. shs. Number of votes per sh. increased to 15 from one, effective Jan. 1, 1983.
Transfer Agent: CIBC Mellon Trust Company
Registrar: CIBC Mellon Trust Company
Exchanges: TSX-VEN
Symbol: SNI.PR.A
CUSIP: 835640202

Sun Life Financial Inc.

4.45% Non-Cum. Class A Pref., Series 3

DBRS Rating:	Pfd-2 high	Oct 24, 2023	
Issued:	10,000,000 shs.	Jan 13, 2006	$25.000
O/S:	10,000,000 shs.	Dec 31, 2023	
Dividend:	$1.1125 (Q)	Mar 31/Jun 30/Sep 30/Dec 31	

Redemption: Redeem. on and after the following dates on min. 30 and max. 60 days' notice, conditional on the approval of the Superintendent of Financial Institutions, as follows:
Mar 31, 2011..$26.00   Mar 31, 2012..$25.75
Mar 31, 2013..$25.50   Mar 31, 2014..$25.25
Mar 31, 2015..$25.00
Exchange: Exchange. on min. 30 days' notice into 1 new pfd per pref. sh, being an exchange price per new pfd of $25.00.
Lead Underwriter(s): CIBC World Markets Inc.
Transfer Agent: TSX Trust Company
Registrar: TSX Trust Company
Exchanges: TSX
Symbol: SLF.PR.C
CUSIP: 866796402

4.45% Non-Cum. Class A Pref., Series 4

DBRS Rating:	Pfd-2 high	Oct 24, 2023	
Issued:	12,000,000 shs.	Oct 10, 2006	$25.000
O/S:	12,000,000 shs.	Dec 31, 2023	
Dividend:	$1.1125 (Q)	Mar 31/Jun 30/Sep 30/Dec 31	

Redemption: Redeem. on and after the following dates on min. 30 and max. 60 days' notice, conditional on the approval of the Superintendent of Financial Institutions, as follows:
Dec 31, 2011..$26.00   Dec 31, 2012..$25.75
Dec 31, 2013..$25.50   Dec 31, 2014..$25.25
Dec 31, 2015..$25.00
Exchange: Exchange. on min. 30 days' notice into 1 new pfd per pref. sh, being an exchange price per new pfd of $25.00.

Lead Underwriter(s): RBC Capital Markets, BMO Capital Markets, CIBC World Markets Inc., National Bank Financial Inc., Scotia Capital Inc., TD Securities Inc.
Transfer Agent: TSX Trust Company
Registrar: TSX Trust Company
Exchanges: TSX
Symbol: SLF.PR.D
CUSIP: 866796501

4.5% Non-Cum. Class A Pref., Series 5

DBRS Rating:	Pfd-2 high	Oct 24, 2023
Issued:	10,000,000 shs.	Feb 2, 2007	$25.000
O/S:	10,000,000 shs.	Dec 31, 2023
Dividend:	$1.125 (Q)	Mar 31/Jun 30/Sep 30/Dec 31

Redemption: Redeem. on and after the following dates on min. 30 and max. 60 days' notice, conditional on the approval of the Superintendent of Financial Institutions, as follows:
Mar 31, 2012...$26.00 Mar 31, 2013..$25.75
Mar 31, 2014...$25.50 Mar 31, 2015..$25.25
Mar 31, 2016...$25.00

Exchange: Exchange. on min. 30 days' notice into 1 new pfd per pref. sh, being an exchange price per new pfd of $25.00.
Lead Underwriter(s): RBC Capital Markets
Transfer Agent: TSX Trust Company
Registrar: TSX Trust Company
Exchanges: TSX
Symbol: SLF.PR.E
CUSIP: 866796600

1.825% Non-Cum. 5-Year Rate Reset Class A Pref., Series 8R

DBRS Rating:	Pfd-2 high	Oct 24, 2023
Issued:	11,200,000 shs.	May 25, 2010	$25.000
O/S:	6,217,331 shs.	Dec 31, 2023
Dividend:	$0.45625 (Q)	Mar 31/Jun 30/Sep 30/Dec 31

Dividend Details: Reset on Jun 30, 2025. Dividend rate will be reset in every fifth year thereafter. The annual dividend rate will be equal to the sum of the five-year Government of Canada Bond Yield plus 1.41%. Previously, annual divd. rate was 0.568750 per sh until Jun 29, 2020.

Redemption: Redeem. on the following dates on min. 30 and max. 60 days' notice as follows:
Jun 30, 2015...$25.00 Jun 30, 2020..$25.00
Redeem. on June 30 in every fifth year thereafter on min. 30 and max. 60 days' notice at $25.00 per share. All redemptions are subject to the provisions of the Insurance Companies Act (Canada), including the requirement of obtaining the prior consent of the Superintendent of Financial Institutions.

Exchange: Exchange. on min. 30 days' notice into pfd A ser 9QR sh as follows:
On Jun 30, 2015......................$25.00........................1 On Jun 30, 2020.......................$25.00.......................1
On Jun 30, 2025......................$25.00........................1

Exchange. on June 30 in every fifth year thereafter. Also exchange. on the company's notice at any time on min. 30 days' notice into one new preferred share per class A pref. sh., series 8R, being an exchange price per new preferred share of $25.00.
Lead Underwriter(s): Scotia Capital Inc., RBC Capital Markets, TD Securities Inc.
Transfer Agent: TSX Trust Company
Registrar: TSX Trust Company
Exchanges: TSX
Symbol: SLF.PR.G
CUSIP: 866796881

2.967% Non-Cum. 5-Year Rate Reset Class A Pref., Series 10R

DBRS Rating:	Pfd-2 high	Oct 24, 2023
Issued:	8,000,000 shs.	Aug 12, 2011	$25.000
O/S:	6,838,672 shs.	Dec 31, 2023
Dividend:	$0.74175 (Q)	Mar 31/Jun 30/Sep 30/Dec 31

Dividend Details: Reset on Sep 30, 2026. Dividend rate will be reset in every fifth year thereafter. The annual dividend rate will be equal to the sum of the five-year Government of Canada Bond Yield plus 2.17%. Previously, annual divd. rate was 0.710500 per sh until Sep 29, 2021.

Redemption: Redeem. on the following dates on min. 30 and max. 60 days' notice as follows:
Sep 30, 2016................................$25.00   Sep 30, 2021................................$25.00
Redeem. on Sept. 30 in every fifth year thereafter on min. 30 and max. 60 days' notice at $25.00 per share. All redemptions are subject to the provisions of the Insurance Companies Act (Canada), including the requirement of obtaining the prior consent of the Superintendent of Financial Institutions.

Exchange: Exchange. on min. 30 days' notice into pfd A ser 11QR as follows:
On Sep 30, 2016..................$25.00....................1   On Sep 30, 2021....................$25.00....................1
On Sep 30, 2026..................$25.00....................1
Exchange. on Sept. 30 in every fifth year thereafter. Also exchange. on the company's notice at any time on min. 30 days' notice into one new preferred share per class A pref. sh., series 10R, being an exchange price per new preferred share of $25.00.

Lead Underwriter(s): Scotia Capital Inc., BMO Capital Markets, RBC Capital Markets
Transfer Agent: TSX Trust Company
Registrar: TSX Trust Company
Exchanges: TSX
Symbol: SLF.PR.H
CUSIP: 866796865

Floating Rate Pref., Series 9QR

Issued:	6,007,314 shs.	Jun 30, 2015	$25.000
O/S:	4,982,669 shs.	Dec 31, 2023	
Dividend:	F.R. (Q)	Mar 31/Jun 30/Sep 30/Dec 31	

Dividend Details: Quarterly divd. rate is T-bill plus 1.41%.

Redemption: Redeem. on the following dates on min. 30 and max. 60 days' notice as follows:
Jun 30, 2020................................$25.00   Jun 30, 2025................................$25.00
Redeem. on June 30 in every fifth year thereafter on min. 30 and max. 60 days' notice at $25.00 per share. All redemptions are subject to the provisions of the Insurance Companies Act (Canada), including the requirement of obtaining the prior consent of the Superintendent of Financial Institutions.

Exchange: Exchange. on min. 30 days' notice into pfd A ser 8R sh as follows:
On Jun 30, 2020..................$25.00....................1   On Jun 30, 2025....................$25.00....................1
Exchange. on June 30 in every fifth year thereafter. Also exchange. on the company's notice at any time on min. 30 days' notice into one new preferred share per class A pref. sh., series 9QR, being an exchange price per new preferred share of $25.00.

Note: Issued upon exchange of an equal number of First Preferred Shares, Series 8R.
Transfer Agent: TSX Trust Company
Registrar: TSX Trust Company
Exchanges: TSX
Symbol: SLF.PR.J
CUSIP: 866796873

Floating Rate Non-Cum. Class A Pref., Series 11QR

DBRS Rating:	Pfd-2 high	Oct 24, 2023	
Issued:	1,080,072 shs.	Sep 30, 2016	$25.000
O/S:	1,161,328 shs.	Dec 31, 2023	
Dividend:	F.R. (Q)	Mar 31/Jun 30/Sep 30/Dec 31	

Dividend Details: Quarterly divd. rate is T-bill plus 2.17%.

Redemption: Redeem. on the following dates on min. 30 and max. 60 days' notice as follows:
Sep 30, 2021................................$25.00   Sep 30, 2026................................$25.00
Redeem. on Sept. 30 in every fifth year thereafter on min. 30 and max. 60 days' notice at (i) $25.00 per share, or (ii) $25.50 in the case of redemption on any other date after Sept. 30, 2016, in each case plus all declared and unpaid dividends. All redemptions are subject to the provisions of the Insurance Companies Act (Canada), including the requirement of obtaining the prior consent of the Superintendent of Financial Institutions.

Exchange: Exchange. on min. 30 days' notice into pfd A ser 10R sh as follows:
On Sep 30, 2021.....................$25.00.....................1   On Sep 30, 2026.....................$25.00.....................1
Exchange. on Sept. 30 in every fifth year thereafter. Also exchange. on the company's notice at any time on min. 30 days' notice into one new preferred share per class A pref. sh., series 11QR, being an exchange price per new preferred share of $25.00.
Note: Issued upon exchange of an equal number of cl A ser. 10R pf shs.
Transfer Agent: TSX Trust Company
Registrar: TSX Trust Company
Exchanges: TSX
Symbol: SLF.PR.K
CUSIP: 866796857

TC Energy Corporation

3.479% Cum. 5-Year Rate Reset First Pref., Series 1

DBRS Rating:	Pfd-3 high	Jul 25, 2023
Issued:	22,000,000 shs.	Sep 30, 2009	$25.000
O/S:	14,577,184 shs.	Dec 31, 2023
Dividend:	$0.86975 (Q)	Mar 31/Jun 30/Sep 30/Dec 31

Dividend Details: Reset on Dec 31, 2024. Dividend rate will be reset in every fifth year thereafter. The annual dividend rate will be equal to the sum of the five-year Government of Canada Bond Yield plus 1.92%. Previously, annual divd. rate was 0.816500 per sh until Dec 30, 2019.
Redemption: Redeem. on the following dates on min. 30 and max. 60 days' notice as follows:
Dec 31, 2014...$25.00   Dec 31, 2019...$25.00
Redeem. on Dec. 31 in every fifth year thereafter on min. 30 and max. 60 days' notice at $25.00 per share.
Exchange: Was exchange. on min. 30 days' notice into pfd 1st ser 2 as follows:
On Dec 31, 2014.....................$25.00.....................1   On Dec 31, 2019.....................$25.00.....................1
Exchange. on Dec. 31 in every fifth year thereafter.
Lead Underwriter(s): Scotia Capital Inc., RBC Capital Markets
Transfer Agent: Computershare Trust Company of Canada Inc.
Registrar: Computershare Trust Company of Canada Inc.
Exchanges: TSX
Symbol: TRP.PR.A
CUSIP: 87807B206

1.694% Cum. 5-Year Rate Reset First Pref., Series 3

DBRS Rating:	Pfd-3 high	Jul 25, 2023
Issued:	14,000,000 shs.	Mar 11, 2010	$25.000
O/S:	9,997,177 shs.	Dec 31, 2023
Dividend:	$0.4235 (Q)	Mar 31/Jun 30/Sep 30/Dec 31

Dividend Details: Reset on Jun 30, 2025. Dividend rate will be reset in every fifth year thereafter. The annual dividend rate will be equal to the sum of the five-year Government of Canada Bond Yield plus 1.28%. Previously, annual divd. rate was 0.538000 per sh until Jun 29, 2020.
Redemption: Redeem. on the following dates on min. 30 and max. 60 days' notice as follows:
Jun 30, 2015...$25.00   Jun 30, 2020...$25.00
Redeem. on June 30 in every fifth year thereafter on min. 30 and max. 60 days' notice at $25.00 per share.
Exchange: Was exchange. on min. 30 days' notice into pfd 1st ser 4 sh as follows:
On Jun 30, 2015.....................$25.00.....................1   On Jun 30, 2020.....................$25.00.....................1
Exchange. on June 30 in every fifth year thereafter.
Lead Underwriter(s): Scotia Capital Inc., RBC Capital Markets
Transfer Agent: Computershare Trust Company of Canada Inc.
Registrar: Computershare Trust Company of Canada Inc.
Exchanges: TSX
Symbol: TRP.PR.B
CUSIP: 87807B404

1.949% Cum. 5-Year Rate Reset First Pref., Series 5

DBRS Rating:	Pfd-3 high	Jul 25, 2023
Issued:	14,000,000 shs.	Jun 29, 2010	$25.000
O/S:	12,070,593 shs.	Dec 31, 2023
Dividend:	$0.48725 (Q)	Jan 30/Apr 30/Jul 30/Oct 30

Dividend Details: Reset on Jan 30, 2026. Dividend rate will be reset in every fifth year thereafter. The annual dividend rate will be equal to the sum of the five-year Government of Canada Bond Yield plus 1.54%. Previously, annual divd. rate was 0.565750 per sh until Jan 29, 2021.
Redemption: Redeem. on the following dates on min. 30 and max. 60 days' notice as follows:
Jan 30, 2016...$25.00   Jan 30, 2021...$25.00
Redeem. on Jan. 30 in every fifth year thereafter on min. 30 and max. 60 days' notice at $25.00 per share.
Exchange: Was exchange. on min. 30 days' notice into pfd 1st ser 6 as follows:
On Jan 30, 2016....................$25.00....................1   On Jan 30, 2021.....................$25.00.....................1
Exchange. on Jan. 30 in every fifth year thereafter.
Lead Underwriter(s): Scotia Capital Inc., RBC Capital Markets, BMO Capital Markets
Transfer Agent: Computershare Trust Company of Canada Inc.
Registrar: Computershare Trust Company of Canada Inc.
Exchanges: TSX
Symbol: TRP.PR.C
CUSIP: 87807B602

5.985% Cum. 5-Year Rate Reset First Pref., Series 7

DBRS Rating:	Pfd-3 high	Jul 25, 2023	
Issued:	24,000,000 shs.	Mar 4, 2013	$25.000
O/S:	24,000,000 shs.	Dec 31, 2023	
Dividend:	$1.49625 (Q)	Jan 30/Apr 30/Jul 30/Oct 30	

Dividend Details: Reset on Apr 30, 2029. Dividend rate will be reset in every fifth year thereafter. The annual dividend rate will be equal to the sum of the five-year Government of Canada Bond Yield plus 2.38%. Previously, annual divd. rate was 0.975750 per sh until Apr 29, 2024.
Redemption: Redeem. on the following dates on min. 30 and max. 60 days' notice as follows:
Apr 30, 2019...$25.00   Apr 30, 2024...$25.00
Redeem. on April 30 in every fifth year thereafter on min. 30 and max. 60 days' notice at $25.00 per share.
Exchange: Was exchange. on min. 30 days' notice into pfd 1st ser 8 as follows:
On Apr 30, 2019....................$25.00....................1   On Apr 30, 2024.....................$25.00.....................1
Exchange. on April 30 in every fifth year thereafter.
Lead Underwriter(s): Scotia Capital Inc., BMO Capital Markets, RBC Capital Markets
Transfer Agent: Computershare Trust Company of Canada Inc.
Registrar: Computershare Trust Company of Canada Inc.
Exchanges: TSX
Symbol: TRP.PR.D
CUSIP: 87807B800

3.762% Cum. 5-Year Rate Reset First Pref., Series 9

DBRS Rating:	Pfd-3 high	Jul 25, 2023	
Issued:	18,000,000 shs.	Jan 20, 2014	$25.000
O/S:	18,000,000 shs.	Dec 31, 2023	
Dividend:	$0.9405 (Q)	Jan 30/Apr 30/Jul 30/Oct 30	

Dividend Details: Reset on Oct 30, 2024. Dividend rate will be reset in every fifth year thereafter. The annual dividend rate will be equal to the sum of the five-year Government of Canada Bond Yield plus 2.35%. Previously, annual divd. rate was 1.062500 per sh until Oct 29, 2019.
Redemption: Redeem. on the following dates on min. 30 and max. 60 days' notice as follows:
Oct 30, 2019...$25.00   Oct 30, 2024...$25.00
Redeem. on Oct. 30 in every fifth year thereafter on min. 30 and max. 60 days' notice at $25.00 per share.
Exchange: Exchange. on min. 30 days' notice into pfd 1st ser 10 as follows:
On Oct 30, 2019....................$25.00....................1   On Oct 30, 2024.....................$25.00.....................1
Exchange. on Oct. 30 in every fifth year thereafter.
Lead Underwriter(s): Scotia Capital Inc., BMO Capital Markets, RBC Capital Markets
Transfer Agent: Computershare Trust Company of Canada Inc.
Registrar: Computershare Trust Company of Canada Inc.
Exchanges: TSX
Symbol: TRP.PR.E
CUSIP: 87807B875

Floating Rate Cum. Pref., Series 2

Issued:	12,501,577 shs.	Dec 31, 2014	$25.000
O/S:	7,422,816 shs.	Dec 31, 2023	
Dividend:	F.R. (Q)	Mar 31/Jun 30/Sep 30/Dec 31	

Dividend Details: Quarterly divd. rate is T-bill plus 1.92%.
Redemption: Redeem. on the following dates on min. 30 and max. 60 days' notice as follows:
Dec 31, 2019..$25.00   Dec 31, 2024...$25.00
Redeem. on Dec. 31 in every fifth year thereafter on min. 30 and max. 60 days' notice at $25.00 per share. After Dec. 31, 2014, other than an Exchange Date, redeem. at $25.50 per sh. plus accrued and unpaid dividends thereon to but excluding the date fixed for redemption.
Exchange: Exchange. on min. 30 days' notice into pfd 1st ser 1 sh as follows:
On Dec 31, 2019....................$25.00....................1   On Dec 31, 2024......................$25.00......................1
Exchange. on Dec. 31 in every fifth year thereafter.
Note: Issued upon exchange of an equal number of First Preferred Shares, Series 1.
Transfer Agent: Computershare Trust Company of Canada Inc.
Registrar: Computershare Trust Company of Canada Inc.
Exchanges: TSX
Symbol: TRP.PR.F
CUSIP: 87807B305

3.351% Cum. 5-Year Rate Reset First Pref., Series 11

DBRS Rating:	Pfd-3 high	Jul 25, 2023	
Issued:	10,000,000 shs.	Mar 2, 2015	$25.000
O/S:	10,000,000 shs.	Dec 31, 2023	
Dividend:	$0.83775 (Q)	Feb 28/May 31/Aug 31/Nov 30	

Dividend Details: Reset on Nov 30, 2025. Dividend rate will be reset in every fifth year thereafter. The annual dividend rate will be equal to the sum of the five-year Government of Canada Bond Yield plus 2.96%. Previously, annual divd. rate was 0.950000 per sh until Nov 29, 2020.
Redemption: Redeem. on the following dates on min. 30 and max. 60 days' notice as follows:
Nov 30, 2020..$25.00   Nov 30, 2025...$25.00
Redeem. on Nov. 30 in every fifth year thereafter on min. 30 and max. 60 days' notice at $25.00 per share.
Exchange: Exchange. on min. 30 days' notice into pfd 1st ser 12 as follows:
On Nov 30, 2020....................$25.00....................1   On Nov 30, 2025......................$25.00......................1
Exchange. on Nov. 30 in every fifth year thereafter.
Lead Underwriter(s): Scotia Capital Inc., RBC Capital Markets
Transfer Agent: Computershare Trust Company of Canada Inc.
Registrar: Computershare Trust Company of Canada Inc.
Exchanges: TSX
Symbol: TRP.PR.G
CUSIP: 87807B859

Floating Rate Cum. Pref., Series 4

Issued:	5,466,595 shs.	Jun 30, 2015	$25.000
O/S:	4,002,823 shs.	Dec 31, 2023	
Dividend:	F.R. (Q)	Mar 31/Jun 30/Sep 30/Dec 31	

Dividend Details: Quarterly divd. rate is T-bill plus 1.28%.
Redemption: Redeem. on the following dates on min. 30 and max. 60 days' notice as follows:
Jun 30, 2020..$25.00   Jun 30, 2025...$25.00
Redeem. on June 30 in every fifth year thereafter on min. 30 and max. 60 days' notice at $25.00 per share.
Exchange: Exchange. on min. 30 days' notice into pfd 1st ser 3 sh as follows:
On Jun 30, 2020....................$25.00....................1   On Jun 30, 2025......................$25.00......................1
Exchange. on June 30 in every fifth year thereafter.
Note: Issued upon exchange of an equal number of First Preferred Shares, Series 3.
Transfer Agent: Computershare Trust Company of Canada Inc.
Registrar: Computershare Trust Company of Canada Inc.
Exchanges: TSX
Symbol: TRP.PR.H
CUSIP: 87807B503

Floating Rate Cum. Pref., Series 6

Issued:	1,285,739 shs.	Feb 1, 2016	$25.000
O/S:	1,929,407 shs.	Dec 31, 2023	
Dividend:	F.R. (Q)	Jan 30/Apr 30/Jul 30/Oct 30	

Dividend Details: Quarterly divd. rate is T-bill plus 1.54%.
Redemption: Redeem. on the following dates on min. 30 and max. 60 days' notice as follows:
Jan 30, 2021...$25.00   Jan 30, 2026...$25.00
Redeem. on Jan. 30 in every fifth year thereafter on min. 30 and max. 60 days' notice at $25.00 per share. After Jan. 30, 2016, other than on an Exchange Date, redeem. at $25.50 per sh., plus declared and unpaid dividends thereon to the date of redemption.
Exchange: Exchange. on min. 30 days' notice into pfd 1st ser 5 sh as follows:
On Jan 30, 2021....................$25.00....................1   On Jan 30, 2026.....................$25.00....................1
Exchange. on Jan. 30 in every fifth year thereafter.
Note: Issued upon exchange of an equal number of First Preferred Shares, Series 5.
Transfer Agent: Computershare Trust Company of Canada Inc.
Registrar: Computershare Trust Company of Canada Inc.
Exchanges: TSX
Symbol: TRP.PR.I
CUSIP: 87807B701

Thomson Reuters Corporation

Floating Rate Cum. Pfce., Series II

DBRS Rating:	Pfd-3 high	Nov 7, 2023	
Issued:	6,000,000 shs.	Dec 30, 1986	$25.000
O/S:	6,000,000 shs.	Dec 31, 2023	
Dividend:	F.R. (Q)	Mar 31/Jun 30/Sep 30/Dec 31	

Dividend Details: Quarterly divd. rate is one quarter of 70% of prime times $25.00.
Redemption: Redeem. on and after the following dates as follows:
Dec 31, 1989...$25.50   Dec 31, 1990...$25.25
Dec 31, 1992...$25.00
Transfer Agent: Computershare Trust Company of Canada Inc.
Registrar: Computershare Trust Company of Canada Inc.
Exchanges: TSX
Symbol: TRI.PR.B
CUSIP: 884903303

The Toronto-Dominion Bank

3.662% Non-Cum. 5-Year Rate Reset Class A First Pref., Series 1

DBRS Rating:	Pfd-2 high	May 3, 2024	
Issued:	20,000,000 shs.	Jun 4, 2014	$25.000
O/S:	20,000,000 shs.	Jan 31, 2024	
Dividend:	$0.9155 (Q)	Jan 31/Apr 30/Jul 31/Oct 31	

Dividend Details: Reset on Oct 31, 2024. Dividend rate will be reset in every fifth year thereafter. The annual dividend rate will be equal to the sum of the five-year Government of Canada Bond Yield plus 2.24%. Previously, annual divd. rate was 0.975000 per sh until Oct 30, 2019.
Redemption: Redeem. on the following dates on min. 30 and max. 60 days' notice, conditional on the approval of the Superintendent of Financial Institutions, as follows:
Oct 31, 2019...$25.00   Oct 31, 2024...$25.00
Redeem. on Oct. 31 in every fifth year thereafter on min. 30 and max. 60 days' notice at $25.00 per share, conditional on approval of the Superintendent of Financial Institutions.
Convertible: Automatically convertible into common shares upon occurrence of a Non-Viability Contingent Capital (NVCC) trigger event as defined by OFSI.
Exchange: Exchange. on min. 30 days' notice into pfd 1st A ser 2 as follows:
On Oct 31, 2019....................$25.00....................1   On Oct 31, 2024.....................$25.00....................1
Exchange. on Oct. 31 in every fifth year thereafter. Exchange. after notice from the Bank given with approval from the Superintendent of Financial Institutions.

Lead Underwriter(s): TD Securities Inc.
Transfer Agent: TSX Trust Company
Registrar: TSX Trust Company
Exchanges: TSX
Symbol: TD.PF.A
CUSIP: 891145690

3.681% Non-Cum. 5-Year Rate Reset Class A First Pref., Series 3

DBRS Rating:	Pfd-2 high	May 3, 2024	
Issued:	20,000,000 shs.	Jul 31, 2014	$25.000
O/S:	20,000,000 shs.	Jan 31, 2024	
Dividend:	$0.92025 (Q)	Jan 31/Apr 30/Jul 31/Oct 31	

Dividend Details: Reset on Jul 31, 2024. Dividend rate will be reset in every fifth year thereafter. The annual dividend rate will be equal to the sum of the five-year Government of Canada Bond Yield plus 2.27%. Previously, annual divd. rate was 0.950000 per sh until Jul 30, 2019.

Redemption: Redeem. on the following dates on min. 30 and max. 60 days' notice, conditional on the approval of the Superintendent of Financial Institutions, as follows:
Jul 31, 2019...$25.00   Jul 31, 2024...$25.00
Redeem. on July 31 in every fifth year thereafter on min. 30 and max. 60 days' notice at $25.00 per share, conditional on approval of the Superintendent of Financial Institutions.

Convertible: Automatically convertible into common shares upon occurrence of a Non-Viability Contingent Capital (NVCC) trigger event as defined by OFSI.

Exchange: Exchange. on min. 30 days' notice into pfd 1st A ser 4 as follows:
On Jul 31, 2019.....................$25.00......................1   On Jul 31, 2024.......................$25.00........................1
Exchange. on July 31 in every fifth year thereafter. Exchange. after notice from the Bank given with approval from the Superintendent of Financial Institutions.

Lead Underwriter(s): TD Securities Inc.
Transfer Agent: TSX Trust Company
Registrar: TSX Trust Company
Exchanges: TSX
Symbol: TD.PF.B
CUSIP: 891145674

3.876% Non-Cum. 5-Year Rate Reset Class A First Pref., Series 5

DBRS Rating:	Pfd-2 high	May 3, 2024	
Issued:	20,000,000 shs.	Dec 16, 2014	$25.000
O/S:	20,000,000 shs.	Jan 31, 2024	
Dividend:	$0.969 (Q)	Jan 31/Apr 30/Jul 31/Oct 31	

Dividend Details: Reset on Jan 31, 2025. Dividend rate will be reset in every fifth year thereafter. The annual dividend rate will be equal to the sum of the five-year Government of Canada Bond Yield plus 2.25%. Previously, annual divd. rate was 0.937500 per sh until Jan 30, 2020.

Redemption: Redeem. on the following dates on min. 30 and max. 60 days' notice, conditional on the approval of the Superintendent of Financial Institutions, as follows:
Jan 31, 2020...$25.00   Jan 31, 2025...$25.00
Redeem. on Jan. 31 in every fifth year thereafter on min. 30 and max. 60 days' notice at $25.00 per share, conditional on approval of the Superintendent of Financial Institutions.

Convertible: Automatically convertible into common shares upon occurrence of a Non-Viability Contingent Capital (NVCC) trigger event as defined by OFSI.

Exchange: Exchange. on min. 30 days' notice into pfd 1st A ser 6 as follows:
On Jan 31, 2020.....................$25.00......................1   On Jan 31, 2025.......................$25.00........................1
Exchange. on Jan. 31 in every fifth year thereafter. Exchange. after notice from the Bank given with approval from the Superintendent of Financial Institutions.

Lead Underwriter(s): TD Securities Inc., RBC Capital Markets
Transfer Agent: TSX Trust Company
Registrar: TSX Trust Company
Exchanges: TSX
Symbol: TD.PF.C
CUSIP: 891145658

FP Equities — Preferreds & Derivatives 2024   105

3.201% Non-Cum. 5-Year Rate Reset Class A First Pref., Series 7

DBRS Rating: Pfd-2 high   May 3, 2024
  Issued: 14,000,000 shs.   Mar 10, 2015 $25.000
  O/S: 14,000,000 shs.   Jan 31, 2024
  Dividend: $0.80025 (Q)   Jan 31/Apr 30/Jul 31/Oct 31

Dividend Details: Reset on Jul 31, 2025. Dividend rate will be reset in every fifth year thereafter. The annual dividend rate will be equal to the sum of the five-year Government of Canada Bond Yield plus 2.79%. Previously, annual divd. rate was 0.900000 per sh until Jul 30, 2020.

Redemption: Redeem. on the following dates on min. 30 and max. 60 days' notice, conditional on the approval of the Superintendent of Financial Institutions, as follows:
Jul 31, 2020...$25.00   Jul 31, 2025..$25.00
Redeem. on July 31 in every fifth year thereafter on min. 30 and max. 60 days' notice at $25.00 per share, conditional on approval of the Superintendent of Financial Institutions.

Convertible: Automatically convertible into common shares upon occurrence of a Non-Viability Contingent Capital (NVCC) trigger event as defined by OFSI.

Exchange: Exchange. on min. 30 days' notice into pfd 1st ser 8 as follows:
On Jul 31, 2020.....................$25.00.....................1   On Jul 31, 2025.....................$25.00.....................1
Exchange. on July 31 in every fifth year thereafter. Exchange. after notice from the Bank given with approval from the Superintendent of Financial Institutions.

Lead Underwriter(s): TD Securities Inc., RBC Capital Markets, Scotia Capital Inc.
Transfer Agent: TSX Trust Company
Registrar: TSX Trust Company
Exchanges: TSX
Symbol: TD.PF.D
CUSIP: 891145633

3.242% Non-Cum. 5-Year Rate Reset Class A First Pref., Series 9

DBRS Rating: Pfd-2 high   May 3, 2024
  Issued: 8,000,000 shs.   Apr 24, 2015 $25.000
  O/S: 8,000,000 shs.   Jan 31, 2024
  Dividend: $0.8105 (Q)   Jan 31/Apr 30/Jul 31/Oct 31

Dividend Details: Reset on Oct 31, 2025. Dividend rate will be reset in every fifth year thereafter. The annual dividend rate will be equal to the sum of the five-year Government of Canada Bond Yield plus 2.87%. Previously, annual divd. rate was 0.925000 per sh until Oct 30, 2020.

Redemption: Redeem. on the following dates on min. 30 and max. 60 days' notice, conditional on the approval of the Superintendent of Financial Institutions, as follows:
Oct 31, 2020...$25.00   Oct 31, 2025...$25.00
Redeem. on Oct. 31 in every fifth year thereafter on min. 30 and max. 60 days' notice at $25.00 per share, conditional on approval of the Superintendent of Financial Institutions.

Convertible: Automatically convertible into common shares upon occurrence of a Non-Viability Contingent Capital (NVCC) trigger event as defined by OFSI.

Exchange: Exchange. on min. 30 days' notice into pfd 1st ser 10 as follows:
On Oct 31, 2020.....................$25.00.....................1   On Oct 31, 2025.....................$25.00.....................1
Exchange. on Oct. 31 in every fifth year thereafter. Exchange. after notice from the Bank given with approval from the Superintendent of Financial Institutions.

Lead Underwriter(s): TD Securities Inc., RBC Capital Markets, Scotia Capital Inc.
Transfer Agent: TSX Trust Company
Registrar: TSX Trust Company
Exchanges: TSX
Symbol: TD.PF.E
CUSIP: 891145617

6.301% Non-Cum. 5-Year Rate Reset Class A First Pref., Series 16

DBRS Rating: Pfd-2 high   May 3, 2024
  Issued: 14,000,000 shs.   Jul 14, 2017 $25.000
  O/S: 14,000,000 shs.   Jan 31, 2024
  Dividend: $1.57525 (Q)   Jan 31/Apr 30/Jul 31/Oct 31

Dividend Details: Reset on Oct 31, 2027. Dividend rate will be reset in every fifth year thereafter. The annual dividend rate will be equal to the sum of the five-year Government of Canada Bond Yield plus 3.01%. Previously, annual divd. rate was 1.125000 per sh until Oct 30, 2022.

Redemption: Redeem. on the following dates on min. 30 and max. 60 days' notice, conditional on the approval of the Superintendent of Financial Institutions, as follows:
Oct 31, 2022..$25.00   Oct 31, 2027..$25.00
Redeem. on Oct. 31 in every fifth year thereafter on min. 30 and max. 60 days' notice at $25.00 per share, conditional on approval of the Superintendent of Financial Institutions.

Convertible: Automatically convertible into common shares upon occurrence of a Non-Viability Contingent Capital (NVCC) trigger event as defined by OFSI.

Exchange: Exchange. on min. 30 days' notice into pfd 1st A ser 17 as follows:
On Oct 31, 2022....................$25.00....................1   On Oct 31, 2027....................$25.00....................1
Exchange. on Oct. 31 in every fifth year thereafter. Exchange. after notice from the Bank given with approval from the Superintendent of Financial Institutions.

Lead Underwriter(s): TD Securities Inc.
Transfer Agent: TSX Trust Company
Registrar: TSX Trust Company
Exchanges: TSX
Symbol: TD.PF.I
CUSIP: 891160640

5.747% Non-Cum. 5-Year Rate Reset Class A First Pref., Series 18

DBRS Rating:	Pfd-2 high	May 3, 2024
Issued:	14,000,000 shs.	Mar 14, 2018 $25.000
O/S:	14,000,000 shs.	Jan 31, 2024
Dividend:	$1.43675 (Q)	Jan 31/Apr 30/Jul 31/Oct 31

Dividend Details: Reset on Apr 30, 2028. Dividend rate will be reset in every fifth year thereafter. The annual dividend rate will be equal to the sum of the five-year Government of Canada Bond Yield plus 2.70%. Previously, annual divd. rate was 1.175000 per sh until Apr 29, 2023.

Redemption: Redeem. on the following dates on min. 30 and max. 60 days' notice, conditional on the approval of the Superintendent of Financial Institutions, as follows:
Apr 30, 2023..$25.00   Apr 30, 2028..$25.00
Redeem. on April 30 in every fifth year thereafter on min. 30 and max. 60 days' notice at $25.00 per share, conditional on approval of the Superintendent of Financial Institutions.

Convertible: Automatically convertible into common shares upon occurrence of a Non-Viability Contingent Capital (NVCC) trigger event as defined by OFSI.

Exchange: Exchange. on min. 30 days' notice into pfd 1st A ser 19 as follows:
On Apr 30, 2023....................$25.00....................1   On Apr 30, 2028....................$25.00....................1
Exchange. on April 30 in every fifth year thereafter. Exchange. after notice from the Bank given with approval from the Superintendent of Financial Institutions.

Lead Underwriter(s): TD Securities Inc.
Transfer Agent: TSX Trust Company
Registrar: TSX Trust Company
Exchanges: TSX
Symbol: TD.PF.J
CUSIP: 891160624

5.10% Non-Cum. 5-Year Rate Reset Class A Pref., Series 24

DBRS Rating:	Pfd-2 high	May 3, 2024
Issued:	18,000,000 shs.	Jun 4, 2019 $25.000
O/S:	18,000,000 shs.	Jan 31, 2024
Dividend:	$1.275 (Q)	Jan 31/Apr 30/Jul 31/Oct 31

Dividend Details: Reset on Jul 31, 2024. Dividend rate will be reset in every fifth year thereafter. The annual dividend rate will be equal to the sum of the five-year Government of Canada Bond Yield plus 3.56%.

Redemption: Redeem. on the following dates on min. 30 and max. 60 days' notice, conditional on the approval of the Superintendent of Financial Institutions, as follows:
Jul 31, 2024..$25.00   Jul 31, 2029..$25.00
Redeem. on July 31 in every fifth year thereafter on min. 30 and max. 60 days' notice at $25.00 per share, conditional on approval of the Superintendent of Financial Institutions.

Convertible: Automatically convertible into common shares upon occurrence of a Non-Viability Contingent Capital (NVCC) trigger event as defined by OFSI.

Exchange: Exchange. on min. 30 days' notice into pfd 1st A ser 25 as follows:
On Jul 31, 2024.....................$25.00.....................1   On Jul 31, 2029.....................$25.00.....................1
Exchange. on July 31 in every fifth year thereafter. Exchange. after notice from the Bank given with approval from the Superintendent of Financial Institutions.
Lead Underwriter(s): TD Securities Inc., RBC Capital Markets, Scotia Capital Inc.
Transfer Agent: TSX Trust Company
Registrar: TSX Trust Company
Exchanges: TSX
Symbol: TD.PF.M
CUSIP: 891160541

TransAlta Corporation

2.877% Cum. 5-Year Rate Reset First Pref., Series A

DBRS Rating:	Pfd-3 low	Dec 4, 2023	
Issued:	12,000,000 shs.	Dec 10, 2010	$25.000
O/S:	9,629,913 shs.	Dec 31, 2023	
Dividend:	$0.71925 (Q)	Mar 31/Jun 30/Sep 30/Dec 31	

Dividend Details: Reset on Mar 31, 2026. Dividend rate will be reset in every fifth year thereafter. The annual dividend rate will be equal to the sum of the five-year Government of Canada Bond Yield plus 2.03%. Previously, annual divd. rate was 0.677250 per sh until Mar 30, 2021.
Redemption: Redeem. on the following dates on min. 30 and max. 60 days' notice as follows:
Mar 31, 2016..$25.00   Mar 31, 2021..$25.00
Redeem. on March 31 in every fifth year thereafter on min. 30 and max. 60 days' notice at $25.00 per share.
Exchange: Was exchange. on min. 30 days' notice into pfd 1st ser B as follows:
On Mar 31, 2016....................$25.00.....................1   On Mar 31, 2021.....................$25.00.....................1
Exchange. on March 31 in every fifth year thereafter.
Lead Underwriter(s): CIBC World Markets Inc., RBC Capital Markets, Scotia Capital Inc.
Transfer Agent: Computershare Trust Company of Canada Inc.
Registrar: Computershare Trust Company of Canada Inc.
Exchanges: TSX
Symbol: TA.PR.D
CUSIP: 89346D768

5.854% Cum. 5-Year Rate Reset First Pref., Series C

DBRS Rating:	Pfd-3 low	Dec 4, 2023	
Issued:	11,000,000 shs.	Nov 30, 2011	$25.000
O/S:	9,955,701 shs.	Dec 31, 2023	
Dividend:	$1.4635 (Q)	Mar 31/Jun 30/Sep 30/Dec 31	

Dividend Details: Reset on Jun 30, 2027. Dividend rate will be reset in every fifth year thereafter. The annual dividend rate will be equal to the sum of the five-year Government of Canada Bond Yield plus 3.10%. Previously, annual divd. rate was 1.006750 per sh until Jun 29, 2022.
Redemption: Redeem. on the following dates on min. 30 and max. 60 days' notice as follows:
Jun 30, 2017..$25.00   Jun 30, 2022..$25.00
Redeem. on June 30 in every fifth year thereafter on min. 30 and max. 60 days' notice at $25.00 per share.
Exchange: Was exchange. into pfd 1st ser D as follows:
On Jun 30, 2017....................$25.00.....................1   On Jun 30, 2022.....................$25.00.....................1
Exchange. on June 30 in every fifth year thereafter.
Lead Underwriter(s): CIBC World Markets Inc., RBC Capital Markets, Scotia Capital Inc.
Transfer Agent: Computershare Trust Company of Canada Inc.
Registrar: Computershare Trust Company of Canada Inc.
Exchanges: TSX
Symbol: TA.PR.F
CUSIP: 89346D735

6.894% Cum. 5-Year Rate Reset First Pref., Series E

DBRS Rating:	Pfd-3 low	Dec 4, 2023	
Issued:	9,000,000 shs.	Aug 10, 2012	$25.000
O/S:	9,000,000 shs.	Dec 31, 2023	
Dividend:	$1.7235 (Q)	Mar 31/Jun 30/Sep 30/Dec 31	

Dividend Details: Reset on Sep 30, 2027. Dividend rate will be reset in every fifth year thereafter. The annual dividend rate will be equal to the sum of the five-year Government of Canada Bond Yield plus 3.65%. Previously, annual divd. rate was 1.298500 per sh until Sep 29, 2022.
Redemption: Redeem. on the following dates on min. 30 and max. 60 days' notice as follows:
Sep 30, 2017...$25.00   Sep 30, 2022..$25.00
Redeem. on Sept. 30 in every fifth year thereafter on min. 30 and max. 60 days' notice at $25.00 per share.
Exchange: Was exchange. on min. 30 days' notice into pfd 1st ser F as follows:
On Sep 30, 2017......................$25.00.....................1   On Sep 30, 2022........................$25.00........................1
Exchange. on Sept. 30 in every fifth year thereafter.
Lead Underwriter(s): CIBC World Markets Inc., RBC Capital Markets, Scotia Capital Inc.
Transfer Agent: Computershare Trust Company of Canada Inc.
Registrar: Computershare Trust Company of Canada Inc.
Exchanges: TSX
Symbol: TA.PR.H
CUSIP: 89346D727

4.988% Cum. 5-Year Rate Reset First Pref., Series G

DBRS Rating:	Pfd-3 low	Dec 4, 2023
Issued:	6,600,000 shs.	Aug 15, 2014 $25.000
O/S:	6,600,000 shs.	Dec 31, 2023
Dividend:	$1.247 (Q)	Mar 31/Jun 30/Sep 30/Dec 31

Dividend Details: Reset on Sep 30, 2024. Dividend rate will be reset in every fifth year thereafter. The annual dividend rate will be equal to the sum of the five-year Government of Canada Bond Yield plus 3.80%. Previously, annual divd. rate was 1.325000 per sh until Sep 29, 2019.
Redemption: Redeem. on the following dates on min. 30 and max. 60 days' notice as follows:
Sep 30, 2019...$25.00   Sep 30, 2024..$25.00
Redeem. on Sept. 30 in every fifth year thereafter on min. 30 and max. 60 days' notice at $25.00 per share.
Exchange: Exchange. on min. 30 days' notice into pfd 1st ser H as follows:
On Sep 30, 2019......................$25.00.....................1   On Sep 30, 2024........................$25.00........................1
Exchange. on Sept. 30 in every fifth year thereafter.
Lead Underwriter(s): RBC Capital Markets, CIBC World Markets Inc., Scotia Capital Inc.
Transfer Agent: Computershare Trust Company of Canada Inc.
Registrar: Computershare Trust Company of Canada Inc.
Exchanges: TSX
Symbol: TA.PR.J
CUSIP: 89346D677

Floating Rate Cum. First Pref., Series B

Issued:	1,824,620 shs.	Mar 31, 2016 $25.000
O/S:	2,370,087 shs.	Dec 31, 2023
Dividend:	F.R. (Q)	Mar 31/Jun 30/Sep 30/Dec 31

Dividend Details: Quarterly divd. rate is T-bill plus 2.03%.
Redemption: Redeem. on the following dates on min. 30 and max. 60 days' notice as follows:
Mar 31, 2021...$25.00   Mar 31, 2026..$25.00
Redeem. on March 31 in every fifth year thereafter on min. 30 and max. 60 days' notice at $25.00 per share. After March 31, 2021, other than on an Exchange Date, redeem. at $25.50 per sh., plus declared and unpaid dividends thereon to the date of redemption.
Exchange: Exchange. on min. 30 days' notice into pfd 1st ser A sh as follows:
On Mar 31, 2021......................$25.00.....................1   On Mar 31, 2026........................$25.00........................1
Exchange. on March 31 in every fifth year thereafter.
Note: Issued upon exchange of an equal number of First Preferred Shares, Series A.
Transfer Agent: Computershare Trust Company of Canada Inc.
Registrar: Computershare Trust Company of Canada Inc.
Exchanges: TSX
Symbol: TA.PR.E
CUSIP: 89346D750

Floating Rate Cum. First Pref., Series D

Issued:	1,044,299 shs.	Jun 30, 2022 $25.000
O/S:	1,044,299 shs.	Dec 31, 2023
Dividend:	F.R. (Q)	Mar 31/Jun 30/Sep 30/Dec 31

Dividend Details: Quarterly divd. rate is T-bill plus 3.1%.
Redemption: Redeem. on the following dates on min. 30 and max. 60 days' notice as follows:
Jun 30, 2022...$25.00   Jun 30, 2027..$25.00
Redeem. on June 30 in every fifth year thereafter on min. 30 and max. 60 days' notice at $25.00 per share. After June 30, 2022, other than on an Exchange Date, redeem. at $25.50 per sh., plus declared and unpaid dividends thereon to the date of redemption.
Exchange: Exchange. into pfd 1st ser C sh as follows:
On Jun 30, 2022....................$25.00....................1   On Jun 30, 2027....................$25.00....................1
Note: Issued upon exchange of an equal number of First Preferred Shares, Series C.
Transfer Agent: Computershare Trust Company of Canada Inc.
Registrar: Computershare Trust Company of Canada Inc.
Exchanges: TSX
Symbol: TA.PR.G
CUSIP: 89346D743

United Corporations Limited

5% Cum. Voting First Pref.

Issued:	52,237 shs.	May 6, 1933	$30.000
O/S:	52,237 shs.	Dec 31, 2023	
Dividend:	$1.50 (Q)	Feb 15/May 15/Aug 15/Nov 15	

Redemption: Redeem. on and after Jan 1, 1933 on min. 60 days' notice at $30.00 per sh.
Transfer Agent: Computershare Investor Services Inc.
Registrar: Computershare Investor Services Inc.
Exchanges: TSX
Symbol: UNC.PR.A
CUSIP: 910144104

$1.50 Cum. Second Pref., 1959 Series

Issued:	80,290 shs.	Jan 1, 1959	$30.000
O/S:	80,290 shs.	Dec 31, 2023	
Dividend:	$1.50 (Q)	Feb 15/May 15/Aug 15/Nov 15	

Redemption: Redeem. at any time on min. 30 days' notice at $30.00 per sh.
Transfer Agent: Computershare Investor Services Inc.
Registrar: Computershare Investor Services Inc.
Exchanges: TSX
Symbol: UNC.PR.B
CUSIP: 910144302

$1.50 Cum. Second Pref., 1963 Series

Issued:	119,710 shs.	Jan 1, 1963	$30.000
O/S:	119,710 shs.	Dec 31, 2023	
Dividend:	$1.50 (Q)	Feb 15/May 15/Aug 15/Nov 15	

Redemption: Redeem. at any time on min. 30 days' notice at $31.50 per sh.
Transfer Agent: Computershare Investor Services Inc.
Registrar: Computershare Investor Services Inc.
Exchanges: TSX
Symbol: UNC.PR.C
CUSIP: 910144401

VersaBank

6.772% Non-Cum. 5-Year Rate Reset Pref., Series 1

Issued:	1,461,460 shs.	Oct 30, 2014	$10.000
O/S:	1,461,460 shs.	Jan 31, 2024	
Dividend:	$0.6772 (Q)	Jan 31/Apr 30/Jul 31/Oct 31	

Dividend Details: Reset on Nov 1, 2024. Dividend rate will be reset in every fifth year thereafter. The annual dividend rate will be equal to the sum of the five-year Government of Canada Bond Yield plus 5.43%. Previously, annual divd. rate was 0.700000 per sh until Oct 31, 2019.

Redemption: Redeem. on the following dates on min. 30 and max. 60 days' notice, conditional on the approval of the Superintendent of Financial Institutions, as follows:
Oct 31, 2019...$10.00   Oct 31, 2024...$10.00
Redeem. on Oct. 31 in every fifth year thereafter on min. 30 and max. 60 days' notice at $10.00 per share, conditional on approval of the Superintendent of Financial Institutions.
Convertible: Automatically convertible into common shares upon occurrence of a Non-Viability Contingent Capital (NVCC) trigger event as defined by OFSI.
Exchange: Exchange. on min. 30 days' notice into pfd ser 2 as follows:
On Oct 31, 2019...................$10.00......................1   On Oct 31, 2024.....................$10.00.....................1
Exchange. on Oct. 31 in every fifth year thereafter.
Lead Underwriter(s): iA Private Wealth Inc.
Transfer Agent: Computershare Investor Services Inc.
Registrar: Computershare Investor Services Inc.
Exchanges: TSX
Symbol: VBNK.PR.A
CUSIP: 92512J205

George Weston Limited

5.8% Cum. Pref., Series I

DBRS Rating: Pfd-3   Jun 26, 2023
Issued: 9,400,000 shs.   Dec 4, 2001 $25.000
O/S: 9,400,000 shs.   Dec 31, 2023
Dividend: $1.45 (Q)   Mar 15/Jun 15/Sep 15/Dec 15

Redemption: Redeem. on and after the following dates on min. 30 and max. 60 days' notice as follows:
Dec 15, 2006...$26.00   Dec 15, 2007...$25.75
Dec 15, 2008...$25.50   Dec 15, 2009...$25.25
Dec 15, 2010...$25.00
Exchange: Exchange. on min. 45 days' notice into 1 new pfd per pref. sh, being an exchange price per new pfd of $25.00.
Lead Underwriter(s): RBC Capital Markets
Transfer Agent: Computershare Investor Services Inc.
Registrar: Computershare Investor Services Inc.
Exchanges: TSX
Symbol: WN.PR.A
CUSIP: 961148889

5.2% Cum. Pref., Series III

DBRS Rating: Pfd-3   Jun 26, 2023
Issued: 8,000,000 shs.   Apr 18, 2005 $25.000
O/S: 8,000,000 shs.   Dec 31, 2023
Dividend: $1.30 (Q)   Jan 1/Apr 1/Jul 1/Oct 1

Redemption: Redeem. on and after the following dates on min. 30 and max. 60 days' notice as follows:
Jul 1, 2010...$26.00   Jul 1, 2011...$25.75
Jul 1, 2012...$25.50   Jul 1, 2013...$25.25
Jul 1, 2014...$25.00
Exchange: Exchange. on min. 45 days' notice into 1 new pfd per pref. sh, being an exchange price per new pfd of $25.00.
Lead Underwriter(s): RBC Capital Markets
Transfer Agent: Computershare Investor Services Inc.
Registrar: Computershare Investor Services Inc.
Exchanges: TSX
Symbol: WN.PR.C
CUSIP: 961148863

5.2% Cum. Pref., Series IV

DBRS Rating: Pfd-3   Jun 26, 2023
Issued: 8,000,000 shs.   Aug 2, 2005 $25.000
O/S: 8,000,000 shs.   Dec 31, 2023
Dividend: $1.30 (Q)   Jan 1/Apr 1/Jul 1/Oct 1

Redemption: Redeem. on and after the following dates on min. 30 and max. 60 days' notice as follows:
Oct 1, 2010..$26.00   Oct 1, 2011...$25.75
Oct 1, 2012..$25.50   Oct 1, 2013...$25.25
Oct 1, 2014..$25.00

Exchange: Exchange. on min. 45 days' notice into 1 new pfd per pref. sh, being an exchange price per new pfd of $25.00.
Lead Underwriter(s): RBC Capital Markets
Transfer Agent: Computershare Investor Services Inc.
Registrar: Computershare Investor Services Inc.
Exchanges: TSX
Symbol: WN.PR.D
CUSIP: 961148855

4.75% Cum. Pref., Series V

DBRS Rating:	Pfd-3	Jun 26, 2023
Issued:	8,000,000 shs.	Apr 19, 2006 $25.000
O/S:	8,000,000 shs.	Dec 31, 2023
Dividend:	$1.1875 (Q)	Jan 1/Apr 1/Jul 1/Oct 1

Redemption: Redeem. on and after the following dates on min. 30 and max. 60 days' notice as follows:
Jul 1, 2011...$26.00   Jul 1, 2012..$25.75
Jul 1, 2013...$25.50   Jul 1, 2014..$25.25
Jul 1, 2015...$25.00

Exchange: Exchange. on min. 45 days' notice into 1 new pfd per pref. sh, being an exchange price per new pfd of $25.00.
Lead Underwriter(s): RBC Capital Markets
Transfer Agent: Computershare Investor Services Inc.
Registrar: Computershare Investor Services Inc.
Exchanges: TSX
Symbol: WN.PR.E
CUSIP: 961148848

Pending Redemptions

At press time, this list of securities had been called for redemption at the dates shown in the table.

Call Date	Issuer	Issue	Call Price
May 24, 2024	Royal Bank of Canada	pfd 1st ser AZ	$25.00
May 27, 2024	Bank of Montreal	pfd B ser 27	$25.00
May 27, 2024	Bank of Montreal	pfd B ser 46	$25.00

Convertible Preferred Shares

Issuer	Description	Conversion Basis (per $1,000)	Conversion Price (per Share)	Exchanges	Symbol
Brookfield Corp	pfd A ser 17	See write-up		T	BN.PR.M

Retractable Preferred Shares and Structured Products

Issuer	Description	Retraction Date	Retraction Price (per Share)	Exchanges	Symbol
Brookfield Property Split	pfd A ser 1	Anytime	US$23.75	T	BPS.PR.U
Brookfield Property Split	pfd A ser 2	Anytime	$23.75	T	BPS.PR.A
Brookfield Property Split	pfd A ser 3	Anytime	$23.75	T	BPS.PR.B
Brookfield Property Split	pfd A ser 4	Anytime	$23.75	T	BPS.PR.C
Canoe EIT Income Fund	pfd ser 1	Anytime	$25.00	T	EIT.PR.A
Canoe EIT Income Fund	pfd ser 2	Mar 15, 2025	$25.00	T	EIT.PR.B

Exchangeable Preferred Shares

Issuer	Description	Exchange Basis (per Preferred share)	Exchange Price (per Share)	Exchanges	Symbol
Aimia Inc	pfd ser 4	1 pfd ser 3 on Mar 31, 2029	$25.00	T	AIM.PR.D
AltaGas Ltd	pfd ser B	1 pfd ser A on Sep 30, 2025	$25.00	T	ALA.PR.B
AltaGas Ltd	pfd ser G	1 pfd ser H on Sep 30, 2024	$25.00	T	ALA.PR.G
AltaGas Ltd	pfd ser H	1 pfd ser G on Sep 30, 2024	$25.00	T	ALA.PR.H
Artis REIT	pfd ser I	1 pfd ser J on Apr 30, 2028	$25.00	T	AX.PR.I
BCE Inc	pfd 1st ser AL	1 pfd 1st ser AK on Dec 31, 2026	$25.00	T	BCE.PR.L
BCE Inc	pfd 1st ser AN	1 pfd 1st ser AM on Mar 31, 2026	$25.00	T	BCE.PR.N
BCE Inc	pfd 1st ser T	1 pfd 1st ser S on Nov 01, 2025	$25.00	T	BCE.PR.T
BIP Investment Corp	pfd ser 1	1 pfd ser 2 on Mar 31, 2029	$25.00	T	BIK.PR.A
Bank of Montreal	pfd B ser 27	1 pfd B ser 28 on May 25, 2024	$25.00	T	BMO.PR.S
Bank of Montreal	pfd B ser 29	1 pfd B ser 30 on Aug 25, 2024	$25.00	T	BMO.PR.T
Bank of Montreal	pfd B ser 31	1 pfd B ser 32 on Nov 25, 2024	$25.00	T	BMO.PR.W
Bank of Montreal	pfd B ser 33	1 pfd B ser 34 on Aug 25, 2025	$25.00	T	BMO.PR.Y
Bank of Montreal	pfd B ser 44	1 pfd B ser 45 on Nov 25, 2028	$25.00	T	BMO.PR.E
Bank of Montreal	pfd B ser 46	1 pfd B ser 47 on May 25, 2024	$25.00	T	BMO.PR.F
Bombardier Inc	pfd ser 2	1 pfd ser 3 on Aug 01, 2027	$25.00	T	BBD.PR.B
Bombardier Inc	pfd ser 3	1 pfd ser 2 on Aug 01, 2027	$25.00	T	BBD.PR.D
Bombardier Inc	pfd ser 4	1 new pfd	$25.00	T	BBD.PR.C
Brookfield Corp	pfd A ser 17	1 new pfd	$25.00	T	BN.PR.M
Brookfield Corp	pfd A ser 18	1 new pfd	$25.00	T	BN.PR.N
Brookfield Corp	pfd A ser 38	1 pfd A ser 39 on Mar 31, 2025	$25.00	T	BN.PF.E
Brookfield Corp	pfd A ser 40	1 pfd A ser 41 on Sep 30, 2024	$25.00	T	BN.PF.F
Brookfield Corp	pfd A ser 42	1 pfd A ser 43 on Jun 30, 2025	$25.00	T	BN.PF.G
Brookfield Corp	pfd A ser 44	1 pfd A ser 45 on Dec 31, 2025	$25.00	T	BN.PF.H
Brookfield Corp	pfd A ser 46	1 pfd A ser 47 on Mar 31, 2027	$25.00	T	BN.PF.I
Brookfield Corp	pfd A ser 48	1 pfd A ser 49 on Dec 31, 2027	$25.00	T	BN.PF.J
Brookfield Infrastructure	pfd A ser 1	1 pfd A ser 2 on Jun 30, 2025	$25.00	T	BIP.PR.A

Exchangeable Preferred Shares

Issuer	Description	Exchange Basis (per Preferred share)	Exchange Price (per Share)	Exchanges	Symbol
Brookfield Infrastructure	pfd A ser 11	1 pfd A ser 12 on Dec 31, 2028	$25.00	T	BIP.PR.F
Brookfield Infrastructure	pfd A ser 3	1 pfd A ser 4 on Dec 31, 2025	$25.00	T	BIP.PR.B
Brookfield Infrastructure	pfd A ser 9	1 pfd A ser 10 on Mar 31, 2028	$25.00	T	BIP.PR.E
Brookfield Office Pptys	pfd AAA ser AA	1 pfd AAA ser BB on Dec 31, 2024	$25.00	T	BPO.PR.A
Brookfield Office Pptys	pfd AAA ser CC	1 pfd AAA ser DD on Jun 30, 2026	$25.00	T	BPO.PR.C
Brookfield Office Pptys	pfd AAA ser EE	1 pfd AAA ser FF on Mar 31, 2027	$25.00	T	BPO.PR.E
Brookfield Office Pptys	pfd AAA ser GG	1 pfd AAA ser HH on Jun 30, 2027	$25.00	T	BPO.PR.G
Brookfield Office Pptys	pfd AAA ser II	1 pfd AAA ser JJ on Dec 31, 2027	$25.00	T	BPO.PR.I
Brookfield Renew Pwr Pfd	pfd A ser 2	1 pfd A ser 1 on Apr 30, 2025	$25.00	T	BRF.PR.B
Brookfield Renew Pwr Pfd	pfd A ser 3	1 pfd A ser 4 on Jul 31, 2024	$25.00	T	BRF.PR.C
Canadian Imp Bank of Comm	pfd A ser 39	1 pfd A ser 40 on Jul 31, 2024	$25.00	T	CM.PR.O
Canadian Imp Bank of Comm	pfd A ser 41	1 pfd A ser 42 on Jan 31, 2025	$25.00	T	CM.PR.P
Canadian Imp Bank of Comm	pfd A ser 43	1 pfd A ser 44 on Jul 31, 2025	$25.00	T	CM.PR.Q
Canadian Imp Bank of Comm	pfd A ser 47	1 pfd A ser 48 on Jan 31, 2028	$25.00	T	CM.PR.S
Canadian Imp Bank of Comm	pfd A ser 51	1 pfd A ser 52 on Jul 31, 2024	$25.00	T	CM.PR.Y
Canadian Utilities Ltd	pfd 2nd ser FF	1 pfd 2nd ser GG on Dec 01, 2025	$25.00	T	CU.PR.I
Canadian Western Bank	pfd ser 5	1 pfd ser 6 on Apr 30, 2029	$25.00	T	CWB.PR.B
Canadian Western Bank	pfd ser 9	1 pfd ser 10 on Apr 30, 2029	$25.00	T	CWB.PR.D
Capital Power Corp	pfd ser 11	1 pfd ser 12 on Jun 30, 2024	$25.00	T	CPX.PR.K
Cenovus Energy Inc	pfd 1st ser 1	1 pfd 1st ser 2 on Mar 31, 2026	$25.00	T	CVE.PR.A
Cenovus Energy Inc	pfd 1st ser 2	1 pfd 1st ser 1 on Mar 31, 2026	$25.00	T	CVE.PR.B
Cenovus Energy Inc	pfd 1st ser 3	1 pfd 1st ser 4 on Dec 31, 2024	$25.00	T	CVE.PR.C
Cenovus Energy Inc	pfd 1st ser 5	1 pfd 1st ser 6 on Mar 31, 2025	$25.00	T	CVE.PR.E
Cenovus Energy Inc	pfd 1st ser 7	1 pfd 1st ser 8 on Jun 30, 2025	$25.00	T	CVE.PR.G
Co-operators Gen Ins Co	pfd E ser C	1 new pfd	$25.00	T	CCS.PR.C
Dundee Corp	pfce 1st ser 3	1 pfce 1st ser 2 on Sep 30, 2024	$25.00	T	DC.PR.D
ECN Capital Corp	pfd ser C	1 pfd ser D on Jun 30, 2027	$25.00	T	ECN.PR.C

Exchangeable Preferred Shares

Issuer	Description	Exchange Basis (per Preferred share)	Exchange Price (per Share)	Exchanges	Symbol
EQB Inc	pfd ser 3	1 pfd ser 4 on Sep 30, 2024	$25.00	T	EQB.PR.C
Element Fleet Mgmt Corp	pfd ser C	1 pfd ser D on Jun 30, 2024	$25.00	T	EFN.PR.C
Element Fleet Mgmt Corp	pfd ser E	1 pfd ser F on Sep 30, 2024	$25.00	T	EFN.PR.E
Emera Inc	pfd 1st ser B	1 pfd 1st ser A on Aug 15, 2025	$25.00	T	EMA.PR.B
Emera Inc	pfd 1st ser F	1 pfd ist ser G on Feb 15, 2025	$25.00	T	EMA.PR.F
Emera Inc	pfd 1st ser H	1 pfd 1st ser I on Aug 15, 2028	$25.00	T	EMA.PR.H
Emera Inc	pfd 1st ser J	1 Pfd 1st ser K on May 15, 2026	$25.00	T	EMA.PR.J
Empire Life Insurance Co	pfd ser 3	1 pfd ser 4 on Jan 17, 2028			
Enbridge Inc	pfd ser 11	1 pfd ser 12 on Mar 01, 2025	$25.00	T	ENB.PF.C
Enbridge Inc	pfd ser 13	1 pfd ser 14 on Jun 01, 2025	$25.00	T	ENB.PF.E
Enbridge Inc	pfd ser 15	1 pfd ser 16 on Sep 01, 2025	$25.00	T	ENB.PF.G
Enbridge Inc	pfd ser 19	1 pfd ser 20 on Mar 01, 2028	$25.00	T	ENB.PF.K
Enbridge Inc	pfd ser 3	1 pfd ser 4 on Sep 01, 2024	$25.00	T	ENB.PR.Y
Enbridge Inc	pfd ser 9	1 pfd ser 10 on Dec 01, 2024	$25.00	T	ENB.PF.A
Enbridge Inc	pfd ser G	1 pfd ser F on Jun 01, 2028	$25.00	T	ENB.PR.G
Enbridge Inc	pfd ser I	1 pfd ser H on Sep 01, 2028	$25.00	T	ENB.PR.I
Enbridge Inc	pfd ser R	1 pfd ser S on Jun 01, 2024	$25.00	T	ENB.PR.T
Fairfax Finl Holdings Ltd	pfd ser D	1 pfd ser C on Dec 31, 2024	$25.00	T	FFH.PR.D
Fairfax Finl Holdings Ltd	pfd ser F	1 pfd ser E on Mar 31, 2025	$25.00	T	FFH.PR.F
Fairfax Finl Holdings Ltd	pfd ser H	1 pfd ser G on Sep 30, 2025	$25.00	T	FFH.PR.H
Fairfax Finl Holdings Ltd	pfd ser J	1 pfd ser I on Dec 31, 2025	$25.00	T	FFH.PR.J
Fairfax Finl Holdings Ltd	pfd ser M	1 pfd ser N on Mar 31, 2025	$25.00	T	FFH.PR.M
First National Finl Corp	pfd A ser 2	1 pfd A ser 1 on Mar 31, 2026	$25.00	T	FN.PR.B
Fortis Inc	pfd 1st ser I	1 pfd 1st ser H on Jun 01, 2025	$25.00	T	FTS.PR.I
Fortis Inc	pfd 1st ser M	1 pfd 1st ser N on Dec 01, 2024	$25.00	T	FTS.PR.M
Indl Alliance Ins & Finl	pfd A ser B	1 new pfd	$25.00	T	IAF.PR.B

Exchangeable Preferred Shares

Issuer	Description	Exchange Basis (per Preferred share)	Exchange Price (per Share)	Exchanges	Symbol
Intact Financial Corp	pfd A ser 7	1 pfd A ser 8 on Jun 30, 2028	$25.00	T	IFC.PR.G
Laurentian Bank of Canada	pfd A ser 13	1 pfd A ser 14 on Jun 15, 2024	$25.00	T	LB.PR.H
Manulife Financial Corp	pfd 1 ser 15	1 pfd 1 ser 16 on Jun 19, 2024	$25.00	T	MFC.PR.L
Manulife Financial Corp	pfd 1 ser 17	1 pfd 1 ser 18 on Dec 19, 2024	$25.00	T	MFC.PR.M
Manulife Financial Corp	pfd 1 ser 19	1 pfd 1 ser 20 on Mar 19, 2025	$25.00	T	MFC.PR.N
Manulife Financial Corp	pfd A ser 2	1 new pfd	$25.00	T	MFC.PR.B
Manulife Financial Corp	pfd 1 ser 25	1 pfd 1 ser 26 on Jun 19, 2028	$25.00	T	MFC.PR.Q
Manulife Financial Corp	pfd A ser 3	1 new pfd	$25.00	T	MFC.PR.C
Manulife Financial Corp	pfd 1 ser 4	1 pfd 1 ser 3 on Jun 19, 2026	$25.00	T	MFC.PR.P
National Bank of Canada	pfd 1st ser 30	1 pfd 1st ser 31 on May 15, 2024	$25.00	T	NA.PR.S
National Bank of Canada	pfd 1st ser 32	1 pfd 1st ser 33 on Feb 15, 2025	$25.00	T	NA.PR.W
National Bank of Canada	pfd 1st ser 38	1 pfd 1st ser 39 on Nov 15, 2027	$25.00	T	NA.PR.C
National Bank of Canada	pfd 1st ser 40	1 pfd 1st ser 41 on May 15, 2028	$25.00	T	NA.PR.E
National Bank of Canada	pfd 1st ser 42	1 pfd 1st ser 43 on Nov 15, 2028	$25.00	T	NA.PR.G
Northland Power Inc	pfd ser 2	1 pfd ser 1 on Sep 30, 2025	$25.00	T	NPI.PR.B
Pembina Pipeline Corp	pfd A ser 15	1 pfd A ser 16 on Sep 30, 2027	$25.00	T	PPL.PR.O
Pembina Pipeline Corp	pfd A ser 19	1 pfd A ser 20 on Jun 30, 2025	$25.00	T	PPL.PR.S
Pembina Pipeline Corp	pfd A ser 21	1 pfd A ser 22 on Mar 01, 2028	$25.00	T	PPL.PF.A
Pembina Pipeline Corp	pfd A ser 22	1 pfd A ser 21 on Mar 01, 2028	$25.00	T	PPL.PF.B
Pembina Pipeline Corp	pfd A ser 25	1 pfd A ser 26 on Feb 15, 2028	$25.00	T	PPL.PF.E
Pembina Pipeline Corp	pfd A ser 5	1 pfd A ser 6 on Jun 01, 2024	$25.00	T	PPL.PR.E
Pembina Pipeline Corp	pfd A ser 7	1 pfd A ser 8 on Dec 01, 2024	$25.00	T	PPL.PR.G
Pembina Pipeline Corp	pfd A ser 9	1 pfd A ser 10 on Dec 01, 2025	$25.00	T	PPL.PR.I
Power Financial Corp	pfd 1st ser Q	1 pfd 1st ser P on Jan 31, 2026	$25.00	T	PWF.PR.Q
Royal Bank of Canada	pfd 1st ser AZ	1 pfd 1st ser BA on May 24, 2024	$25.00	T	RY.PR.Z
Royal Bank of Canada	pfd 1st ser BB	1 pfd 1st ser BC on Aug 24, 2024	$25.00	T	RY.PR.H
Royal Bank of Canada	pfd 1st ser BD	1 pfd 1st ser BE on May 24, 2025	$25.00	T	RY.PR.J

Exchangeable Preferred Shares

Issuer	Description	Exchange Basis (per Preferred share)	Exchange Price (per Share)	Exchanges	Symbol
Royal Bank of Canada	pfd 1st ser BF	1 pfd 1st ser BG on Nov 24, 2025	$25.00	T	RY.PR.M
Royal Bank of Canada	pfd 1st ser BH	1 new pfd sh	$25.00	T	RY.PR.N
Royal Bank of Canada	pfd 1st ser BI	1 new pfd sh	$25.00	T	RY.PR.O
Royal Bank of Canada	pfd 1st ser BO	1 pfd 1st ser BP on Feb 24, 2029	$25.00	T	RY.PR.S
Sun Life Financial Inc	pfd A ser 10R	1 pfd A ser 11QR on Sep 30, 2026	$25.00	T	SLF.PR.H
Sun Life Financial Inc	pfd A ser 11QR	1 pfd A ser 10R on Sep 30, 2026	$25.00	T	SLF.PR.K
Sun Life Financial Inc	pfd A ser 3	1 new pfd	$25.00	T	SLF.PR.C
Sun Life Financial Inc	pfd A ser 4	1 new pfd	$25.00	T	SLF.PR.D
Sun Life Financial Inc	pfd A ser 5	1 new pfd	$25.00	T	SLF.PR.E
Sun Life Financial Inc	pfd A ser 8R	1 pfd A ser 9QR on Jun 30, 2025	$25.00	T	SLF.PR.G
Sun Life Financial Inc	pfd A ser 9QR	1 pfd A ser 8R on Jun 30, 2025	$25.00	T	SLF.PR.J
TC Energy Corp	pfd 1st ser 11	1 pfd 1st ser 12 on Nov 30, 2025	$25.00	T	TRP.PR.G
TC Energy Corp	pfd 1st ser 2	1 pfd 1st ser 1 on Dec 31, 2024	$25.00	T	TRP.PR.F
TC Energy Corp	pfd 1st ser 4	1 pfd 1st ser 3 on Jun 30, 2025	$25.00	T	TRP.PR.H
TC Energy Corp	pfd 1st ser 6	1 pfd 1st ser 5 on Jan 30, 2026	$25.00	T	TRP.PR.I
TC Energy Corp	pfd 1st ser 9	1 pfd 1st ser 10 on Oct 30, 2024	$25.00	T	TRP.PR.E
TD Bank	pfd 1st A ser 1	1 pfd 1st A ser 2 on Oct 31, 2024	$25.00	T	TD.PF.A
TD Bank	pfd 1st A ser 16	1 pfd 1st A ser 17 on Oct 31, 2027	$25.00	T	TD.PF.I
TD Bank	pfd 1st A ser 18	1 pfd 1st A ser 19 on Apr 30, 2028	$25.00	T	TD.PF.J
TD Bank	pfd 1st A ser 24	1 pfd 1st A ser 25 on Jul 31, 2024	$25.00	T	TD.PF.M
TD Bank	pfd 1st A ser 3	1 pfd 1st A ser 4 on Jul 31, 2024	$25.00	T	TD.PF.B
TD Bank	pfd 1st A ser 5	1 pfd 1st A ser 6 on Jan 31, 2025	$25.00	T	TD.PF.C
TD Bank	pfd 1st A ser 7	1 pfd 1st ser 8 on Jul 31, 2025	$25.00	T	TD.PF.D
TD Bank	pfd 1st A ser 9	1 pfd 1st ser 10 on Oct 31, 2025	$25.00	T	TD.PF.E
TransAlta Corp	pfd 1st ser B	1 pfd 1st ser A on Mar 31, 2026	$25.00	T	TA.PR.E
TransAlta Corp	pfd 1st ser D	1 pfd 1st ser C on Jun 30, 2027	$25.00	T	TA.PR.G

Exchangeable Preferred Shares

Issuer	Description	Exchange Basis (per Preferred share)	Exchange Price (per Share)	Exchanges	Symbol
TransAlta Corp	pfd 1st ser G	1 pfd 1st ser H on Sep 30, 2024	$25.00	T	TA.PR.J
VersaBank	pfd ser 1	1 pfd ser 2 on Oct 31, 2024	$10.00	T	VBNK.PR.A
George Weston Ltd	pfd ser I	1 new pfd	$25.00	T	WN.PR.A
George Weston Ltd	pfd ser III	1 new pfd	$25.00	T	WN.PR.C
George Weston Ltd	pfd ser IV	1 new pfd	$25.00	T	WN.PR.D
George Weston Ltd	pfd ser V	1 new pfd	$25.00	T	WN.PR.E

DBRS Rating Scale: Preferred Shares

DOMINION BOND RATING SERVICE

The following tables itemize the latest ratings as provided by Dominion Bond Rating Service Limited.

The DBRS preferred share rating scale is used in the Canadian securities market and is meant to give an indication of the risk that a borrower will not fulfill its full obligations in a timely manner, with respect to both dividend and principal commitments. Every DBRS rating is based on quantitative and qualitative considerations relevant to the borrowing entity. Each rating category is denoted by the subcategories "high" and "low". The absence of either a "high" or "low" designation indicates the rating is in the middle of the category.

The Preferred Share Rating Scale is as follows:

Pfd-1 Preferred shares rated Pfd-1 are of superior credit quality, and are supported by entities with strong earnings and balance sheet characteristics. Pfd-1 securities generally correspond with companies whose senior bonds are rated in the AAA or AA categories. As is the case with all rating categories, the relationship between senior debt ratings and preferred share ratings should be understood as one where the senior debt rating effectively sets a ceiling for the preferred shares issued by the entity. However, there are cases where the preferred share rating could be lower than the normal relationship with the issuer's senior debt rating.

Pfd-2 Preferred shares rated Pfd-2 are of satisfactory credit quality. Protection of dividends and principal is still substantial, but earnings, the balance sheet, and coverage ratios are not as strong as Pfd-1 rated companies. Generally, Pfd-2 ratings correspond with companies whose senior bonds are rated in the A category.

Pfd-3 Preferred shares rated Pfd-3 are of adequate credit quality. While protection of dividends and principal is still considered acceptable, the issuing entity is more susceptible to adverse changes in financial and economic conditions, and there may be other adverse conditions present which detract from debt protection. Pfd-3 ratings generally correspond with companies whose senior bonds are rated in the higher end of the BBB category.

Pfd-4 Preferred shares rated Pfd-4 are speculative, where the degree of protection afforded to dividends and principal is uncertain, particularly during periods of economic adversity. Companies with preferred shares rated Pfd-4 generally coincide with entities that have senior bond ratings ranging from the lower end of the BBB category through the BB category.

Pfd-5 Preferred shares rated Pfd-5 are highly speculative and the ability of the entity to maintain timely dividend and principal payments in the future is highly uncertain. Entities with a Pfd-5 rating generally have senior bond ratings of B or lower. Preferred shares rated Pfd-5 often have characteristics that, if not remedied, may lead to default.

D A security rated D implies the issuer has either not met a scheduled dividend or principal payment or the issuer has made it clear it will miss such a payment in the near future. In some cases, DBRS may not assign a D rating under a bankruptcy announcement scenario, as allowances for grace periods may exist in the underlying legal documentation. Once assigned, the D rating will continue as long as the missed payment continues to be in arrears, and until such time as the rating is suspended, discontinued, or reinstated by DBRS.

DBRS Preferred Share/Securities Ratings, by Issuer

Issuer	Description	DBRS Rating	Last Update
Algonquin Power & Utils	Preferred Shares	Pfd-3	Feb 6, 2024
Artis REIT	Preferred Trust Units	Pfd-3 low	Feb 2, 2024
BCE Inc	First Preferred Shares	Pfd-3	Mar 28, 2024
Bank of Montreal	NVCC Preferred Shares	Pfd-2	Jun 2, 2023
Big Pharma Split Corp	Preferred Shares	Pfd-3 high	Sep 7, 2023
Brompton Lifeco Split	5.25% Preferred Shares	Pfd-3 low	Mar 28, 2024
Brompton Split Banc Corp	5.25% Preferred Shares	Pfd-3	Aug 8, 2023
Brookfield Corp	Cum. & Non-Cum. Preference Shares, Class A and Preferred Securities	Pfd-2	Nov 22, 2023
Brookfield Invts Corp	Senior Preferred Shares	Pfd-2	Nov 22, 2023
Brookfield Office Pptys	Preferred Shares, Class AAA	Pfd-3 low	May 15, 2023
Brookfield Renew Pwr Pfd	Preferred Shares, Series 1	Pfd-3 high	May 26, 2023
CU Inc	Preferred Shares	Pfd-2 high	Jul 25, 2023
Canadian Banc Corp	Floating Rate Preferred Shares	Pfd-3 low	Nov 16, 2023
Canadian Imp Bank of Comm	NVCC Preferred Shares	Pfd-2	Jun 1, 2023
Cdn Large Capital Leaders	Preferred Shares	Pfd-3 high	Dec 20, 2023
Canadian Utilities Ltd	Second Preferred Shares	Pfd-2	Aug 29, 2023
Canadian Western Bank	NVCC Preferred Shares	Pfd-3	Nov 14, 2023
Canoe EIT Income Fund	Preferred Units	Pfd-2 high	Jan 31, 2024
Capital Power Corp	Preferred Shares	Pfd-3 low	Apr 5, 2024
Cenovus Energy Inc	Preferred Shares	Pfd-3 high	Dec 18, 2023
Co-operators Gen Ins Co	Non-Cum. Preferred Shares, Class E	Pfd-2	Oct 26, 2023
Dividend 15 Split Corp	Preferred Shares	Pfd-3	Apr 11, 2024
Dividend 15 Split Corp II	Preferred Shares	Pfd-3 low	Jun 28, 2023
Divid Growth Split Corp	5.25% Preferred Shares	Pfd-3 low	Jun 21, 2023
E Split Corp	Preferred Shares	Pfd-3 high	Jun 6, 2023
ECN Capital Corp	Preferred	Pfd-4 high	Aug 24, 2023
Element Fleet Mgmt Corp	Perpetual Preferred Shares	Pfd-3 high	Sep 27, 2023
Empire Life Insurance Co	Preferred Shares	Pfd-2	May 25, 2023

DBRS Preferred Share/Securities Ratings, by Issuer

Issuer	Description	DBRS Rating	Last Update
Enbridge Inc	Preferred Shares	Pfd-3 high	Sep 6, 2023
Fairfax Finl Holdings Ltd	Preferred Shares	Pfd-2 low	Dec 1, 2023
Financial 15 Split Corp	Preferred Shares	Pfd-4	Feb 15, 2024
First National Finl Corp	Class A Preferred Shares	Pfd-3	Mar 12, 2024
Fortis Inc	First Preference Shares	Pfd-2 low	May 3, 2024
Global Divid Growth Split	Preferred Shares	Pfd-3 high	May 29, 2023
Great-West Lifeco Inc	Non-Cum. First Preferred Shares	Pfd-2 high	Sep 22, 2023
Intl Alliance Ins & Finl	Non-Cum. Preferred Shares, Class A	Pfd-1 low	Feb 27, 2024
Intact Financial Corp	Preferred Shares	Pfd-2 high	Oct 10, 2023
Laurentian Bank of Canada	NVCC Preferred Shares	Pfd-3	Dec 15, 2023
Life & Banc Split Corp	Preferred Shares	Pfd-3	Feb 14, 2024
Loblaw Cos Ltd	Second Preferred Shares	Pfd-3 high	May 18, 2023
Manulife Financial Corp	Non-Cum. Class A Preferred Shares	Pfd-2 high	Jul 19, 2023
National Bank of Canada	NVCC Preferred Shares	Pfd-2	Apr 26, 2024
North Amern Finl 15 Split	Preferred Shares	Pfd-4	Feb 15, 2024
Partners Value Split Corp	Preferred Shares	Pfd-2	Mar 8, 2024
Pembina Pipeline Corp	Preferred Shares	Pfd-3 high	Apr 26, 2024
Power Corp of Canada	Cum. & Non-Cum. First Preferred Shares	Pfd-2	Nov 2, 2023
Power Financial Corp	Cum. & Non-Cum. First Preferred Shares	Pfd-2 high	Nov 2, 2023
Prime Dividend Corp	Floating Rate Cum. Preferred Shares	Pfd-3	May 16, 2023
RF Capital Group Inc	Preferred Shares	Pfd-4 high	Jun 28, 2023
Real Estate Split Corp	Preferred Shares	Pfd-3 high	Oct 24, 2023
Royal Bank of Canada	NVCC Preferred Shares	Pfd-2 high	May 12, 2023
Sagen MI Canada Inc	Preferred Shares	Pfd-2 high	Apr 26, 2024
Sun Life Financial Inc	Class A Preferred Shares	Pfd-2 high	Oct 24, 2023
Sustainable Power	Preferred Shares	Pfd-3	Mar 15, 2024
TC Energy Corp	Preferred Shares	Pfd-3 high	Jul 25, 2023

DBRS Preferred Share/Securities Ratings, by Issuer

Issuer	Description	DBRS Rating	Last Update
Thomson Reuters Corp	Preference Shares, Series II	Pfd-3 high	Nov 7, 2023
TD Bank	NVCC Preferred Shares	Pfd-2 high	May 3, 2024
TransAlta Corp	Preferred Shares	Pfd-3 low	Dec 4, 2023
George Weston Ltd	Preferred Shares	Pfd-3	Jun 26, 2023

DBRS Preferred Share/Securities Ratings, by Rating

DBRS Rating	Issuer	Description	Last Update
Pfd-1 low	Indl Alliance Ins & Finl	Non-Cum. Preferred Shares, Class A	Feb 27, 2024
Pfd-2 high	CU Inc	Preferred Shares	Jul 25, 2023
Pfd-2 high	Canoe EIT Income Fund	Preferred Units	Jan 31, 2024
Pfd-2 high	Great-West Lifeco Inc	Non-Cum. First Preferred Shares	Sep 22, 2023
Pfd-2 high	Intact Financial Corp	Preferred Shares	Oct 10, 2023
Pfd-2 high	Manulife Financial Corp	Non-Cum. Class A Preferred Shares	Jul 19, 2023
Pfd-2 high	Power Financial Corp	Cum. & Non-Cum. First Preferred Shares	Nov 2, 2023
Pfd-2 high	Royal Bank of Canada	NVCC Preferred Shares	May 12, 2023
Pfd-2 high	Sagen MI Canada Inc	Preferred Shares	Apr 26, 2024
Pfd-2 high	Sun Life Financial Inc	Class A Preferred Shares	Oct 24, 2023
Pfd-2 high	TD Bank	NVCC Preferred Shares	May 3, 2024
Pfd-2	Bank of Montreal	NVCC Preferred Shares	Jun 2, 2023
Pfd-2	Brookfield Corp	Cum. & Non-Cum. Preference Shares, Class A and Preferred Securities	Nov 22, 2023
Pfd-2	Brookfield Invts Corp	Senior Preferred Shares	Nov 22, 2023
Pfd-2	Canadian Imp Bank of Comm	NVCC Preferred Shares	Jun 1, 2023
Pfd-2	Canadian Utilities Ltd	Second Preferred Shares	Aug 29, 2023
Pfd-2	Co-operators Gen Ins Co	Non-Cum. Preferred Shares, Class E	Oct 26, 2023
Pfd-2	Empire Life Insurance Co	Preferred Shares	May 25, 2023
Pfd-2	National Bank of Canada	NVCC Preferred Shares	Apr 26, 2024
Pfd-2	Partners Value Split Corp	Preferred Shares	Mar 8, 2024
Pfd-2	Power Corp of Canada	Cum. & Non-Cum. First Preferred Shares	Nov 2, 2023
Pfd-2 low	Fairfax Finl Holdings Ltd	Preferred Shares	Dec 1, 2023
Pfd-2 low	Fortis Inc	First Preference Shares	May 3, 2024
Pfd-3 high	Big Pharma Split Corp	Preferred Shares	Sep 7, 2023
Pfd-3 high	Brookfield Renew Pwr Pfd	Preferred Shares, Series 1	May 26, 2023
Pfd-3 high	Cdn Large Capital Leaders	Preferred Shares	Dec 20, 2023
Pfd-3 high	Cenovus Energy Inc	Preferred Shares	Dec 18, 2023

DBRS Preferred Share/Securities Ratings, by Rating

DBRS Rating	Issuer	Description	Last Update
Pfd-3 high	E Split Corp	Preferred Shares	Jun 6, 2023
Pfd-3 high	Element Fleet Mgmt Corp	Perpetual Preferred Shares	Sep 27, 2023
Pfd-3 high	Enbridge Inc	Preferred Shares	Sep 6, 2023
Pfd-3 high	Global Divid Growth Split	Preferred Shares	May 29, 2023
Pfd-3 high	Loblaw Cos Ltd	Second Preferred Shares	May 18, 2023
Pfd-3 high	Pembina Pipeline Corp	Preferred Shares	Apr 26, 2024
Pfd-3 high	Real Estate Split Corp	Preferred Shares	Oct 24, 2023
Pfd-3 high	TC Energy Corp	Preferred Shares	Jul 25, 2023
Pfd-3 high	Thomson Reuters Corp	Preference Shares, Series II	Nov 7, 2023
Pfd-3	Algonquin Power & Utils	Preferred Shares	Feb 6, 2024
Pfd-3	BCE Inc	First Preferred Shares	Mar 28, 2024
Pfd-3	Brompton Split Banc Corp	5.25% Preferred Shares	Aug 8, 2023
Pfd-3	Canadian Western Bank	NVCC Preferred Shares	Nov 14, 2023
Pfd-3	Dividend 15 Split Corp	Preferred Shares	Apr 11, 2024
Pfd-3	First National Finl Corp	Class A Preferred Shares	Mar 12, 2024
Pfd-3	Laurentian Bank of Canada	NVCC Preferred Shares	Dec 15, 2023
Pfd-3	Life & Banc Split Corp	Preferred Shares	Feb 14, 2024
Pfd-3	Prime Dividend Corp	Floating Rate Cum. Preferred Shares	May 16, 2023
Pfd-3	Sustainable Power	Preferred Shares	Mar 15, 2024
Pfd-3	George Weston Ltd	Preferred Shares	Jun 26, 2023
Pfd-3 low	Artis REIT	Preferred Trust Units	Feb 2, 2024
Pfd-3 low	Brompton Lifeco Split	5.25% Preferred Shares	Mar 28, 2024
Pfd-3 low	Brookfield Office Pptys	Preferred Shares, Class AAA	May 15, 2023
Pfd-3 low	Canadian Banc Corp	Floating Rate Preferred Shares	Nov 16, 2023
Pfd-3 low	Capital Power Corp	Preferred Shares	Apr 5, 2024
Pfd-3 low	Dividend 15 Split Corp II	Preferred Shares	Jun 28, 2023
Pfd-3 low	Divid Growth Split Corp	5.25% Preferred Shares	Jun 21, 2023

DBRS Preferred Share/Securities Ratings, by Rating

DBRS Rating	Issuer	Description	Last Update
Pfd-3 low	TransAlta Corp	Preferred Shares	Dec 4, 2023
Pfd-4 high	ECN Capital Corp	Preferred	Aug 24, 2023
Pfd-4 high	RF Capital Group Inc	Preferred Shares	Jun 28, 2023
Pfd-4	Financial 15 Split Corp	Preferred Shares	Feb 15, 2024
Pfd-4	North Amern Finl 15 Split	Preferred Shares	Feb 15, 2024

Preferred Securities

This table is an alphabetical listing of all exchange-listed preferred securities issued by Canadian corporations. These securities are a hybrid security that combine certain characteristics of both debt and equity. The security is a junior unsecured subordinated debenture and pays interest, not dividends. It is equity-like because it is long-term (generally 49 years), has few obligations (the issuer can defer interest payments for up to 20 quarters without being put into bankruptcy by the holder) and is deeply subordinated.

From an issuer's perspective, preferred securities provide preferential treatment by ratings agencies and accounting authorities: the issuer can include the capital raised as equity for accounting purposes. The issuer is in effect issuing tax-deductible equity. The cost to the issuer is a higher rate on the securities than would be required on senior secured debt, assuming the issuer could issue such a security.

The securities are primarily aimed at tax-free investors, particularly retail investors through their RRSPs. The securities provide the opportunity for the investor to receive a higher yield by going down the capital structure of a higher-grade issuer instead of purchasing a higher yielding debt from a lower-grade issuer. These securities also provide a pricing advantage over debt as they are listed on stock exchanges.

References for Table

Amount Outstanding	See the detailed description of the individual securities for the "as at" date of the particular issue.
Recent Price	Latest closing price to May 9, 2024
Rate	Total annual interest payable per preferred security.
Mandatory Redemption	Date at which all outstanding securities will be redeemed.

Preferred Securities

Issuer	Description	Amount Outstanding	Recent Price	Rate	Mandatory Redemption	DBRS Rating	Exch.	Symbol
Algonquin Power & Utils	nt 6.2% 2079/07/01	14,000,000	US$6.20		Jul 01, 2079			
Top 10 Split Trust	pfd 6.25%	499,532	$11.37	$0.78125	Mar 31, 2026		T	TXT.PR.A

Derivatives

Algonquin Power & Utilities Corp.

6.20% Fixed/Floating Rate Subordinated Notes, Series 2019-A, due July 1, 2079

Issued:	14,000,000 shs.	May 23, 2019	US$25.000
O/S:	14,000,000 shs.	Dec 31, 2023	
Interest:	US$6.20 (Q)	Jan 1/Apr 1/Jul 1/Oct 1	

Interest Details: Beginning Jul 1, 2024 quarterly divd. rate will be plus 4.01%.

Redemption: Redeem. on and after Jul 1, 2024 on min. 30 and max. 60 days' notice at US$25.00 per sh, conditional on tax changes. Redeem. at any time on min. 30 and max. 60 days' notice at par, conditional on tax changes.

Lead Underwriter(s): Merrill Lynch, Pierce, Fenner & Smith Incorporated, J.P. Morgan Securities LLC, RBC Capital Markets, LLC, Wells Fargo Securities, LLC

Transfer Agent: Equiniti Trust Company, LLC

CUSIP: 015857808

Top 10 Split Trust

6.25% Preferred Securities, due Mar. 31, 2021

Issued:	4,379,931 shs.	Dec 7, 2005	
O/S:	499,532 shs.	Dec 31, 2023	
Interest:	$0.78125 (Q)	Mar 31/Jun 30/Sep 30/Dec 31	

Redemption: No details available.

Retraction: Retract. together with the surrender of a capital unit under a Concurrent Retraction or a Special Annual Retraction. Under a concurrent retraction right, the retraction price is equal to 95% of the Combined Value (the amount determined on a particular business day equal to the NAV per Capital Unit plus the Repayment Price (the principal amount of the Preferred Security, together with any accrued and unpaid interest thereon)), less $0.50. Under a Special Annual Retraction right in December, if both a preferred share and a capital share are retracted together, entitled to a cash price equal to the Combined Value.

Note: The Portfolio Shares consist of common shares of the six largest Canadian banks (Bank of Montreal, The Bank of Nova Scotia, Canadian Imperial Bank of Commerce, National Bank of Canada Royal Bank of Canada, and The Toronto-Dominion Bank) and the four largest Canadian life insurance companies (Great-West Lifeco Inc., Industrial Alliance Insurance and Financial Services Inc., Manulife Financial Corporation, and Sun Life Financial Inc.) by market capitalization. The principal amount of $12.50 per Preferred Security will be repaid on termination of the Fund. The term of the fund was extended from an original maturity date of Mar. 31, 2011 and will be automatically extended for successive five-year terms after March 31, 2016.

Transfer Agent: Computershare Trust Company of Canada Inc.

Registrar: Computershare Trust Company of Canada Inc.

Exchanges: TSX

Symbol: TXT.PR.A

CUSIP: 890520117

Structured Products

Structured products is a term applied to categorize an investment vehicle which is created using a dual security structure—Preferred Shares/Securities and Capital Shares/Units— to provide investors with greater ability to choose the tax character of distributions received.

Preferred Shares/Securities provide holders with (a) fixed quarterly dividend/interest payments and (b) repayment of the original subscription price at maturity.

Capital Shares/Units provide holders with (a) tax efficient monthly cash distributions, a significant portion of which is tax deferred; and (b) repayment of the original subscription price at maturity. Capital unit holders may also be entitled to an amount, at maturity, representing capital appreciation of the portfolio of securities held.

These split shares are offered on a particular issuer (such as a bank) or a group of similar issuers (such as financial institutions or resource companies). The net proceeds of the offering are invested in specified securities, however, a portion of the investments (usually 15%-20% of net asset value) may be invested in other companies which meet stated investment criteria. The investment holdings may be rebalanced (or substituted for) on a quarterly basis or as necessary from time to time.

Investment criteria which limit the portfolio of securites to be acquired are set out in the Trust Agreement and may not be changed without the prior approval by the unitholders. Some examples of these criteria are: (a) qualifying assets for purchase; (b) asset/security weightings in the portfolio; and (c) minimum market capitalization of qualifying companies held in the portfolio.

In certain cases, (a) cash or cash equivalents may be held; (b) covered call options may be written and also (c) borrowing may be allowed, from time to time, for working capital purposes, provided that the aggregate amount of such borrowings may not exceed a specified percentage of the total assets.

Closed-end investment trusts differ from mutual funds in a number of respects, most notably as follows: (a) units may be surrendered for redemption only once a year, upon the holder providing notice, whereas the securities of most mutual funds are redeemable daily; (b) the units are to have a stock exchange listing, whereas the securities of most mutual funds do not; (c) unlike most mutual funds, the units will not be offered on a continuous basis; and (d) the trust is permitted to borrow, whereas mutual funds are not permitted to do so.

For companies technically to be considered **mutual fund** corporations, they are not conventional mutual funds and have obtained exemptions from certain requirements, such as (a), (b) and (c) above.

Other Structured Products which have been issued as preferred securities can be found in the Preferred Securities section, beginning on page 129.

Big Banc Split Corp.

8.4% Pref.

Issued:	1,814,104 shs.	Jun 26, 2020	$10.000
O/S:	1,340,004 shs.	Dec 31, 2023	
Dividend:	$0.84 (M)	Payable on the last day of each month	

Dividend Details: Previously, annual divd. rate was 0.600000 per sh until Nov 30, 2023.

Note: Portfolio consists of common shares of Bank of Montreal, Canadian Imperial Bank of Commerce, National Bank of Canada, Royal Bank of Canada, The Bank of Nova Scotia and The Toronto-Dominion Bank. Issued concurrently with an equal number of capital shares.

Lead Underwriter(s): National Bank Financial Inc.
Transfer Agent: TSX Trust Company
Exchanges: TSX
Symbol: BNK.PR.A
CUSIP: 088893201

Big Pharma Split Corp.

5% Pref.

DBRS Rating:	Pfd-3 high	Sep 7, 2023	
Issued:	1,745,200 shs.	Nov 24, 2017	$10.000
O/S:	1,029,738 shs.	Dec 31, 2023	
Dividend:	$0.50 (Q)	Jan 15/Apr 15/Jul 15/Oct 15	

Dividend Details: Dividends are funded entirely from dividends received on the shares in the Portfolio.

Retraction: Retract. at any time to receive payment on the Retraction Payment Date (15th business day following such Retraction Date). Retraction price is equal to 96% of the lesser of (i) the NAV per Unit determined as of the Retraction Date (second last business day of each month), less the cost to the company of the purchase of a class A share in the market for cancellation and (ii) $10.00. Under an annual retraction right in June, if both a preferred share and a class A share are retracted together, entitled to a cash price equal to the NAV per Unit on that date.

Note: Invests in a portfolio consisting of equity securities of 10 dividend-paying healthcare and pharmaceutical companies listed on a North American stock exchange as selected by the portfolio manager. Issued concurrently with an equal number of capital shares.

Lead Underwriter(s): BMO Capital Markets, CIBC World Markets Inc., Scotia Capital Inc., National Bank Financial Inc.
Transfer Agent: TSX Trust Company
Registrar: TSX Trust Company
Exchanges: TSX
Symbol: PRM.PR.A
CUSIP: 08934P207

Brompton Energy Split Corp.
(formerly Brompton Oil Split Corp.)

8.25% Cum. Pref.

Issued:	3,349,800 shs.	Feb 24, 2015	$10.000
O/S:	822,414 shs.	Dec 31, 2023	
Dividend:	$0.825 (Q)	Mar 15/Jun 15/Sep 15/Dec 15	

Dividend Details: Previously, annual divd. rate was 0.800000 per sh until Mar 31, 2024.

Retraction: Retract. at any time to receive payment on the Retraction Payment Date (10th business day following such Retraction Date). Retraction price is equal to 96% of the lesser of (i) the NAV per Unit determined as of the Retraction Date (second last business day of each month), less the cost to the company of the purchase of a class A share in the market for cancellation and (ii) $10.00. Under an annual retraction right in March, if both a preferred share and a class A share are retracted together, entitled to a cash price equal to the NAV per Unit on that date.

Note: Portfolio of equity securities of at least 15 large capitalization North American oil and gas issuers selected by the Manager from the S&P 500 Index and the S&P/TSX Composite Index. The Portfolio will be focused primarily on oil and gas issuers that have significant exposure to oil.

Brompton Lifeco Split Corp.

7% Cum. Pref.

DBRS Rating:	Pfd-3 low	Mar 28, 2024	
Issued:	13,620,018 shs.	Apr 18, 2007	$10.000
O/S:	8,158,215 shs.	Dec 31, 2023	
Dividend:	$0.70 (Q)	Feb 15/May 15/Aug 15/Nov 15	

Dividend Details: Distributions will be paid on or before the 10th business in February, May, August and November. Distributions may consist of ordinary dividends, capital gains dividends, or returns of capital. Previously, annual divd. rate was 0.625000 per sh until Apr 30, 2024.

Redemption: All outstanding preferred shares will be redeemed on min. 30 days' notice on April 29, 2024 at a price equal to the lesser of (i) $10.00 plus any accrued and unpaid distributions thereon and (ii) the NAV of the company on that date divided by the total number of preferred shares then outstanding.

Retraction: Retract. at any time to receive payment on the Retraction Payment Date (tenth business day in the month following a Retraction Date). Retraction price per share will equal to 96% of the lesser of (i) the NAV per Unit determined as of the Retraction Date (second last business day of each month), less the cost to the company of the purchase of a class A share in the market for cancellation and (ii) $10.00. Under an annual retraction right in April, if both a preferred share and a class A share are retracted together, entitled to a cash price equal to the NAV per Unit on that date, less any costs associated with the retraction.

Note: The Portfolio Shares consist of common shares (equally weighted) of the following Canadian life insurance companies: Great-West Lifeco Inc., Industrial Alliance Insurance and Financial Services Inc., Manulife Financial Corporation, and Sun Life Financial Inc. On or about Dec. 1, 2012, the "Termination Date", holders will receive $10.00 for each preferred share held. Issued concurrently with an equal number of class A shares.

Lead Underwriter(s): RBC Capital Markets, CIBC World Markets Inc.
Transfer Agent: Computershare Investor Services Inc.
Registrar: Computershare Investor Services Inc.
Exchanges: TSX
Symbol: LCS.PR.A
CUSIP: 112216205

Brompton Split Banc Corp.

6.25% Cum. Pref.

DBRS Rating:	Pfd-3	Aug 8, 2023	
Issued:	26,669,430 shs.	Nov 16, 2005	$10.000
O/S:	21,180,497 shs.	Dec 31, 2023	
Dividend:	$0.625 (Q)	Jan 15/Apr 15/Jul 15/Oct 15	

Dividend Details: Distributions may consist of ordinary dividends, capital gains dividends or non-taxable returns of capital. Distributions are payable on or before the tenth business day in the month following the end of the period in respect of which the distribution is payable. Previously, annual divd. rate was 0.500000 per sh until Nov 29, 2022.

Redemption: All outstanding preferred shares will be redeemed on min. 30 days' notice on Nov. 29, 2022 at a price equal to the lesser of (i) $10.00 plus any accrued and unpaid distributions thereon and (ii) the NAV of the company on that date divided by the total number of preferred shares then outstanding.

Retraction: Retract. at any time to receive payment on the Retraction Payment Date (10th business day following such Retraction Date). Retraction price is equal to 96% of the lesser of (i) the NAV per Unit determined as of the Retraction Date (second last business day of each month), less the cost to the company of the purchase of a class A share in the market for cancellation and (ii) $10.00. Under an annual retraction right in December, if both a preferred share and a class A share are retracted together, entitled to a cash price equal to the NAV per Unit on that date.

Note: The portfolio will consist of, on an equally weighted basis, common shares of the Bank of Montreal, Canadian Imperial Bank of Commerce, National Bank of Canada, Royal Bank of Canada, The Bank of Nova Scotia and The Toronto-Dominion Bank. Issued concurrently with an equal number of class A shares.

Lead Underwriter(s): Scotia Capital Inc., CIBC World Markets Inc., RBC Capital Markets
Transfer Agent: Haventree Bank
Registrar: Haventree Bank
Exchanges: TSX
Symbol: ESP.PR.A
CUSIP: 11222U201

Lead Underwriter(s): CIBC World Markets Inc., RBC Capital Markets
Transfer Agent: Computershare Investor Services Inc.
Registrar: Computershare Investor Services Inc.
Exchanges: TSX
Symbol: SBC.PR.A
CUSIP: 11221E208

Canadian Banc Corp.

Floating Rate Cum. Pref.

DBRS Rating:	Pfd-3 low	Nov 16, 2023	
Issued:	30,735,952 shs.	Jul 15, 2005	$10.000
O/S:	36,456,182 shs.	Nov 30, 2023	
Dividend:	F.R. (M)	Payable on the 10th day of each month	

Dividend Details: Monthly divd. rate is prime times $10.00 plus 0.75%. Dividends will be paid within 10 days of the Dividend Record Date (the last business day of each month). The minimum rate per annum is 5% and the maximum rate is 7%.

Retraction: Retract. at any time to receive payment on the Retraction Payment Date (15th business day following such Retraction Date). Retraction price is equal to the lesser of (i) $10.00; and (ii) 96% of the NAV per Unit determined as of the Retraction Date (last business day of each month), less the cost to the company of the purchase of a class A share in the market for cancellation. Under an annual retraction right in July, if both a preferred share and a class A share are retracted together, the Retraction Price will be equal to the NAV per Unit on that date, less any related commissions and other costs related to liquidating the Portfolio to pay such amount.

Note: The Portfolio Shares consist primarily of common shares of the following Canadian banks, each representing no less than 5% and no more than 20% of the NAV of the company: Bank of Montreal, The Bank of Nova Scotia, Canadian Imperial Bank of Commerce, National Bank of Canada, Royal Bank of Canada, and The Toronto-Dominion Bank. Up to 20% of the NAV of the company may be invested in equity securities of Canadian or foreign financial services corporations other than the Portfolio Companies. The company may substitute Portfolio Companies in extraordinary circumstances. To supplement the dividends earned on the portfolio and to reduce risk, the company will from time to time write covered call options in respect of all or part of the portfolio. On or about Dec. 1, 2012, the "Termination Date", holders will receive $10.00 for each preferred share held.

Lead Underwriter(s): CIBC World Markets Inc., RBC Capital Markets
Transfer Agent: Computershare Investor Services Inc.
Registrar: Computershare Investor Services Inc.
Exchanges: TSX
Symbol: BK.PR.A
CUSIP: 13536V206

Canadian Large Cap Leaders Split Corp.

7.50% Cum. Pref.

DBRS Rating:	Pfd-3 high	Dec 20, 2023	
Issued:	1,850,633 shs.	Feb 22, 2024	$10.000
O/S:	1,850,633 shs.	Feb 22, 2024	
Dividend:	$0.75 (Q)	Mar 31/Jun 30/Sep 30/Dec 31	

Redemption: All outstanding preferred shares will be redeemed on min. 60 days' notice on Feb. 28, 2029 at a price equal to the lesser of (i) $10.00 plus any accrued and unpaid distributions thereon and (ii) the NAV of the company on that date divided by the total number of preferred shares then outstanding.

Retraction: Retract. at any time to receive payment on the Retraction Payment Date (15th business day following such Retraction Date). Retraction price is equal to 96% of the lesser of (i) the NAV per Unit determined as of such Retraction Date (second last business day of the month), less the cost to the company of the purchase of a class A share in the market for cancellation and (ii) $10.00. Under an annual concurrent retraction (one class A share and one preferred share) beginning in February 2026, entitled to a retraction price per unit equal to the NAV per Unit on that date, less any costs associated with the retraction, including commissions and other such costs if any, related to the liquidation of any portion of the Portfolio required to fund such retraction.

Note: Invests in an initially equally weighted portfolio consisting primarily of equity securities of Canadian dividend growth companies as selected by the portfolio manager.

Lead Underwriter(s): RBC Capital Markets
Transfer Agent: TSX Trust Company
Registrar: TSX Trust Company
Exchanges: TSX
Symbol: NPS.PR.A
CUSIP: 13625G201

Canadian Life Companies Split Corp.

7.95% Cum. 2012 Pref.

Issued:	7,776,613 shs.	Jun 25, 2012	$10.000
O/S:	11,624,001 shs.	Nov 30, 2023	
Dividend:	$0.80 (M)		

Dividend Details: Dividends will be paid within 15 days of the Dividend Record Date (the last business day of each month). Previously, annual divd. rate was 0.795000 per sh until Dec 22, 2022.

Retraction: Retract. at any time to receive payment on the Retraction Payment Date (15th business day following a Retraction Date). Retraction price per share will be equal to the lesser of (i) 98% of the NAV per Unit determined as of such Retraction Date (last business day of a month) less the cost to the company, including commissions, of purchasing a class A share in the market and (ii) $10.00. Under an annual retraction right in March, if both a preferred share and a class A share are retracted together, entitled to a cash price equal to the NAV per Unit on that date plus accrued and unpaid dividends.

Note: Issued upon exchange of the 5.25% preferred shares following a capital reorganization.
Transfer Agent: Computershare Investor Services Inc.
Registrar: Computershare Investor Services Inc.
Exchanges: TSX
Symbol: LFE.PR.B
CUSIP: 136290301

Canoe EIT Income Fund

4.80% Cum. Pref. Units, Series 1

DBRS Rating:	Pfd-2 high	Jan 31, 2024	
Issued:	5,635,000 shs.	Mar 14, 2017	$25.000
O/S:	5,635,000 shs.	Dec 31, 2023	
Dividend:	$1.20 (Q)	Mar 15/Jun 12/Sep 15/Dec 15	

Redemption: Redeem. on and after the following dates on min. 30 and max. 60 days' notice as follows:
Mar 15, 2022..$25.75   Mar 15, 2023..$25.50
Mar 15, 2024..$25.00

Retraction: Retract. on and after Mar 15, 2024 at $25.00 per sh.
Lead Underwriter(s): Scotia Capital Inc., RBC Capital Markets
Transfer Agent: Alliance Trust Company
Registrar: Alliance Trust Company
Exchanges: TSX
Symbol: EIT.PR.A
CUSIP: 13780R208

4.80% Cum. Pref. Units, Series 2

DBRS Rating:	Pfd-2 high	Jan 31, 2024	
Issued:	3,220,000 shs.	Apr 17, 2018	$25.000
O/S:	3,220,000 shs.	Dec 31, 2023	
Dividend:	$1.20 (Q)	Mar 15/Jun 15/Sep 15/Dec 15	

Redemption: Redeem. on and after the following dates on min. 30 and max. 60 days' notice as follows:
Mar 15, 2023..$25.75   Mar 15, 2024..$25.50
Mar 15, 2025..$25.00

Retraction: Retract. on and after Mar 15, 2025 at $25.00 per sh.
Lead Underwriter(s): Scotia Capital Inc.
Transfer Agent: Alliance Trust Company
Registrar: Alliance Trust Company
Exchanges: TSX
Symbol: EIT.PR.B
CUSIP: 13780R133

Dividend 15 Split Corp.

5.5% Cum. Pref.

DBRS Rating:	Pfd-3	Apr 11, 2024
Issued:	85,557,733 shs.	Mar 16, 2004 $10.000
O/S:	119,416,216 shs.	Nov 30, 2023
Dividend:	$0.55 (M)	Payable on the 10th day of each month

Dividend Details: Dividends will be paid within 15 days of the Dividend Record Date (the last business day of each month). Previously, annual divd. rate was 0.525000 per sh until Nov 30, 2019.

Retraction: Retract. at any time to receive payment on the Retraction Payment Date (15th day following such Retraction Date). Retraction price per share will equal the lesser of (i) 96% of the NAV per Unit determined as of the Retraction Date (last business day of each month), less the cost to the company of the purchase of a class A share in the market for cancellation and less any other applicable costs and (ii) $10.00. Under an annual retraction right in August, if both a preferred share and a class A share are retracted together, entitled to a cash price equal to the NAV per Unit on that date.

Note: The company invests in a portfolio of dividend-yielding common shares of the following companies (with weightings between 4% and 8%): Bank of Montreal, The Bank of Nova Scotia, BCE Inc., CI Financial Corp., Canadian Imperial Bank of Commerce, Enbridge Inc., Manulife Financial Corporation, National Bank of Canada, Royal Bank of Canada, Sun life Financial Inc., TELUS Corporation, Thomson Reuters Corp., The Toronto-Dominion Bank, TransAlta Corporation, and TransCanada Corporation. In addition, up to 15% of the NAV of the company may be invested in equity securities of issuers other than the Portfolio Companies. The company may substitute Portfolio Companies as necessary to reflect changes in dividend yields or in extraordinary circumstances. On or about Dec. 1, 2014 (extended from Dec. 1, 2009), the "Termination Date", holders will receive $10.00 for each preferred share held. Issued concurrently with an equal number of class A shares. Effective June 3, 2013, the termination date was extended for an additional five years to Dec. 1, 2019. The termination date may then be further extended for additional successive terms of five years each in the discretion of the Board of Directors.

Lead Underwriter(s): CIBC World Markets Inc., RBC Capital Markets, BMO Capital Markets, TD Securities Inc.
Transfer Agent: Computershare Investor Services Inc.
Registrar: Computershare Investor Services Inc.
Exchanges: TSX
Symbol: DFN.PR.A
CUSIP: 25537R208

Dividend 15 Split Corp. II

5.75% Cum. Pref.

DBRS Rating:	Pfd-3 low	Jun 28, 2023
Issued:	20,455,750 shs.	Nov 16, 2006 $10.000
O/S:	24,907,707 shs.	Nov 30, 2023
Dividend:	$0.575 (M)	Payable on the 10th day of each month

Dividend Details: Dividends will be paid within 15 days of the Dividend Record Date (the last business day of each month). Previously, annual divd. rate was 0.525000 per sh until Nov 30, 2019.

Retraction: Retract. at any time to receive payment on the Retraction Payment Date (15th business day following such Retraction Date). Retraction price per share will equal the lesser of (i) 96% of the NAV per Unit determined as of the Retraction Date (last business day of each month), less the cost to the company of the purchase of a class A share in the market for cancellation and (ii) $10.00. Under an annual retraction right in August, if both a preferred share and a class A share are retracted together, entitled to a cash price equal to the NAV per Unit on that date.

Note: The Portfolio Shares consist principally of publicly traded equity securities which include each of the following Canadian issuers: Bank of Montreal, The Bank of Nova Scotia, BCE Inc., Canadian Imperial Bank of Commerce, CI Financial Corp., Enbridge Inc., Manulife Financial Corporation, National Bank of Canada, Royal Bank of Canada, Sun Life Financial Inc., TELUS Corporation, Thomson Reuters Corporation, The Toronto-Dominion Bank, TransAlta Corporation, and TransCanada Corporation. The Portfolio will be rebalanced from time to time. On or about Dec. 1, 2014, the "Termination Date", holders will receive $10.00 for each preferred share held. Issued concurrently with an equal number of class A shares.

Lead Underwriter(s): CIBC World Markets Inc., RBC Capital Markets
Transfer Agent: Computershare Investor Services Inc.
Registrar: Computershare Investor Services Inc.
Exchanges: TSX
Symbol: DF.PR.A
CUSIP: 25537W207

FP Equities — Preferreds & Derivatives 2024   137

Dividend Growth Split Corp.

5.5% Cum. Pref.

DBRS Rating:	Pfd-3 low	Jun 21, 2023	
Issued:	53,262,015 shs.	Dec 3, 2007	$10.000
O/S:	43,624,329 shs.	Dec 31, 2023	
Dividend:	$0.55 (Q)	Mar 15/Jun 15/Sep 15/Dec 15	

Dividend Details: Distributions will be paid on or before the 10th business day following the end of the period in respect of which the distribution is payable. Previously, annual divd. rate was 0.525000 per sh until Nov 28, 2019.

Redemption: All outstanding preferred shares will be redeemed on min. 30 days' notice on Sept. 27, 2024 at a price equal to the lesser of (i) $10.00 plus any accrued and unpaid distributions thereon and (ii) the NAV of the company on that date divided by the total number of preferred shares then outstanding.

Retraction: Retract. at any time to receive payment on the Retraction Payment Date (10th business day following such Retraction Date). Retraction price is equal to 96% of the lesser of (i) the NAV per Unit determined as of such Retraction Date (second last business day of the month), less the cost to the company of the purchase of a class A share in the market for cancellation and (ii) $10.00. Under a quarterly concurrent retraction (one class A share and one preferred share) beginning in February 2008, entitled to a retraction price per unit equal to the NAV per Unit on that date, less any costs associated with the retraction, including commissions and other such costs if any, related to the liquidation of any portion of the Portfolio required to fund such retraction.

Note: The Portfolio Shares initially consist of common shares of 20 large capitalization Canadian equities selected from those TSX-listed equities that have demonstrated the highest dividend growth rate over a five-year period and have a current dividend yield of at least 2% per annum. The Portfolio Universe will be rebalanced at least annually. Issued concurrently with an equal number of class A shares. In 2008, Dividend Growth Split Corp. merged with YEARS Financial Trust.

Lead Underwriter(s): RBC Capital Markets, CIBC World Markets Inc., Scotia Capital Inc.
Transfer Agent: Computershare Investor Services Inc.
Registrar: Computershare Investor Services Inc.
Exchanges: TSX
Symbol: DGS.PR.A
CUSIP: 25537Y203

E Split Corp.

7% Pref.

DBRS Rating:	Pfd-3 high	Jun 6, 2023	
Issued:	31,424,056 shs.	Jun 29, 2018	$10.000
O/S:	24,294,982 shs.	Apr 19, 2024	
Dividend:	$0.70 (Q)	Mar 31/Jun 30/Sep 30/Dec 31	

Dividend Details: Previously, annual divd. rate was 0.525000 per sh until Jun 29, 2023.
Note: The Portfolio Shares consist of common shares of Enbridge Inc. Issued concurrently with an equal number of class A shares.
Lead Underwriter(s): CIBC World Markets Inc., RBC Capital Markets
Exchanges: TSX
Symbol: ENS.PR.A
CUSIP: 26916F203

Financial 15 Split Corp.

9.25% Cum. Pref.

DBRS Rating:	Pfd-4	Feb 15, 2024	
Issued:	56,912,066 shs.	Nov 14, 2003	$10.000
O/S:	47,357,527 shs.	Nov 30, 2023	
Dividend:	$0.925 (M)	Payable on the 10th day of each month	

Dividend Details: Dividends will be paid within 15 days of the Dividend Record Date (the last business day of each month). Previously, annual divd. rate was 0.750000 per sh until Nov 30, 2023.

Retraction: Retract. at any time to receive payment on the Retraction Payment Date (15th day following such Retraction Date). Retraction price per share will equal the lesser of (i) 96% of the NAV per Unit determined as of the Retraction Date (last business day of each month), less the cost to the company of the purchase of a class A share in the market for cancellation and less any other applicable costs and (ii) $10.00. Under an annual retraction right in October, if both a preferred share and a class A share are retracted together, entitled to a cash price equal to the NAV per Unit on that date.

Note: The company invests primarily in a portfolio of common shares of the following financial services companies: Bank of Montreal, The Bank of Nova Scotia, Canadian Imperial Bank of Commerce, Royal Bank of Canada, The Toronto-Dominion Bank, National Bank of Canada, Manulife Financial Corporation, Sun Life Financial Inc., Great-West Lifeco Inc., CI Financial Corp., Bank of America Corp., Citigroup Inc., Goldman Sachs Group Inc., JPMorgan Chase & Co., and Wells Fargo & Co. The Portfolio will be rebalanced as necessary from time to time. Up to 15% of the NAV of the company may be invested in equity securities of issuers other than the Portfolio Companies. The company will limit its holdings of U.S. issuers to ensure that its shares will not be foreign property for Canadian tax purposes. The company may substitute Portfolio Companies in extraordinary circumstances. On or about Dec. 1, 2015 (extended from Dec. 1, 2008), the "Termination Date", holders will receive $10.00 for each preferred share held. Issued concurrently with an equal number of class A shares.

Lead Underwriter(s): CIBC World Markets Inc.
Transfer Agent: Computershare Investor Services Inc.
Registrar: Computershare Investor Services Inc.
Exchanges: TSX
Symbol: FTN.PR.A
CUSIP: 317504108

Global Dividend Growth Split Corp.

5% Cum. Pref.

DBRS Rating:	Pfd-3 high	May 29, 2023	
Issued:	15,828,781 shs.	Jun 15, 2018	$10.000
O/S:	15,703,501 shs.	Dec 31, 2023	
Dividend:	$0.50 (Q)	Mar 31/Jun 30/Sep 30/Dec 31	

Redemption: All outstanding preferred shares will be redeemed on June 30, 2026 at a price equal to the lesser of (i) $10.00 plus any accrued and unpaid distributions thereon and (ii) the NAV of the company on that date divided by the total number of preferred shares then outstanding.

Retraction: Retract. at any time to receive payment on the Retraction Payment Date (10th business day following such Retraction Date). Retraction price is equal to 96% of the lesser of (i) the NAV per Unit determined as of such Retraction Date (second last business day of the month), less the cost to the company of the purchase of a class A share in the market for cancellation and (ii) $10.00. Under an annual concurrent retraction (one class A share and one preferred share) beginning in June 2020, entitled to a retraction price per unit equal to the NAV per Unit on that date, less any costs associated with the retraction, including commissions and other such costs if any, related to the liquidation of any portion of the Portfolio required to fund such retraction.

Note: Diversified portfolio consisting of equity securities of at least 20 large capitalization global dividend growth companies with a minimum market capitalization of US$10 billion and a history of dividend growth. Issued concurrently with an equal number of class A shares.

Lead Underwriter(s): RBC Capital Markets, CIBC World Markets Inc., National Bank Financial Inc., Scotia Capital Inc.
Transfer Agent: TSX Trust Company
Registrar: TSX Trust Company
Exchanges: TSX
Symbol: GDV.PR.A
CUSIP: 379444201

Life & Banc Split Corp.

7.25% Cum. Pref.

DBRS Rating:	Pfd-3	Feb 14, 2024	
Issued:	59,294,871 shs.	Oct 17, 2006	$10.000
O/S:	43,196,934 shs.	Apr 25, 2024	
Dividend:	$0.725 (Q)	Jan 15/Apr 15/Jul 15/Oct 15	

Dividend Details: Distributions may consist of ordinary dividends, capital gains dividends, or returns of capital. Previously, annual divd. rate was 0.545000 per sh until Oct 30, 2023.

Redemption: All outstanding preferred shares will be redeemed on min. 30 days' notice on Nov. 29, 2018, unless the term of the Fund is extended, at a price equal to the lesser of (i) $10.00 plus any accrued and unpaid distributions thereon and (ii) the NAV of the company on that date divided by the total number of preferred shares then outstanding.

Retraction: Retract. at any time to receive payment on the Retraction Payment Date (10th business day in the month). Retraction price per share will equal to 96% of the lesser of (i) the NAV per Unit determined as of the Retraction Date (second last business day of each month), less the cost to the company of the purchase of a class A share in the market for cancellation and less any other applicable costs and (ii) $10.00. Under an annual retraction right in November, if both a preferred share and a class A share are retracted together, entitled to a cash price equal to the NAV per Unit on that date, less any costs associated with the retraction.

Note: The company invests, on an equally weighted basis, in a portfolio consisting of common shares of the following six Canadian banks and four Canadian life insurance companies: Bank of Montreal, Canadian Imperial Bank of Commerce, National Bank of Canada, Royal Bank of Canada, The Bank of Nova Scotia, The Toronto-Dominion Bank, Great-West Lifeco Inc., Industrial Alliance Insurance and Financial Services Inc., Manulife Financial Corporation, and Sun Life Financial Inc. Issued concurrently with an equal number of class A shares.

Lead Underwriter(s): CIBC World Markets Inc., RBC Capital Markets
Transfer Agent: Computershare Investor Services Inc.
Registrar: Computershare Investor Services Inc.
Exchanges: TSX
Symbol: LBS.PR.A
CUSIP: 53184C118

M Split Corp.

Cum. Class I Pref.

Issued:	2,846,795 shs.	Mar 23, 2010	$5.000
O/S:	2,275,889 shs.	Nov 30, 2023	
Dividend:	$0.375 (M)	Payable on the 10th day of each month	

Retraction: Retract. at any time at a price per class I preferred share equal to the sum of (i) the lessor of (a) $5.00, and (b) 97% of an amount equal to the NAV per Unit determined as of the applicable Retraction Date less the cost to the company of purchasing a class II preferred share and a capital share in the market for cancellation, plus (ii) all accrued and unpaid and declared and unpaid dividends on a class I preferred share to be retracted to but excluding the Retraction Date. Under a concurrent retraction (one capital share, one class I preferred share and one class II preferred share), on the October Retraction Date, entitled to an aggregate price equal to (i) the NAV per Unit calculated on such Retraction Date, less any commissions and other applicable costs, plus (ii) all accrued and unpaid and declared and unpaid dividends in respect of the class I preferred shares, class II preferred shares and capital shares so surrendered for retraction.

Note: The Portfolio Shares consist of Manulife Financial Corporation common shares. On Dec. 1, 2014, the "Termination Date", holders will receive (i) the lesser of (a) $5.00 and (b) the NAV of the company, divided by the number of class I preferred shares then outstanding, plus (ii) all accrued and unpaid and declared and unpaid dividends thereon. Issued as a result of a reorganization effective Mar. 23, 2010 converting each Priority Equity share outstanding on that date into one class I preferred share, one class II preferred share, one 2011 warrant and one 2012 warrant.

Transfer Agent: Computershare Investor Services Inc.
Registrar: Computershare Investor Services Inc.
Exchanges: TSX
Symbol: XMF.PR.B
CUSIP: 55376A503

Class II Pref.

Issued:	2,735,138 shs.	Aug 25, 2014
O/S:	2,275,889 shs.	Nov 30, 2023

Dividend Details: Pays monthly distributions of $0.03125 if and when the net asset value per unit (one class I preferred share, one class II preferred share and one capital share) exceeds $10.00.

Retraction: Retract. at any time at a price per class II preferred share equal to the sum of (i) the lessor of (a) $5.00, and (b) 97% of an amount equal to the NAV per Unit determined as of the applicable Retraction Date less the cost to the company of purchasing a class I preferred share and a capital share in the market for cancellation, plus (ii) all accrued and unpaid and declared and unpaid dividends on a class II preferred share to be retracted to but excluding the Retraction Date. Under a concurrent retraction (one capital share, one class I preferred share and one class II preferred share), on the October Retraction Date, entitled to an aggregate price equal to (i) the NAV per Unit calculated on such Retraction Date, less any commissions and other applicable costs, plus (ii) all accrued and unpaid and declared and unpaid dividends in respect of the class I preferred shares, class II preferred shares and capital shares so surrendered for retraction.

Note: The Portfolio Shares consist of Manulife Financial Corporation common shares. On Dec. 1, 2019, the "Termination Date", holders will receive (i) the lesser of (a) $5.00 and (b) the NAV of the company less the amount required to redeem all class I preferred shares then outstanding, divided by the number of class II preferred shares then outstanding, plus (ii) all accrued and unpaid and declared and unpaid dividends thereon. Issued as a result of a reorganization effective August 25, 2014 converting each class II preferred share outstanding on that date into one new class II preferred share and one 2014 warrant.

Transfer Agent: Computershare Investor Services Inc.
Registrar: Computershare Investor Services Inc.
Exchanges: TSX
Symbol: XMF.PR.C
CUSIP: 55376A800

New Commerce Split Fund

6% Cum. Class I Pref.

Issued:	3,824,009 shs.	Mar 26, 2010	$5.000
O/S:	896,532 shs.	Nov 30, 2023	
Dividend:	$0.30 (M)	Payable on the 10th day of each month	

Dividend Details: Previously, annual divd. rate was 0.375000 per sh until Dec 16, 2014.

Retraction: Retract. at any time to receive payment on the Retraction Payment Date (fifteenth business day following such Retraction Date). Retraction price will equal the lesser of (i) $5.00; and (ii) 97% of the net asset value per New Unit determined as of the Retraction Date (last business day of each month), less the cost to the company of the purchase of a class II preferred share and a capital share in the market for cancellation. Under an annual retraction right in October, if a class I preferred shares, a class II preferred share and a capital share are retracted together, entitled to a cash price equal to the NAV per New Unit calculated as of such date, plus all accrued and unpaid and declared and unpaid dividends to but excluding such Retraction Date.

Note: The Portfolio Shares consist of Canadian Imperial Bank of Commerce common shares. On or about Dec. 1, 2019, the "Termination Date", holders will receive the lesser of $5.00 and the net asset value per unit for each preferred share held.

Transfer Agent: Computershare Investor Services Inc.
Registrar: Computershare Investor Services Inc.
Exchanges: TSX
Symbol: YCM.PR.A
CUSIP: 200701506

Class II Pref.

Issued:	3,824,009 shs.	Mar 26, 2010	$5.000
O/S:	896,532 shs.	Nov 30, 2023	
Dividend:	V.R. (M)	Payable on the 10th day of each month	

Dividend Details: Pays monthly distributions of $0.03125 if and when the net asset value per unit (one class I preferred share, one class II preferred share and one capital share) exceeds $10.

FP Equities — Preferreds & Derivatives 2024   141

Retraction: Retract. at any time to receive payment on the Retraction Payment Date (fifteenth business day following such Retraction Date). Retraction price will equal the lesser of (i) $5.00; and (ii) 97% of the net asset value per New Unit determined as of the Retraction Date (last business day of each month), less the cost to the company of the purchase of a class II preferred share and a capital share in the market for cancellation. Under an annual retraction right in October, if a class I preferred shares, a class II preferred share and a capital share are retracted together, entitled to a cash price equal to the NAV per New Unit calculated as of such date, plus all accrued and unpaid and declared and unpaid dividends to but excluding such Retraction Date.

Note: The Portfolio Shares consist of Canadian Imperial Bank of Commerce common shares. On or about Dec. 1, 2019, the "Termination Date", holders will receive the lesser of $5.00 and the net asset value per unit for each preferred share held.

Transfer Agent: Computershare Investor Services Inc.
Registrar: Computershare Investor Services Inc.
Exchanges: TSX
Symbol: YCM.PR.B
CUSIP: 200701605

North American Financial 15 Split Corp.

9.5% Cum. Pref.

DBRS Rating:	Pfd-4	Feb 15, 2024	
Issued:	35,121,400 shs.	Oct 15, 2004	$10.000
O/S:	52,028,792 shs.	Nov 30, 2023	
Dividend:	$0.95 (M)	Payable on the 10th day of each month	

Dividend Details: Dividends will be paid within 10 days of the Dividend Record Date (the last business day of each month). Previously, annual divd. rate was 0.775000 per sh until Dec 19, 2023.

Retraction: Retract. at any time to receive payment on the Retraction Payment Date (15th day following such Retraction Date). Retraction price per share will equal the lesser of (i) 96% of the NAV per Unit determined as of the Retraction Date (last business day of each month), less the cost to the company of the purchase of a class A share in the market for cancellation and less any other applicable costs and (ii) $10.00. Under an annual retraction right in October, if both a preferred share and a class A share are retracted together, entitled to a cash price equal to the NAV per Unit on that date.

Note: The company invests primarily in a portfolio of common shares of the following financial services companies: Bank of Montreal, The Bank of Nova Scotia, Canadian Imperial Bank of Commerce, Royal Bank of Canada, The Toronto-Dominion Bank, National Bank of Canada, Manulife Financial Corporation, Sun Life Financial Inc., Great-West Lifeco Inc., CI Financial Corp., Bank of America Corp., Citigroup Inc., JPMorgan Chase & Co., Goldman Sachs Group Inc. and Wells Fargo & Co. The Portfolio will be rebalanced as necessary from time to time. Up to 15% of the NAV of the company may be invested in equity securities of issuers other than the Portfolio Companies. The company will limit its holdings of U.S. issuers to ensure that its shares will not be foreign property for Canadian tax purposes. The company may substitute Portfolio Companies in extraordinary circumstances. On or about Dec. 1, 2014 (extended from Dec. 1, 2009), the "Termination Date", holders will receive $10.00 for each preferred share held. Issued concurrently with an equal number of class A shares.

Lead Underwriter(s): CIBC World Markets Inc.
Transfer Agent: Computershare Investor Services Inc.
Registrar: Computershare Investor Services Inc.
Exchanges: TSX
Symbol: FFN.PR.A
CUSIP: 65685J103

Partners Value Split Corp.

4.40% Cum. Class AA Pref., Series 12

DBRS Rating:	Pfd-2	Mar 8, 2024	
Issued:	6,900,000 shs.	Apr 12, 2021	$25.000
O/S:	6,900,000 shs.	Dec 31, 2023	
Dividend:	$1.10 (Q)	Mar 7/Jun 7/Sep 7/Dec 7	

142   FP Equities — Preferreds & Derivatives 2024

Redemption: Redeem. on and after the following dates on min. 15 days' notice as follows:
Feb 28, 2026...$25.50   Feb 28, 2027..$25.00
Redeem. prior to Feb. 28, 2026 for $26.00 per share plus accrued and unpaid dividends if, and will not redeem Series 12 Preferred Shares prior to Feb. 28, 2026 unless: (i) capital shares have been retracted; or (ii) there is a takeover bid for the Brookfield Asset Management Inc. shares and the Board of Directors of the company determines that such bid is in the best interest of the holders of the capital shares. All outstanding preferred shares will be redeemed on Feb. 29, 2028 at a price equal to the lesser of (i) $25.00 plus accrued and unpaid distributions and (ii) the NAV per unit.

Retraction: Retract. at any time to receive payment on the Retraction Payment Date (15th day of the month). The Preferred Share Retraction Price will be equal to the lesser of (i) NAV per Unit and (ii) $25.00. A holder who surrenders a Series 12 preferred share for retraction will receive on the Retraction Payment Date that number of Series 10 Debentures determined by dividing the holder's aggregate Preferred Share Retraction Price by $25.00. The Series 10 Debentures will be issued by, at the company's option in respect of each retraction, either the company or, if agreed to by Partners Value Investments, Partners Value Investments. In lieu of fractional debentures, cash payment will be made.

Lead Underwriter(s): Scotia Capital Inc., BMO Capital Markets, CIBC World Markets Inc., RBC Capital Markets, TD Securities Inc.
Transfer Agent: TSX Trust Company
Registrar: TSX Trust Company
Exchanges: TSX
Symbol: PVS.PR.J
CUSIP: 70214J855

4.45% Cum. Class AA Pref., Series 13

DBRS Rating:	Pfd-2	Mar 8, 2024	
Issued:	6,000,000 shs.	Mar 25, 2022	$25.000
O/S:	6,000,000 shs.	Dec 31, 2023	
Dividend:	$1.1125 (Q)	Mar 7/Jun 7/Sep 7/Dec 7	

Redemption: Redeem. on and after the following dates on min. 15 days' notice as follows:
May 31, 2027...$25.50   May 31, 2028..$25.00
Redeem. prior to May 31, 2027 for $26.00 per share plus accrued and unpaid dividends if, and will not redeem Series 13 Preferred Shares prior to May 31, 2027 unless: (i) capital shares have been retracted; or (ii) there is a takeover bid for the Brookfield Asset Management Inc. shares and the Board of Directors of the company determines that such bid is in the best interest of the holders of the capital shares. All outstanding preferred shares will be redeemed on May 31, 2029 at a price equal to the lesser of (i) $25.00 plus accrued and unpaid distributions and (ii) the NAV per unit.

Retraction: Retract. at any time to receive payment on the Retraction Payment Date (15th day of the month). The Preferred Share Retraction Price will be equal to the lesser of (i) NAV per Unit and (ii) $25.00. A holder who surrenders a Series 13 preferred share for retraction will receive on the Retraction Payment Date that number of Series 11 Debentures determined by dividing the holder's aggregate Preferred Share Retraction Price by $25.00. The Series 11 Debentures will be issued by, at the company's option in respect of each retraction, either the company or, if agreed to by Partners Value Investments, Partners Value Investments. In lieu of fractional debentures, cash payment will be made.

Lead Underwriter(s): Scotia Capital Inc., BMO Capital Markets, CIBC World Markets Inc., RBC Capital Markets, TD Securities Inc.
Transfer Agent: TSX Trust Company
Registrar: TSX Trust Company
Exchanges: TSX
Symbol: PVS.PR.K
CUSIP: 70214J848

4.80% Cum. Class AA Pref., Series 8

DBRS Rating:	Pfd-2	Mar 8, 2024	
Issued:	6,000,000 shs.	Sep 18, 2017	$25.000
O/S:	5,999,300 shs.	Dec 31, 2023	
Dividend:	$1.20 (Q)	Mar 7/Jun 7/Sep 7/Dec 7	

Redemption: Redeem. on and after the following dates on min. 15 days' notice as follows:
Sep 30, 2022..$25.50   Sep 30, 2023..$25.00
Redeem. prior to Sept. 30, 2022 for $26.00 per share plus accrued and unpaid dividends if, and will not redeem Series 8 Preferred Shares prior to Sept. 30, 2022 unless: (i) capital shares have been retracted; or (ii) there is a takeover bid for the Brookfield Asset Management Inc. shares and the Board of Directors of the company determines that such bid is in the best interest of the holders of the capital shares. All outstanding preferred shares will be redeemed on Sept. 30, 2024 at a price equal to the lesser of (i) $25.00 plus accrued and unpaid distributions and (ii) the NAV per unit.

Retraction: Retract. at any time to receive payment on the Retraction Payment Date (15th day of the month). The Preferred Share Retraction Price will be equal to the lesser of (i) NAV per Unit and (ii) $25.00. A holder who surrenders a Series 8 preferred share for retraction will receive on the Retraction Payment Date that number of Series 6 Debentures determined by dividing the holder's aggregate Preferred Share Retraction Price by $25.00. The Series 6 Debentures will be issued by, at the company's option in respect of each retraction, either the company or, if agreed to by Partners Value Investments, Partners Value Investments. In lieu of fractional debentures, cash payment will be made.

Lead Underwriter(s): Scotia Capital Inc., CIBC World Markets Inc., RBC Capital Markets, TD Securities Inc.
Transfer Agent: TSX Trust Company
Registrar: TSX Trust Company
Exchanges: TSX
Symbol: PVS.PR.F
CUSIP: 70214J806

4.75% Cum. Class AA Pref., Series 11

DBRS Rating:	Pfd-2	Mar 8, 2024	
Issued:	6,000,000 shs.	Oct 6, 2020	$25.000
O/S:	6,000,000 shs.	Dec 31, 2023	
Dividend:	$1.1875 (Q)	Mar 7/Jun 7/Sep 7/Dec 7	

Redemption: Redeem. on and after the following dates on min. 15 days' notice as follows:
Oct 31, 2023..$25.50   Oct 31, 2024..$25.00
Redeem. prior to Oct. 31, 2023 for $26.00 per share plus accrued and unpaid dividends if, and will not redeem Series 11 Preferred Shares prior to Oct. 31, 2023 unless: (i) capital shares have been retracted; or (ii) there is a takeover bid for the Brookfield Asset Management Inc. shares and the Board of Directors of the company determines that such bid is in the best interest of the holders of the capital shares. All outstanding preferred shares will be redeemed on Oct. 31, 2025 at a price equal to the lesser of (i) $25.00 plus accrued and unpaid distributions and (ii) the NAV per unit.

Retraction: Retract. at any time to receive payment on the Retraction Payment Date (15th day of the month). The Preferred Share Retraction Price will be equal to the lesser of (i) NAV per Unit and (ii) $25.00. A holder who surrenders a Series 11 preferred share for retraction will receive on the Retraction Payment Date that number of Series 9 Debentures determined by dividing the holder's aggregate Preferred Share Retraction Price by $25.00. The Series 9 Debentures will be issued by, at the company's option in respect of each retraction, either the company or, if agreed to by Partners Value Investments, Partners Value Investments. In lieu of fractional debentures, cash payment will be made.

Lead Underwriter(s): Scotia Capital Inc., BMO Capital Markets, CIBC World Markets Inc., RBC Capital Markets, TD Securities Inc.
Transfer Agent: TSX Trust Company
Registrar: TSX Trust Company
Exchanges: TSX
Symbol: PVS.PR.I
CUSIP: 70214J863

4.90% Cum. Class AA Pref., Series 9

DBRS Rating:	Pfd-2	Mar 8, 2024	
Issued:	6,000,000 shs.	Nov 26, 2018	$25.000
O/S:	5,996,800 shs.	Dec 31, 2023	
Dividend:	$1.225 (Q)	Mar 7/Jun 7/Sep 7/Dec 7	

Redemption: Redeem. on and after the following dates on min. 15 days' notice as follows:
Feb 28, 2024..................................$25.50   Feb 28, 2025....................................$25.00
Redeem. prior to Feb. 28, 2024 for $26.00 per share plus accrued and unpaid dividends if, and will not redeem Series 9 Preferred Shares prior to Feb. 28, 2024 unless: (i) capital shares have been retracted; or (ii) there is a takeover bid for the Brookfield Asset Management Inc. shares and the Board of Directors of the company determines that such bid is in the best interest of the holders of the capital shares. All outstanding preferred shares will be redeemed on Feb. 28, 2026 at a price equal to the lesser of (i) $25.00 plus accrued and unpaid distributions and (ii) the NAV per unit.

Retraction: Retract. at any time to receive payment on the Retraction Payment Date (15th day of the month). The Preferred Share Retraction Price will be equal to the lesser of (i) NAV per Unit and (ii) $25.00. A holder who surrenders a Series 9 preferred share for retraction will receive on the Retraction Payment Date that number of Series 7 Debentures determined by dividing the holder's aggregate Preferred Share Retraction Price by $25.00. The Series 7 Debentures will be issued by, at the company's option in respect of each retraction, either the company or, if agreed to by Partners Value Investments, Partners Value Investments. In lieu of fractional debentures, cash payment will be made.

Lead Underwriter(s): Scotia Capital Inc., BMO Capital Markets, CIBC World Markets Inc., RBC Capital Markets, TD Securities Inc.
Transfer Agent: TSX Trust Company
Registrar: TSX Trust Company
Exchanges: TSX
Symbol: PVS.PR.G
CUSIP: 70214J889

4.70% Cum. Class AA Pref., Series 10

DBRS Rating:	Pfd-2	Mar 8, 2024	
Issued:	6,000,000 shs.	Mar 2, 2020	$25.000
O/S:	6,000,000 shs.	Dec 31, 2023	
Dividend:	$1.175 (Q)	Mar 7/Jun 7/Sep 7/Dec 7	

Redemption: Redeem. on and after the following dates on min. 15 days' notice as follows:
Feb 28, 2025..................................$25.50   Feb 28, 2026....................................$25.00
Redeem. prior to Feb. 28, 2025 for $26.00 per share plus accrued and unpaid dividends if, and will not redeem Series 10 Preferred Shares prior to Feb. 28, 2025 unless: (i) capital shares have been retracted; or (ii) there is a takeover bid for the Brookfield Asset Management Inc. shares and the Board of Directors of the company determines that such bid is in the best interest of the holders of the capital shares. All outstanding preferred shares will be redeemed on Feb. 28, 2027 at a price equal to the lesser of (i) $25.00 plus accrued and unpaid distributions and (ii) the NAV per unit.

Retraction: Retract. at any time to receive payment on the Retraction Payment Date (15th day of the month). The Preferred Share Retraction Price will be equal to the lesser of (i) NAV per Unit and (ii) $25.00. A holder who surrenders a Series 10 preferred share for retraction will receive on the Retraction Payment Date that number of Series 8 Debentures determined by dividing the holder's aggregate Preferred Share Retraction Price by $25.00. The Series 8 Debentures will be issued by, at the company's option in respect of each retraction, either the company or, if agreed to by Partners Value Investments, Partners Value Investments. In lieu of fractional debentures, cash payment will be made.

Lead Underwriter(s): Scotia Capital Inc., BMO Capital Markets, CIBC World Markets Inc., RBC Capital Markets, TD Securities Inc.
Transfer Agent: TSX Trust Company
Registrar: TSX Trust Company
Exchanges: TSX
Symbol: PVS.PR.H
CUSIP: 70214J871

Premium Income Corporation

5.75% Cum. Pref.

Issued:	23,496,946 shs.	Oct 30, 1996	$15.000
O/S:	15,310,591 shs.	Oct 31, 2023	
Dividend:	$0.8625 (Q)	Jan 31/Apr 30/Jul 31/Oct 31	

Redemption: All outstanding preferred shares will be redeemed on Nov. 1, 2017 at a price equal to the lesser of (i) $15.00 and (ii) the NAV per share.

Retraction: Retract. monthly on five days' notice prior to the last business day of the month at 96% of the lesser of (i) $15.00 and (ii) NAV per share less the cost of purchase for cancellation of the shares to be redeemed on the stock exchange.

Note: The Portfolio Shares consist of common shares issued by Bank of Montreal, The Bank of Nova Scotia, Canadian Imperial Bank of Commerce, Royal Bank of Canada and The Toronto-Dominion Bank, and may also include covered options written against all or part of the portfolio securities. The termination date was extended initially to Nov. 1, 2010 (from Nov. 1, 2003), then subsequently to Nov. 1, 2017. Issued concurrently with an equal number of class A shares.

Lead Underwriter(s): Richardson Greenshields of Canada Limited
Transfer Agent: Computershare Investor Services Inc.
Registrar: Computershare Investor Services Inc.
Exchanges: TSX
Symbol: PIC.PR.A
CUSIP: 740910203

Prime Dividend Corp.

Floating Rate Cum. Pref.

DBRS Rating:	Pfd-3	May 16, 2023	
Issued:	2,400,000 shs.	Nov 16, 2005	$10.000
O/S:	854,254 shs.	Nov 30, 2023	
Dividend:	F.R. (M)	Payable on the 10th day of each month	

Dividend Details: Monthly divd. rate is prime times $10.00 plus 0.75%. The minimum annual dividend rate is 5% and the maximum annual rate is 7%.

Retraction: Retract. at any time to receive payment on the Retraction Payment Date (15th business day following such Retraction Date). Retraction price is equal to the lesser of (i) 96% of the NAV per Unit determined as of the Retraction Date (last business day of each month), less the cost to the company of the purchase of a class A share in the market for cancellation and (ii) $10.00. Under an annual retraction right in April, if both a preferred share and a class A share are retracted together, entitled to a cash price equal to the NAV per Unit on that date.

Note: The company invests in a portfolio of dividend-paying companies which will primarily include the following: BANKS: Bank of Montreal, The Bank of Nova Scotia, Canadian Imperial Bank of Commerce, National Bank of Canada, Royal Bank of Canada, The Toronto-Dominion Bank; LIFE INSURANCE COMPANIES: Great-West Lifeco Inc., Manulife Financial Corporation, Sun Life Financial Inc.; UTILITIES & OTHER: BCE Inc., Power Financial Corporation, TransAlta Corporation, TransCanada Corporation, TMX Group Inc.; and INVESTMENT MANAGEMENT COMPANIES: AGF Management Limited, CI Financial Corp. and IGM Financial Inc. Up to 20% of the Net Asset Value of the company may be invested in equity securities of issuers in the financial services or utilities sectors in Canada or the United States, other than the Portfolio Companies. On or about Dec. 1, 2012, the "Termination Date", holders will receive $10.00 for each preferred share held. Issued concurrently with an equal number of class A shares.

Lead Underwriter(s): CIBC World Markets Inc., RBC Capital Markets
Transfer Agent: Computershare Investor Services Inc.
Registrar: Computershare Investor Services Inc.
Exchanges: TSX
Symbol: PDV.PR.A
CUSIP: 74161F205

Real Estate Split Corp.
(formerly Real Estate & E-Commerce Split Corp.)

Pref.

DBRS Rating:	Pfd-3 high	Oct 24, 2023	
Issued:	7,271,022 shs.	Nov 19, 2020	$10.000
O/S:	7,365,572 shs.	Apr 23, 2024	
Dividend:	$0.525 (Q)	Jan 15/Apr 15/Jul 15/Oct 15	

Lead Underwriter(s): CIBC World Markets Inc., RBC Capital Markets
Transfer Agent: Middlefield Capital Corporation
Exchanges: TSX
Symbol: RS.PR.A
CUSIP: 75602C206

S Split Corp.

5.25% Cum. Pref.

Issued:	4,750,000 shs.	May 17, 2007	$10.00
O/S:	412,473 shs.	Dec 31, 2023	
Dividend:	$0.525 (M)	Payable on the last day of each month	

Redemption: All outstanding preferred shares may be redeemed on min. 30 days' notice on Dec. 1, 2021 at a price equal to the lesser of (i) $10.00 plus any accrued and unpaid distributions thereon and (ii) the NAV of the company on that date divided by the total number of preferred shares then outstanding.

Retraction: Retract. at any time to receive payment on the Retraction Payment Date (fifteenth business day of the month). Retraction price per share will equal 95% of the lesser of (i) the NAV per Unit determined as of the Valuation Date (ten business days prior to the last business day of the month), less the cost to the company of the purchase of a class A share in the market for cancellation and (ii) $10.00. Under an annual retraction right in June, if both a preferred share and a class A share are retracted together, entitled to a cash price equal to the NAV per Unit on that date, less any costs associated with the retraction.

Note: The Portfolio Shares consist of The Bank of Nova Scotia common shares. Issued concurrently with an equal number of class A shares. Termination date extended to November 30, 2021 and may be further extended for successive terms of up to seven years after November 30, 2021.

Lead Underwriter(s): RBC Capital Markets, CIBC World Markets Inc., Scotia Capital Inc.
Transfer Agent: Computershare Investor Services Inc.
Registrar: Computershare Investor Services Inc.
Exchanges: TSX
Symbol: SBN.PR.A
CUSIP: 784732208

Sustainable Power & Infrastructure Split Corp.

5% Pref.

DBRS Rating:	Pfd-3	Mar 15, 2024	
Issued:	3,732,166 shs.	May 21, 2021	$10.000
O/S:	3,546,366 shs.	Dec 31, 2023	
Dividend:	$0.50 (Q)	Mar 31/Jun 30/Sep 30/Dec 31	

Note: Invests in a globally diversified and actively managed portfolio consisting primarily of dividend-paying securities of power and infrastructure companies, whose assets, products and services the manager believes are facilitating the multi-decade transition toward decarbonization and environmental sustainability. Issued concurrently with an equal number of Class A shares.

Lead Underwriter(s): RBC Capital Markets, CIBC World Markets Inc., National Bank Financial Inc., Scotia Capital Inc.
Transfer Agent: TSX Trust Company
Registrar: TSX Trust Company
Exchanges: TSX
Symbol: PWI.PR.A
CUSIP: 86934R209

TDb Split Corp.

Priority Equity Shares

Issued:	7,062,012 shs.	Aug 7, 2007	$10.000
O/S:	7,217,560 shs.	Nov 30, 2023	
Dividend:	$0.525 (M)	Payable on the 10th day of each month	

Dividend Details: Dividends will be paid within 10 days of the Dividend Record Date (the last business day of each month).

Retraction: Retract. at any time to receive payment on the Retraction Payment Date (fifteenth business day following such Retraction Date). Retraction price per share will equal the lesser of (i) 96% of the NAV per Unit determined as of the Retraction Date (last business day of each month), less the cost to the company of the purchase of a class A share in the market for cancellation and less any other applicable costs and (ii) $10.00. Under an annual retraction right in December, if both a preferred share and a class A share are retracted together, entitled to a cash price equal to the NAV per Unit on that date.

Note: The Portfolio Shares consist of The Toronto-Dominion Bank common shares. On or about Dec. 1, 2014, the "Termination Date", holders will, to the extent possible, receive $10.00 for each priority equity share held. Issued concurrently with an equal number of class A shares.

FP Equities — Preferreds & Derivatives 2024   147

Lead Underwriter(s): CIBC World Markets Inc., RBC Capital Markets
Transfer Agent: Computershare Investor Services Inc.
Registrar: Computershare Investor Services Inc.
Exchanges: TSX
Symbol: XTD.PR.A
CUSIP: 87234Y100

US Financial 15 Split Corp.

2012 Cum. Pref.

Issued:	2,207,399 shs.	Jun 25, 2012	$10.000
O/S:	1,900,817 shs.	Nov 30, 2023	
Dividend:	V.R. (M)	Payable on the 10th day of each month	

Dividend Details: Monthly dividend rate is equal to 5.25% per annum, based on the net asset value per Unit calculated as at the end of the preceding month (maximum of $0.04375 per month per Preferred share). Dividends will be paid within 10 days of the Dividend Record Date (the last business day of each month).

Retraction: Retract. at any time to receive payment on the Retraction Payment Date (15th day following a Retraction Date). Retraction price per share will equal the lesser of (i) 98% of the NAV per Unit determined as of such Retraction Date (last business day of each month), less the cost to the company of the purchase of a class A share in the market for cancellation and less any other applicable costs and (ii) $10.00. Under an annual retraction right in February, if both a preferred share and a class A share are retracted together, entitled to a cash price equal to the NAV per Unit on that date plus accrued and unpaid dividends.

Note: Issued upon exchange of the 5.25% preferred shares following a capital reorganization.

Transfer Agent: Computershare Investor Services Inc.
Registrar: Computershare Investor Services Inc.
Exchanges: TSX
Symbol: FTU.PR.B
CUSIP: 90341H309

World Financial Split Corp.

5.25% Cum. Pref.

Issued:	18,850,000 shs.	Feb 17, 2004	$10.000
O/S:	862,417 shs.	Dec 31, 2023	
Dividend:	$0.525 (Q)	Mar 31/Jun 30/Sep 30/Dec 31	

Dividend Details: Distributions may consist of ordinary dividends, capital gains dividends or non-taxable returns of capital or any combination thereof.

Redemption: All outstanding preferred shares will be redeemed on min. 30 days' notice on June 30, 2018 at a price equal to the lesser of (i) $10.00 and (ii) the NAV of the company on that date divided by the total number of preferred shares then outstanding.

Retraction: Retract. at any time to receive payment on the Retraction Payment Date (eighth business day following a Valuation Date). Retraction price per share will equal 96% of the lesser of (i) the NAV per Unit determined as of such Valuation Date (five business days prior to the last day of a month) less the cost to the company, including commissions, of purchasing a class A share in the market and (ii) $10.00. Under an annual retraction right in June, if both a preferred share and a class A share are retracted together, entitled to a cash price equal to the NAV per Unit on that date.

Note: The company invests in a portfolio which includes common equity securities selected from the ten largest financial services companies by market capitalization in each of Canada, the United States and the Rest of the World. In addition, the issuers of the securities in the portfolio, other than those of Canadian issuers, must have a minimum credit rating of "A" from Standard & Poor's Rating Services or a comparable rating from an equivalent rating agency. In addition, up to 20% of the NAV of the company may be invested in common shares of financial services companies that have a market capitalization at the time of investment of at least US$10 billion and for non-Canadian issuers, a minimum local currency issuer credit rating of "A-" from Standard & Poor's or a comparable rating from an equivalent rating agency. The Portfolio Universe will be reset on an annual basis on Dec. 31. Issued concurrently with an equal number of class A shares. The term of the fund was extended from June 30, 2011 to June 30, 2018 and the term will be automatically extended for successive seven-year terms after June 30, 2018.

Lead Underwriter(s): RBC Capital Markets
Transfer Agent: Computershare Investor Services Inc.
Registrar: Computershare Investor Services Inc.
Exchanges: TSX
Symbol: WFS.PR.A
CUSIP: 98146P202

Income Trusts

Income Trusts are designed as a higher-risk alternative to fixed-income securities. Distributions, based on performance of the fund's underlying assets, can vary substantially depending upon commodity prices, as well as volume of business and costs of production.

This section is an alphabetical listing of securities which are neither preferred, nor common, but are in effect units of a special type of incorporated body, known as a trust. Under the terms of their creation, these investment vehicles have special tax status, by virtue of their goal of distributing their annual income to the unit holders, on a tax-advantaged basis.

Oil & Gas Royalty Trusts are investments that provide exposure to resource sectors. The trust purchases a royalty, typically 99%, from a company with producing oil and gas properties. The trust receives royalty income, essentially net cash flow (cash flow, net of certain deductions, such as administrative expenses and management fees). Depending on the tax position of the trust—how much of its income is sheltered with Canadian Oil and Gas Property Expense or other tax pools—unitholders may receive all, or a portion of, the distributions as a return of capital. Under Canadian tax rules, this would reduce the adjusted cost base of the Income Trusts, and the unitholder could have to pay capital gains tax when the units are sold or deemed to be sold. A portion of the distributions can also be deemed a return on capital, and taxable as income.

Structured Products are structured to own debt and/or equity of a company engaged in a resource-oriented or other business. Whereas a royalty trust distributes the bulk of its cash flow derived from royalty income, an income trust distributes cash flow through interest on debentures and dividends from shares. Unlike a royalty trust, a tax shield on distributions is not available to an income trust.

Real Estate Investment Trusts are closed-end investment trusts that normally invest in income-producing properties. They often operate with balance sheets that are more conservative than those of traditional real estate companies. Typically, borrowing is limited to no more than 50% of adjusted assets, and they do not normally invest in raw land or engage in speculative development. REITs typically pay out 90% of distributable income. The capital cost allowance available to the REIT will reduce taxable income at the trust level but will not affect the amount of cash that can be distributed to unitholders of the REIT. The portion of distributed income which is not immediately taxable to the unitholder is treated as a return of capital and reduces the unitholder's cost base.

This table is organized into five trust groupings as follows:
(1) Business Trusts, (2) Oil & Gas Royalty Trusts, (3) Real Estate Investment Trusts, (4) Structured Products.

References for Table

Recent Price	Latest closing price to May 9, 2024
Rate	Total distributions declared in the last twelve months, or less if recently issued. (n.a. - new issue, no distributions declared yet)
DRIP	Dividend Reinvestment Plan. At their option, unitholder can elect to receive additional units in lieu of cash payment.
NAV	Net Asset Value. Holders have the option to request redemption at NAV. In other cases, some funds are redeemable under specific circumstances and others are not redeemable until termination.
Termination Date	Date at which the trust will be wound up and the assets divided.
Assets held in Portfolio	Describes the holdings, or purpose of the trust.
Note 1	o/s amounts do not include shares or other securities exchangeable into trust untits.

Trust Units

Business Trusts

Issuer	O/S Amount	O/S Date	Recent Price	Rate	DRIP	Redeem.	Termination Date	Exchange	Symbol	Assets held in Portfolio
A&W Rev Royalties Incm Fd	20,383,114	Dec 31, 2023	$29.59	$1.92	yes			T	AW.UN	Royalties of 3% on sales generated by A&W restaurants in the Royalty Pool
Alaris Eqty Ptnrs Incm Tr	45,498,191	Dec 31, 2023	$16.17	$1.36				T	AD.UN	Provides alternative financing primarily to private companies in North America in return for royalties or distributions.
Boston Pizza Royalties	21,278,563	Dec 31, 2023	$15.80	$1.356				T	BPF.UN	Royalties of 4% on total sales from Boston Pizza restaurants in the Royalty Pool
Chemtrade Logistics Incm	115,536,668	Dec 31, 2023	$8.71	$0.66	yes			T	CHE.UN	Chemical by-product removal, storage, marketing and distribution services, primarily to the mining industry
DRI Healthcare Trust	56,358,240	Dec 31, 2023	US$16.16	US$0.34				T	DHT.UN	Owns and acquires pharmaceutical royalties.
Dream Impact Trust	17,571,967	Dec 31, 2023	$3.84	$0.64				T	MPCT.UN	Invests in hard asset alternative investments with a focus on real estate lending and infrastructure, including renewable power.
Keg Royalties Income Fund	11,353,500	Dec 31, 2023	$14.70	$1.1352				T	KEG.UN	Royalties of 4% of gross sales from the Keg restaurants in the Royalty Pool
Richards Pkg Income Fund	10,955,007	Dec 31, 2023	$31.68	$1.32				T	RPI.UN	Full-service rigid packaging distributor targeting small and medium-sized North American businesses
SIR Royalty Income Fund	8,375,567	Dec 31, 2023	$13.27	$1.14				T	SRV.UN	Royalties of 6% of the pooled revenues from SIR Restaurants in Canada (including Jack Astor's Bar and Grill, Canyon Creek Chop House, Alice Fazooli's! Italian Crabshack and reds Bistro & Bar)

Real Estate Investment Trusts

Trust Units

Issuer	O/S Amount	O/S Date	Recent Price	Rate	DRIP	Redeem.	Termination Date	Exchange	Symbol	Assets held in Portfolio
Allied Properties REIT	127,955,983	Dec 31, 2023	$16.99	$1.80	yes			T	AP.UN	Class I urban office properties in downtown Toronto
American Hotel Incm Pptys	79,026,415	Dec 31, 2023	US$0.57					T	HOT.UN	Hotels in the United States focused on providing railroad crew accommodation.
Artis REIT	107,950,866	Dec 31, 2023	$6.38	$0.60				T	AX.UN	Owns a portfolio of real estate properties, including commercial, multi-family residential, industrial, office and mixed-use properties in western Canada, primarily in Alberta
Automotive Pptys REIT	39,727,346	Dec 31, 2023	$9.96	$0.80				T	APR.UN	Owns primarily income-producing automotive dealership properties across Canada.
BSR Real Estate Invt Tr	33,141,180	Dec 31, 2023	US$11.14	US$0.52				T	HOM.U	Garden-style, multi-family residential properties primarily in the sunbelt region of the United States.
BTB REIT	86,705,901	Dec 31, 2023	$3.18	$0.30	yes			T	BTB.UN	Mid-market office, industrial, and retail properties in both primary and secondary markets across Canada with an initial focus on geographic markets east of Ottawa, Ontario
Boardwalk REIT	49,388,174	Dec 31, 2023	$72.75	$1.44				T	BEI.UN	Owns and operates multi-family residential communities within Canada
CT Real Estate Invt Trust	108,321,650	Dec 31, 2023	$13.89	$0.9252	yes			T	CRT.UN	Commercial properties in Canada.
Canadian Apt Pptys REIT	167,614,292	Dec 31, 2023	$45.50	$1.45	yes			T	CAR.UN	Multi-unit residential properties
Cdn Net Real Estate Invt	20,528,502	Dec 31, 2023	$4.95	$0.345				V	NET.UN	Owns commercial property along Highway 20 in Mont St-Hilaire, St-Jean-sur-le-Richelieu and Rivière-du-Loup, Que.
Choice Pptys REIT	327,859,972	Dec 31, 2023	$13.13	$0.75				T	CHP.UN	Owns income-producing commercial properties in Canada.

Trust Units

Issuer	O/S Amount	O/S Date	Recent Price	Rate	DRIP	Redeem.	Termination Date	Exchange	Symbol	Assets held in Portfolio
Crombie REIT	106,905,347	Dec 31, 2023	$12.97	$0.89004	yes			T	CRR.UN	Retail, office and mixed-use properties located in Canada, primarily retail properties in Ontario and western Canada
Dream Indl REIT	273,243,349	Dec 31, 2023	$12.96	$0.70	yes			T	DIR.UN	Industrial properties in Canada
Dream Office REIT	16,313,218	Feb 27, 2024	$18.15	$1.00	yes			T	D.UN	Central business district office properties primarily in downtown Toronto, Ont.
Dream Residential Real	12,645,268	Dec 31, 2023	US$6.26	US$0.42				T	DRR.U	Multi-residential properties in the United States.
European Residential REIT	91,470,111	Dec 31, 2023	€2.30	€0.12				T	ERE.UN	Owns and invests in residential and commercial properties in Europe.
Firm Cap Apt REIT	7,604,375	Dec 31, 2023	US$5.35	US$0.246	yes			V	FCA.UN	Acquires and manages multi-unit residential properties in major cities across the United States.
Firm Capital Property Tr	36,925,682	Dec 31, 2023	$5.03	$0.52	yes			T	FCD.UN	Owns industrial, retail, medical office and multi-residential properties across Canada.
First Capital REIT	212,184,309	Dec 31, 2023	$15.17	$0.864	yes			T	FCR.UN	Develops, owns and operates mixed-use real estate properties in major urban centres across Canada, with tenants including grocery stores, pharmacies, liquor stores, banks, restaurants, cafés, fitness centres, medical, childcare facilities and professional and personal services.
Flagship Communities REIT	15,492,056	Dec 31, 2023	US$15.00	US$0.5904				T	MHC.U	Owns and acquires manufactured home communities (MHCs) and related assets in the U.S.
H&R REIT	261,867,587	Dec 31, 2023	$9.27	$0.60				T	HR.UN	Commercial and residential properties across Canada and in the United States.
Inovalis REIT	32,594,711	Dec 31, 2023	$1.06	$0.4125	yes			T	INO.UN	Office properties primarily in France and Germany.
InterRent REIT	144,783,151	Dec 31, 2023	$11.92	$0.378	yes			T	IIP.UN	Multi-unit residential income properties in southern and eastern Ontario

Trust Units

Issuer	O/S Amount	O/S Date	Recent Price	Rate	DRIP	Redeem.	Termination Date	Exchange	Symbol	Assets held in Portfolio
Killam Apartment REIT	118,298,478	Dec 31, 2023	$17.20	$0.69996	yes			T	KMP.UN	Acquires, manages and develops multi-family residential apartment buildings and manufactured home communities in Atlantic Canada, Ontario and Alberta.
Lanesborough REIT	680,473,620	Dec 31, 2023	$0.01					V	LRT.UN	Retail, residential, industrial and office properties located across Canada
Marwest Apt REIT	8,657,564	Dec 31, 2023	$0.77	$0.0153				V	MAR.UN	Owns and operates multi-family residential properties in western Canada.
Melcor REIT	12,963,169	Dec 31, 2023	$2.98					T	MR.UN	Retail, office and industrial properties.
Minto Apt REIT	39,898,612	Dec 31, 2023	$15.15	$0.505				T	MI.UN	Owns income-producing multi-residential properties in urban markets in Canada.
Morguard NA Res REIT	37,735,959	Dec 31, 2023	$16.12	$0.74004	yes			T	MRG.UN	Owns multi-unit residential properties in Canada and the United States
Morguard REIT	64,267,901	Dec 31, 2023	$5.35	$0.24	yes			T	MRT.UN	Office, industrial and retail properties across Canada
NexPoint Hospitality Tr	29,352,055	Dec 31, 2023	US$0.01	US$0.0497				V	NHT.U	Acquires, owns, renovates and operates hotel properties in the United States, with a focus on select-service and extended stay hotels.
Nexus Industrial REIT	68,589,606	Dec 31, 2023	$7.18	$0.64	yes			T	NXR.UN	Industrial properties in Canada.
Northview Residential	3,280,000	Dec 31, 2023	$14.20	$1.09375				T	NRR.UN	Acquires, owns and operates income-producing multi-residential suites, commercial real estate and execusuites located primarily in secondary markets within British Columbia, Alberta, Saskatchewan, Québec, New Brunswick, Newfoundland and Labrador, the Northwest Territories and Nunavut.

Trust Units

Issuer	O/S Amount	O/S Date	Recent Price	Rate	DRIP	Redeem.	Termination Date	Exchange	Symbol	Assets held in Portfolio
NorthWest Healthcare REIT	243,292,126	Dec 31, 2023	$5.07	$0.36	yes			T	NWH.UN	Portfolio of income-producing properties with a focus on leasing space to doctors, dentists, other medical professionals and related healthcare service providers such as pharmacies, laboratories and diagnostic imaging clinics
PRO Real Estate Invt Tr	59,249,207	Dec 31, 2023	$5.08	$0.45	yes			T	PRV.UN	Commercial properties in Canada, primarily in Québec, Atlantic Canada and Ontario.
Pine Trail Real Estate	35,442,657	Dec 31, 2023	$0.04		yes			V	PINE.UN	Owns and acquires healthcare properties in Canada with a focus on medical office buildings and seniors housing.
Plaza Retail REIT	110,368,000	Dec 31, 2023	$3.50	$0.28	yes			T	PLZ.UN	Unenclosed and enclosed retail real estate throughout Canada with a focus on eastern Canada.
Primaris Real Estate Invt	96,585,736	Dec 31, 2023	$13.71	$0.84				T	PMZ.UN	Enclosed shopping centres located in major urban markets and major secondary cities across Canada.
RioCan REIT	300,455,000	Dec 31, 2023	$17.66	$1.11				T	REI.UN	Primarily retail properties
Slate Grocery REIT	58,985,408	Dec 31, 2023	US$10.73	US$0.864	yes			T	SGR.UN	Grocery anchored shopping centres in secondary markets in the United States.
Slate Office REIT	80,049,062	Dec 31, 2023	$0.68		yes			T	SOT.UN	Industrial, office and retail properties primarily in western Canada.
SmartCentres Real Estate	144,625,322	Dec 31, 2023	$22.78	$1.85				T	SRU.UN	Mid-market retail, office and industrial rental properties
Sun Residential REIT	203,338,999	Dec 31, 2023	$0.04	$0.0038				V	SRES	Owns and operates multi-family residential properties primarily in the sunbelt region of the United States.
True North Coml Real	15,676,644	Dec 31, 2023	$9.62		yes			T	TNT.UN	Owns commercial properties.

Trust Units

Issuer	O/S Amount	O/S Date	Recent Price	Rate	DRIP	Redeem.	Termination Date	Exchange	Symbol	Assets held in Portfolio
Structured Products										
Bitcoin Fund	6,440,080	Dec 31, 2023	US$63.75					T	QBTC.U	Invests in the digital currency bitcoin.
Bloom Select Income Fund	1,174,060	Dec 31, 2023	$7.35	$0.50	yes			T	BLB.UN	Diversified portfolio comprised primarily of publicly listed or traded Canadian securities, primarily of eligible high dividend paying Canadian common equity securities, income trusts and REITs that have a Beta of less than 1.0 at the time of investment
Blue Ribbon Income Fund	8,515,572	Dec 31, 2023	$7.66	$0.48	yes			T	RBN.UN	Canadian royalty trusts, income funds, real estate investment trusts and limited partnerships
Brookfield Glo Infra Fd	16,227,350	Dec 31, 2023	$4.30	$0.60	yes			T	BGI.UN	Invests primarily in equity securities of publicly traded global infrastructure companies.
Cdn High Income Equity Fd	1,072,760	Dec 31, 2023	$6.40	$0.48	yes			T	CIQ.UN	Portfolio consisting primarily of the many undervalued high income investment opportunities in the income trust sector and on the expanding high-income common equity market
Canoe EIT Income Fund	177,791,829	Feb 23, 2024	$13.84	$1.20	yes		Dec 31, 2050	T	EIT.UN	Royalty and income trusts and real estate investment trusts
Canso Credit Income Fund	9,093,749	Dec 31, 2023	$14.90	$0.50				T	PBY.UN	Primarily consists of corporate bonds and other credit instruments, but will also, from time to time, hold other securities (such as convertible and distressed bonds) in the portfolio as a result of exchanges, recapitalization and other reorganizations

Trust Units

Issuer	O/S Amount	O/S Date	Recent Price	Rate	DRIP	Redeem.	Termination Date	Exchange	Symbol	Assets held in Portfolio
Citadel Income Fund	3,117,698	Dec 31, 2023	$2.50	$0.12	yes	NAV		T	CTF.UN	Portfolio of income funds, approximately equally weighted except for oil & gas trusts and REITs (which will be equally weighted within their respective sectors), with each fund comprising the Portfolio being publicly rated (with a rating of SR-5 or higher) and having a minimum float capitalization of $400 million and a yield of at least 6% per annum
Energy Income Fund	2,338,790	Dec 31, 2023	$1.51	$0.12	yes	NAV		T	ENI.UN	Oil and gas trusts and oil and gas corporations
Ether Fund	4,278,182	Dec 31, 2023	US$48.75					T	QETH.U	Invests in the digital currency Ether.
Healthcare Special	1,568,800	Dec 31, 2023	$13.00	$0.24068				T	MDS.UN	Invests primarily in publicly traded issuers and private issuers that derive a significant portion of their revenue or earnings from medical and healthcare products and/or services.
Income Financial Trust	3,349,070	Dec 31, 2023	$7.60	$0.768		NAV	Jan 01, 2029	T	INC.UN	Shares of companies included in the TSX Financial Services Index, the S&P Financials Index and the S&P Midcap Financials Index
JFT Strategies Fund	2,967,442	Dec 31, 2023	$25.34	$0.25	yes			T	JFS.UN	Portfolio will consist of long/short positions in any one or a combination of equities, debt securities or other securities that seek to generate positive returns by selecting what the Portfolio Manager believes to be superior quality investments for long positions and inferior quality investments for short positions
MINT Income Fund	10,923,499	Dec 31, 2023	$6.81	$0.48	yes			T	MID.UN	Primarily high yield equities, supplemented by high yield debt

Trust Units

Issuer	O/S Amount	O/S Date	Recent Price	Rate	DRIP	Redeem.	Termination Date	Exchange	Symbol	Assets held in Portfolio
Marret High Yield Strat	36,729,002	Dec 31, 2023	$0.01					O	MHY.UN	Portfolio focused primarily on high yield debt securities to generate returns consistent with the long-term performance of equity indices, but with the volatility and risk characteristics consistent with 10 year U.S. Treasury notes
Marret Multi-Strategy	3,301,850	Dec 31, 2023	$0.01					O	MMF.UN	Provides exposure to five diversified, actively managed investment portfolios consisting primarily of income generating securities
Middlefid Glo Real Asset	3,510,152	Dec 31, 2023	$7.11	$0.50	yes			T	RA.UN	Invests primarily in dividend paying securities of global issuers focused on, involved in or that derive a significant portion of their revenue from physical real estate or infrastructure assets.
PIMCO Global Inc Opp	36,546,016	Dec 31, 2023	$7.49	$0.68256	yes			T	PGI.UN	Actively managed portfolio consisting primarily of fixed-income securities across multiple global fixed-income sectors.
PIMCO Multi-Sector Income	25,613,259	Dec 31, 2023	$8.01	$0.78456	yes			T	PIX.UN	Actively managed portfolio consisting primarily of fixed income securities selected from multiple global fixed income sectors.
PIMCO Tactical Income Fd	34,476,468	Dec 31, 2023	$6.67	$0.6698	yes			T	PTI.UN	Actively managed portfolio consisting primarily of fixed income securities selected from multiple global fixed income sectors.
PIMCO Tactical Incm Fd	37,619,995	Dec 31, 2023	$7.22	$0.68508	yes			T	PTO.UN	Actively managed portfolio of debt obligations and other income-producing securities and instruments of any type and credit quality with varying maturities and related derivatives, and real estate-related investments.

Trust Units

Issuer	O/S Amount	O/S Date	Recent Price	Rate	DRIP	Redeem.	Termination Date	Exchange	Symbol	Assets held in Portfolio
Picton Mahoney Tactical	1,941,197	Dec 31, 2023	$6.89	$0.36	yes			T	PMB.UN	Diversified portfolio of income producing securities, primarily consisting of long and short positions in high-yield and investment grade bonds and, to a more limited extent, government bonds, convertible bonds, preferred shares and dividend paying equities, with a focus on North American issuers
Precious Metals & Mng Tr	10,676,487	Dec 31, 2023	$1.77	$0.12	yes	NAV		T	MMP.UN	Portfolio of mining issuers focusing on companies engaged in the exploration, mining and production of gold, diamonds, uranium, copper, zinc and other metals and minerals listed on North American stock exchanges
Ravensource Fund	1,296,075	Dec 31, 2023	$15.97					T	RAV.UN	Debt securities of issuers in Australia, New Zealand and other Asian countries
Sprott Physical Gold Tr	401,306,562	Dec 31, 2023	17.88					T	PHYS.U	Invests and holds substantially all of its assets in physical gold bullion
Sprott Physical Platinum	10,872,372	Dec 31, 2023	9.80					T	SPPP.U	Invests in and holds physical platinum and palladium.
Sprott Physical Silver Tr	487,602,694	Dec 31, 2023	9.30					T	PSLV.U	Invests and holds substantially all of its assets in physical silver bullion
Sustainable Inno Hlth Div	2,902,353	Dec 31, 2023	$11.91	$0.39996	yes			T	SIH.UN	Invests primarily in dividend paying securities of global technology and healthcare companies, including initially those which the fund's advisor believes are positioned to benefit long-term from the trends and changing consumer behaviours resulting from the COVID-19 global pandemic.

Trust Units

Issuer	O/S Amount	O/S Date	Recent Price	Rate	DRIP	Redeem.	Termination Date	Exchange	Symbol	Assets held in Portfolio
Sustainable Real Estate	2,259,526	Dec 31, 2023	$6.83	$0.50004				T	MSRE.UN	Diversified, actively managed portfolio consisting primarily of dividend paying securities of international issuers focused on, involved in, or that derive a significant portion of their revenue from business models that are creating and transforming the green property and related sectors by employing or developing sustainable property management practices or materials.
Symphony Floating Rate Sr	6,880,403	Dec 31, 2023	$6.87	$0.60	yes			T	SSF.UN	Provides exposure to a diversified portfolio consisting primarily of short-duration floating rate senior corporate debt instruments, including senior secured loans and other senior debt obligations of North American non-investment grade corporate borrowers

Warrants

A warrant represents the option to buy shares of the issuing company at a stated price (the exercise price) to a specified date (the expiry date). Most warrants are exercisable for a period of several years from their date of issue. Warrants issued by junior resource companies are a notable exception, usually expiring within one year of their date of issue. Perpetual warrants are another exception but are extremely rare.

Variations of the basic warrant include warrants with extended expiry dates, and piggyback warrants which entitle the holder to acquire additional warrants on exercise of the original. While they usually represent the right to buy common shares of the issuer, in recent years warrants have been issued entitling holders to acquire flow-through shares, preferred shares, corporate debt instruments, gold, silver, U.S. dollars and even Government of Canada Bonds.

Warrants may be attached to new debt and preferred share issues to increase the marketability of such issues. These warrants are usually detachable. Also, warrants are frequently offered to the public in units which combine common shares with warrants to acquire additional common shares. Warrants issued in this manner are usually separable from the stock at some later date and can then be traded separately.

The value of a warrant at any given time depends upon its exercise price, the market value of the underlying shares and the time left to expiry. When the market value of the shares exceeds the warrant exercise price, the warrant has an intrinsic value equal to the excess of market value over the warrant exercise price. When the market value of the shares is less than the warrant exercise price, the warrant carries a premium equal to the excess cost of acquiring stock by exercising the warrant over the cost of acquiring stock directly. The premium or speculative value of a warrant diminishes as the expiry date draws near. On expiration, all warrants are worthless.

A warrant's leverage potential is its most attractive feature. Leverage refers to the appreciation or loss potential of a warrant. Because of the relatively low cost of investing in warrants, any increase in the value of the underlying stock will result in a much greater increase in the value of the warrant. The greater the leverage, the greater the warrant's appreciation potential when the value of the stock rises and conversely, the greater the warrant's loss potential when the value of the stock falls.

Warrants can be traded in the market for capital gains or they can be exercised to acquire shares at a cost lower than market value. Low cost, versatility, and the high potential for capital gain make warrants an interesting and attractive investment option.

Warrants, by Expiry Date

Expiry Date	Issuer	Basis	Exercise Price	Exchange	Symbol
May 12, 2024	Cardiol Therapeutics Inc	1 wt to buy 1 cl. A sh	$4.60	T	CRDL.WT.A
May 13, 2024	American Lithium Corp	1 wt to buy 1 com sh	$3.00	V	LI.WT
May 16, 2024	FRX Innovations Inc	1 wt to buy 1 com sh	$1.30	V	FRXI.WT
May 27, 2024	Reconnaissance Energy	1 wt to buy 1 com sh	$14.00	V	RECO.WT.A
May 30, 2024	HIVE Digital Tchnlgys Ltd	5 wts to buy 1 com sh	$30.00	V	HIVE.WT
Jun 12, 2024	BZAM Ltd	1 wt to buy 1 com sh	$0.50	O	BZAM.WR
Jun 16, 2024	Millennial Precious Mtls	1 wt to buy 0.092 com sh	$1.38	V	MPM.MT
Jun 16, 2024	Stack Capital Group Inc	1 wt to buy 1 com sh	$15.00	T	STCK.WT
Jun 28, 2024	AnalytixInsight Inc	1 wt to buy 1 com sh	$0.90	V	ALY.WT
Jun 29, 2024	VSBLTY Grpe Tchnlgys Corp	1 wt to buy 1 com sh	$0.65	O	VSBY.WT.A
Jul 08, 2024	Choom Holdings Inc	1 wt to buy 1 com sh	$0.12		
Jul 15, 2024	Mexican Gold Mining Corp	10 wts to buy 1 com sh	$1.20	V	MEX.WT
Jul 28, 2024	Red Light Holland Corp	1 wt to buy 1 com sh	$0.38	O	TRIP.WT
Aug 16, 2024	Tidewater Midstream	1 wt to buy 1 com sh	$1.44	T	TWM.WT
Aug 22, 2024	Theralase Tchnlgys Inc	1 wt to buy 1 com sh	$0.35	V	TLT.WT
Sep 02, 2024	Graphene Mfg Group Ltd	1 wt to buy 1 ord	$2.60	V	GMG.WT
Sep 16, 2024	Decibel Cannabis Co Inc	1 wt to buy 1 com sh	$0.40	V	DB.WT.A
Sep 26, 2024	Jackpot Digital Inc	1 wt to buy 1 com sh	$1.00	V	JJ.WT.B
Sep 30, 2024	Nevada Copper Corp	1 wt to buy 1 com sh	$0.34	T	NCU.WT.C
Oct 06, 2024	Volatus Aerospace Corp	1 wt to buy 1 com sh	$0.50	V	VOL.WT.A
Oct 24, 2024	Avanti Helium Corp	1 wt to buy 1 com sh	$0.80	V	AVN.WT
Oct 26, 2024	WonderFi Technologies Inc	1 wt to buy 1 com sh	$2.55	T	WNDR.WT.B
Nov 15, 2024	Tokens.com Corp	1 wt to buy 1 com sh	$1.15	V	COIN.WT
Nov 23, 2024	Wellfield Tchnlgys Inc	1 wt to buy 1 com sh	$2.00	V	WFLD.WT
Nov 23, 2024	Wildpack Beverage Inc	1 wt to buy 1 com sh	$1.26	V	CANS.WT.A
Dec 05, 2024	Sagicor Financial Co Ltd	1 wt to buy 1 com sh	$11.50	T	SFC.WT

Derivatives

Warrants, by Expiry Date

Expiry Date	Issuer	Basis	Exercise Price	Exchange	Symbol
Dec 06, 2024	Uranium Royalty Corp	1 wt to buy 1 com sh	$2.00	T	URC.WT
Dec 15, 2024	Cross River Ventures Corp	1 wt to buy 1 com sh	$0.20	O	CRVC.WT
Dec 17, 2024	Blackhawk Growth Corp	1 wt to buy 1 com sh	$0.05	O	BLR.WT
Dec 23, 2024	Eat Well Invt Group Inc	1 wt to buy 1 com sh	$0.75	O	EWG.WT
Jan 14, 2025	mCloud Technologies Corp	3 wts to buy 1 com sh	$16.20	V	MCLD.WT.H
Feb 04, 2025	Exro Technologies Inc	1 wt to buy 1 com sh	$2.00	T	EXRO.WT
Feb 06, 2025	Avanti Helium Corp	1 wt to buy 1 com sh	$1.00	V	AVN.WT.A
Feb 08, 2025	Giga Metals Corp	1 wt to buy 1 com sh	$0.45	V	GIGA.WT.A
Feb 16, 2025	LithiumBank Res Corp	1 wt to buy 1 com sh	$2.00	V	LBNK.WT
Mar 04, 2025	ROK Resources Inc	1 wt to buy 1 cl. B sh	$0.25	V	ROK.WT
Mar 10, 2025	Saturn Oil & Gas Inc	1 wt to buy 1 com sh	$4.00	T	SOIL.WT.A
Mar 24, 2025	Desert Mountain Enrg Corp	1 wt to buy 1 com sh	$2.70	V	DME.WT
Mar 30, 2025	Nepra Foods Inc	1 wt to buy 1 sub vtg	$0.70	O	NPRA.WT
Apr 06, 2025	Hertz Energy Inc	1 wt to buy 1 com sh	$0.25	O	HZ.WT
Apr 13, 2025	Decisive Dividend Corp	1 wt to buy 1 com sh	$7.09	V	DE.WT
May 01, 2025	Total Helium Ltd	1 wt to buy 1 com sh	$0.75	V	TOH.WT.A
Jun 01, 2025	Aurora Cannabis Inc	10 wts to buy 1 com sh	US$32.00	T	ACB.WS.U
Jun 29, 2025	Trillion Energy Intl Inc	1 wt to buy 1 com sh	$0.50	O	TCF.WT
Jul 28, 2025	VSBLTY Grpe Tchnlgys Corp	1 wt to buy 1 com sh	$0.50	O	VSBY.WT.B
Jul 29, 2025	Aris Mining Corp	1 wt to buy 0.5 com sh	$2.75	T	ARIS.WT.A
Aug 19, 2025	Rock Tech Lithium Inc	1 wt to buy 1 com sh	$4.50	V	RCK.WT
Oct 05, 2025	NowVertical Group Inc	1 wt to buy 1 com sh	$1.25	V	NOW.WT.A
Oct 22, 2025	BZAM Ltd	1 wt to buy 1 com sh	$0.30	O	BZAM.WA
Nov 11, 2025	Lion One Metals Ltd	1 wt to buy 1 com sh	$1.25	V	LIO.WT
Nov 20, 2025	Jackpot Digital Inc	1 wt to buy 1 com sh	$0.10	V	JJ.WT.C
Nov 24, 2025	Emerge Commerce Ltd	1 wt to buy 1 com sh	$0.25	V	ECOM.WT

Warrants, by Expiry Date

Expiry Date	Issuer	Basis	Exercise Price	Exchange	Symbol
Nov 26, 2025	Khiron Life Sciences Corp	1 wt to buy 1 com sh	$0.75	V	KHRN.WT.H
Dec 10, 2025	BZAM Ltd	1 wt to buy 1 com sh	$0.35	O	BZAM.WB
Jan 01, 2026	Cenovus Energy Inc	1 wt to buy 1 com sh	$6.54	T / N	CVE.WT / CVE.WS
Jan 06, 2026	Hempfusion Wellness Inc	1 wt to buy 1 com sh	US$1.20		
Jan 16, 2026	Gold Flora Corp	1 wt to buy 1 com sh	US$11.50	W	GRAM.WT.U
Feb 07, 2026	Ayr Wellness Inc	1 wt to buy 1 sub vtg	US$2.12	O	AYR.WT.U
Feb 09, 2026	Silver Mountain Res Inc	1 wt to buy 1 com sh	$0.45	V	AGMR.WT.A
Feb 13, 2026	Glass House Brands Inc	1 wt to buy 1 cl. A sh	US$11.50	W	GLAS.WT.U
Feb 28, 2026	NowVertical Group Inc	1 wt to buy 1 com sh	$0.80	V	NOW.WT.B
Mar 02, 2026	Carbon Streaming Corp	5 wts to buy 1 com sh	$7.50	W	NETZ.WT
Mar 02, 2026	Ionic Brands Corp	1 wt to buy 1 com sh	$0.30	O	IONC.WT
Mar 02, 2026	Osisko Development Corp	1 wt to buy 1 com sh	$8.55	V	ODV.WT.B
Mar 09, 2026	Eupraxia Phrmctcls Inc	1 wt to buy 1 com sh	$11.20	T	EPRX.WT
Mar 17, 2026	Denarius Metals Corp	10 wts to buy 1 com sh	$8.00	W	DMET.WT
Apr 20, 2026	Eupraxia Phrmctcls Inc	1 wt to buy 1 com sh	$3.00	T	EPRX.WT.A
Apr 21, 2026	Taiga Motors Corp	1 wt to buy 1 com sh	$17.25	T	TAIG.WT
May 06, 2026	Lion Electric Co	1 wt to buy 1 com sh	US$11.50	T / N	LEV.WT / LEV.WS
Jun 07, 2026	Vintage Wine Estates Inc	1 wt to buy 1 cl A unit	US$11.50		
Jun 21, 2026	Replenish Nutrients Hldg	1 wt to buy 1 com sh	$0.32	O	ERTH.WT
Jul 02, 2026	NextPoint Financial Inc	1 wt to buy 1 com sh	US$11.50		
Aug 03, 2026	Highwood Asset Mgmt Ltd	1 wt to buy 1 com sh	$7.50	V	HAM.WT
Aug 15, 2026	LNG Energy Group Corp	1 wt to buy 1 com sh	$0.60	V	LNGE.WT
Oct 19, 2026	Algoma Steel Group Inc	1 wt to buy 1 com sh	US$11.50	T / Q	ASTL.WT / ASTLW

Warrants, by Expiry Date

Expiry Date	Issuer	Basis	Exercise Price	Exchange	Symbol
Oct 20, 2026	Else Nutrition Hldgs Inc	1 wt to buy 1 com sh	$2.70	T	BABY.WT.A
Oct 21, 2026	Aurania Resources Ltd	1 wt to buy 1 com sh	$2.20	V	ARU.WT.B
Nov 07, 2026	Leafly Holdings Inc	1 wt to buy 1 com sh	US$11.50	Q	LFLYW
Nov 08, 2026	Total Helium Ltd	1 wt to buy 1 com sh	$2.00	V	TOH.WT
Nov 14, 2026	Royal Helium Ltd	1 wt to buy 1 com sh	$0.31	V	RHC.WT.A
Nov 29, 2026	Freeman Gold Corp	1 wt to buy 1 com sh	US$0.65	V	FMAN.WT.U
Dec 06, 2026	Radio Fuels Energy Corp	1 wt to buy 1 com sh	$0.50	O	CAKE.WT
Mar 02, 2027	Osisko Development Corp	1 wt to buy 1 com sh	$14.75	V	ODV.WT.A
Mar 13, 2027	Integra Resources Corp	1 wt to buy 1 com sh	$1.20	V	ITR.WT
Mar 24, 2027	Elevation Gold Mng Corp	1 wt to buy 1 com sh	$0.70	V	ELVT.WT.A
Apr 24, 2027	Xtract One Tchnlgys Inc	1 wt to buy 1 com sh	$0.64	T	XTRA.WT
May 12, 2027	Anfield Energy Inc	1 wt to buy 1 com sh	$0.18	V	AEC.WT
May 20, 2027	NG Energy Intl Corp	1 wt to buy 1 com sh	$1.40	V	GASX.WT.A
May 27, 2027	Osisko Development Corp	1 wt to buy 1 com sh	US$10.70	V	ODV.WT.U
				Q	ODVWZ
Jul 08, 2027	Cielo Waste Solutions	15 wts to buy 1 com sh	$1.35	V	CMC.WT
Aug 16, 2027	Graphene Mfg Group Ltd	1 wt to buy 1 ord	$2.20	V	GMG.WT.A
Dec 09, 2027	KWESST Micro Systems Inc	1 wt to buy 1 com sh	US$5.00	V	KWE.WT.U
Dec 16, 2027	Lion Electric Co	1 wt to buy 1 com sh	US$2.80	T	LEV.WT.A
				N	LEV.WS.A
Apr 30, 2028	i-80 Gold Corp	1 wt to buy 1 com sh	$2.15	T	IAU.WT
Jun 16, 2028	Razor Energy Corp	1 wt to buy 1 com sh	$1.20	V	RZE.WT.H
Oct 05, 2028	Bear Creek Mining Corp	1 wt to buy 1 com sh	$0.42	V	BCM.WT
Mar 07, 2029	Planet 13 Holdings Inc	1 wt to buy 1 com sh	US$0.77	O	PLTH.WT
May 16, 2029	FG Acquisition Corp	1 wt to buy 1 cl. A sh	US$11.50	T	FGAA.WT.U
Jul 25, 2029	Agrinam Acquisition Corp	1 wt to buy 1 cl. A sh	US$11.50	T	AGRI.WT.U

Warrants, by Issuer

Issuer	Basis	Exercise Price	Expiry Date	Exchange	Symbol
Agrinam Acquisition Corp	1 wt to buy 1 cl. A sh	US$11.50	Jul 25, 2029	T	AGRI.WT.U
Algoma Steel Group Inc	1 wt to buy 1 com sh	US$11.50	Oct 19, 2026	T	ASTL.WT
American Lithium Corp	1 wt to buy 1 com sh	$3.00	May 13, 2024	V	LI.WT
Analytixinsight Inc	1 wt to buy 1 com sh	$0.90	Jun 28, 2024	V	ALY.WT
Anfield Energy Inc	1 wt to buy 1 com sh	$0.18	May 12, 2027	V	AEC.WT
Aris Mining Corp	1 wt to buy 0.5 com sh	$2.75	Jul 29, 2025	T	ARIS.WT.A
Aurania Resources Ltd	1 wt to buy 1 com sh	$2.20	Oct 21, 2026	V	ARU.WT.B
Aurora Cannabis Inc	10 wts to buy 1 com sh	US$32.00	Jun 01, 2025	T	ACB.WS.U
Avanti Helium Corp	1 wt to buy 1 com sh	$0.80	Oct 24, 2024	V	AVN.WT
Avanti Helium Corp	1 wt to buy 1 com sh	$1.00	Feb 06, 2025	V	AVN.WT.A
Ayr Wellness Inc	1 wt to buy 1 sub vtg	US$2.12	Feb 07, 2026	O	AYR.WT.U
BZAM Ltd	1 wt to buy 1 com sh	$0.30	Oct 22, 2025	O	BZAM.WA
BZAM Ltd	1 wt to buy 1 com sh	$0.35	Dec 10, 2025	O	BZAM.WB
BZAM Ltd	1 wt to buy 1 com sh	$0.50	Jun 12, 2024	O	BZAM.WR
Bear Creek Mining Corp	1 wt to buy 1 com sh	$0.42	Oct 05, 2028	V	BCM.WT
Blackhawk Growth Corp	1 wt to buy 1 com sh	$0.05	Dec 17, 2024	O	BLR.WT
Carbon Streaming Corp	5 wts to buy 1 com sh	$7.50	Mar 02, 2026	W	NETZ.WT
Cardiol Therapeutics Inc	1 wt to buy 1 cl. A sh	$4.60	May 12, 2024	T	CRDL.WT.A
Cenovus Energy Inc	1 wt to buy 1 com sh	$6.54	Jan 01, 2026	T	CVE.WT
				N	CVE.WS
Choom Holdings Inc	1 wt to buy 1 com sh	$0.12	Jul 08, 2024		
Cielo Waste Solutions	15 wts to buy 1 com sh	$1.35	Jul 08, 2027	V	CMC.WT
Cross River Ventures Corp	1 wt to buy 1 com sh	$0.20	Dec 15, 2024	O	CRVC.WT
Decibel Cannabis Co Inc	1 wt to buy 1 com sh	$0.40	Sep 16, 2024	V	DB.WT.A
Decisive Dividend Corp	1 wt to buy 1 com sh	$7.09	Apr 13, 2025	V	DE.WT

Warrants, by Issuer

Issuer	Basis	Exercise Price	Expiry Date	Exchange	Symbol
Denarius Metals Corp	10 wts to buy 1 com sh	$8.00	Mar 17, 2026	W	DMET.WT
Desert Mountain Enrg Corp	1 wt to buy 1 com sh	$2.70	Mar 24, 2025	V	DME.WT
Eat Well Invt Group Inc	1 wt to buy 1 com sh	$0.75	Dec 23, 2024	O	EWG.WT
Elevation Gold Mng Corp	1 wt to buy 1 com sh	$0.70	Mar 24, 2027	V	ELVT.WT.A
Else Nutrition Hldgs Inc	1 wt to buy 1 com sh	$2.70	Oct 20, 2026	T	BABY.WT.A
Emerge Commerce Ltd	1 wt to buy 1 com sh	$0.25	Nov 24, 2025	V	ECOM.WT
Eupraxia Phrmctcls Inc	1 wt to buy 1 com sh	$3.00	Apr 20, 2026	T	EPRX.WT.A
Eupraxia Phrmctcls Inc	1 wt to buy 1 com sh	$11.20	Mar 09, 2026	T	EPRX.WT
Exro Technologies Inc	1 wt to buy 1 com sh	$2.00	Feb 04, 2025	T	EXRO.WT
FG Acquisition Corp	1 wt to buy 1 cl. A sh	US$11.50	May 16, 2029	T	FGAA.WT.U
FRX Innovations Inc	1 wt to buy 1 com sh	$1.30	May 16, 2024	V	FRX.WT
Freeman Gold Corp	1 wt to buy 1 com sh	US$0.65	Nov 29, 2026	V	FMAN.WT.U
Giga Metals Corp	1 wt to buy 1 com sh	$0.45	Feb 08, 2025	V	GIGA.WT.A
Glass House Brands Inc	1 wt to buy 1 cl. A sh	US$11.50	Feb 13, 2026	W	GLAS.WT.U
Gold Flora Corp	1 wt to buy 1 com sh	US$11.50	Jan 16, 2026	W	GRAM.WT.U
Graphene Mfg Group Ltd	1 wt to buy 1 ord	$2.60	Sep 02, 2024	V	GMG.WT
Graphene Mfg Group Ltd	1 wt to buy 1 ord	$2.20	Aug 16, 2027	V	GMG.WT.A
HIVE Digital Tchnlgys Ltd	5 wts to buy 1 com sh	$30.00	May 30, 2024	V	HIVE.WT
Hempfusion Wellness Inc	1 wt to buy 1 com sh	US$1.20	Jan 06, 2026		
Hertz Energy Inc	1 wt to buy 1 com sh	$0.25	Apr 06, 2025	O	HZ.WT
Highwood Asset Mgmt Ltd	1 wt to buy 1 com sh	$7.50	Aug 03, 2026	V	HAM.WT
i-80 Gold Corp	1 wt to buy 1 com sh	$2.15	Apr 30, 2028	T	IAU.WT
Integra Resources Corp	1 wt to buy 1 com sh	$1.20	Mar 13, 2027	V	ITR.WT
Ionic Brands Corp	1 wt to buy 1 com sh	$0.30	Mar 02, 2026	O	IONC.WT
Jackpot Digital Inc	1 wt to buy 1 com sh	$1.00	Sep 26, 2024	V	JJ.WT.B
Jackpot Digital Inc	1 wt to buy 1 com sh	$0.10	Nov 20, 2025	V	JJ.WT.C
KWESST Micro Systems Inc	1 wt to buy 1 com sh	US$5.00	Dec 09, 2027	V	KWE.WT.U

FP Equities — Preferreds & Derivatives 2024

Warrants, by Issuer

Issuer	Basis	Exercise Price	Expiry Date	Exchange	Symbol
Khiron Life Sciences Corp	1 wt to buy 1 com sh	$0.75	Nov 26, 2025	V	KHRN.WT.H
LNG Energy Group Corp	1 wt to buy 1 com sh	$0.60	Aug 15, 2026	V	LNGE.WT
Leafly Holdings Inc	1 wt to buy 1 com sh	US$11.50	Nov 07, 2026	Q	LFLYW
Lion Electric Co	1 wt to buy 1 com sh	US$11.50	May 06, 2026	T	LEV.WT
				N	LEV.WS
Lion Electric Co	1 wt to buy 1 com sh	US$2.80	Dec 16, 2027	T	LEV.WT.A
				N	LEV.WS.A
Lion One Metals Ltd	1 wt to buy 1 com sh	$1.25	Nov 11, 2025	V	LIO.WT
LithiumBank Res Corp	1 wt to buy 1 com sh	$2.00	Feb 16, 2025	V	LBNK.WT
mCloud Technologies Corp	3 wts to buy 1 com sh	$16.20	Jan 14, 2025	V	MCLD.WT.H
Mexican Gold Mining Corp	10 wts to buy 1 com sh	$1.20	Jul 15, 2024	V	MEX.WT
Millennial Precious Mtls	1 wt to buy 0.092 com sh	$1.38	Jun 16, 2024	V	MPM.WT
NG Energy Intl Corp	1 wt to buy 1 com sh	$1.40	May 20, 2027	V	GASX.WT.A
Nepra Foods Inc	1 wt to buy 1 sub vtg	$0.70	Mar 30, 2025	O	NPRA.WT
Nevada Copper Corp	1 wt to buy 1 com sh	$0.34	Sep 30, 2024	T	NCU.WT.C
NextPoint Financial Inc	1 wt to buy 1 com sh	US$11.50	Jul 02, 2026		
NowVertical Group Inc	1 wt to buy 1 com sh	$1.25	Oct 05, 2025	V	NOW.WT.A
NowVertical Group Inc	1 wt to buy 1 com sh	$0.80	Feb 28, 2026	V	NOW.WT.B
Osisko Development Corp	1 wt to buy 1 com sh	$8.55	Mar 02, 2026	V	ODV.WT.B
Osisko Development Corp	1 wt to buy 1 com sh	$14.75	Mar 02, 2027	V	ODV.WT.A
Osisko Development Corp	1 wt to buy 1 com sh	US$10.70	May 27, 2027	V	ODV.WT.U
				Q	ODVWZ
Planet 13 Holdings Inc	1 wt to buy 1 com sh	US$0.77	Mar 07, 2029	O	PLTH.WT
ROK Resources Inc	1 wt to buy 1 cl. B sh	$0.25	Mar 04, 2025	V	ROK.WT
Radio Fuels Energy Corp	1 wt to buy 1 com sh	$0.50	Dec 06, 2026	O	CAKE.WT
Razor Energy Corp	1 wt to buy 1 com sh	$1.20	Jun 16, 2028	V	RZE.WT.H

Derivatives

Warrants, by Issuer

Issuer	Basis	Exercise Price	Expiry Date	Exchange	Symbol
Reconnaissance Energy	1 wt to buy 1 com sh	$14.00	May 27, 2024	V	RECO.WT.A
Red Light Holland Corp	1 wt to buy 1 com sh	$0.38	Jul 28, 2024	O	TRIP.WT
Replenish Nutrients Hldg	1 wt to buy 1 com sh	$0.32	Jun 21, 2026	O	ERTH.WT
Rock Tech Lithium Inc	1 wt to buy 1 com sh	$4.50	Aug 19, 2025	V	RCK.WT
Royal Helium Ltd	1 wt to buy 1 com sh	$0.31	Nov 14, 2026	V	RHC.WT.A
Sagicor Financial Co Ltd	1 wt to buy 1 com sh	$11.50	Dec 05, 2024	T	SFC.WT
Saturn Oil & Gas Inc	1 wt to buy 1 com sh	$4.00	Mar 10, 2025	T	SOIL.WT.A
Silver Mountain Res Inc	1 wt to buy 1 com sh	$0.45	Feb 09, 2026	V	AGMR.WT.A
Stack Capital Group Inc	1 wt to buy 1 com sh	$15.00	Jun 16, 2024	T	STCK.WT
Taiga Motors Corp	1 wt to buy 1 com sh	$17.25	Apr 21, 2026	T	TAIG.WT
Theralase Tchnlgys Inc	1 wt to buy 1 com sh	$0.35	Aug 22, 2024	V	TLT.WT
Tidewater Midstream	1 wt to buy 1 com sh	$1.44	Aug 16, 2024	T	TWM.WT
Tokens.com Corp	1 wt to buy 1 com sh	$1.15	Nov 15, 2024	V	COIN.WT
Total Helium Ltd	1 wt to buy 1 com sh	$0.75	May 01, 2025	V	TOH.WT.A
Total Helium Ltd	1 wt to buy 1 com sh	$2.00	Nov 08, 2026	V	TOH.WT
Trillion Energy Intl Inc	1 wt to buy 1 com sh	$0.50	Jun 29, 2025	O	TCF.WT
Uranium Royalty Corp	1 wt to buy 1 com sh	$2.00	Dec 06, 2024	T	URC.WT
VSBLTY Grpe Tchnlgys Corp	1 wt to buy 1 com sh	$0.65	Jun 29, 2024	O	VSBY.WT.A
VSBLTY Grpe Tchnlgys Corp	1 wt to buy 1 com sh	$0.50	Jul 28, 2025	O	VSBY.WT.B
Vintage Wine Estates Inc	1 wt to buy 1 cl A unit	US$11.50	Jun 07, 2026		
Volatus Aerospace Corp	1 wt to buy 1 com sh	$0.50	Oct 06, 2024	V	VOL.WT.A
Wellfield Tchnlgys Inc	1 wt to buy 1 com sh	$2.00	Nov 23, 2024	V	WFLD.WT
Wildpack Beverage Inc	1 wt to buy 1 com sh	$1.26	Nov 23, 2024	V	CANS.WT.A
WonderFi Technologies Inc	1 wt to buy 1 com sh	$2.55	Oct 26, 2024	T	WNDR.WT.B
Xtract One Tchnlgys Inc	1 wt to buy 1 com sh	$0.64	Apr 24, 2027	T	XTRA.WT

CANADA'S INFORMATION RESOURCE CENTRE (CIRC)

Access all these great resources online, all the time, at Canada's Information Resource Centre (CIRC)
http://circ.greyhouse.ca

Canada's Information Resource Centre (CIRC) integrates all of Grey House Canada's award-winning reference content into one easy-to-use online resource. With **over 100,000 Canadian organizations** and **over 140,600 contacts**, plus thousands of additional facts and figures, CIRC is the most comprehensive resource for specialized database content in Canada! Access all 20 databases, including the recently revised *Careers & Employment Canada*, with Canada Info Desk Complete - it's the total package!

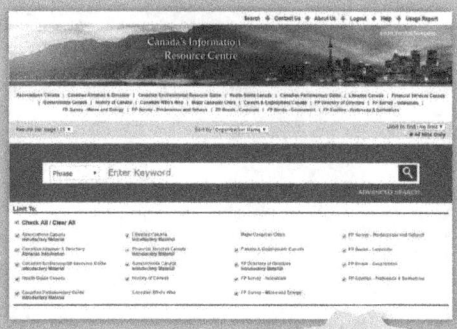

KEY ADVANTAGES OF CIRC:

- Seamlessly cross-database search content from select databases
- Save search results for future reference
- Link directly to websites or email addresses
- Clear display of your results makes compiling and adding to your research easier than ever before

DESIGN YOUR OWN CUSTOM CONTACT LISTS!

CIRC gives you the option to define and extract your own lists in seconds. Find new business leads, do keyword searches, locate upcoming conference attendees; all the information you want is right at your fingertips.

Brand new Major Canadian Cities data!

CHOOSE BETWEEN KEYWORD AND ADVANCED SEARCH!

With CIRC, you can choose between Keyword and Advanced search to pinpoint information. Designed for both beginner and advanced researchers, you can conduct simple text searches as well as powerful Boolean searches.

PROFILES IN CIRC INCLUDE:

- Phone numbers, email addresses, fax numbers and full addresses for all branches of the organization
- Social media accounts, such as Twitter and Facebook
- Key contacts based on job titles
- Budgets, membership fees, staff sizes and more!

Search CIRC using common or unique fields, customized to your needs!

ONLY GREY HOUSE DIRECTORIES PROVIDE SPECIAL CONTENT YOU WON'T FIND ANYWHERE ELSE!

- **Associations Canada:** finances/funding sources, activities, publications, conferences, membership, awards, member profile
- **Canadian Parliamentary Guide:** private and political careers of elected members, complete list of constituencies and representatives
- **Financial Services:** type of ownership, number of employees, year founded, assets, revenue, ticker symbol
- **Libraries Canada:** staffing, special collections, services, year founded, national library symbol, regional system
- **Governments Canada:** municipal population
- **Canadian Who's Who:** birth city, publications, education (degrees, alma mater), career/occupation and employer
- **Major Canadian Cities:** demographics, ethnicity, immigration, language, education, housing, income, labour and transportation
- **Health Guide Canada:** chronic and mental illnesses, general resources, appendices and statistics
- **Cannabis Canada:** firm type, foreign activity, type of ownership, revenue sources
- **Canadian Environmental Resource Guide:** organization scope, budget, number of employees, activities, regulations, areas of environmental specialty
- **Careers & Employment Canada:** career associations, career employment websites, expanded employers, recruiters, awards and scholarships, and summer jobs
- **FP Directory of Directors:** names, directorships, educational and professional backgrounds and email addresses of top Canadian directors; list of major companies and complete company contact information
- **FPbonds:** bond information in PDF form and with sortable tables
- **FPsurvey:** detailed profiles of current publicly traded companies, as well as past corporate changes

The new CIRC provides easier searching and faster, more pinpointed results of all of our great resources in Canada, from Associations and Government to Major Companies to Zoos and everything in between. Whether you need fully detailed information on your contact or just an email address, you can customize your search query to meet your needs.

Contact us now for a **free trial** subscription or visit http://circ.greyhouse.ca

---

GREY HOUSE PUBLISHING CANADA
For more information please contact Grey House Publishing Canada
Tel.: (866) 433-4739 or (416) 644-6479 Fax: (416) 644-1904 | info@greyhouse.ca | www.greyhouse.ca

CENTRE DE DOCUMENTATION DU CANADA (CDC)

Consultez en tout temps toutes ces excellentes ressources en ligne grâce au Centre de documentation du Canada (CDC) à http://circ.greyhouse.ca

Le Centre de documentation du Canada (CDC) regroupe sous une seule ressource en ligne conviviale tout le contenu des ouvrages de référence primés de Grey House Canada. Répertoriant plus de **100 000 entreprises canadiennes, et plus de 140 600 personnes-ressources**, faits et chiffres, il s'agit de la ressource la plus complète en matière de bases de données spécialisées au Canada! Grâce à l'ajout de sept bases de données, le Canada Info Desk Complete est plus avantageux que jamais alors qu'il coûte 50 % que l'abonnement aux ouvrages individuels. Accédez aux 20 bases de données dès maintenant — le Canadian Info Desk Complete vous offre un ensemble complet!

Nouvelles données sur les Principales villes canadiennes!

PRINCIPAUX AVANTAGES DU CDC

- Recherche transversale efficace dans le contenu des bases de données
- Sauvegarde des résultats de recherche pour consultation future
- Lien direct aux sites Web et aux adresses électroniques
- Grâce à l'affichage lisible de vos résultats, il est dorénavant plus facile de compiler les résultats ou d'ajouter des critères à vos recherches

CONCEPTION PERSONNALISÉE DE VOS LISTES DE PERSONNES-RESSOURCES!

Le CDC vous permet de définir et d'extraire vos propres listes, et ce, en quelques secondes. Découvrez des clients potentiels, effectuez des recherches par mot-clé, trouvez les participants à une conférence à venir : l'information dont vous avez besoin, au bout de vos doigts.

CHOISISSEZ ENTRE RECHERCHES MOT-CLÉ ET AVANCÉE!

Grâce au CDC, vous pouvez choisir entre une recherche Mot-clé ou Avancée pour localiser l'information avec précision. Vous avez la possibilité d'effectuer des recherches en texte simple ou booléennes puissantes — les recherches sont conçues à l'intention des chercheurs débutants et avancés.

LES PROFILS DU CDC COMPRENNENT :

- Numéros de téléphone, adresses électroniques, numéros de télécopieur et adresses complètes pour toutes les succursales d'un organisme
- Comptes de médias sociaux, comme Twitter et Facebook
- Personnes-ressources clés en fonction des appellations d'emploi
- Budgets, frais d'adhésion, tailles du personnel et plus!

Effectuez des recherches dans le CDC à l'aide de champs uniques ou communs, personnalisés selon vos besoins!

SEULS LES RÉPERTOIRES DE GREY HOUSE VOUS OFFRENT UN CONTENU PARTICULIER QUE VOUS NE TROUVEREZ NULLE PART AILLEURS!

- **Le répertoire des associations du Canada** : sources de financement, activités, publications, congrès, membres, prix, profil de membre
- **Guide parlementaire canadien** : carrières privées et politiques des membres élus, liste complète des comtés et des représentants
- **Services financiers** : type de propriétaire, nombre d'employés, année de la fondation, immobilisations, revenus, symbole au téléscripteur
- **Bibliothèques Canada** : personnel, collections particulières, services, année de la fondation, symbole de bibliothèque national, système régional
- **Gouvernements du Canada** : population municipale
- **Canadian Who's Who** : ville d'origine, publication, formation (diplômes et alma mater), carrière/emploi et employeur
- **Principales villes canadiennes** : données démographiques, ethnicité, immigration, langue, éducation, logement, revenu, main-d'œuvre et transport
- **Guide canadien de la santé** : maladies chroniques et mentales, ressources generales, annexes et statistiques
- **Cannabis au Canada** : type d'entreprise, activité à l'étranger, type de propriété, sources de revenus
- **Guide des ressources environnementales canadiennes** : périmètre organisationnel, budget, nombre d'employés, activités, réglementations, domaines de spécialité environnementale
- **Carrières et emplois Canada** : associations professionnelles, sites Web d'emplois, employeurs, recruteurs, bourses, et emplois d'été
- **Répertoire des administrateurs** : prénom, nom de famille, poste de cadre et d'administrateur, parcours scolaire et professionnel et adresse électronique des cadres supérieurs canadiens; liste des sociétés les plus importantes au Canada et l'information complète des compagnies
- **FPbonds** : information sur les obligations en format PDF, avec tableaux à trier
- **FPsurvey** : profils détaillés de sociétés cotées en bourse et changements organisationnels antérieurs

Le nouveau CDC facilite la recherche au sein de toutes nos ressources au Canada et procure plus rapidement des résultats plus poussés – des associations au gouvernement en passant par les principales entreprises et les zoos, sans oublier tout un éventail d'organisations! Que vous ayez besoin d'information très détaillée au sujet de votre personne-ressource ou d'une simple adresse électronique, vous pouvez personnaliser votre requête afin qu'elle réponde à vos besoins. Contactez-nous sans tarder pour obtenir un **essai gratuit** ou visitez http://circ.greyhouse.ca

---

GREY HOUSE PUBLISHING CANADA

Pour obtenir plus d'information, veuillez contacter Grey House Publishing Canada par tél. : 1 866 433-4739 ou 416 644-6479 par téléc. : 416 644-1904 | info@greyhouse.ca | www.greyhouse.ca

Canadian Almanac & Directory
The Definitive Resource for Facts & Figures About Canada

The *Canadian Almanac & Directory* has been Canada's most authoritative sourcebook for 177 years. Published annually since 1847, it continues to be widely used by publishers, business professionals, government offices, researchers, information specialists and anyone needing current, accessible information on every imaginable topic relevant to those who live and work in Canada.

A directory and a guide, the *Canadian Almanac & Directory* provides the most comprehensive picture of Canada, from physical attributes to economic and business summaries, leisure and recreation. It combines textual materials, charts, colour photographs and directory listings with detailed profiles, all verified and organized for easy retrieval. The *Canadian Almanac & Directory* is a wealth of general information, displaying national statistics on population, employment, CPI, imports and exports, as well as images of national awards, Canadian symbols, flags, emblems and Canadian parliamentary leaders.

For important contacts throughout Canada, for any number of business projects or for that once-in-a-while critical fact, the *Canadian Almanac & Directory* will help you find the leads you didn't even know existed—quickly and easily!

ALL THE INFORMATION YOU'LL EVER NEED, ORGANIZED INTO 17 DISTINCT CATEGORIES FOR EASY NAVIGATION!

Almanac—a fact-filled snapshot of Canada, including History, Geography, Economics and Vital Statistics.

Arts & Culture—includes 9 topics from Galleries to Zoos.

Associations—thousands of organizations arranged in over 120 different topics, from Accounting to Youth.

Broadcasting—Canada's major Broadcasting Companies, Provincial Radio and Television Stations, Cable Companies, and Specialty Broadcasters.

Business & Finance—Accounting, Banking, Insurance, Canada's Major Companies and Stock Exchanges.

Education—arranged by Province and includes Districts, Government Agencies, Specialized and Independent Schools, Universities and Technical facilities.

Government—spread over three sections, with a Quick Reference Guide, Federal and Provincial listings, County and Municipal Districts and coverage of Courts in Canada.

Health—Government agencies, hospitals, community health centres, retirement care and mental health facilities.

Law Firms—all Major Law Firms, followed by smaller firms organized by Province and listed alphabetically.

Libraries—Canada's main Library/Archive and Government Departments for Libraries, followed by Provincial listings and Regional Systems.

Publishing—Books, Magazines and Newspapers organized by Province, including frequency and circulation figures.

Religion—broad information about religious groups and associations from 37 different denominations.

Sports—Associations in 110 categories, with detailed League and Team listings.

Transportation—complete listings for all major modes.

Utilities—Associations, Government Agencies and Provincial Utility Companies.

PRINT OR ONLINE – QUICK AND EASY ACCESS TO ALL THE INFORMATION YOU NEED!

Available in hardcover print or electronically via the web, the *Canadian Almanac & Directory* provides instant access to the people you need and the facts you want every time.

Canadian Almanac & Directory print edition is verified and updated annually. Ongoing changes are added to the web version on a regular basis. The web version allows you to narrow your search by using index fields such as name or type of organization, subject, location, contact name or title and postal code.

Online subscribers have the option to instantly generate their own contact lists and export them into spreadsheets for further use—a great alternative to high cost list broker services.

GREY HOUSE PUBLISHING CANADA

For more information please contact Grey House Publishing Canada
Tel.: (866)-433-4739 or (416) 644-6479 Fax: (416) 644-1904 | info@greyhouse.ca | www.greyhouse.ca

Répertoire et almanach canadien
La ressource de référence au sujet des données et des faits relatifs au Canada

Le *Répertoire et almanach canadien* constitue le guide canadien le plus rigoureux depuis 177 ans. Publié annuellement depuis 1847, il est toujours grandement utilisé dans le monde des affaires, les bureaux gouvernementaux, par les spécialistes de l'information, les chercheurs, les éditeurs ou quiconque est à la recherche d'information actuelle et accessible sur tous les sujets imaginables à propos des gens qui vivent et travaillent au Canada.

À la fois répertoire et guide, le *Répertoire et almanach canadien* dresse le tableau le plus complet du Canada, des caractéristiques physiques jusqu'aux revues économique et commerciale, en passant par les loisirs et les activités récréatives. Il combine des documents textuels, des représentations graphiques, des photographies en couleurs et des listes de répertoires accompagnées de profils détaillés. Autant d'information pointue et organisée de manière à ce qu'elle soit facile à obtenir. Le *Répertoire et almanach canadien* foisonne de renseignements généraux. Il présente des statistiques nationales sur la population, l'emploi, l'IPC, l'importation et l'exportation ainsi que des images des prix nationaux, des symboles canadiens, des drapeaux, des emblèmes et des leaders parlementaires canadiens.

Si vous cherchez des personnes-ressources essentielles un peu partout au Canada, peu importe qu'il s'agisse de projets d'affaires ou d'une question factuelle anecdotique, le Répertoire et almanach canadien vous fournira les pistes dont vous ignoriez l'existence – rapidement et facilement!

TOUTE L'INFORMATION DONT VOUS AUREZ BESOIN, ORGANISÉE EN 17 CATÉGORIES DISTINCTES POUR UNE CONSULTATION FACILE!

Almanach—un aperçu informatif du Canada, notamment l'histoire, la géographie, l'économie et les statistiques essentielles.

Arts et culture—comprends 9 sujets, des galeries aux zoos.

Associations—des milliers d'organisations classées selon plus de 120 sujets différents, de l'actuariat au jeunesse.

Radiodiffusion—les principales sociétés de radiodiffusion au Canada, les stations radiophoniques et de télévision ainsi que les entreprises de câblodistribution et les diffuseurs thématiques.

Commerce et finance—comptabilité, services bancaires, assurances, principales entreprises et bourses canadiennes.

Éducation—organisé par province et comprend les arrondissements scolaires, les organismes gouvernementaux, les écoles spécialisées et indépendantes, les universités et les établissements techniques.

Gouvernement—s'étend sur trois sections et comprend un guide de référence, des listes fédérales et provinciales, les comtés et arrondissements municipaux ainsi que les cours canadiennes.

Santé—organismes gouvernementaux, hôpitaux, centres de santé communautaires, établissements de soins pour personnes retraitées et de soins de santé mentale.

Sociétés d'avocats—toutes les principales sociétés d'avocats, suivies des sociétés plus petites, classées par province et en ordre alphabétique.

Bibliothèques—la bibliothèque et les archives principales du Canada ainsi que les bibliothèques des ministères, suivis des listes provinciales et des systèmes régionaux.

Édition—livres, magazines et journaux classés par province, y compris leur fréquence et les données relatives à leur diffusion.

Religion—information générale au sujet des groupes religieux et des associations religieuses de 37 dénominations.

Sports—associations de 110 sports distincts; comprend des listes de ligues et d'équipes.

Transport—des listes complètes des principaux modes de transport.

Services publics—associations, organismes gouvernementaux et entreprises de services publics provinciales.

FORMAT PAPIER OU EN LIGNE— ACCÈS RAPIDE À TOUS LES RENSEIGNEMENTS DONT VOUS AVEZ BESOIN!

Offert sous couverture rigide ou en format électronique grâce au web, le *Répertoire et almanach canadien* offre invariablement un accès instantané aux représentants du gouvernement et aux faits qui font l'objet de vos recherches.

La version imprimée du Répertoire et almanach canadien est vérifiée et mise à jour annuellement. La version en ligne est mise à jour mensuellement. Cette version vous permet de circonscrire la recherche grâce aux champs de l'index comme le nom ou le type d'organisme, le sujet, l'emplacement, le nom ou le titre de la personne-ressource et le code postal.

Les abonnés au service en ligne peuvent générer instantanément leurs propres listes de contacts et les exporter en format feuille de calcul pour une utilisation approfondie – une solution de rechange géniale aux services dispendieux d'un commissionnaire en publipostage.

GREY HOUSE PUBLISHING CANADA

Pour obtenir plus d'information, veuillez contacter GREY HOUSE Publishing Canada par tél. : 1 866 433-4739 ou 416 644-6479 par téléc. : 416 644-1904 | info@greyhouse.ca | www.greyhouse.ca

Major Canadian Cities
Compared & Ranked

New edition with 2021 census data!

Major Canadian Cities provides the user with numerous ways to rank and compare 50 major cities across Canada. All statistical information is at your fingertips; you can access details about the cities, each with a population of 100,000 or more. On Canada's Information Resource Centre (CIRC), you can instantly rank cities according to your preferences and make your own analytical tables with the data provided. There are hundreds of questions that these ranking tables will answer: Which cities have the youngest population? Where is the economic growth the strongest? Which cities have the best labour statistics?

A city profile for each location offers additional insights into the city to provide a sense of the location, its history, its recreational and cultural activities. Following the profile are rankings showing its uniqueness in the spectrum of cities across Canada: interesting notes about the city and how it ranks amongst the top 50 in different ways, such as most liveable, wealthiest and coldest! These reports are available only from Grey House Publishing Canada and only with your subscription to this exciting product!

AVAILABLE ONLINE!

Major Canadian Cities is available electronically via the Web, providing instant access to the facts you want about each city, as well as some interesting points showing how the city scores compared with others.

Use the online version to search statistics and create your own tables, or view pre-prepared tables in pdf form. This can help with research for academic work, infrastructure development or pure interest, with all the data you need in one, modifiable source.

MAJOR CANADIAN CITIES SHOWS YOU THESE STATISTICAL TABLES:

Demographics
- Population Growth
- Age Characteristics
- Male/Female Ratio
- Marital Status

Housing
- Household Type & Size
- Housing Age & Value

Labour
- Labour Force
- Occupation
- Industry
- Place of Work

Ethnicity, Immigration & Language
- Mother Tongue
- Knowledge of Official Languages
- Language Spoken at Home
- Minority Populations
- Education
- Education Attainment

Income
- Median Income
- Median Income After Taxes
- Median Income by Family Type
- Median Income After Taxes by Family Type

Transportation
- Mode of Transportation to Work

GREY HOUSE PUBLISHING CANADA

For more information please contact Grey House Publishing Canada
Tel.: (866)-433-4739 or (416) 644-6479 Fax: (416) 644-1904 | info@greyhouse.ca | www.greyhouse.ca

Principales villes canadiennes
Comparaison et classement

Nouvelle édition avec les données du recensement de 2021 !

Principales villes canadiennes offre à l'utilisateur de nombreuses manières de classer et de comparer 50 villes principales du Canada. Toute l'information statistique se trouve au bout de vos doigts : vous pouvez obtenir des détails sur les villes, chacune comptant 100 000 habitants ou plus. Dans le Centre de documentation du Canada (CDC), vous pouvez classer instantanément les villes selon vos préférences et créer vos propres tableaux analytiques à l'aide des données fournies. Ces tableaux de classement répondent à des centaines de questions, notamment : quelles villes comptent la population la plus jeune? À quel endroit la croissance économique est-elle la plus forte? Quelles villes présentent les meilleures statistiques en matière de main-d'œuvre?

Un profil de ville offre des renseignements supplémentaires afin de vous donner une idée de son emplacement, de son histoire, de ses activités récréatives et culturelles. Suivent des classements qui démontrent l'unicité de la ville dans un spectre de villes qui se trouvent partout au Canada. Vous trouverez également des remarques intéressantes au sujet de la ville et de son classement parmi les 50 principales villes, par exemple selon celle où il fait le mieux vivre, où se trouvent les plus riches et où il fait le plus froid. Ces rapports sont disponibles uniquement auprès de Grey House Publishing Canada et dans le cadre de votre abonnement à ce produit emballant!

PRINCIPALES VILLES CANADIENNES COMPREND CES TABLEAUX STATISTIQUES :

Données démographiques
- Croissance de la population
- Caractéristiques relatives à l'âge
- Ratio homme/femme
- État matrimonial

Logement
- Type et taille du logement
- Âge et valeur du logement

Main-d'œuvre
- Population active
- Emploi
- Industrie
- Lieu de travail

Ethnicité, immigration et langue
- Langue maternelle
- Connaissance des langues officielles
- Langue parlée à la maison
- Populations minoritaires
- Formation
- Niveau scolaire

Revenu
- Revenu médian
- Revenu médian après impôts
- Revenu médian par type de famille
- Revenu médian après impôts par type de famille

Transport
- Moyen de transport vers le travail

OFFERT EN VERSION ÉLECTRONIQUE!

Principales villes canadiennes est offert en version électronique sur le Web. Vous accédez donc instantanément aux faits dont vous avez besoin pour chaque ville, de même que des éléments intéressants qui illustrent la comparaison entre les villes.

Servez-vous de la version en ligne pour effectuer des recherches parmi les statistiques et créer vos propres tableaux, ou consulter les tableaux déjà prêts en format PDF. Elle peut vous aider dans le cadre de recherches pour des travaux universitaires, pour le développement d'infrastructures ou consultez-la par simple curiosité – autant de données réunies en une source modifiable.

GREY HOUSE PUBLISHING CANADA

Pour obtenir plus d'information, veuillez contacter Grey House Publishing Canada
par tél. : 1 866 433-4739 ou 416 644-6479 par téléc. : 416 644-1904 | info@greyhouse.ca | www.greyhouse.ca

Canadian Who's Who

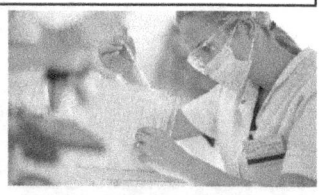

Canadian Who's Who is the only authoritative publication of its kind in Canada, offering access to the top 10 000 notable Canadians in all walks of life. Published annually to provide current and accurate information, the familiar bright-red volume is recognized as the standard reference source of contemporary Canadian biography.

Documenting the achievement of Canadians from a wide variety of occupations and professions, *Canadian Who's Who* records the diversity of culture in Canada. These biographies are organized alphabetically and provide detailed information on the accomplishments of notable Canadians, from coast to coast. All who are interested in the achievements of Canada's most influential citizens and their significant contributions to the country and the world beyond should acquire this reference title.

Detailed entries give date and place of birth, education, family details, career information, memberships, creative works, honours, languages, and awards, together with full addresses. Included are outstanding Canadians from business, academia, politics, sports, the arts and sciences, etc.

Every year the publisher invites new individuals to complete questionnaires from which new biographies are compiled. The publisher also gives those already listed in earlier editions an opportunity to update their biographies. Those listed are selected because of the positions they hold in Canadian society, or because of the contributions they have made to Canada.

AVAILABLE ONLINE!

Canadian Who's Who is also available online, through Canada's Information Resource Centre (CIRC). Readers can access this title's in-depth and vital networking content in the format that best suits their needs—in print, by subscription or online.

The print edition of *Canadian Who's Who 2024* contains 10,000 entries, while the online edition gives users access to over 27,500 biographies, including all current listings and over 15,800 archived biographies dating back to 1999.

GREY HOUSE PUBLISHING CANADA For more information please contact Grey House Publishing Canada
Tel.: (866)-433-4739 or (416) 644-6479 Fax: (416) 644-1904 | info@greyhouse.ca | www.greyhouse.ca

Canadian Who's Who

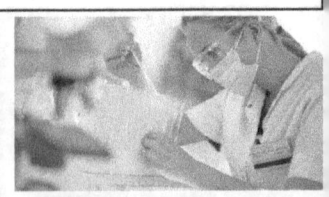

Canadian Who's Who est la seule publication digne de foi de son genre au Canada. Elle donne accès 10 000 dignitaires canadiens de tous les horizons. L'ouvrage annuel rouge vif bien connu, rempli d'information à jour et exacte, est la référence standard en matière de biographies canadiennes contemporaines.

Canadian Who's Who, qui porte sur les réalisations de Canadiens occupant une vaste gamme de postes et de professions, illustre la diversité de la culture canadienne. Ces biographies sont classées en ordre alphabétique et donnent de l'information détaillée sur les réalisations de Canadiens éminents, d'un océan à l'autre. Tous ceux qui s'intéressent aux réalisations des citoyens les plus influents au Canada et à leurs contributions importantes au pays et partout dans le monde doivent se procurer cet ouvrage de référence.

Les entrées détaillées indiquent la date et le lieu de la naissance, traitent de l'éducation, de la famille, de la carrière, des adhésions, des œuvres de création, des distinctions, des langues et des prix - en plus des adresses complètes. Elles comprennent des Canadiens exceptionnels du monde des affaires, des universités, de la politique, des sports, des arts, des sciences et plus encore!

Chaque année, l'éditeur invite de nouvelles personnes à remplir les questionnaires à partir desquels il prépare les nouvelles biographies. Il le remet également aux personnes qui font partie de numéros antérieurs afin de leur permettre d'effectuer une mise à jour. Les personnes retenues le sont en raison des postes qu'elles occupent dans la société canadienne ou de leurs contributions au Canada.

OFFERT EN FORMAT ÉLECTRONIQUE!

Canadian Who's Who est également offert en ligne par l'entremise du Centre de documentation du Canada (CDC). Les lecteurs peuvent accéder au contenu approfondi et essentiel au réseautage de cet ouvrage dans le format qui leur convient le mieux - version imprimée, en ligne ou par abonnement.

L'édition imprimée de Canadian Who's Who 2024 compte 10 000 entrées tandis qu'en consultant la version en ligne, les utilisateurs ont accès à 27 500 biographies, dont fi ches d'actualité et plus de 15 800 biographies archives qui remontent jusqu'à 1999.

Pour obtenir plus d'information, veuillez contacter Grey House Publishing Canada par tél. : 1 866 433-4739 ou 416 644-6479 par téléc. : 416 644-1904 | info@greyhouse.ca | www.greyhouse.ca

Canadian Parliamentary Guide
Your Number One Source for All General Federal Elections Results!

Published annually since before Confederation, the *Canadian Parliamentary Guide* is an indispensable directory, providing biographical information on elected and appointed members in federal and provincial government. Featuring government institutions such as the Governor General's Household, Privy Council and Canadian legislature, this comprehensive collection provides historical and current election results with statistical, provincial and political data.

AVAILABLE IN PRINT AND NOW ONLINE!

THE CANADIAN PARLIAMENTARY GUIDE IS BROKEN DOWN INTO FIVE COMPREHENSIVE CATEGORIES

Monarchy—biographical information on His Majesty King Charles III, The Royal Family and the Governor General

Federal Government—a separate chapter for each of the Privy Council, Senate and House of Commons (including a brief description of the institution, its history in both text and chart format and a list of current members), followed by unparalleled biographical sketches*

General Elections

1867–2019
- information is listed alphabetically by province then by riding name
- notes on each riding include: date of establishment, date of abolition, former division and later divisions, followed by election year and successful candidate's name and party
- by-election information follows

2021
- information for the 2021 election is organized in the same manner but also includes information on all the candidates who ran in each riding, their party affiliation and the number of votes won

Provincial and Territorial Governments—Each provincial chapter includes:
- statistical information
- description of Legislative Assembly
- biographical sketch of the Lieutenant Governor or Commissioner
- list of current Cabinet Members
- dates of legislatures since confederation
- current Members and Constituencies
- biographical sketches*
- general election and by-election results, including the most recent provincial and territorial elections.

Courts: Federal—each court chapter includes a description of the court (Supreme, Federal, Federal Court of Appeal, Court Martial Appeal and Tax Court), its history and a list of its judges followed by biographical sketches*

* Biographical sketches follow a concise yet in-depth format:

Personal Data—place of birth, education, family information

Political Career—political career path and services

Private Career—work history, organization memberships, military history

Available in hardcover print, the *Canadian Parliamentary Guide* is also available electronically via the Web, providing instant access to the government officials you need and the facts you want every time. Use the web version to narrow your search with index fields such as institution, province and name.

Create your own contact lists! Online subscribers can instantly generate their own contact lists and export information into spreadsheets for further use. A great alternative to high cost list broker services!

Photo of the Rt. Hon. Justin Trudeau by Adam Scotti, provided by the Office of the Prime Minister © Her Majesty the Queen in Right of Canada, 2021.

GREY HOUSE PUBLISHING CANADA For more information please contact Grey House Publishing Canada
Tel.: (866)-433-4739 or (416) 644-6479 Fax: (416) 644-1904 | info@greyhouse.ca | www.greyhouse.ca

Guide parlementaire canadien

Votre principale source d'information en matière de résultats d'élections fédérales!

Publié annuellement depuis avant la Confédération, le *Guide parlementaire canadien* est une source fondamentale de notices biographiques des membres élus et nommés aux gouvernements fédéral et provinciaux. Il y est question, notamment, d'établissements gouvernementaux comme la résidence du gouverneur général, le Conseil privé et la législature canadienne. Ce recueil exhaustif présente les résultats historiques et actuels accompagnés de données statistiques, provinciales et politiques.

OFFERT EN FORMAT PAPIER ET DÉSORMAIS ÉLECTRONIQUE!

LE GUIDE PARLEMENTAIRE CANADIEN EST DIVISÉ EN CINQ CATÉGORIES EXHAUSTIVES:

La monarchie—des renseignements biographiques sur Sa Majesté le Roi Charles III, la famille royale et le gouverneur général.

Le gouvernement fédéral—un chapitre distinct pour chacun des sujets suivants: Conseil privé, sénat, Chambre des communes (y compris une brève description de l'institution, son historique sous forme de textes et de graphiques et une liste des membres actuels) suivi de notes biographiques sans pareil.*

Les élections fédérales

1867–2019

- Les renseignements sont présentés en ordre alphabétique par province puis par circonscription.
- Les notes de chaque circonscription comprennent : La date d'établissement, la date d'abolition, l'ancienne circonscription, les circonscriptions ultérieures, etc. puis l'année d'élection ainsi que le nom et le parti des candidats élus.
- Viennent ensuite des renseignements sur l'élection partielle.

2021

- Les renseignements de l'élection 2021 sont organisés de la même manière, mais comprennent également de l'information sur tous les candidats qui se sont présentés dans chaque circonscription, leur appartenance politique et le nombre de voix récoltées.

Gouvernements provinciaux et territoriaux—Chaque chapitre portant sur le gouvernement provincial comprend :

- des renseignements statistiques
- une description de l'Assemblée législative
- des notes biographiques sur le lieutenant-gouverneur ou le commissaire
- une liste des ministres actuels
- les dates de périodes législatives depuis la Confédération
- une liste des membres et des circonscriptions
- des notes biographiques*
- les résultats d'élections générales et partielles, y compris les dernières élections provinciales et territoriales.

Cours : fédérale—chaque chapitre comprend : une description de la cour (suprême, fédérale, cour d'appel fédérale, cour d'appel de la cour martiale et cour de l'impôt), son histoire, une liste des juges qui y siègent ainsi que des notes biographiques.*

* Les notes biographiques respectent un format concis, bien qu'approfondi :

Renseignements personnels—lieu de naissance, formation, renseignements familiaux

Carrière politique—cheminement politique et service public

Carrière privée—antécédents professionnels, membre d'organisations, antécédents militaires

Offert sous couverture rigide ou en format électronique grâce au web, le *Guide parlementaire canadien* donne invariablement un accès instantané aux représentants du gouvernement et aux faits qui font l'objet de vos recherches. Servez-vous de la version en ligne afin de circonscrire vos recherches grâce aux champs spéciaux de l'index comme l'institution, la province et le nom.

Créez vos propres listes! Les abonnés au service en ligne peuvent générer instantanément leurs propres listes de contacts et les exporter en format feuille de calcul pour une utilisation approfondie – une solution de rechange géniale aux services dispendieux d'un commissionnaire en publipostage!

Photo de le très honorable Justin Trudeau par Adam Scotti. Photo fournie par le Bureau du Premier ministre © Sa Majesté la Reine du Chef du Canada, 2021.

GREY HOUSE PUBLISHING CANADA

Pour obtenir plus d'information, veuillez contacter Grey House Publishing Canada
par tél. : 1 866 433-4739 ou 416 644-6479 par téléc. : 416 644-1904 | info@greyhouse.ca | www.greyhouse.ca

Directory of Directors
Your Best Source for Hard-to-Find Business Information

Since 1931, the *Financial Post Directory of Directors* has been recognizing leading Canadian companies and their execs. Today, this title is one of the most comprehensive resources for hard-to-find Canadian business information, allowing readers to access roughly 16,800 executive contacts from Canada's top 1,400 corporations. This prestigious title offers a definitive list of directorships and offices held by noteworthy Canadian business people. It also provides details on leading Canadian companies—publicly traded and privately-owned, including company name, contact information and the names of their executive officers and directors.

ACCESS THE COMPANIES & DIRECTORS YOU NEED IN NO TIME!

The updated 2024 edition of the *Directory of Directors* is jam-packed with information, including:

- **ALL-NEW front matter**: An infographic drawn from data in the book, a report on diversity disclosure practices, reports on what defines a modern board chair and improving boardroom use of technology, and rankings from the FP500.

- **Personal listings**: First name, last name, gender, birth date, degrees, schools attended, executive positions and directorships, previous positions held, main business address and more.

- **Company listings**: Boards of directors and executive officers, head office address, phone and fax numbers, toll-free number, web and email addresses.

Powerful indexes enabling researchers to target just the information they need include:

- An **industrial classification index**: List of key Canadian companies, sorted by industry type according to the Global Industry Classification Standard (GICS®).

- A **geographic location index** grouping all companies in the Company Listings section according to the city and province/state of the head office; and

- An **alphabetical list of abbreviations** providing definitions of common abbreviations used for terms, titles, organizations, honours/fellowships and degrees throughout the Directory.

AVAILABLE ONLINE!

The Directory is also available online, through Canada's Information Resource Centre. Readers can access this title's in-depth and vital networking content in the format that best suits their needs—in print, by subscription or online.

Create your own contact lists! Online subscribers can instantly generate their own contact lists and export information into spreadsheets for further use. A great alternative to high cost list broker services!

GREY HOUSE PUBLISHING CANADA
For more information please contact Grey House Publishing Canada
Tel.: (866)-433-4739 or (416) 644-6479 Fax: (416) 644-1904 | info@greyhouse.ca | www.greyhouse.ca

Répertoire des administrateurs
Votre source par excellence de renseignements professionnels difficiles à trouver

Depuis 1931, le Financial Post Directory of Directors (Répertoire des administrateurs du Financial Post) reconnaît les sociétés canadiennes importantes et leur haute direction. De nos jours, cet ouvrage compte parmi certaines des ressources les plus exhaustives lorsqu'il est question des renseignements d'affaires canadiens difficiles à trouver. Il permet aux lecteurs d'accéder à environ 16 800 coordonnées d'administrateurs provenant des 1 400 sociétés les plus importantes au Canada. Ce document prestigieux comprend une liste définitive des postes d'administrateurs et des fonctions que ces gens d'affaires canadiens remarquables occupent. Il offre également des détails sur des sociétés canadiennes importantes – privées ou négociées sur le marché – y compris le nom de l'entreprise, ses coordonnées et le nombre des membres de sa haute direction et de ses administrateurs.

UN ACCÈS RAPIDE ET FACILE À TOUS LES ENTREPRISES ET DIRECTEURS DONT VOUS AVEZ BESOIN!

La version mise à jour de 2024 du Répertoire des administrateurs du Financial Post est remplie d'information, notamment:

- **NOUVELLE section de textes préliminaires** –une infographie inspirée des données de l'ouvrage; un rapport sur les pratiques de divulgation de la diversité; des rapports sur ce qui définit un président de conseil d'administration moderne et l'amélioration de l'utilisation de la technologie dans les conseils d'administration; le classement le plus récent au FP500.
- **Données personnelles** – prénom, nom de famille, sexe, date de naissance, diplômes, écoles fréquentées, poste de cadre et d'administrateur, postes occupés préalablement, adresse professionnelle principale et plus encore.
- **Listes de sociétés** – conseils d'administration et cadres supérieurs, adresse du siège social, numéros de téléphone et de télécopieur, numéro sans frais, adresse électronique et site Web.

Des index puissants permettent aux utilisateurs de cibler l'information dont ils ont besoin, notamment:

- **Index de classement industriel** - énumère les sociétés classées par type d'industrie général selon le Global Industry Classification Standard (GICS^{MD}).
- l'**Index des emplacements géographiques** qui comprend toutes les sociétés de la section Liste des sociétés en fonction de la ville et de la province/de l'état où se trouve le siège social;
- une **liste des abréviations en ordre alphabétique** définit les abréviations courantes pour la terminologie, les titres, les organisations, les distinctions/fellowships et les diplômes mentionnés dans le Répertoire.

OFFERT EN FORMAT ÉLECTRONIQUE!

Le Répertoire est également accessible en ligne par l'entremise du Centre de documentation du Canada. Les lecteurs peuvent accéder au contenu approfondi et essentiel au réseautage de cet ouvrage dans le format qui leur convient le mieux - version imprimée, en ligne ou par abonnement.

Créez vos propres listes! Les abonnés au service en ligne peuvent générer instantanément leurs propres listes de contacts et les exporter en format feuille de calcul pour une utilisation approfondie – une solution de rechange géniale aux services dispendieux d'un commissionnaire en publipostage.

GREY HOUSE PUBLISHING CANADA

Pour obtenir plus d'information, veuillez contacter Grey House Publishing Canada
par tél. : 1 866 433-4739 ou 416 644-6479 par téléc. : 416 644-1904 | info@greyhouse.ca | www.greyhouse.ca

Associations Canada
Makes Researching Organizations Quick and Easy

Associations Canada is an easy-to-use compendium, providing detailed indexes, listings and abstracts on over 20,500 local, regional, provincial, national and international organizations (identifying location, budget, founding date, management, scope of activity and funding source—just to name a few).

POWERFUL INDEXES HELP YOU TARGET THE ORGANIZATIONS YOU WANT

There are a number of criteria you can use to target specific organizations. Organized with the user in mind, Associations Canada is broken down into a number of indexes to help you find what you're looking for quickly and easily.

- **Subject Index**—listing of Canadian and foreign association headquarters, alphabetically by subject and keyword
- **Acronym Index**—an alphabetical listing of acronyms and corresponding Canadian and foreign associations, in both official languages
- **Budget Index**—Canadian associations, alphabetical within eight budget categories
- **Conferences & Conventions Index**—meetings sponsored by Canadian and foreign associations, listed alphabetically by conference name
- **Executive Name Index**—alphabetical listing of key contacts of Canadian associations, for both headquarters and branches
- **Geographic Index**—listing of headquarters, branch offices, chapters and divisions of Canadian associations, alphabetical within province and city
- **Mailing List Index**—associations that offer mailing lists, alphabetical by subject
- **Registered Charitable Organizations Index**—listing of associations that are registered charities, alphabetical by subject

PRINT OR ONLINE—QUICK AND EASY ACCESS TO ALL THE INFORMATION YOU NEED!

Available in softcover print or electronically via the web, Associations Canada provides instant access to the people you need and the facts you want every time. Whereas the print edition is verified and updated annually, ongoing changes are added to the web version on a regular basis. The web version allows you to narrow your search by using index fields such as name or type of organization, subject, location, contact name or title and postal code.

Create your own contact lists! Online subscribers have the option to instantly generate their own contact lists and export them into spreadsheets for further use—a great alternative to high cost list broker services.

ASSOCIATIONS CANADA PROVIDES COMPLETE ACCESS TO THESE HIGHLY LUCRATIVE MARKETS:

Travel & Tourism
- Who's hosting what event...when and where?
- Check on events up to three years in advance

Journalism and Media
- Pure research—What do they do? Who is in charge? What's their budget?
- Check facts and sources in one step

Libraries
- Refer researchers to the most complete Canadian association reference anywhere

Business
- Target your market, research your interests, compile profiles and identify membership lists
- Warm up your cold calls with all the background you need to sell your product or service
- Preview prospects by budget, market interest or geographic location

Association Executives
- Look for strategic alliances with associations of similar interest
- Spot opportunities or conflicts with convention plans

Research & Government
- Scan interest groups or identify charities in your area of concern
- Check websites, publications and speaker availability
- Evaluate mandates, affiliations and scope

GREY HOUSE PUBLISHING CANADA For more information please contact Grey House Publishing Canada
Tel.: (866)-433-4739 or (416) 644-6479 Fax: (416) 644-1904 | info@greyhouse.ca | www.greyhouse.ca

Associations du Canada
La recherche d'organisations simplifiée

Il s'agit d'un recueil facile d'utilisation qui offre des index, des fiches descriptives et des résumés exhaustifs de plus de 20 500 organismes locaux, régionaux, provinciaux, nationaux et internationaux. Il donne, entre autres, des détails sur leur emplacement, leur budget, leur date de mise sur pied, l'éventail de leurs activités et leurs sources de financement.

En plus d'affecter plus d'un milliard de dollars annuellement aux frais de transport, à la participation à des congrès et à la mise en marché, *Associations du Canada* débourse des millions de dollars dans sa quête pour répondre aux intérêts de ses membres.

DES INDEX PUISSANTS QUI VOUS AIDENT À CIBLER LES ORGANISATIONS VOULUES

Vous pouvez vous servir de plusieurs critères pour cibler des organisations précises. C'est avec l'utilisateur en tête qu'*Associations du Canada* a été divisé en plusieurs index pour vous aider à trouver, rapidement et facilement, ce que vous cherchez.

- **Index des sujets**—liste des sièges sociaux d'associations canadiennes et étrangères; sujets classés en ordre alphabétique et mot-clé.
- **Index des acronymes**—liste alphabétique des acronymes et des associations canadiennes et étrangères équivalentes; présenté dans les deux langues officielles.
- **Index des budgets**—associations canadiennes classées en ordre alphabétique parmi huit catégories de budget.
- **Index des congrès**—rencontres commanditées par des associations canadiennes et étrangères; classées en ordre alphabétique selon le titre de l'événement.
- **Index des directeurs**—liste alphabétique des principales personnes-ressources des associations canadiennes, aux sièges sociaux et aux succursales.
- **Index géographique**—liste des sièges sociaux, des succursales, des sections régionales et des divisions des associations canadiennes; ordre alphabétique au sein des provinces et des villes.
- **Index des listes de distribution**—liste des associations qui offrent des listes de distribution; en ordre alphabétique selon le sujet.
- **Index des œuvres de bienfaisance enregistrées**—liste des associations enregistrées en tant qu'œuvres de bienfaisance; en ordre alphabétique selon le sujet.

OFFERT EN FORMAT PAPIER OU EN LIGNE—UN ACCÈS RAPIDE ET FACILE À TOUS LES RENSEIGNEMENTS DONT VOUS AVEZ BESOIN!

Offert sous couverture souple ou en format électronique grâce au web, *Associations du Canada* donne invariablement un accès instantané aux personnes et aux faits dont vous avez besoin. Si la version imprimée est vérifiée et mise à jour annuellement, des changements continus sont apportés mensuellement à la base de données en ligne. Servez-vous de la version en ligne afin de circonscrire vos recherches grâce à des champs spéciaux de l'index comme le nom de l'organisation ou son type, le sujet, l'emplacement, le nom de la personne-ressource ou son titre et le code postal.

Créez vos propres listes! Les abonnés au service en ligne peuvent générer instantanément leurs propres listes de contacts et les exporter en format feuille de calcul pour une utilisation approfondie – une solution de rechange géniale aux services dispendieux d'un commissionnaire en publipostage.

ASSOCIATIONS DU CANADA OFFRE UN ACCÈS COMPLET À CES MARCHÉS HAUTEMENT LUCRATIFS

Voyage et tourisme
- Renseignez-vous sur les hôtes des événements... sur les dates et les endroits.
- Consultez les événements trois ans au préalable.

Journalisme et médias
- Recherche authentique—quel est leur centre d'activité? Qui est la personne responsable? Quel est leur budget?
- Vérifiez les faits et sources en une seule étape.

Bibliothèques
- Orientez les chercheurs vers la référence la plus complète en ce qui concerne les associations canadiennes.

Commerce
- Ciblez votre marché, faites une recherche selon vos sujets de prédilection, compilez des profils et recensez des listes des membres.
- Préparez votre sollicitation au hasard en obtenant les renseignements dont vous avez besoin pour offrir votre produit ou service.
- Obtenez un aperçu de vos clients potentiels selon les budgets, les intérêts au marché ou l'emplacement géographique.

Directeurs d'associations
- Recherchez des alliances stratégiques avec des associations partageant vos intérêts.
- Repérez des occasions ou des conflits dans le cadre de la planification des congrès.

Recherche et gouvernement
- Parcourez les groupes d'intérêts ou identifiez les organismes de bienfaisance de votre domaine d'intérêt.
- Consultez les sites Web, les publications et vérifiez la disponibilité des conférenciers.
- Évaluez les mandats, les affiliations et le champ d'application.

GREY HOUSE PUBLISHING CANADA Pour obtenir plus d'information, veuillez contacter Grey House Publishing Canada
par tél. : 1 866 433-4739 ou 416 644-6479 par téléc. : 416 644-1904 | info@greyhouse.ca | www.greyhouse.ca

Canadian Environmental Resource Guide
The Only Complete Guide to the Business of Environmental Management

The *Canadian Environmental Resource Guide* provides data on every aspect of the environment industry in unprecedented detail. It's one-stop searching for details on government offices and programs, information sources, product and service firms and trade fairs that pertain to the business of environmental management. All information is fully indexed and cross-referenced for easy use. The directory features current information and key contacts in Canada's environmental industry including:

ENVIRONMENTAL UP-DATE

- Information on prominent environmentalists, environmental abbreviations and a summary of recent environmental events
- Updated articles, rankings, statistics and charts on all aspects of the environmental industry
- Trade shows, conferences and seminars for the current year and beyond

ENVIRONMENTAL INDUSTRY RESOURCES

- Comprehensive listings for companies and firms producing and selling products and services in the environmental sector, including markets served, working language and percentage of revenue sources: public and private
- Environmental law firms, with lawyers' areas of speciality
- Detailed indexes by subject, geography and ISO

ENVIRONMENTAL GOVERNMENT LISTINGS

- Information on important intergovernmental offices and councils, and listings of environmental trade representatives abroad
- In-depth listings of environmental information at the municipal level, including population and number of households, water and waste treatment, landfill statistics and special by-laws and bans, as well as key environmental contacts for each municipality

Available in softcover print or electronically via the web, the *Canadian Environmental Resource Guide* provides instant access to the people you need and the facts you want every time. The *Canadian Environmental Resource Guide* is verified and updated annually. Ongoing changes are added to the web version on a regular basis.

CANADIAN ENVIRONMENTAL RESOURCE GUIDE OFFERS EVEN MORE CONTENT ONLINE!

Environmental Information Resources—Extensive listings of special libraries and thousands of environmental associations, with information on membership, environmental activities, key contacts and more.

Government Listings—Every federal and provincial department and agency influencing environmental initiatives and purchasing policies.

The web version allows you to narrow your search by using index fields such as name or type of organization, subject, location, contact name or title and postal code.

Create your own contact lists! Online subscribers have the option to instantly generate their own contact lists and export them into spreadsheets for further use—a great alternative to high cost list broker services.

GREY HOUSE PUBLISHING CANADA For more information please contact Grey House Publishing Canada
Tel.: (866)-433-4739 or (416) 644-6479 Fax: (416) 644-1904 | info@greyhouse.ca | www.greyhouse.ca

Guide des ressources environnementales canadiennes
Le seul guide complet dédié à la gestion de l'environnement

Le *Guide des ressources environnementales canadiennes* offre de l'information relative à tous les aspects de l'industrie de l'environnement dans les moindres détails. Il permet d'effectuer une recherche de données complètes sur les bureaux et programmes gouvernementaux, les sources de renseignements, les entreprises de produits et de services et les foires commerciales qui portent sur les activités de la gestion de l'environnement. Toute l'information est entièrement indexée et effectue un double renvoi pour une consultation facile. Le répertoire présente des renseignements actualisés et les personnes-ressources clés de l'industrie de l'environnement au Canada, y compris les suivants.

MISE À JOUR SUR L'INDUSTRIE DE L'ENVIRONNEMENT
- De l'information sur d'éminents environnementalistes, les abréviations utilisées dans le domaine de l'environnement et un résumé des événements environnementaux récents
- Des articles, des classements, des statistiques et des graphiques mis à jour sur tous les aspects de l'industrie verte
- Les salons professionnels, conférences et séminaires qui ont lieu cette année et ceux qui sont prévus

RESSOURCES DE L'INDUSTRIE ENVIRONNEMENTALE
- Des listes exhaustives des entreprises et des cabinets qui fabriquent ou offrent des produits et des services dans le domaine de l'environnement, y compris les marchés desservis, la langue de travail et la ventilation des sources de revenus – publics et privés
- Une liste complète des cabinets spécialisés en droit environnemental
- Des index selon le sujet, la géographie et la certification ISO

LISTES GOUVERNEMENTALES RELATIVES À L'ENVIRONNEMENT
- De l'information sur les bureaux et conseils intergouvernementaux importants ainsi que des listes des représentants de l'éco-commerce à l'extérieur du pays
- Des listes approfondies portant sur l'information environnementale au palier municipal, notamment la population et le nombre de ménages, le traitement de l'eau et des déchets, des statistiques sur les décharges, des règlements et des interdictions spéciaux ainsi que des personnes-ressources clés en environnement pour chaque municipalité

Offert sous couverture rigide ou en format électronique grâce au Web, le *Guide des ressources environnementales canadiennes* offre invariablement un accès instantané aux représentants du gouvernement et aux faits qui font l'objet de vos recherches. Il est vérifié et mis à jour annuellement. La version en ligne est mise à jour mensuellement.

LE GUIDE DES RESSOURCES ENVIRONNEMENTALES CANADIENNES DONNE ACCÈS À PLUS DE CONTENU EN LIGNE!

Des ressources informationnelles sur l'environnement—Des bibliothèques et des centres de resources spécialisés, et des milliers d'associations environnementales, avec de l'information sur l'adhésion, les activités environnementales, les personnes-ressources principales et plus encore.

Listes gouvernementales—Toutes les agences et tous les services gouvernementaux fédéraux et provinciaux qui exercent une influence sur les initiatives en matière d'environnement et de politiques d'achat.

Servez-vous de la version en ligne afin de circonscrire vos recherches grâce à des champs spéciaux de l'index comme le nom de l'organisation ou son type, le sujet, l'emplacement, le nom de la personne-ressource ou son titre et le code postal.

Créez vos propres listes! Les abonnés au service en ligne peuvent générer instantanément leurs propres listes de contacts et les exporter en format feuille de calcul pour une utilisation approfondie—une solution de rechange géniale aux services dispendieux d'un commissionnaire en publipostage.

GREY HOUSE PUBLISHING CANADA Pour obtenir plus d'information, veuillez contacter Grey House Publishing Canada
par tél. : 1 866 433-4739 ou 416 644-6479 par téléc. : 416 644-1904 | info@greyhouse.ca | www.greyhouse.ca

Libraries Canada

Gain Access to Complete and Detailed Information on Canadian Libraries

Libraries Canada brings together the most current information from across the entire Canadian library sector, including libraries and branch libraries, educational libraries, regional systems, resource centres, archives, related periodicals, library schools and programs, provincial and governmental agencies and associations.

As the nation's leading library directory for over 35 years, *Libraries Canada* gives you access to almost 10,000 names and addresses of contacts in these institutions. Also included are valuable details such as library symbol, number of staff, operating systems, library type and acquisitions budget, hours of operation—all thoroughly indexed and easy to find.

INSTANT ACCESS TO CANADIAN LIBRARY SECTOR INFORMATION

Developed for publishers, advocacy groups, computer hardware suppliers, internet service providers and other diverse groups which provide products and services to the library community; associations that need to maintain a current list of library resources in Canada; and research departments, students and government agencies which require information about the types of services and programs available at various research institutions, *Libraries Canada* will help you find the information you need—quickly and easily.

EXPERT SEARCH OPTIONS AVAILABLE WITH ONLINE VERSION...

Available in print and online, *Libraries Canada* delivers easily accessible, quality information that has been verified and organized for easy retrieval. Five easy-to-use indexes assist you in navigating the print edition while the online version utilizes multiple index fields that help you get results.

Available on Grey House Publishing Canada's CIRC interface, you can choose between Keyword and Advanced search to pinpoint information. Designed for both novice and advanced researchers, you can conduct simple text searches as well as powerful Boolean searches, plus you can narrow your search by using index fields such as name or type of institution, headquarters, location, area code, contact name or title and postal code. Save your searches to build on at a later date or use the mark record function to view, print, e-mail or export your selected records.

Online subscribers have the option to instantly generate their own contact lists and export them into spreadsheets for further use. A great alternative to high cost list broker services.

LIBRARIES CANADA GIVES YOU ALL THE ESSENTIALS FOR EACH INSTITUTION:

Name, address, contact information, key personnel, number of staff

Collection information, type of library, acquisitions budget, subject area, special collection

User services, number of branches, hours of operation, ILL information, photocopy and microform facilities, for-fee research, Internet access

Systems information, details on electronic access, operating and online systems, Internet and e-mail software, Internet connectivity, access to electronic resources

Additional information including associations, publications and regional systems

With almost 60% of the data changing annually it has never been more important to have the latest version of *Libraries Canada*.

GREY HOUSE PUBLISHING CANADA For more information please contact Grey House Publishing Canada
Tel.: (866)-433-4739 or (416) 644-6479 Fax: (416) 644-1904 | info@greyhouse.ca | www.greyhouse.ca

Bibliothèques Canada

Accédez aux renseignements complets et détaillés au sujet des bibliothèques canadiennes

Bibliothèques Canada combine les renseignements les plus à jour provenant du secteur des bibliothèques de partout au Canada, y compris les bibliothèques et leurs succursales, les bibliothèques éducatives, les systèmes régionaux, les centres de ressources, les archives, les périodiques pertinents, les écoles de bibliothéconomie et leurs programmes, les organismes provinciaux et gouvernementaux ainsi que les associations.

Principal répertoire des bibliothèques depuis plus de 35 ans, *Bibliothèques Canada* vous donne accès à près de 10 000 noms et adresses de personnes-ressources pour ces établissements. Il comprend également des détails précieux comme le symbole d'identification de bibliothèque, le nombre de membres du personnel, les systèmes d'exploitation, le type de bibliothèque et le budget attribué aux acquisitions, les heures d'ouverture – autant d'information minutieusement indexée et facile à trouver.

Offert en version imprimée et en ligne, *Bibliothèques Canada* offre des renseignements de qualité, facile d'accès, qui ont été vérifiés et organisés afin de les obtenir facilement. Cinq index conviviaux vous aident dans la navigation du numéro imprimé tandis que la version en ligne vous permet de saisir plusieurs champs d'index pour vous aider à découvrir l'information voulue.

ACCÈS INSTANTANÉ AUX RENSEIGNEMENTS DU DOMAINE DES BIBLIOTHÈQUES CANADIENNES

Conçu pour les éditeurs, les groupes de revendication, les fournisseurs de matériel informatique, les fournisseurs de services Internet et autres groupes qui offrent produits et services aux bibliothèques; les associations qui ont besoin de conserver une liste à jour des ressources bibliothécaires au Canada; les services de recherche, les organismes étudiants et gouvernementaux qui ont besoin d'information au sujet des types de services et de programmes offerts par divers établissements de recherche, *Bibliothèques Canada* vous aide à trouver l'information nécessaire – rapidement et simplement.

LA VERSION EN LIGNE COMPREND DES OPTIONS DE RECHERCHE POUSSÉES...

À partir de l'interface du Centre de documentation du Canada de Grey House Publishing Canada, vous pouvez choisir entre la recherche poussée et rapide pour cibler votre information. Vous pouvez effectuer des recherches par texte simple, conçues à la fois pour les chercheurs débutants et chevronnés, ainsi que des recherches booléennes puissantes. Vous pouvez également restreindre votre recherche à l'aide des champs d'index, comme le nom ou le type d'établissement, le siège social, l'emplacement, l'indicatif régional, le nom de la personne-ressource ou son titre et le code postal. Enregistrez vos recherches pour vous en servir plus tard ou utilisez la fonction de marquage pour afficher, imprimer, envoyer par courriel ou exporter les dossiers sélectionnés.

Les abonnés au service en ligne peuvent générer instantanément leurs propres listes de contacts et les exporter en format feuille de calcul pour une utilisation approfondie – une solution de rechange géniale aux services dispendieux d'un commissionnaire en publipostage.

BIBLIOTHÈQUES CANADA VOUS DONNE TOUS LES RENSEIGNEMENTS ESSENTIELS RELATIFS À CHAQUE ÉTABLISSEMENT :

Leurs nom et adresse, les coordonnées de la personne-ressource, les membres clés du personnel, le nombre de membres du personnel

L'information relative aux collections, le type de bibliothèque, le budget attribué aux acquisitions, le domaine, les collections particulières

Les services aux utilisateurs, le nombre de succursales, les heures d'ouverture, les renseignements relatifs au PEB, les services de photocopie et de microforme, la recherche rémunérée, l'accès à Internet

L'information relative aux systèmes, des détails sur l'accès électronique, les systèmes d'exploitation et ceux en ligne, Internet et le logiciel de messagerie électronique, la connectivité à Internet, l'accès aux ressources électroniques

L'information supplémentaire, y compris les associations, les publications et les systèmes régionaux

Alors que près de 60 % des données sont modifiées annuellement, il est plus important que jamais de posséder la plus récente version de *Bibliothèques Canada*.

GREY HOUSE PUBLISHING CANADA

Pour obtenir plus d'information, veuillez contacter Grey House Publishing Canada
par tél. : 1 866 433-4739 ou 416 644-6479 par téléc. : 416 644-1904 | info@greyhouse.ca | www.greyhouse.ca

Financial Services Canada
Unparalleled Coverage of the Canadian Financial Service Industry

With corporate listings for over 30,000 organizations and hard-to-find business information, *Financial Services Canada* is the most up-to-date source for names and contact numbers of industry professionals, senior executives, portfolio managers, financial advisors, agency bureaucrats and elected representatives.

Financial Services Canada is the definitive resource for detailed listings—providing valuable contact information including: name, title, organization, profile, associated companies, telephone and fax numbers, e-mail and website addresses. Use our online database and refine your search by stock symbol, revenue, year founded, assets, ownership type or number of employees.

POWERFUL INDEXES HELP YOU LOCATE THE CRUCIAL FINANCIAL INFORMATION YOU NEED.

Organized with the user in mind, *Financial Services Canada* contains categorized listings and 4 easy-to-use indexes:

Alphabetic—financial organizations listed in alphabetical sequence by company name

Geographic—financial institutions broken down by town or city

Executive Name—all officers, directors and senior personnel in alphabetical order by surname

Insurance class—lists all companies by insurance type

Reduce the time you spend compiling lists, researching company information and searching for e-mail addresses. Whether you are interested in contacting a finance lawyer regarding international and domestic joint ventures, need to generate a list of foreign banks in Canada or want to contact the Toronto Stock Exchange—*Financial Services Canada* gives you the power to find all the data you need.

PRINT OR ONLINE—QUICK AND EASY ACCESS TO ALL THE INFORMATION YOU NEED!

Available in softcover print or electronically via the web, *Financial Services Canada* provides instant access to the people you need and the facts you want every time.

Financial Services Canada print edition is verified and updated annually. Ongoing changes are added to the web version on a regular basis. The web version allows you to narrow your search by using index fields such as name or type of organization, subject, location, contact name or title and postal code.

Create your own contact lists! Online subscribers have the option to instantly generate their own contact lists and export them into spreadsheets for further use—a great alternative to high cost list broker services.

ACCESS TO CURRENT LISTINGS FOR...

Banks and Depository Institutions
- Domestic and savings banks
- Foreign banks and branches
- Foreign bank representative offices
- Trust companies
- Credit unions

Non-Depository Institutions
- Bond rating companies
- Collection agencies
- Credit card companies
- Financing and loan companies
- Trustees in bankruptcy

Investment Management Firms, including securities and commodities
- Financial planning / investment management companies
- Investment dealers
- Investment fund companies
- Pension/money management companies
- Stock exchanges
- Holding companies

Insurance Companies, including federal and provincial
- Reinsurance companies
- Fraternal benefit societies
- Mutual benefit companies
- Reciprocal exchanges

Accounting and Law
- Accountants
- Actuary consulting firms
- Law firms (specializing in finance)

Major Canadian Companies
- Key financial contacts for public, private and Crown corporations

Associations
- Associations and institutes serving the financial services sector

Financial Technology & Services
- Companies involved in financial software and other technical areas.

Access even more content online:
Government and Publications
- Federal, provincial and territorial contacts
- Leading publications serving the financial services industry

---

GREY HOUSE PUBLISHING CANADA For more information please contact Grey House Publishing Canada
Tel.: (866)-433-4739 or (416) 644-6479 Fax: (416) 644-1904 | info@greyhouse.ca | www.greyhouse.ca

Services financiers au Canada
Une couverture sans pareille de l'industrie des services financiers canadiens

Grâce à plus de 30 000 organisations et renseignements commerciaux rares, *Services financiers du Canada* est la source la plus à jour de noms et de coordonnées de professionnels, de membres de la haute direction, de gestionnaires de portefeuille, de conseillers financiers, de fonctionnaires et de représentants élus de l'industrie.

Services financiers du Canada intègre les plus récentes modifications à l'industrie afin de vous offrir les détails les plus à jour au sujet de chaque entreprise, notamment le nom, le titre, l'organisation, les numéros de téléphone et de télécopieur, le courriel et l'adresse du site Web. Servez-vous de la base de données en ligne et raffinez votre recherche selon le symbole, le revenu, l'année de création, les immobilisations, le type de propriété ou le nombre d'employés.

DES INDEX PUISSANTS VOUS AIDENT À TROUVER LES RENSEIGNEMENTS FINANCIERS ESSENTIELS DONT VOUS AVEZ BESOIN.

C'est avec l'utilisateur en tête que Services financiers au Canada a été conçu; il contient des listes catégorisées et quatre index faciles d'utilisation :

Alphabétique—les organisations financières apparaissent en ordre alphabétique, selon le nom de l'entreprise.

Géographique—les institutions financières sont détaillées par ville.

Nom de directeur—tous les agents, directeurs et cadres supérieurs sont classés en ordre alphabétique, selon leur nom de famille.

Classe d'assurance—toutes les entreprises selon leur type d'assurance.

Passez moins de temps à préparer des listes, à faire des recherches ou à chercher des contacts et des courriels. Que vous soyez intéressé à contacter un avocat en droit des affaires au sujet de projets conjoints internationaux et nationaux, que vous ayez besoin de générer une liste des banques étrangères au Canada ou que vous souhaitiez communiquer avec la Bourse de Toronto, *Services financiers au Canada* vous permet de trouver toutes les données dont vous avez besoin.

OFFERT EN FORMAT PAPIER OU EN LIGNE – UN ACCÈS RAPIDE ET FACILE À TOUS LES RENSEIGNEMENTS DONT VOUS AVEZ BESOIN!

Offert sous couverture rigide ou en format électronique grâce au Web, Services financiers du Canada donne invariablement un accès instantané aux personnes et aux faits dont vous avez besoin. Si la version imprimée est vérifiée et mise à jour annuellement, des changements continus sont apportés mensuellement à la base de données en ligne. Servez-vous de la version en ligne afin de circonscrire vos recherches grâce à des champs spéciaux de l'index comme le nom de l'organisation ou son type, le sujet, l'emplacement, le nom de la personne-ressource ou son titre et le code postal.

Créez vos propres listes! Les abonnés au service en ligne peuvent générer instantanément leurs propres listes de contacts et les exporter en format feuille de calcul pour une utilisation approfondie – une solution de rechange géniale aux services dispendieux d'un commissionnaire en publipostage.

ACCÉDEZ AUX LISTES ACTUELLES...

Banques et institutions de dépôt
- Banques nationales et d'épargne
- Banques étrangères et leurs succursales
- Bureaux des représentants de banques étrangères
- Sociétés de fiducie
- Coopératives d'épargne et de crédit

Établissements financiers
- Entreprises de notation des obligations
- Agences de placement
- Compagnies de carte de crédit
- Sociétés de financement et de prêt
- Syndics de faillite

Sociétés de gestion de placements, y compris les valeurs et marchandises
- Entreprises de planification financière et de gestion des investissements
- Maisons de courtage de valeurs
- Courtiers en épargne collective
- Entreprises de gestion de la pension/de trésorerie
- Bourses
- Sociétés de portefeuille

Compagnies d'assurance, fédérales et provinciales
- Compagnies de réassurance
- Sociétés fraternelles
- Sociétés de secours mutuel
- Échanges selon la formule de réciprocité

Comptabilité et droit
- Comptables
- Cabinets d'actuaires-conseils
- Cabinets d'avocats (spécialisés en finance)

Principales entreprises canadiennes
- Principaux contacts financiers pour les sociétés de capitaux publiques, privées et de la Couronne

Les associations et Technologie et services financiers

Accès à plus de contenu en ligne: Gouvernement et Publications
- Personnes-ressources aux paliers fédéral, provinciaux et territoriaux
- Principales publications qui desservent l'industrie des services financiers

---

GREY HOUSE PUBLISHING CANADA

Pour obtenir plus d'information, veuillez contacter Grey House Publishing Canada
par tél. : 1 866 433-4739 ou 416 644-6479 par téléc. : 416 644-1904 | info@greyhouse.ca | www.greyhouse.ca

Careers & Employment Canada

Careers & Employment Canada is the go-to resource for job-seekers across Canada, with detailed, current information on everything from industry associations to summer job opportunities. Divided into five helpful sections, this guide contains 10,000 organizations and 20,000 industry contacts to aid in research and jump-start careers in a variety of fields.

ADDITIONAL RESOURCES INCLUDE:

- **Associations**
- **Employers**
  - Arts & Culture
  - Business & Finance
  - Education
  - Environmental
  - Government
  - Healthcare
  - Legal
  - Major Corporations in Canada
  - Telecommunications & Media
  - Transportation
- **Recruiters**
- **Summer Jobs**
- **Career & Employment Websites**
  - National & Regional
  - Industry
  - Topic-Specific
  - Employment Options
  - Clientele
  - Where to Get Resources

AVAILABLE ONLINE!

This content is also available online on Canada's Information Resource Centre (CIRC), where users can search, sort, save and export the thousands of listings available. Please visit www.greyhouse.ca to sign up for a free trial.

Rounding off this guide are 70 pages of reports on the current job market in Canada, a list of industry Awards and Honours, as well as Entry, Executive, and Government Contact indexes for even easier reference. Valuable for employment professionals, librarians, teachers, and job-seekers alike, *Careers & Employment Canada* helps take the strain out of job searching by providing a direct link to the organizations and contacts that matter most.

A CLOSER LOOK AT WHAT'S INSIDE:

Reports on the Job Market—A series of articles on the current job market sourced from Statistics Canada—everything from equity in the workplace to the many ways in which the COVID-19 pandemic has affected the labour market.

Associations—Nearly 800 national associations covering an array of industries and professions.

Employers—Need-to-know companies and organizations broken down into 11 master categories such as Arts & Culture, Education, Government, and Telecommunications & Media.

Recruiters—Top recruiting firms across Canada, organized by national and provincial scope.

Summer Jobs—National and regional summer job opportunities—everything from government agencies to summer camps

Career & Employment Websites—Includes hiring and job board platforms broken down by industry, employment tools, and resources by job type and specialized clientele such as Indigenous, New Canadians, People with Disabilities, Women, and Youth.

GREY HOUSE PUBLISHING CANADA

For more information please contact Grey House Publishing Canada
Tel.: (866)-433-4739 or (416) 644-6479 Fax: (416) 644-1904 | info@greyhouse.ca | www.greyhouse.ca

Carrières et emploi Canada

Carrières et emploi Canada est la ressource privilégiée pour les personnes en recherche d'emploi partout au Canada. Elle contient de l'information détaillée et actuelle, des associations de l'industrie aux offres d'emploi d'été. Divisé en cinq sections pratiques, ce guide comprend 10 000 contacts d'organisations et 20 000 d'industrie pour aider à la recherche d'emploi et démarrer des carrières dans divers domaines.

LES RESSOURCES SUPPLÉMENTAIRES COMPRENNENT :

- **Associations**
- **Employeurs**
    - Arts et culture
    - Affaires et finances
    - Formation
    - Environnement
    - Gouvernement
    - Soins de santé
    - Domaine juridique
    - Grandes entreprises au Canada
    - Télécommunications et médias
    - Transport
- **Recruteurs**
- **Emplois d'été**
- **Sites sur les carrières et l'emploi**
    - À l'échelle nationale et régionale
    - Industrie
    - Relatif à un sujet précis
    - Possibilités d'emploi
    - Communauté
    - Où trouver les ressources

OFFERT EN LIGNE!

Ce contenu est également offert en ligne sur le centre de documentation du Canada (CIRC) où les utilisateurs peuvent effectuer des recherches, trier, sauvegarder et exporter des milliers d'entrées disponibles. Veuillez visiter www.greyhouse.ca (en anglais uniquement) pour vous inscrire afin d'en faire un essai gratuit.

À la fin de ce guide, vous trouverez 70 pages de rapports sur le marché de l'emploi actuel au Canada, une liste des prix remis par l'industrie ainsi que des index classés par entrée, direction et contact gouvernemental pour en faciliter davantage la consultation. Outil précieux pour les professionnels de l'emploi, bibliothécaires, enseignants et chercheurs d'emploi, *Carrières et emploi Canada* aide à alléger la recherche d'emploi en offrant un lien direct avec les organisations et personnes-ressources plus essentielles que jamais.

UN EXAMEN PLUS APPROFONDI DU CONTENU :

Rapports sur le marché de l'emploi—Une série d'articles sur le marché du travail actuel provenant de Statistiques Canada : de l'équité en milieu de travail aux divers impacts de la pandémie de la COVID-19 sur le marché de l'emploi.

Associations—Près de 800 associations nationales portant sur une gamme d'industries et de professions.

Employeurs—Les entreprises et organisations essentielles, divisées en 11 catégories principales comme les arts et la culture, l'éducation, le gouvernement, les télécommunications et les médias.

Recruteurs—Les principales agences de recrutement partout au Canada, selon leur portée nationale et provinciale.

Emplois d'été—Les occasions d'emploi d'été, à l'échelle nationale et régionale; des agences gouvernementales aux camps d'été.

Sites Web professionnels et d'emplois—Comprend les plateformes d'embauche et d'offres d'emploi, divisées par industrie, outils d'embauche et les ressources par type d'emploi et communautés précises, notamment les Autochtones, nouveaux Canadiens, personnes handicapées, femmes et jeunes.

GREY HOUSE PUBLISHING CANADA

Pour obtenir plus d'information, veuillez contacter Grey House Publishing Canada
par tél. : 1 866 433-4739 ou 416 644-6479 par téléc. : 416 644-1904 | info@greyhouse.ca | www.greyhouse.ca

Cannabis Canada

Cannabis Canada is a one-of-a-kind resource covering all aspects of this growing industry. Featuring a wide-ranging collection of reports and statistics, you'll find everything you need to know about this now-legal marketplace, including need-to-know international information.

This first edition includes the State of the Cannabis Industry 2019, exploring the history of marijuana, current regulations, insightful reports, and listings of upcoming trade shows and conferences.

Readers will also discover the brand new Cannabis Industry Buyer's Guide, featuring everything from Licensed Producers to consulting firms, equipment manufacturers to security firms, and more. All listings include specialized fields that go far beyond name and address, and boast crucial, current key contacts.

ADDITIONAL RESOURCES INCLUDE:

- Industry associations
- Financial and venture capital firms
- Law firms
- Government agencies
- Post-secondary schools
- Healthcare and treatment facilities
- Publications

Rounding out the book are Appendices containing detailed statistics, and multiple Indexes to help you navigate this comprehensive body of work.

A CLOSER LOOK AT WHAT'S INSIDE:

State of the Cannabis Industry 2019—A large, detailed section containing everything from the history of cannabis to current legal regulations. Objective reports on all aspects of the industry are also included, as are listings of Canadian and foreign trade shows and conferences.

Cannabis Industry Buyer's Guide—In-depth company listings covering all essential aspects of the industry. This is your go-to source for crucial contacts you need to expand your business, grow your network, or answer your research questions.

Associations—Everything from professional associations to health organizations, including international bodies essential to the industry.

Finance and Venture Capital—All the information you need on insurance, banking, and industry investment.

Law Firms—Find out which law firms offer services in the cannabis space, right down to specific lawyers' specialties!

Government—Federal and provincial departments and agencies that regulate and oversee the cannabis industry in Canada. This is your source for the best contacts in government.

Education—Colleges, universities and specialized schools that offer or are planning to offer cannabis-related courses.

Health—Locations of specialized health facilities, including mental health and addiction treatment programs across the country.

Publications—Listings of Canadian and foreign magazines, both in print and online, serving members of the cannabis community.

AVAILABLE ONLINE!

The *Canadian Cannabis Guide* is also available online on Canada's Information Resource Centre (CIRC). Thousands of companies and contacts are just a click away! Search by name or type of organization, subject, location, contact name or title and postal code. Export results and create mailing lists with this easy-to-use online database – an essential tool for researchers, students, marketing professionals and industry experts alike.

GREY HOUSE PUBLISHING CANADA

For more information please contact Grey House Publishing Canada
Tel.: (866)-433-4739 or (416) 644-6479 Fax: (416) 644-1904 | info@greyhouse.ca | www.greyhouse.ca

Cannabis au Canada

Cannabis du Canada est une ressource unique qui porte sur tous les aspects de cette industrie en pleine expansion. Il comprend des entrées exhaustives ainsi qu'une vaste gamme de rapports et de statistiques : vous y trouverez tout ce qu'il y a à savoir sur ce marché désormais légal, y compris des renseignements à portée internationale.

La première édition inclut le document l'État de l'industrie du cannabis 2019 sur l'histoire de la marijuana, les réglementations en vigueur ainsi que des rapports éclairants et des annonces de salons commerciaux et de congrès à venir.

Les lecteurs découvriront également le tout nouveau guide de l'acheteur de l'industrie du cannabis qui couvre un vaste éventail de sujets : des producteurs autorisés aux sociétés de conseil en passant par les sociétés de sécurité et plus encore. Toutes les entrées comprennent des champs spécialisés qui vont bien plus loin que le nom et l'adresse : elles regorgent de contacts essentiels et actuels.

PARMI LES RESSOURCES SUPPLÉMENTAIRES, MENTIONNONS :

- Associations de l'industrie
- Sociétés financières et de capital de risque
- Cabinets d'avocats
- Agences gouvernementales
- Établissements de soins de santé et de traitement
- Publications

Des annexes avec des statistiques détaillées et plusieurs index vous aident à parcourir cet ouvrage exhaustif.

OFFERT EN LIGNE!

Le *Guide canadien du cannabis* sera également offert en ligne dans le Centre de documentation du Canada (CIRC). Un seul clic vous donne accès à des milliers d'entreprises et de personnes-ressources! Effectuez une recherche par nom ou par type d'organisation, par sujet, par emplacement, par code postal, par personne-ressource ou par titre. Exportez les résultats pour créer des listes d'envoi grâce à cette base de données en ligne conviviale, un outil essentiel tant pour les chercheurs, étudiants, professionnels du marketing que pour les experts de l'industrie.

UN EXAMEN PLUS APPROFONDI DU CONTENU :

L'état de l'industrie du cannabis en 2019—Une section détaillée volumineuse : de l'histoire du cannabis à la réglementation actuelle. S'y trouvent également des rapports objectifs portant sur tous les aspects de l'industrie, des entrées relatives aux salons professionnels ainsi qu'aux conférences, au Canada et à l'étranger.

Guide de l'acheteur—Industrie du cannabis : entrées commerciales exhaustives sur tous les aspects essentiels de l'industrie. Il constitue votre source d'information par excellence de personnes-ressources essentielles à l'expansion de votre entreprise et de votre réseau ou à la recherche de réponses.

Associations—Des associations professionnelles aux organismes de santé, y compris les organismes internationaux essentiels à l'industrie.

Finances et capital-risque—Toute l'information dont vous avez besoin au sujet de l'assurance, des services bancaires et du secteur des placements.

Cabinets d'avocats—Découvrez les cabinets d'avocats qui offrent des services reliés aux enjeux du cannabis, jusqu'aux domaines de spécialité d'avocats précis!

Gouvernement—Les agences et ministères fédéraux et provinciaux qui réglementent et surveillent l'industrie du cannabis au Canada. Cette source vous offre les meilleurs contacts à l'échelle du gouvernement.

Enseignement—Collèges, universités et écoles spécialisées qui offrent des cours ayant trait au cannabis ou qui comptent le faire.

Santé—L'emplacement d'établissements de santé spécialisés, notamment en santé mentale et en programmes de traitement des dépendances, partout au pays.

Publications—Listes de magazines, canadiens et étrangers, imprimés et en ligne, que peuvent consulter les participants du secteur du cannabis.

GREY HOUSE PUBLISHING CANADA

Pour obtenir plus d'information, veuillez contacter Grey House Publishing Canada
par tél. : 1 866 433-4739 ou 416 644-6479 par téléc. : 416 644-1904 | info@greyhouse.ca | www.greyhouse.ca

Health Guide Canada
An Informative Handbook on Health Services in Canada

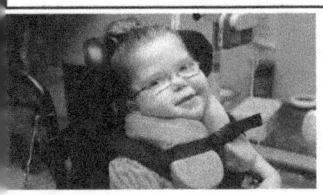

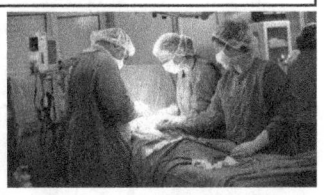

Health Guide Canada: An informative handbook on chronic and mental illnesses and health services in Canada offers a comprehensive overview of 107 chronic and mental illnesses, from Addison's to Wilson's disease. Each chapter includes an easy-to-understand medical description, plus a wide range of condition-specific support services and information resources that deal with the variety of issues concerning those with a chronic or mental illness, as well as those who support the illness community.

Health Guide Canada contains thousands of ways to deal with the many aspects of chronic or mental health disorder. It includes associations, government agencies, libraries and resource centres, educational facilities, hospitals and publications. In addition to chapters dealing with specific chronic or mental conditions, there is a chapter relevant to the health industry in general, as well as others dealing with charitable foundations, death and bereavement groups, homeopathic medicine, indigenous issues and sports for the disabled.

Specific sections include:

- Educational Material
- Section I: Chronic & Mental Illnesses
- Section II: General Resources
- Section III: Appendices
- Section IV: Statistics

Each listing will provide a description, address (including website, email address and social media links, if possible) and executives' names and titles, as well as a number of details specific to that type of organization.

In addition to patients and families, hospital and medical centre personnel can find the support they need in their work or study. *Health Guide Canada* is full of resources crucial for people with chronic illness as they transition from diagnosis to home, home to work, and work to community life.

PRINT OR ONLINE – QUICK AND EASY ACCESS TO ALL THE INFORMATION YOU NEED!

Available in softcover print or electronically via the web, *Health Guide Canada* provides instant access to the people you need and the facts you want every time. Whereas the print edition is verified and updated annually, ongoing changes are added to the web version on a regular basis. The web version allows you to narrow your search by using index fields such as name or type of organization, subject, location, contact name or title and postal code.

HEALTH GUIDE CANADA HELPS YOU FIND WHAT YOU NEED WITH THESE VALUABLE SOURCING TOOLS!

Entry Name Index—An alphabetical list of all entries, providing a quick and easy way to access any listing in this edition.

Tabs—Main sections are tabbed for easy look-up. Headers on each page make it easy to locate the data you need.

Create your own contact lists! Online subscribers have the option to instantly generate their own contact lists and export them into spreadsheets for further use—a great alternative to high cost list broker services.

GREY HOUSE PUBLISHING CANADA
For more information please contact Grey House Publishing Canada
Tel.: (866)-433-4739 or (416) 644-6479 Fax: (416) 644-1904 | info@greyhouse.ca | www.greyhouse.ca

Guide canadien de la santé

Un manuel informatif au sujet des services en santé au Canada

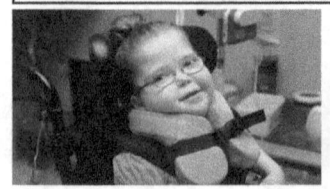

Le *Guide canadien de la santé : un manuel informatif au sujet des maladies chroniques et mentales de même que des services en santé au Canada* donne un aperçu exhaustif de 107 maladies chroniques et mentales, de la maladie d'Addison à celle de Wilson. Chaque chapitre comprend une description médicale facile à comprendre, une vaste gamme de services de soutien particuliers à l'état et des ressources documentaires qui portent sur diverses questions relatives aux personnes qui sont prises avec une maladie chronique ou mentale et à ceux qui soutiennent la communauté liée à cette maladie.

Le *Guide canadien de la santé* contient des milliers de moyens pour composer avec divers aspects d'une maladie chronique ou d'un problème de santé mentale. Il comprend des associations, des organismes gouvernementaux, des bibliothèques et des centres de documentation, des services d'éducation, des hôpitaux et des publications. En plus des chapitres qui portent sur des états chroniques ou mentaux, un chapitre traite de l'industrie de la santé en général; d'autres abordent les fondations qui réalisent des rêves, les groupes de soutien axés sur le décès et le deuil, la médecine homéopathique, les questions autochtones et les sports pour les personnes handicapées. Les sections incluent

- Matériel didactique
- Section I : Les maladies chroniques ou mentales
- Section II : Les ressources génériques
- Section III : Les annexes
- Section IV : Les statistiques

Chaque entrée comprend une description, une adresse (y compris le site Web, le courriel et les liens des médias sociaux, lorsque possible), les noms et titres des directeurs de même que plusieurs détails particuliers à ce type d'organisme.

Les membres du personnel des hôpitaux et des centres médicaux peuvent trouver, au même titre que parents et familles, le soutien dont ils ont besoin dans le cadre de leur travail ou de leurs études. Le *Guide canadien de la santé* est rempli de ressources capitales pour les personnes qui souffrent d'une maladie chronique alors qu'elles passent du diagnostic au retour à la maison, de la maison au travail et du travail à la vie au sein de la communauté.

OFFERT EN FORMAT PAPIER OU EN LIGNE—UN ACCÈS RAPIDE ET FACILE À TOUS LES RENSEIGNEMENTS DONT VOUS AVEZ BESOIN!

Offert sous couverture souple ou en format électronique grâce au web, le *Guide canadien de la santé* donne invariablement un accès instantané aux personnes et aux faits dont vous avez besoin. Si la version imprimée est vérifiée et mise à jour annuellement, des changements continus sont apportés mensuellement à la base de données en ligne. Servez-vous de la version en ligne afin de circonscrire vos recherches grâce à des champs spéciaux de l'index comme le nom de l'organisation ou son type, le sujet, l'emplacement, le nom de la personne-ressource ou son titre et le code postal.

LE GUIDE CANADIEN DE LA SANTÉ VOUS AIDERA À TROUVER CE DONT VOUS AVEZ BESOIN GRÂCE À CES OUTILS DE REPÉRAGE PRÉCIEUX!

Répertoire nominatif—une list alphabétique offrant un moyen rapide et facile d'accéder à toute liste de cette edition.

Onglets—les sections principals possèdent un onglet pour une consultation facile. Les notes en tête de chaque page vous aident à trouver les données voulues.

Créez vos propres listes! Les abonnés au service en ligne peuvent générer instantanément leurs propres listes de contacts et les exporter en format feuille de calcul pour une utilisation approfondie – une solution de rechange géniale aux services dispendieux d'un commissionnaire en publipostage.

GREY HOUSE PUBLISHING CANADA

Pour obtenir plus d'information, veuillez contacter Grey House Publishing Canada par tél. : 1 866 433-4739 ou 416 644-6479 par téléc. : 416 644-1904 | info@greyhouse.ca | www.greyhouse.ca

THE FACTS FOUND FAST!

Tap into FP Corporate Surveys and access all the facts and figures you need to make better informed decisions.

Covering over 6,300 publicly traded Canadian companies, FP Survey - Industrials and FP Survey - Mines & Energy are loaded with financial and operational information. Discover companies' financial results, capital and debt structure, key corporate developments, major shareholders, directors and executive officers, subsidiaries and more!

The ideal complement, FP Survey - Predecessor & Defunct, provides a comprehensive record of changes to Canadian public corporations dating back almost 90 years.

FP Corporate Surveys are completely unbiased, current and credible - make your investment decisions based on the facts.

ALL THE IN-DEPTH INFORMATION THAT YOU NEED – ALL IN ONE PLACE

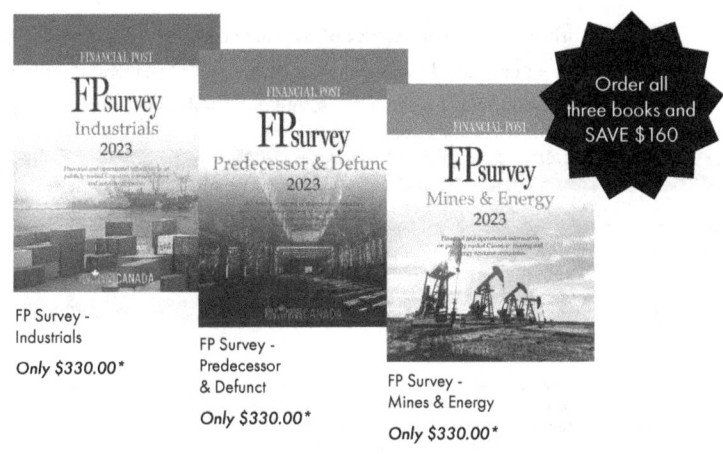

Order all three books and SAVE $160

FP Survey - Industrials
Only $330.00*

FP Survey - Predecessor & Defunct
Only $330.00*

FP Survey - Mines & Energy
Only $330.00*

*Plus shipping and applicable taxes

3 Easy Ways to Order

Phone: 1.866.433.4739 • Fax: 416.644.1904 • Email: info@greyhouse.ca

GREY HOUSE PUBLISHING CANADA

To Order: Toll Free Tel 1.866.433.4739 • Fax 416.644.1904

Financial Post Fixed Income Books are owned by Financial Post Data, a division of Postmedia Network Inc., and are exclusively printed and distributed by Grey House Publishing Canada.

Make Smarter Investment Decisions

FP Advisor

The ultimate online investment and research tool

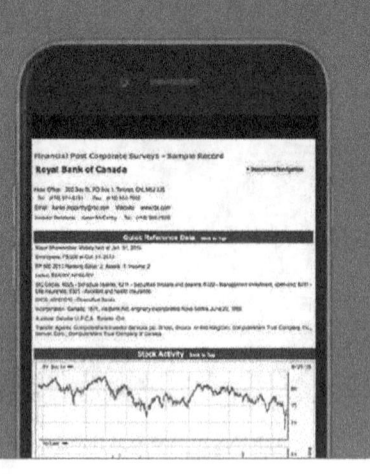

As the most trusted and reliable source of corporate data, FP Advisor provides detailed information about public and private companies across Canada, archival financial data, useful analytical and lead generation tools, and more—all in one convenient place.

FP Advisor includes:

Corporate Snapshots	Historical Reports	Dividends
Corporate Surveys	Industry Reports	New Issues
Corporate Analyzer	Predecessor & Defunct	Fixed Income
Investor Reports	Mergers & Acquisition	Directory of Directors

" FP Advisor is a very important source of information for us. We rely extensively on Predecessor & Defunct and Mergers & Acquisitions to track companies over time. Historical Reports include valuable current operations and ownership details that can be difficult to find elsewhere."
Kathy West, Head, Winspear Business Library, University of Alberta

Get a free trial today!

fpadvisor@postmedia.com | legacy-fpadvisor.financialpost.com

POSTMEDIA